GOD'S WILL is ALWAYS HEALING:

Crushing Theological Barriers to Healing

by Joshua Greeson

2

<u>Acknowledgements</u>

Forgoing the obvious thanks to God, I would like to say a heartfelt thank you to all the writers, preachers, teachers and friends who have poured bits of truth into me over the years. You helped form foundations in me that God could build on.

Thanks to Chuck Parry for his practical advice on this project, and all my other friends who encouraged me along the way.

Thanks to my cousin, Jesse Jordan, who did the cover art for the book. I am totally blown away! Contact: megatrawn@gmail.com

Thanks to Starbucks for the smiling faces, energized room, and tasty drinks that most often fueled my writing process.

A massive thank you to my wife, Jasmine, for listening to my theological ramblings, for proofreading my intentionally-less-than-proper writing, and for patiently understanding that sometimes revelation just flows easier at 2am.

Lastly, thank you to anyone who reads this book. It's long, and I'm thankful for your investment of time. I really do believe you will receive a big return on your investment. It'll probably rattle some of our favorite theological cages along the way; but I pray it will help many more of us (and those we minister to) receive and enjoy more of the freedom that Jesus purchased for us so long ago.

Endorsements

"Of all the books that I read and write endorsements for, this one is close to the top of the list. Joshua Greeson has done an amazing job of laying out with clarity and Scripture, God's will to heal His body. Questions about healing are answered with Scripture very accurately. The reader will come away from this book knowing God's will to heal.

"As I read this book, i thought about F.F. Bosworth's book, <u>Christ The Healer</u>, which is a classic. This takes that book to the next level. I will recommend this book to my staff as a must read. All I can say is, 'Well done, Joshua!'"

--Cal Pierce
Director, Healing Rooms Ministries
Spokane, Washington

"I remember when I first heard, 'It is always God's will to heal', to me it seemed like a false doctrine. I had objections like, 'Some of the most Godly people I know are sick! How would God allow sickness if it is always His will to heal?' Now many years later—after much study and the practical experience of seeing literally thousands of healings occur—I know 'It is *always* God's will to heal.' Thankfully, leaders like Joshua Greeson are paving the way for others to understand this missing truth. Enjoy as you read this groundbreaking book and discover the truth for yourself!"

--Jonathan Welton
Best-Selling Author
Director of The Welton Academy

"<u>God Will is Always Healing</u> is a wonderful and powerful journey through the bible that clearly lays out a theological foundation for Gods heart for healing. Josh has done a great job to help remove the barriers that religion has taught many of us over the years. If you desire to walk in a life of power, demonstrated by miracles and healing, then I *highly* recommend that you read this book. God's Will is Always Healing will help equip, empower and renew your mind, to help prepare you to walk in a supernatural life, so that you will see impossibilities bow the knee to Jesus!"

--Chris Gore
Director of Healing Ministries--
Bethel Church, Redding, CA.

"No matter *where* you stand on the issue of healing, you should take the time to read this book. Josh gives a very solid presentation through Scripture as well as his own examples about this topic. It is evident that a lot of work (and love) went into this. It's well written and structured in a way that is easy to follow. Written from a graceful perspective, Josh digs into Scripture to tackle a question that is close to all of us: Is healing part of the gospel promise, and is it *always* God's will to heal?"

--Mick Mooney
Author of God's Grammar

"I was inspired, I was challenged, and I felt safe when reading this book. You might ask yourself what I mean by 'safe.' Well, the author took care of me as a reader. There was no judgment or condemnation, but instead, love and encouragement. Several things stood out as the theme of this book:

1. God is good
2. Not everything that happens is God's will or His fault
3. As a believer, we have the authority of Jesus and God wants us to pull heaven to earth (literally)

"Joshua Greeson will share his heart, share his passion, and ultimately share the love of Christ! You won't be disappointed and his book has now found a long time spot on my bookshelf, not in the corner, but where I can easily grab and read as this book will take several readings to digest.

"Lord Jesus, thank you for Joshua and his heart behind the message of the words written for everyone to read. Lord, open eyes and open ears to see and hear what You are doing—and have always done—to reach more people through the love of Jesus! Use this book to break chains, break mindsets, and to release more of heaven onto earth.

"Thank you Joshua for sharing this with the world! Well done!"

--Brae Wyckoff
Founder, The Greater News
Author of The Orb of Truth

"<u>God's Will is Always Healing</u> provides in one volume a tremendous compilation of new creation realities. Josh Greeson has done a thorough job of laying a solid theological foundation for not only the doctrine of divine healing, but also for the very nature of a good God and our relationship to Him in a covenant of abundant life. Specific questions regarding healing are answered with ample scriptural evidence, and the study guide included makes this book an ideal resource for church groups, schools and individuals pursuing the revelation of what Jesus' sacrifice has made available to us."

--**Bernadette Ooley**
Bible Teacher & Founding Staff Member,
Bethel School of Supernatural Ministry--Redding, California

"I have said, 'There's no point in writing another book on healing, because they've all been written.' Then, I got a copy of Josh Greeson's book. It does exactly what the subtitle says—*crushes* theological barriers to healing. The chapter on Paul's thorn is the most thorough and enlightening expose on that subject that I have ever read! He also includes two chapters on the believer's union with Christ, (most healing books don't), which help you see that healing is absolutely yours, and also shows you how you are the healing extension of Christ in the earth today! This book is written in a very enjoyable and reader-friendly style. It's suitable for individual and group study with questions after each chapter that will help lock the truths into a person's heart. You will not be disappointed with this very important book!"

--**Steve C Shank**
Founder of City on the Hill Church and Ministries, and
Confirming the Word Bible College in Boulder, Colorado
Author of <u>Schizophrenic God? Finding Reality in Conflict, Confusion, and Contradiction</u>

"I *loved* this book. I think every born-again Believer should have this book in their arsenal. I love the fact that you don't have to dig up all the important Scriptures that support healing—Joshua did all the work so you could just take all the wonderful nuggets! Guys please get this book it is a must have. I wish i would have had this book 3 years ago when I first started seeing the Kingdom of God it would have answered so many questions that I had then. WOW! Wait until the Body gets ahold of this book; it's going to shake things! Thanks brother, I loved it!"

--**Pete Cabrera, Jr.**
Royal Family International

"I have read almost every book on healing there is. If I read this one first, it would have saved me *a lot* of time, money and energy. This work is by far the most in-depth, complete and New Covenant based that I have come across. Joshua has done a fantastic job expounding on such a misunderstood and wrongly taught subject. Whether you know nothing about healing or whether you think you know it all, this book will be a treasure trove of knowledge to reveal even more of God's love and goodness to man!"

--Cornel Marais
Founder of Charisma Ministries
Best Selling Author of <u>So You Think Your Mind Is Renewed</u>?

"Joshua Greeson writes with a straightforward, shoot-from-the-hip style, covering all the basic truths of healing from a Biblical perspective. While <u>God's Will is Always Healing</u> is a hefty 400 pages, it is not wordy, but rather to the point. It reads more like an outline—covering every area of promise, question, debate, argument, and opposition to experiencing God's blessings. He is refreshingly free of technique, and majors in truth, principle and relationship—focusing on the price Jesus paid through His death, and the victory He won for us through His resurrection.

"While we are constantly being transformed by renewing our minds to the truths of Heaven and the One Who is the Truth, we can use this handy resource to look up topics that have been long misunderstood, and questions we've always had about healing, God's goodness, His plans and promises, and our own attempts to reconcile why our circumstances don't always align with Truth. Josh does a great job of expounding on the Scriptures and including other scholarly references. Highly recommended."

--Chuck Parry
Associate Director, Bethel Healing Rooms
Redding, California

Table of Contents

Preface

Why I Wrote This Book

Why another book on healing? There are lots of books about healing; but there are still lots of wrong ideas about healing floating around in the Church. We've heard all kinds of different ideas through the centuries. "Is healing *always* God's will, or isn't it?" "Is it God's timing?" "Is it included with salvation or not?" "If it's God's will, and it's included with salvation, then why am I sick?" "Maybe we're like Job," or "maybe this is like Paul's thorn." "Maybe God is trying to teach us something." There are all kinds of questions and crazy ideas out there that impact our thinking about God, His character, and His will.

As I've traveled to various cities and nations teaching and ministering healing, I've heard and answered these same questions and challenges over and over again. There are solid biblical answers to all of them, I assure you. After repeating myself for a few years, I thought, "Hey, why don't I just write this all down and be done repeating myself? Plus, the book can get to places I might not ever reach, and bring these liberating truths to a lot more of God's kids! Let's do it!" And so this book was born. I pray that it's a great blessing to you!

Big, But Approachable

Yes, this book is BIG; but it's super approachable, and very easy to read. I tried to write it like I might say it to your face if we were chatting over coffee, rather than just outlining a bunch of information and facts on a page. It's presented in a style that's humorous, casual, conversational, and easy to understand for the average Believer; yet it's deep and scholarly enough to challenge even the most highly educated theologians.

A Quick Note About the Scriptures

There is a TON of Scripture contained in these pages. Without it, the book would be much shorter; but with it, I'm hoping people will actually read the Bible with their own eyes, instead of taking my word for it (or someone else's). That way, when someone's theological cages get rattled by the truths explained here, they can just get mad at God and the Bible, instead of getting mad at ME. Hahaha.

I often abbreviate the Scriptures I quote here. Some don't like that; but it's a necessity. Most of the time, it's to save space; but sometimes it's just to bring clarity and keep focused on the point I'm making. For instance, I might give you a chapter-long Bible reference, and only quote to you a few excerpts. That's easy to notice if you're reading the text on a page—you can see the ellipses or "dot, dot, dot" indicating the missing text; but if you're listening to the audio book, for instance, it's not as easy to recognize. Please remember this if you're trying to follow along in your own Bible.

If you are an audio book listener who loves to really *study* the Scriptures, I highly recommend getting either the paperback or electronic (*visual*) versions of this book. Not only will you be able to see the details I am referring to; but you also get all the Endnotes and References, Appendices and charts, and perhaps most importantly, the Study Guide (which you do not get in the audio book version). Not to mention that you will possibly want to reference this book for a long time to come, and that's much easier to do when it's a book on your shelf.

Getting the Most Out of the Book

For those of you that have it, I personally feel that the Study Guide is worth the cost of the whole book. It deeply enhances the experience, and increases the benefit you receive from reading. These Questions for Discussion, Study and Review will be invaluable in helping to digest the material—especially if any of these ideas are new to you. The Study Guide makes this book awesome for individual, family, or group Bible study, devotion and discussion. Do you want to have solidified in your heart that it is always God's will to heal? If you want the maximum mind-renewal experience, and really want to get the truth deeper in the core of your understanding—Please, do the Study Guide Questions!

Aside from that, it might be good to take this book in bite-sized pieces. Read a chapter, and wrestle with it. Do the review questions, and let it all sink in. Talk it out with the Lord if you need to. Then, come back for the next round.

With that—dear readers and listeners—we'll look to the precious Holy Spirit of God to teach us any truth that's contained here. I pray for the full freedom and fruit of it in our lives, and in the lives of those we impact in the years ahead. God bless you.

Introduction

There are Benefits to Knowing God

God is immeasurably good. And from Him come good things. He's made innumerable blessings available to every person on earth, and wants us all to enjoy them! As Believers in Jesus Christ in an everlasting, unbreakable covenant with Him, there are certain benefits that are *promised* to us! There are definitely benefits to knowing this God! Thankfully, we can also take of what He's given us, and give it away to others as well!

Psalm 68:19
Blessed be the Lord, Who daily loads us with benefits, The God of our salvation! Selah.

What Are These Benefits?

There are probably too many benefits to list; and every day, He's pouring it all out on all of us. God is so good and full of blessing! *Every* good thing you can think of comes from God, and is included in our inheritance!

James 1:17
Every good gift and every perfect gift is from above, and comes down from the Father of lights, with whom there is no variation or shadow of turning.

If it's "good," it's included. Even the Old Covenant Israelites had benefits. King David got excited about this, and wrote a song:

Psalm 103:1-5
"Bless the LORD, O my soul;
And all that is within me, bless His holy name!
Bless the LORD, O my soul,
And forget not all His benefits:
Who forgives all your iniquities,
Who heals all your diseases,

15

Who redeems your life from destruction,
Who crowns you with lovingkindness and tender mercies,
Who satisfies your mouth with good things,
So that your youth is renewed like the eagle's...."

He goes on—the list is a long one. But even in this partial list we see that healing is one of the benefits of relationship with God. In fact, it's second on the list, right next to forgiveness of sin! Healing is the main one we'll discuss in this book; but many of the principles we'll cover apply to *all* of the benefits.

So if all of these benefits are available—and even *promised* to the Believer—why doesn't everyone actually *receive* the benefits He's provided? There are many reasons why people don't experience the benefits of salvation; but in this book, we will primarily be dealing with two of them: lack of knowledge and the traditions of men.

Lack of Knowledge

First, there is ignorance—a lack of knowledge. People just don't know all that Jesus accomplished on our behalf, and what He's made available to us.

Hosea 4:6a
"My people are destroyed for lack of knowledge..."

> Most of the benefits of the Kingdom of God don't fall on us like ripe cherries off a tree.

Most of the benefits of the Kingdom of God don't fall on us like ripe cherries off a tree. We need to *learn* what's been made available to us. So how can we know what God is offering? He tells us in the Bible. If we'll get in there and read it, we can find out what He wants for us, and what He's done to secure it. We'll do quite a bit of that together here in this book.

The provisions of this benefits package are already ours in the unseen, eternal realm where God lives. If we are to receive them here in the natural, physical realm, we have a role to play in the process. We must trust what He says more than we trust what we see. Why? Because, "*Without faith it is impossible to please God* (Hebrews 11:6)." It takes faith to connect with God; and having faith requires that we know the will of God. "Faith begins where the will of God is known," said F.F. Bosworth.[1]

It is impossible to believe God for something we are not convinced He is offering. So if we are going to ask God for something, and have any confidence He'll deliver, we must know that what we are asking is the will of God.

1 John 5:14-15
Now this is the confidence that we have in Him, that if we ask anything according to His will, He hears us. And if we know that He hears us, whatever we ask, we know that we have the petitions that we have asked of Him.

It would be difficult to ask Him for something in faith, if we didn't know whether He wants us to have it or not. That would be like trying to write a thousand dollar check when you don't know if you have a dime in your bank account. You can fill it out and cross your fingers, but that's no way to live your life! The bank expects you to be aware of what's in your account before you go out writing checks, and so does God.

Misunderstandings and False Traditions

Another reason Christians don't receive the benefits of salvation is because we've heard bad teaching and religious traditions. Maybe we read about these benefits in the Bible, got excited, and told someone what we discovered. Then well-meaning preachers, friends, and family talked us out of it. They passed along men's traditions, and their own misunderstandings of Scripture.

These bad ideas became "vain imaginations" (2 Corinthians 10:5)—roadblocks that keep us from believing God for His promises to come to pass in our lives.

Matthew 15:6-9
"...You have made the commandment of God of no effect by your tradition... Teaching as doctrines the commandments of men."

> Bad ideas become "vain imaginations"— roadblocks that keep us from believing God for His promises.

Why would they do this? Are they mean-spirited "Grinches" that just want you to go without? Probably not. In most cases, they tried to step out in faith, and got disappointed. Maybe they had a loved one die after they prayed for their healing. They concluded from their experiences that it must not *always* be God's will for His kids to enjoy *all* of these benefits. Then they come across something in the Bible that—if misunderstood, or taken out of context—can seem to justify their own experience of not receiving. Then they share their misconceptions with others, building a doctrine around their shared experiences. Are they being intentionally dishonest? Not in most cases. They are just hurting, and they want their pain and disappointments to make some kind of sense.

Our minds don't experience peace until a puzzle is solved. Even if it's a false rationalization—as long as it "feels" resolved—our brain can settle down. Then we can move on and enjoy being in our comfort zone. But come on Church—God's got something better in mind! Let's not make people's experiences (or lack thereof) the standard we live our lives by. Let's see what our loving Father God says is available, and believe that we can actually experience all of His goodness!

I want to see people experience the love, goodness and power of God. I want to see people experience all the benefits of being children of God. I want to see people FREE! And if you're a Believer, then I know that you do too.

18

Some of the Barriers Addressed in This Book:

God says that healing and health are benefits of the Kingdom. We'll prove that as we go along. But in the meantime, I realize that if you've been a Christian very long, you've probably heard people bring up Scriptural issues that seem to complicate the simple truth that God does not want people to be sick or in pain. I run into them every day as I try to minister healing to people:

- What about Job?
- What about Paul's "thorn in the flesh"?
- What about when the Bible says we'll have "suffering," or "trials and tribulations"?
- Doesn't God use sickness to teach or mature us?
- Weren't there some people that Jesus didn't heal?
- Didn't the gifts of the Spirit stop or fade away a long time ago?
- Isn't everything that happens God's will? If so, then He must *allow* sickness for some "higher purpose," right?

In this book we will tackle all of these specific concerns and more. No longer will these questions sit in the back of your mind and paralyze you from taking action—No more nagging doubts that drag you backward into unbelief, and hold you back from grabbing ahold of the Kingdom and its provisions. You won't have to wonder anymore about whether it's God making you or someone else sick. You will be free to fight sickness and disease, pain and physical malfunctions of any kind; because you will know it's your enemy's handiwork.

John 8:32
And you shall know the truth, and the truth shall make you free.

There's also a saying—"The truth will set you free; but first it will make you mad!" Hold on to your seat! If you are open to truth—however uncomfortable it may make you—You can get free, and help others do the same!

19

While we do address the specific (smaller) arguments against divine healing, first we'll delve into some of the bigger, more foundational Scriptural matters that secure God's provision for our healing and health. In other words we'll establish some pillars of truth—some larger truths that reflect the whole, Biblical counsel of God. This is one of the basic rules of Bible interpretation—Let the Bible interpret itself.

If we think we see something in Scripture that seems to contradict the clear, basic truths, we are misunderstanding or misinterpreting that Scripture. Once the basic framework of the Bible and God's ways gets nailed down, we can't get hung up on isolated Scriptures that—by themselves, taken out of the context of the whole Bible—could seem to justify our doubts. Some of the "larger truths" we'll touch on include:

> If you are open to truth—however uncomfortable it may make you—You can get free, and help others do the same.

- Old Covenant vs. New Covenant
- Invisible Truth vs. Visible Circumstances
- God's Goodness vs. the Devil's Badness
- The Believer's Authority and God's Sovereignty
- Salvation, The Atonement and Christ's Finished Work
- Jesus is our Standard
- Believers are in Union with the Exalted Christ

Once we're grounded in some basic and clear Scriptural truths, we have a filter to judge the less clear, or seemingly contrary Scriptures by. Then we can have unshakeable confidence in God's will to heal. From there, we'll move into the specific questions and see how simple they are to crush in light of the big picture of Scripture.

God's absolute goodness will overshadow any questioning of His character. His love will become the mark by which we know His ways. His finished work and victory will be the foundation and framework we build our lives on. Jesus' example will be the plumb line for all of our theology. Victory over all the works of the devil will become our increasingly consistent experience.

Now let's get to it, and conquer some theological roadblocks that keep Believers from receiving and ministering our God-given inheritance of healing and health... God's will is *always* healing!

Notes:

Notes:

Chapter 1

HUMAN AUTHORITY: Managers of the Earth

A Brief History of the World

If you don't get anything else in this book, please "get" these first couple of chapters. The truths contained here will provide a basic framework for understanding everything else in Scripture and life! Sadly, many Christians haven't been taught this framework at all, while it should really be considered "Christianity 101"!!!

The first chapter could be a book on its own, so I cannot cover these ideas in depth here in a few pages. However—because of their importance in understanding God's will for Healing—It is very necessary for us to at least gain a basic understanding of our role as Believers. Think of it as a basic job description.

1) God Created the World, and Gave Mankind Authority

God created the world and everything in it. Then He made man and told him to take care of the earth and have dominion over it. God created, and delegated! He put man in charge of the operation.

Genesis 1:26-28
26 Then God said, "Let Us make man in Our image, according to Our likeness; *let them have dominion* over the fish of the sea, over the birds of the air, and over the cattle, *over all the earth* and over every creeping thing that creeps on the earth." 27 So God created man in His own image; in the image of God He created him; male and female He created them. 28 Then God blessed them, and God said to them, "Be fruitful and multiply; *fill the earth and subdue it; have dominion* over the fish of the sea, over the birds of the air, and over every living thing that moves on the earth."

So who owns the earth? Man or God? God does!

Psalm 24:1
The earth is the LORD's, and all its fullness, the world and those who dwell therein.

Let's say you own a business. You then put a manager in place to run the business. You give him the tools and resources necessary to operate the business. You trained him well, or at least you gave him a copy of your company policies. Now he should know what your will is for the business, and be able to run it accordingly. Then you say, "OK, now you're in charge. I expect you to run the place like I would and make it prosper." Ultimate authority is yours, but you have now delegated it to the manager. While it still *belongs* to you, the manager is *responsible* for what he does with the business on his watch.

> God created...
> and delegated!

God is the Owner, but people are the Managers. Once we become children of God by faith in God's grace, we become Co-Owners; but we'll get to that later. To stick with the Owner-Manager analogy, the policy manual is the Bible, and the business is the Earth. He has "given" it into our care. He has given us the information and resources we need to run the earth as He wants it to be run. He has delegated the authority over all the earth to *Man*!

Psalm 115:16
The heaven, *even* the heavens, *are* the LORD's; but *the earth He has given to the children of men.*

A lot of people like to say (especially when something bad happens), "Well, God is in control." Folks, God is *not* in control, not like they mean it when they say that. God is in charge; but He's not in control. He set things up, and lets us "control" it. Man is second in command, but right now is in the immediate position to exercise authority—by God's Own Sovereign decree.

Psalm 8:4-6
[4] What is man...? ...You have crowned him with glory and honor. [6] *You have made him to have dominion over the works of Your hands; You have put all things under his feet,*

2) ...Man Gave His Authority to Satan...

Adam and Eve, as the heads of all humanity, yielded to Satan's temptation in the Garden. In choosing to obey Satan rather than God, they subjugated themselves to him. They delegated their authority to Satan—in essence, they chose him as their god. Because all of Creation was under their authority, It was also handed over to the authority of Satan. This sin caused them to break away from fellowship with God. God didn't want that condition to remain forever, so He kicked them out of the Garden and prevented them from returning and eating the fruit of the Tree of Life (Genesis 3:22-24).

When Man sinned, he obeyed Satan instead of God. He chose Satan as his new master. He yielded his God-given authority over to the devil, making Satan his god. As the god of this world/age, Satan influences world events through people yielding to him. This happens when people hear Satan's lies, agree with him, and decide to act in line with his suggestions. Because of Satan becoming ruler, Mankind and all of Creation fell into a state of being cursed (un-blessed). Because Satan is a rebel, when he rules, chaos (the curse) is the result.

> When Man sinned... he yielded his God-given authority over to the devil.

1 John 5:19
We know that we are of God, and *the whole world lies under the sway of the wicked one.*

The idea that Satan became the god of this world bothers many Christians. But that doesn't make it any less true.

25

2 Corinthians 4:3-4

³ But even if our gospel is veiled, it is veiled to those who are perishing,
⁴ whose minds *the god of this age* has blinded, who do not believe, lest the light of the gospel of the glory of Christ, who is the image of God, should shine on them.

Before the Cross, Satan was the god of this world, or the god of that age. In other words, From Adam until Jesus, he had some influence and authority. Mankind gave it to him. Even Jesus recognized that Satan had (temporary) authority on the earth! We see this when Satan came to tempt Jesus in the wilderness. Satan recognized why Jesus had come to the Earth, and offered to give it to Him by means of a shortcut—if only Jesus would worship him, Satan would hand Him the keys!

Luke 4:5-7

⁵ Then the devil, taking Him up on a high mountain, showed Him all the kingdoms of the world in a moment of time. ⁶ And the devil said to Him, "All this authority I will give You, and their glory; for this has been delivered to me, and I give it to whomever I wish. ⁷ Therefore, if You will worship before me, all will be Yours."

Now, if Satan could offer to give Jesus the authority over "all the kingdoms of the world," then he must have had it to give. If he didn't, then Jesus would have known it, and this would not have been a legitimate temptation. If a penniless beggar said to you, "Sign your house over to me today, and I'll give you a million dollars for it tomorrow," you would look at him like he was a fool. You certainly wouldn't be tempted by the offer of a million dollars, because you know that he doesn't have it to give. Jesus knew that Satan had it to give. But He also knew that He had come to earth to get it back legitimately; and that didn't include the shortcut of worshipping the devil.

Still not convinced that Satan was given authority over this world? Check out Jesus' words in the gospel of John:

John 12:31
Now is the judgment of this world; now *the ruler of this world* will be cast out.

John 14:30
I will no longer talk much with you, for *the ruler of this world* is coming, and he has nothing in Me.

John 16:8-11
And when He has come, He will convict the world of sin, and of righteousness, and of judgment... of judgment, because *the ruler of this world* is judged.

Three times Jesus identified Satan as "the ruler of this world." I don't think it gets any plainer than that. But thankfully, that's not the end of the story!

3) ...Jesus Took the Authority Back From Satan...

God originally gave authority over the Earth to Mankind, and Mankind chose to give it away to the devil. Only a Man could take it back—this is one of the reasons why Jesus had to come as a Man—to get the job done "legally." Yes, Jesus is God; but He was *born* as a Man, and *lived* as a Man. He said it was illegal to come into earthly authority and influence any other way:

> Yes, Jesus is God; but He was *born* as a Man, and *lived* as a Man.

John 10:1-6
[1] "Most assuredly, I say to you, he who does not enter the sheepfold by the door, but climbs up some other way, the same is a thief and a robber. [2] But he who enters by the door is the shepherd of the sheep. [3] To him the doorkeeper opens, and the sheep hear his voice; and he calls his own sheep by name and leads them out... [6] Jesus used this illustration, but they did not understand the things which He spoke to them.

Here Jesus identified Himself as the Shepherd. The sheepfold (the pen) is the realm of authority in the Earth. He says, "I'm legit, I'm gaining the authority by coming through the gate (as a Man)!" They didn't get it, so he tried again:

John 10:7-10

[7] Then Jesus said to them again, "Most assuredly, I say to you, I am the door of the sheep. [8] All who *ever* came before Me are thieves and robbers, but the sheep did not hear them. [9] I am the door. If anyone enters by Me, he will be saved, and will go in and out and find pasture. [10] The thief does not come except to steal, and to kill, and to destroy. I have come that they may have life, and that they may have *it* more abundantly.

Here Jesus says, "The one who came into authority before Me (the devil) is a thief. He didn't come as a man and get authority legitimately—he stole it. So I'm here to take it back. Now I am

> No longer is it being born in the flesh that grants authority—it's being born again and identifying with Jesus.

the new door. No longer is it being born in the flesh that grants authority—it's being born again and identifying with Me. This will give the sheep (His People) restored access to authority and life." We see it described again in Hebrews:

Hebrews 2:14-18

[14] Inasmuch then as the children have partaken of flesh and blood, He Himself likewise shared in the same, that through death He might destroy him who had the power of death, that is, the devil, [15] and release those who through fear of death were all their lifetime subject to bondage. [16] For indeed He does not give aid to angels, but He does give aid to the seed of Abraham. [17] Therefore, in all things He had to be made like His brethren, that He might be a merciful and faithful High Priest in things pertaining to God, to make propitiation for the sins of the people. [18] For in that He Himself has suffered, being tempted, He is able to aid those who are tempted.

This Scripture gives us yet another reason why it was vital that Jesus came to the earth in the flesh. He had to come as a man to identify fully with us. If He didn't go through all that we as people have to go through, we would have no right to receive the benefits of identification with Him. But because He was made as one of us, He can relate to us, and have mercy on us; and now the Great Exchange (salvation) is available. He became what we were, so we could become as He is.

This Scripture also clearly talks about how Jesus set us free from the bondage we were under—with the Law against us, and Satan as slavemaster.

Colossians 2:13-15
[13] And you, being dead in your trespasses and the uncircumcision of your flesh, He has made alive together with Him, having forgiven you all trespasses, [14] having wiped out the handwriting of requirements that was against us, which was contrary to us. And He has taken it out of the way, having nailed it to the cross. [15] *Having disarmed principalities and powers, He made a public spectacle of them, triumphing over them in it.*

Thank God, Jesus accomplished all that He came to accomplish. The Son of God became Man, so Man could become sons of God. He became sin, so that we could become righteousness. He became the

> The Son of God became Man, so Man could become sons of God.

condemned, so that we could become the forgiven. He became the cursed, so that we could become blessed. Through His death, burial and resurrection—He conquered the devil on his own turf, and took back the keys of authority!

Revelation 1:18
I am He who lives, and was dead, and behold, I am alive forevermore. Amen. And *I have the keys of Hades and of Death.*

4) ...Then Jesus Gave the Authority Back to Believers!!!

But then we get to where the rubber meets the road for us as New Testament Believers—He gave the authority back to *us*, putting *us* in charge of the earth again. He said in Matthew 28, "OK guys, I've been given all authority. So now *you* go make disciples, teaching them to do everything I taught you to do." Then in Ephesians 1 it

> Jesus regained the authority, then gave it to us, and commissioned us to disciple the Earth!

says that if we are any part of the Body of Christ, then all things are under us. Jesus regained the authority, then gave it to us, and commissioned us to disciple the Earth!

Matthew 10:1
And when He had called His twelve disciples to Him, He *gave them power over unclean spirits, to cast them out, and to heal all kinds of sickness and all kinds of disease*.

Luke 9:1
Then He called His twelve disciples together and *gave them power and authority over all demons, and to cure diseases*.

Luke 10:19
Behold, *I give you the authority* to trample on serpents and scorpions, and over all the power of the enemy, and nothing shall by any means hurt you.

Matthew 16:19
And I will give you the keys of the kingdom of heaven, and whatever you bind on earth will be bound in heaven, and whatever you loose on earth will be loosed in heaven."

Even before He made full salvation available through His death, burial and resurrection, Jesus was able to delegate authority over devils and sickness to His disciples. Jesus was right with God, and thus able to move in increased authority over demons and disease. Now that the Spirit of God resides in us, and we've been made right with God by the blood of Jesus Christ the righteous, we can (and must) walk in the same authority and power!

Now, somebody might look at the above Scriptures and say, "Sure, but he was talking to the disciples." You're right, but first of all—aren't you also a disciple? Were the 12 special? They were certainly privileged, but weren't "special." Even if they were, Jesus commanded them to heal the sick (Matthew 10, Luke 10), right? Yes. Then let's also look again at the "Great Commission" that Jesus gives to us—all Believers—in Matthew 28.

Matthew 28:18-20

[18] And Jesus came and spoke to them, saying, "All authority has been given to Me in heaven and on earth. [19] Go therefore and make disciples of all the nations, baptizing them in the name of the Father and of the Son and of the Holy Spirit, [20] teaching them to observe all things that I have commanded you; and lo, I am with you always, *even* to the end of the age." Amen.

Here, Jesus commanded the disciples to teach Believers to "observe" (that means "DO") "*all things* that I have commanded you." That clearly includes the commands to heal the sick, raise the dead, and cast out devils.

Additionally, the Luke 10 reference above is Jesus commanding not only the 12; but "seventy others." Certainly as a blood-bought son of God, you are endowed with equal or more authority than these Old Testament saints were (Jesus hadn't yet gone to the cross)! We also find that the post-resurrection disciples (even those who were not part of the original 12, and not part of the 70) carried on Jesus' ministry of healing the sick. And it has continued to varying degrees throughout Church History. Sorry, but there is no way around the fact that we are commissioned—and therefore responsible—to obey Jesus' commands to heal the sick!

In Matthew 28, we see Jesus declaring His total victory. How much authority was given to Jesus? "*All* authority." You know what that word "all" means in the Greek? It means "*all*." And if Jesus has *all* authority, then that also means that the devil has *none*. He is a defeated foe. So Jesus has all authority where? "In heaven *and on earth*." Thank God! Jesus fulfilled His mission— He came as a Man, took our place, and got the authority back!!! Hallelujah!!

Power of Attorney

Another way to understand what it meant when Jesus commissioned His disciples is that Jesus provided "power of attorney." What does that mean? He gave the authority to operate on His behalf, in His Name. The dictionary defines power of attorney as "legal authority to act for another person..."[1] That pretty much sums it up, eh?

I remember when I was in the Army, soldiers were required to grant power of attorney to their spouse while they were deployed. This was so life could go on in the soldier's absence. The spouse could get money out of bank accounts, write checks, pay the bills, rent housing, and carry on life-as-usual—in the soldier's name—*as if the soldier himself were doing it*.

In a natural, legal power of attorney situation—if I'm going to be unavailable or otherwise unable to carry on certain activities that need doing—I'd have to grant power of attorney to someone else to do them for me. If I'm smart, I'll choose someone that I'm in relationship with, that knows me, and who will do what I myself would do—in pretty much any given situation that might arise. *Any act that the person with power of attorney does "in the name" of the other party is viewed in the eyes of the law as if that person did it themselves*. The one with power of attorney stands in the stead of the person they represent. In a legal sense, they *become* the other person. This is *exactly* what Jesus has done with us, His bride, His trusted friends, His brothers and sisters and joint heirs! This sounds like the Parable of the Minas, in Luke 19:

Luke 19:12-13
[12] Therefore He said: "A certain nobleman went into a far country to receive for himself a kingdom and to return. [13] So he called ten of his servants, delivered to them ten minas, and said to them, '*Do business till I come.*'

The Nobleman (Jesus) told us, "Do business till I come." We have been given authority to carry on the Family business—in Jesus' Name—until He returns. He apparently trusts us to do what we know that He would do. That is because He recognizes a spiritual truth that most of us have yet to truly wrap our heads around: We are "in Christ." We are to re-present Him. We are

His ambassadors. We act in His Name, on His behalf, with His character and motivation, and with His power and authority to the world.

Humans have a certain amount of authority over the created Earth realm just because of Genesis 1:26 and Psalm 8. Creation is subject to Mankind's authority. Do most people know that? No. Have humans used their authority wisely and responsibly since then? No.

> We have been given authority to carry on the Family business— in Jesus' Name— until He returns.

Beyond that, there is power of attorney. Jesus commissioned others to operate in the same authority that He did Himself, even before the New Covenant was in effect. But here's the thing: There is another step beyond even simple human authority, and beyond delegated authority (or power of attorney)—there is the authority we've inherited as sons and daughters of the King and Owner of the earth Himself!

Notes:

CHAPTER 2

THE BELIEVER'S AUTHORITY:
Heirs of the Earth

We Are No Longer Just Managers—We are Heirs!

We discussed the idea of power of attorney in the last chapter. We mentioned that someone who is smart will only give power of attorney to somebody they trust implicitly. Why does God trust people like this? Because through our identification with Christ, and through union with Him, He sees us as being just like Jesus!! That's because He sees us through His eyes of love (which believes all things, hopes all things, and endures all things)!! And it's because we *are* just like Jesus. We're in Him, and He's in us and we are forever one.

Any human can exercise a measure of authority and dominion over the Earth. While Jesus walked the earth, He delegated some additional authority—as One right with God—to at least 82 other people. After accomplishing our great salvation and bringing us into union with Himself, He made "all authority" available to us as His joint heirs. There is so much to this magnificent union with Christ! Please read and reread the chapters on our union with Christ. If we will get ahold of the truths concerning our identity in Him, most of the other issues we struggle with will work themselves out!

Ephesians 2:4-6
[4] But God, who is rich in mercy, because of His great love with which He loved us, [5] even when we were dead in trespasses, made us alive together with Christ (by grace you have been saved), [6] and raised us up together, and made us sit together in the heavenly places in Christ Jesus,

These verses say that we are sitting together with Christ right now in the heavenly places. This is a present-day reality. The real you, the spirit you, is sitting with Christ where He is. Where, specifically in the "heavenly places" is that?

Ephesians 1:20-23
[20] which He worked in Christ when He raised Him from the dead and seated Him at His right hand in the heavenly places, [21] far above all principality and power and might and dominion, and every name that is named, not only in this age but also in that which is to come. [22] And He put all things under His feet, and gave Him to be head over all things to the church, [23] which is His body, the fullness of Him who fills all in all.

Jesus is sitting at the right hand of God. And so are we; because we are in Him. What does that mean, to sit at someone's "right hand?" It means that we are operating in the authority of the One we sit next to. This is where we get the figure of speech where we say that a person is someone else's "right hand man." So, concerning the subject of authority, if we are in Christ, we are—right now—seated at the right hand of God. We are—right now—in a place of completely restored authority. We are in Christ. We are His very Body! "All things" are under us—right now, as we are submitted to the Father through Jesus!

This Scripture says that Jesus was given a place "far above all principality and power and might and dominion and every name that is named." Then it says that "all things" were put under His feet. Most Believers are fine with all of that. But then it has the audacity to say that Believers are His body, which means that "all things" are under us! Even if you are the pinky toenail on the Body of Christ, "all things" are under you!

> Even if you are the pinky toenail on the Body of Christ, "all things" are under you!

Now, some might say, "OK, well, it sure doesn't look like Believers have authority over 'all things'! If 'all things' are under us as Believers, then why is the world such a mess? Why does the devil get away with so much?" I'm glad you asked. The writer of Hebrews (generally believed to be the Apostle Paul) wondered the same thing:

Hebrews 2:8-10

[8] For in that He put *all* in subjection under him, He left *nothing* that is not put under him. But *now we do not yet see all things put under him.* [9] *But we see Jesus...*"

He's saying, "I realize that although 'all things' are under the authority of Man, we don't yet see it working right. But we do see Jesus, and He showed us how things are supposed to look when we do our part correctly!" So even though we don't see Man exercising authority over the devil the way we should most of the time, we shouldn't misinterpret that to mean that we aren't supposed to grow up and learn how to do it!

Unfortunately, this is what much of the Body of Christ does—We see our own experience—or lack thereof—and interpret Scriptures by our own experience. So when I say "God's Will Is Always Healing," someone always says, "But what about my Aunt Lulu? She was a Christian. She got sick, we prayed, and she still died. So you must be wrong. Sickness can't be under our feet! Plus 'God is in control,' so it must be God's will that she was sick." Then they will invent all kinds of reasons that God must want Aunt Lulu sick, or just wanted to "take her home." No, no, no!

> We need to accept our responsibility to learn how to walk more effectively and consistently in the authority the Bible says is ours in Christ.

Instead of rationalizing and trying to understand everything, we must take the Scriptural truths that are clear, accept and believe them, and work with them the best we know how. Healing is God's character, nature, and will. Sickness is of the devil. We are commanded to heal the sick. Anything that doesn't line up with these simple facts is a mystery we may not understand, but we need to overcome it and expect God's standard anyway. We must simply realize that we haven't got it all figured out yet. Instead, we need to accept our responsibility to learn how to walk more effectively and consistently in the authority the Bible says is ours in Christ. If you can't accept even these basics just yet, it's OK—that's why this book came into existence—So please hang around, keep an open mind and heart to the Scriptures we'll discuss. Keep going!!

Romans 5:17
For if by the one man's offense death reigned through the one, much more those who receive abundance of grace and of the gift of righteousness will reign in life through the One, Jesus Christ.

This verse nicely summarizes this book thus far. Paraphrased: "Adam sinned and brought death on all Mankind; but Jesus brought grace and righteousness to those who will receive it. They will become just like Him, and they will reign in life through Him." Thank you, Brother Paul.

How Long Are We in Authority?

As we discovered in the last chapter, Jesus delivered the "keys" of authority to His Church. Adam was a Manager. Now through Christ, we are no longer mere Managers—We are sons and daughters, heirs of God, and joint-heirs with Jesus Christ. The Earth is our inheritance.

Romans 8:16-17
[16] The Spirit Himself bears witness with our spirit that we are children of God,
[17] and if children, then heirs—heirs of God and joint heirs with Christ, if indeed we suffer with Him, that we may also be glorified together.

We will discuss that later in greater detail. For now, a question: Just how long will this "mess" continue on the earth? Answer: As long as we let it! The Scripture tells us very clearly that Jesus is not returning to take back full authority until His enemies have been brought down, put under subjection to His rule. Now, who did He leave here to accomplish that, by the grace of God? If you said "Us, the Church," you're right!

Psalm 110:1
The LORD said to my Lord, "Sit at My right hand, Till I make Your enemies Your footstool."

Acts 2:34-35
[34] "For David did not ascend into the heavens, but he says himself: 'The LORD said to my Lord," Sit at My right hand, [35] Till I make Your enemies Your footstool."

Hebrews 1:13
But to which of the angels has He ever said: "Sit at My right hand, Till I make Your enemies Your footstool"?

Hebrews 10:12-13
[12] But this Man, after He had offered one sacrifice for sins forever, sat down at the right hand of God, [13] from that time waiting till His enemies are made His footstool.

The fact that this same quote is referenced FOUR times in Scripture should tell us that God sees it as something we should understand, eh? Jesus is seated at the right hand of God—*until* His enemies are made His footstool. God Himself will accomplish it—but He'll do that like He does most everything else—through the Church. So when Jesus commissioned us and gave His authority to us, He was saying, "Round 2: Handle it—You are empowered to make the earth My footstool. Bring my enemies into subjection. When you're done, I'll come back and pick up the keys!"

> Jesus is seated at the right hand of God—until His enemies are made His footstool.

1 Corinthians 15:23-28
[23] But each one in his own order: Christ the firstfruits, afterward those who are Christ's at His coming. [24] Then comes the end, when He delivers the kingdom to God the Father, when He puts an end to all rule and all authority and power. [25] For He must reign till He has put all enemies under His feet. [26] The last enemy that will be destroyed is death. [27] For "He has put all things under His feet." But when He says "all things are put under Him," it is evident that He who put all things under Him is excepted. [28] Now when all things are made subject to Him, then the Son Himself will also be subject to Him who put all things under Him, that God may be all in all.

This Scripture clearly reiterates that once Jesus' enemies are subjected to Him (which He does through US, His Body), then He will hand the Kingdom over to the Father, and things will wrap up.

What Things Does God Control?

This is covered more in depth in the "God's Sovereignty" chapter; but for now, let's touch on it briefly. The question is, if Believers are the Heirs of the Earth, left to "run the Family business", what does God Himself still control? He has proclaimed the end from the beginning, and the ultimate resolution of things has been foreseen and proclaimed by God. The devil loses, God wins, and the redeemed sons and daughters of God will be with Him forever. But until then, He's left us responsible for the "day-to-day operations" of running the earth.

This is exactly parallel to the parable of the talents in Matthew 25:14-30. Here, Jesus says the Kingdom of Heaven is like a man (Jesus) going away on a trip. Before He left, He gave authority and resources to His Managers (us). Then He goes away for a while. We are supposed to take the authority He's given to us to do business on His behalf, and advance His Kingdom. Then He'll come back and "settle accounts." Some will have taken initiative, gone out and acted in the Name and authority of Jesus to accomplish His will—to do what He would have done were He there in their shoes. To them, Jesus will give even more authority.

Meanwhile, others will say, "I knew you to be a hard man, reaping where you have not sown, and gathering where you have not scattered seed. And I was afraid..." People who think that God will get what's His, regardless of what they do or don't do, are simply afraid. But God says, "In one sense, you're right.

I'm going to get it all in the end. But the thing is, I gave you responsibility for doing part of the job. Since you didn't do it, I'll let this other guy handle it for you." What did Jesus call the servant that didn't use the authority given him to conduct business on behalf of the Master? "Lazy" and "unprofitable," among other things (v.26, 30).

2 Corinthians 5:20
Now then, we are ambassadors for Christ, as though God were pleading through us: we implore you on Christ's behalf, be reconciled to God.

We've been given the authority to accomplish the will of God. To do His will, we must know His will. To walk in His ways, we must know His ways. He's given us His Spirit to do just that. He's said, "Here, take care of the earth, make my enemies my footstool. I'm giving you fully sanctioned authority to do what I would do if I were here. You are My sons and daughters, My representatives, My ambassadors. Conduct affairs in the Earth on My behalf; and I'll come back to pick it up when it's time. Thanks!" At that time, He will ask for an accounting of what we did with the authority He gave us. Did we subdue the earth and destroy the devil's works, bringing His enemies into subjection? Or did we figure His will gets done in the end anyway, hide our authority and resources in the dirt (earthly pursuits), and bide our time in fear?

Come on Church, don't let somebody else handle your piece of the puzzle—Let's all do our part. God, in His wisdom and power, has created and designed us for

> Life on Earth is training for reigning!

relationship with Him. He's training us to co-reign with His Only Son! To do so more accurately, we must grow in maturity and authority; because we are destined to reign with Him forever. Life on Earth is "training for reigning!" He's given us a little (our sphere of influence in the Earth), so that He can later make us "lord over much."

41

Relationship Reconciles Man's Will & God's Sovereignty

Many people struggle with understanding the issues surrounding God's Sovereignty and Mankind's authority. There are lots of great Scriptures that can seem to clearly support each point of view. Most see these two sides of truth as contradictory; but unless one is taken to an extreme, I don't think they have to be. Here it is in a nutshell: God, in His Sovereignty, chose to give Man authority. God's will is accomplished when Man willingly partners with God. Understanding this partnership can help reconcile the two parts of the equation—God's Sovereignty and Man's authority—and lots of debatable Scriptures.

> God, in His Sovereignty, chose to give Man authority.

1) We can find Scriptures that tell us essentially, "God does whatever He wants to."

Psalm 115:3
But our God is in heaven; He does whatever He pleases.

Daniel 4:35
All the inhabitants of the earth are reputed as nothing; He does according to His will in the army of heaven and among the inhabitants of the earth. No one can restrain His hand or say to Him, "What have You done?"

Right, God sure does do whatever He wants to, and He does according to His will. He does whatever He has said He will do! And what He chose was to grant Mankind authority on the earth. He chose to give us dominion. He stands by His Word, refuses to break it, and lets us be either wise or foolish with the authority He's given. He will co-labor with those who choose relationship with Him, and bless and deliver us. But if we don't invite Him through relationship, there's not usually much He can do!

2) We can find Scriptures that show things being done that are *against* the will of God.

Genesis 6:5-6
[5] Then the LORD saw that the wickedness of man was great in the earth, and that every intent of the thoughts of his heart was only evil continually. [6] And the LORD was sorry that He had made man on the earth, and He was grieved in His heart.

Matthew 23:37
"O Jerusalem, Jerusalem, the one who kills the prophets and stones those who are sent to her! How often *I wanted* to gather your children together, as a hen gathers her chicks under her wings, *but you were not willing*!

This is because nobody in relationship with God acted on behalf of God to enforce His will. Because God has given us the role of authority in the Earth, He could do nothing. The people just reaped what they had sown. Because God put the rules of sowing and reaping in place, He still appears (in some verses) to be an active participant, even when He's not. But if people had only used our authority to access His help—God's will could have been enforced and evil plans would have been foiled.

3) We can also find Scriptures that show people can make (either good *or* evil) plans of their own, and get the results of their own actions.

Hosea 8:4 (New International Version)
They set up kings without my consent; they choose princes without my approval. With their silver and gold they make idols for themselves to their own destruction.

Matthew 12:35
A good man out of the good treasure of his heart brings forth good things, and an evil man out of the evil treasure brings forth evil things.

Isaiah 32:7-8
[7] Also the schemes of the schemer are evil; He devises wicked plans to destroy the poor with lying words, even when the needy speaks justice. [8] But a generous man devises generous things, and by generosity he shall stand.

43

Luke 7:30a
But the Pharisees and lawyers *rejected the will of God for themselves...*

This last Scripture shows clearly that it is possible to rebel and reject God's will, and do something else entirely.

Good people act and bring blessing out of relationship with God. Others act of their own evil will, and *if nobody acts to stop them*, they (temporarily) get away with it. But (unless they receive God's mercy and forgiveness) eventually they reap the results of the evil they've sown.

4) Some Scriptures say that God only gives good gifts:

Matthew 7:11
If you then, being evil, know how to give good gifts to your children, how much more will your Father who is in heaven give good things to those who ask Him!

James 1:17
Every good gift and every perfect gift is from above, and comes down from the Father of lights, with whom there is no variation or shadow of turning.

When people *trust* God's good nature and will (this is most often expressed through prayers of thanksgiving), His good gifts are accessed. Sometimes, even when people *don't* trust and cooperate, they can *still* receive good from God. It rains on the just *and* the unjust alike.

5) Then of course there are Scriptures that *seem* to say that God is responsible for both good *and* evil.

Ecclesiastes 7:14
In the day of prosperity be joyful, But in the day of adversity consider: Surely God has appointed the one as well as the other, So that man can find out nothing that will come after him.

Isaiah 45:7
I form the light and create darkness, I make peace and create calamity; I, the LORD, do all these things.

God instituted Mankind's authority, and He instituted sowing and reaping, and other natural laws and processes. In this sense, He decided that there must be both good and evil, or He "appointed" evil, simply by setting man in a place of authority where they could choose to sow evil seeds and reap the corresponding evil harvest. But in reality, God appointed the *system*, not the *results* we create with the system He gave us. If we sow an evil seed and get an evil harvest, the *harvest* is not God's will for us; but our *freedom* to sow and reap is. Whether we get the "good" God wills, or the "bad" we sow, most often depends on whether or not we operate from loving, trusting relationship with God through faith.

6) Some Scriptures show that God can take a bad situation that people create, and turn it for good.

Genesis 50:20
You planned evil against me; God planned it for good to bring about the present result—the survival of many people.

Romans 8:28
And we know that all things work together for good to those who love God, to those who are the called according to His purpose.

In both of these contexts, we see that man can invite God into bad situations and He can fix them. *Because He is invited to do so*, He is able to work around the bad situation, and ultimately bring about His good will. But the good end result that He orchestrates is not evidence that He arranged the original bad situation! God doesn't create problems only to fix them.

7) Some Scriptures show that people make choices and plans; but God brings about something different than they planned.

Proverbs 16:9
A man's heart plans his way, But the LORD directs his steps.

Proverbs 19:21
There are many plans in a man's heart, Nevertheless the LORD's counsel—
that will stand.

Genesis 11:1-8
[1] Now the whole earth had one language and one speech... [4] And they said, "Come, let us build ourselves a city, and a tower whose top is in the heavens; let us make a name for ourselves... [5] But the LORD came down to see the city and the tower which the sons of men had built. [6] And the LORD said, "Indeed the people are one and they all have one language, and this is what they begin to do; now nothing that they propose to do will be withheld from them. [7] Come, let Us go down and there confuse their language, that they may not understand one another's speech." [8] So the LORD scattered them abroad from there over the face of all the earth, and they ceased building the city.

Very simply, if one's plans are in line with God's will, and they—through trusting relationship—allow God to protect them and defeat opposition, then they get their plans. The Proverbs 16 verse can even mean that Man chooses his *overall goal*; then God gives Him the *specific steps* to get there. But if someone's plans are against God's will, and another person in relationship with God invites God to intervene, then He can respond and do something different than the people planned.

8) Perhaps most fascinatingly, we also have Scriptures that seem to show Man influencing God to "change" His Own expressed will.

In Exodus 32:9-14, we read that God says He's going to destroy Israel and start a new nation with Moses. Moses has a conversation with God (*faith-filled, relational prayer*) and "changes God's mind."

In Isaiah 38:1-5, we read that God declares that King Hezekiah needs to settle his business; because he's about to die. Hezekiah gets serious with God in *relational conversation (prayer)*, and within a few minutes, God says essentially, "Never mind what I said before. You just got another 15 years." These are just two examples.

46

We can all see clearly that *relationship with God*, yet again, is most often the deciding factor about what takes place in a situation—whether good or evil. God was in a position where people were going to reap what they had sown; but righteous man—through trusting relationship with God—invites God in to intervene and do the good that is really in His heart to do.

> Faith-filled prayer allows God to do the good that is really in His heart to do.

James 5:16b
...The effective, fervent prayer of a righteous man avails much.

So guess what happens when we don't have the effective, fervent prayer of a righteous man? Not much is availed!

Prayer is a Key to God's Will Being Done

James 4:2-3, 6
You lust and do not have. You murder and covet and cannot obtain. You fight and war. *Yet you do not have because you do not ask.* [3] You ask and do not receive, because you ask amiss, that you may spend *it* on your pleasures... [6] But He gives more grace.

We do not have, because we do not ask. Or, if we do take the time to ask, we ask "amiss" (with wrong direction or motivation). Some things we must "ask" for; but for other things, we only need to decree, "Your Kingdom come, Your will be done, on earth as it (already) is in Heaven" (Matthew 6:10). Let this visible world reflect what is accomplished in the invisible world,

Jesus! If something was already accomplished and included in our redemption, then we no longer need to ask for it, we just need to believe it and give thanks! This is how we do our job as Earth's Joint-Owners in Christ.

We must ask, and we must receive these invisible spiritual realities. Again: we do not have, because we do not ask. God requires us to *ask*. John Wesley is quoted as saying, "God will do *nothing* on the earth *except* in answer to believing prayer." Jack Hayford says, "The whole process by which God's will is done on earth depends on an interceding church."[1] To press a bit further, Dr. Lillian B. Yeomans wrote, "(God) has *tied Himself irrevocably* to human cooperation... He has made man's faith a determining factor in the execution of divine purposes."[2] First, Man must pray. Next, his faith trusts that God has answered, and causes him to *act*—Faith without works is dead. Lastly and most importantly, God's *grace* makes our work effective.

Hebrews 4:16
Let us therefore come boldly to the throne of grace, that we may obtain mercy and find grace to help in time of need.

We must receive God's grace, which enables us to act on our faith, which accesses God's help in bringing His ways into the natural realm. God has Sovereignly decided and decreed that the earth is our responsibility and that we as Mankind have dominion and authority here. Thus, He will not violate His Own Word by just doing whatever, whenever. He gave us the power of choice and authority in the earth, and He will honor our God-given right to make choices, even if they are against His will. However, He will also assist us if we ask Him. He patiently waits for our invitation. Relationship is the most supreme privilege of the Believer!

Our Responsibility

Matthew 18:18 (CEV)
I promise you that God in heaven will allow whatever you allow on earth, but he will not allow anything you don't allow.

God will allow whatever we allow? Wow! We make the choice, and God honors our choice, because He has granted us that role on Earth. Stunning! So instead of pointing our fingers at God—or even at the devil, for that matter—We need to point them at *ourselves* as the Church! God doesn't allow sickness, *we do.* Ouch! Really? Yep, I said it. Add to that list: poverty, injustice, perversion, crime, and whatever else goes on here that's out of line with Heaven's ways. And the devil only gets away with it because we don't do anything about it! Any time we try to shift responsibility off of ourselves—and onto God or the devil—for our problems, we know we are believing some religious nonsense. God has ordained that we would grow up and mature until we look exactly like Jesus.

> Any time we try to shift responsibility off of ourselves... we know we are believing some religious nonsense.

Ephesians 4:14-16
[14] that we should no longer be children, tossed to and fro and carried about with every wind of doctrine, by the trickery of men, in the cunning craftiness of deceitful plotting, [15] but, speaking the truth in love, may *grow up in all things into Him who is the head—Christ—* [16] from whom the whole body, joined and knit together by what every joint supplies, according to the effective working by which every part does its share, causes growth of the body for the edifying of itself in love.

Some people say that when I tell them it's our responsibility, it makes them feel condemned or guilty. That is not my intent. Listen, God is not into guilt and condemnation, and neither am I. You can have it one of two ways: One, God's will is responsible for everything, or two, Man has responsibility to run the earth. The problem with option one is that if God wills everything that happens, then we can't do anything... about anything! We'd just have to roll over and let life beat on us; because we know that we can't overpower "God's will." But if Man is in appointed authority and therefore responsible for loosing God's will into a situation, *then* when troubles come, we know that we have it beat with God's help. This is actually an empowering, liberating view, not a condemning one. Let's forget past mistakes and failures, and believe in the higher life God has already given us!

I often joke about the once-trendy "WWJD" ("What Would Jesus Do?") bracelets. I do this because as a new creation with a new nature like His, it should be basically instinctive for us to do what He would do. Our new nature is the very nature of Jesus. But as an analytical test of our theology, that might be a good question: "What *would* Jesus do?" If we ask that question in the face of sickness, we won't come up with some religious, theological nonsense answer. We will actually be one step in the right direction! Jesus is the acid test of any theology.

Jesus is the acid test of any theology.

If we'll consider what Jesus—"the Head"—looks like, and how *He* responds to sickness, for instance—We'll see what *we're* supposed to grow up into. So how does Jesus look? How does He act? How much authority does He have? We are called to represent Him—that means re-present (present again, copycat, imitate, reflect) Jesus! Make conscious decisions to reject the thoughts that don't mirror His. Imitate Him until your new, real, re-created, invisible nature is what comes out most "naturally." This is part of the mind-renewing process—visibly reflecting who we already are invisibly.

People are always waiting for God to do something, even asking Him to do something. Meanwhile, God is waiting for *us* to do the job He empowered and commissioned us to do. He gave us the authority. He gave us the resources. We are in Christ! Let's look again at Ephesians 2:

Ephesians 2:4-6
[4] But God, who is rich in mercy, because of His great love with which He loved us, [5] even when we were dead in trespasses, made us alive together with Christ (by grace you have been saved), [6] and raised us up together, and made us sit together in the heavenly places in Christ Jesus,

Are you in Christ? If so, then all things are under you! Are you in Christ? Then *you are seated at the right hand of God in a place of authority* over all principality and power. Are you in Christ?

Then you have dominion over devils and every sickness and disease. So when the devil is allowed to operate—It isn't God that is allowing it—It's US—The Church! The basic assumption of many people—even Christians—that "God allows sickness", is therefore mistaken. Worse still is the idea that God not only allows it, but wills/approves of it. We'll get to that one later. Everything that God has is ours!! The world *belongs* to us in Christ; and we are commissioned, empowered, and responsible to do our Daddy's business—with the full backing of heaven! God's will is *always* healing!

Notes:

CHAPTER 3

GOD'S SOVEREIGNTY

Understanding What Sovereignty Is And Isn't

For the sake of clarity, I looked up "sovereign" on www.dictionary.com. Here's how it defines the adjective form of the word:

–adjective
5. belonging to or characteristic of a sovereign or sovereignty; royal.
6. having supreme rank, power, or authority.
7. supreme; preeminent; indisputable...
8. greatest in degree; utmost or extreme.
9. being above all others in character, importance, excellence, etc.
10. efficacious; potent... [1]

I completely agree that God is Sovereign, if we're talking about these dictionary definitions. God is royal. God has supreme rank, power, and authority (there is none higher or more powerful than He). He is the greatest, the utmost. He is above all others in character, importance, and excellence. He is efficacious (effective) and potent (powerful). I believe in the Sovereignty of God!

However, when *some* people say, "God is Sovereign," they mean that they can chalk any kind of weirdness that happens up to a mysterious God they don't know very well. When others say "God is Sovereign," they actually mean that everything that happens is the will of God. It doesn't matter if this occurrence is totally against common sense, against the Biblical picture of God and His Character and Nature, against all His promises, against what we see in Heaven and in the Garden, against the perfect picture of God that Jesus provided, and against all that Christ accomplished for us on the cross—they think God did it all. Rubbish!

Now, we wouldn't take that made-up definition of sovereignty, and apply it to any "sovereign" nation on earth! When we say a nation is sovereign, we just mean that they are independent, and that they call the shots and make the rules for their own territory. For instance, the United States is a sovereign nation. We have laws and rules that define how we want things done here. However, does that stop people from breaking the rules? Of course not. Let's say someone commits a murder. We don't blame the President for the criminal's behavior saying, "Hey look, you're the boss of this sovereign nation, so you control every little detail of what goes on. You must have planned for this to happen." Ridiculous! Nowhere in the definition of "sovereign" is "control of every detail" implied.

The government's responsibility is to write the laws that define what is acceptable and not acceptable in this country. They are to establish police forces and a justice system to enforce these laws. These are the folks that have to do the "leg work" of making the nation look like the plan does. This is a fairly decent picture of life in the Kingdom! Redeemed Mankind has the day-to-day duties of running the Kingdom in accordance with the ways of the King. We enforce what God has established and decreed as His will.

As we discussed in the last chapter, God has reserved some things for His Own authority. He gave certain responsibilities to Man, and maintained some other duties for Himself. For instance, in Matthew 24 and Mark 13, we see the disciples asking Jesus about when He'll set up His earthly Kingdom. Part of His response:

Mark 13:32
"But of that day and hour no one knows, not even the angels in heaven, nor the Son, but only the Father.

Nobody knows or handles the timing of that event but the Father—not even the angels or Jesus Himself. God has reserved control of that event for Himself. However, other areas of responsibility He has given to Mankind. But some other folks say that God controls every detail of daily life here on earth. They are saying that everything that happens is God's will and plan. Rape, murder, child molestation, sickening torturous diseases, genocides, pornography, sex trafficking—it doesn't matter what it is—they say He decreed and ordained all of it. To say something is God's will is to say that He *chose* it; and to say that He chose it is to say that He is responsible for it. To say He is *responsible* for it... is... Be careful!!! To break this theory down to its most basic idea: If everything that happens is God's decree and will, then God is responsible for—and therefore guilty of—sin. Come on, does that make any Biblical sense whatsoever? Is God Holy or not? A Holy God is the God of the Bible, and a Holy God is not guilty of sin. This is not rocket science: God has some responsibilities He's kept for Himself, and the rest He's handed to us.

> To say something is God's will is to say that He *chose* it; and to say that He chose it is to say that He is *responsible* for it.

Sovereign Does Not Mean Inconsistent

Some people think that "Sovereignty" means God is some kind of cosmic loose cannon. For instance, if somebody is sick and I show up boldly declaring healing as God's will for them, some people have a problem with that. They take me aside and say things like, "You can't say that for sure. Sometimes God heals and sometimes He doesn't. How can you pretend to know what God wants? You're not God! God is Sovereign, after all." In other words, they're saying, "God is inconsistent." But they must not know that God has already clearly revealed in His Word that His will is always healing. Period. And He never goes back on His Word. I can therefore confidently state that God will do what He says He will do.

Psalm 89:34
My covenant I will not break, nor alter the word that has gone out of My lips.

55

Psalm 119:89
Forever, O LORD, Your word is settled in heaven.

Isaiah 40:8
The grass withers, the flower fades, But the word of our God stands forever."

Numbers 23:19
"God is not a man, that He should lie, Nor a son of man, that He should repent. Has He said, and will He not do? Or has He spoken, and will He not make it good?

When God says something, we can bank on it! When God declared that He gave earth to the children of men, and that we are to have dominion over all the works of His hands, He meant it, and He won't change that. When He says that Healing is His will, and that it's the children's bread, He meant it, and He won't change it!

Listen, "Sovereign" does not mean, "unreliable," or "inconsistent." God does not just do random, unpredictable things—some good, some bad, some indifferent. God is steady. God is sure. God never changes. His Holy and Loving Character and Nature can be clearly seen and known. He has clearly revealed many aspects of His will in His Word. His Word contains promises of what He will do for us. His Word is the basis for true faith. If we believe His Word, we can confidently expect God to come through. God is reliable!

Not only does His Word make us multiple promises of Healing; but if God has ever healed anyone of anything, He'll do it for another; because He is fair, and shows

> If we believe His Word, we can confidently expect God to come through. God is reliable!

no favoritism or partiality to anyone! If He did if for one, He'll do it for another, and He'll do it for you or I; because He is consistent, steady and reliable!

Luke 20:21
Then they asked Him, saying, "Teacher, we know that You say and teach rightly, and *You do not show personal favoritism*, but teach the way of God in truth:

Galatians 2:6
...God shows personal favoritism to no man...

James 2:1, 8-9
[1] My brethren, do not hold the faith of our Lord Jesus Christ, the Lord of glory, with partiality...
[8] If you really fulfill the royal law according to the Scripture, "You shall love your neighbor as yourself," you do well; [9] but *if you show partiality, you commit sin, and are convicted by the law as transgressors.*

If we say that God will heal one; but hold it back from another, then we are saying that God is showing partiality and favoritism. We are either saying that God loves one more than He does another, or He's got some other shady motivation for differentiating. These verses tell us plainly that He does not do that in the New Covenant. They also say that if He did, He would be committing sin and transgressing His Own law! If you know anything about God, then you know that this is utterly impossible!

But some people see some terrible thing happen, and just throw up their hands and say, "Well, the Lord moves in mysterious ways." Folks, that is not in the

> The Infinite God has made Himself intimately knowable.

Bible! Yes, God is amazing! And yes, He does supernatural things that we can't always wrap our heads around. He is certainly beyond natural, finite comprehension in His power and wisdom. But at the same time, we are created in His image; and He made us to know Him. His ways should not be a mystery to His children, His friends, His Bride—and that's us. The Infinite God has made Himself intimately knowable. Then they'll quote this Scripture to me:

1 Corinthians 2:9
Eye has not seen, nor ear heard, nor have entered into the heart of man the things which God has prepared for those who love Him."

But of course they leave off the next three verses:

1 Corinthians 2:10-12
"*But God has revealed them to us through His Spirit.* For the Spirit searches all things, yes, the deep things of God. For what man knows the things of a man except the spirit of the man which is in him? Even so no one knows the things of God except the Spirit of God. Now *we have received*, not the spirit of the world, but *the Spirit who is from God, that we might know the things that have been freely given to us by God.*

The first word is "But." That's an important "but!" Paul is quoting an Old Testament Scripture about the way things were, then clearly contrasts it with our situation in the New Testament. He's saying "It *used to be*, that God was a mystery to our unregenerate selves; but now as born again Believers, He's given us His Own Spirit. Why did God give us His Spirit? So 'that we might know the things that have been freely given to us by God (like healing, for instance)'. God gave us His Spirit so we can know Him, His character, His will, and His ways."

John 15:15
No longer do I call you servants, for a servant does not know what his master is doing; but I have called you friends, for all things that I heard from My Father I have made known to you.

> Jesus said that if we are His friends, He'll tell us everything!

Jesus said that if we are His friends, He'll tell us everything! I've heard all kinds of Christians talk about how, "Christianity is not a religion; it's a relationship!" But what kind of relationship would you have with someone if you never know what to expect of them from one day to the next? Can you trust this person? Will they do what they said they would do? Can you believe the things they tell you? Do you need to "walk on pins and needles" around them; because you never know what kind of crazy mood they'll be in from day to day? If somebody else made some false accusation against them that was totally outside their character, would you know it? Of course you would, because relationship = knowing someone's character and ways. Relationship with God is no different. We can and should know Him, and progressively be getting to know Him more each day.

Sovereign Does Not Mean "Control Freak"

Continuing our discussion on God's Sovereignty... When some people say, "God is Sovereign," they mean that He controls everything that goes on in the world. But listen, "Sovereign" doesn't mean "Control Freak!" For instance, someone gets cancer, and the family says, "This is terrible, but God is Sovereign—He's in control. This must be the will of God." The problem is, God is *not* in control, *not* in the sense that they mean it. They believe that people are essentially puppets and pawns with no influence on the world whatsoever. In other words, they think that God's will is automatic and unavoidable— that everything that happens is the will of God, by His decree and command.

But if everything that happens is God's will, He couldn't justly dish out reward or punishment for things we have no choice about. Also, if everything that happens is God's will, then let's just "eat, drink and be merry, for tomorrow we die"--"God's will is going to happen anyway," right? Wrong! This hyper-sovereign view has rightly been called, "The arch-enemy of soul winning."

> If everything that happens is God's will, why should we do anything at all?

Now, I know that the people who believe this stuff answer, "We do it because God commands it, and to disobey Him would be sin." I understand that; but come on, what would be the purpose of God commanding us to pray, for instance, if His will would happen whether we cooperated or not? "Because He wants us to obey and grow up," they say. The purpose of growing up into Christ is to operate like He does—to be like Him. Not only to "be" like Him; but to "do" like Him—to rule and reign *with* Him. But guess what? If there is nothing to rule over—nothing opposing the will of God—then what is the purpose of growing up and learning to rule (do things) like He does? But I say that there *is* something to rule over—the forces that oppose God's will.

Luke 11:2
So He said to them, "When you pray, say: Our Father in heaven, Hallowed be Your name. Your kingdom come. *Your will be done on earth as it is in heaven.*

Why would Jesus tell us to pray, "Your Kingdom come, Your will be done, on earth as it is in Heaven," if His will were already being done? Why would He tell us to pray for something we are already experiencing? That would make this prayer a purposeless exercise. Heaven looks like God's will. He wants it to be that way on earth. We have to pray in order for it to be done, which means it isn't already being done. There are things happening here that are not the will of God, or the Lord's prayer would be meaningless. There are opposing influences (Satan and demons, fallen Creation, and the will of men not yielded to God) still to be brought in line with His will.

> Why would Jesus tell us to pray, "Your Kingdom come, Your will be done, on earth as it is in Heaven," if His will were already being done?

There are 10 times in the New Testament where the Lord mentions those Believers who "overcome" (1 John 5:4, 5, Rev. 2:7, 11, 17, 26, 3:5, 12, 21, and 21:6). In Romans 8:37, He calls us "more than conquerors." The obvious question to me is—If God's will is already being done, then what are we overcoming and conquering? God? His will? Of course not! We are overcoming and conquering the forces that *oppose* God, His will, and us—His people.

60

Look at what the Scripture says in Ephesians:

Ephesians 6:12
For we do not wrestle against flesh and blood, but against principalities, against powers, against the rulers of the darkness of this age, against spiritual hosts of wickedness in the heavenly places.

Why are we wrestling? If God's will is automatic, then there is no need to fight the devil, right? Wrong! These "spiritual hosts of wickedness" are obviously doing something God opposes, or He wouldn't be having us "wrestle against" them. If they were doing God's will, and we wrestled against them, then we would be wrestling against God Himself. Was God saying we should fight against Him? Of course not!

> If God's will is automatic, then there is no need to fight the devil, right? Wrong!

Think about this: What does it look like when God is in control of things? We must look at Heaven. Now, there are "heavenly places" (or "the heavens") where Satan and his demons rebelled and fell, and they obviously are doing stuff that is not in line with God's will there. But I'm talking about the third heaven (2 Corinthians 12:2)—the place where God Himself dwells. Heaven is a place that reflects the way God wants things to look. There is no sickness there, no crying, no pain. He commanded us to pray, "Your Kingdom come, Your will be done, on earth as it is in Heaven." In other words, He wants to answer the prayer that Earth would become like Heaven, completely yielded to His way of doing things. Why would we have to pray this if His will was already being done? That—again—would be a fruitless exercise. There is no sickness allowed in Heaven, God wants our prayers to release that reality so that there is no sickness allowed on Earth either. This is the real essence of prayers of binding and loosing, or the "Keys of the Kingdom."

Matthew 16:19 (AMP)
[19]I will give you the keys of the kingdom of heaven; and whatever you bind (declare to be improper and unlawful) on earth must be what is already

61

bound in heaven; and whatever you loose (declare lawful) on earth must be what is already loosed in heaven.

Matthew 18:18 (NASB)
"Truly I say to you, whatever you bind on earth *shall have been* bound in heaven; and whatever you loose on earth *shall have been* loosed in heaven.

I realize that the Amplified or New American Standard translations might alter your previous understanding of these verses; but even the footnotes in the NIV and NKJV verify this as the most correct translation. Jesus says that we should know what is already allowed/not allowed in Heaven, and allow/not allow it here on Earth, so that Earth reflects Heaven. Again, this confirms our understanding of the Lord's Prayer in Luke 11:2— "Your Kingdom come, Your will be done on earth, as it is in Heaven."

Examples: Purity, Salvation and Healing

God has given us multiple examples in Scripture of things happening that are directly opposed to His clearly expressed will.

1 Thessalonians 4:3-8
³ For *this is the will of God, your sanctification: that you should abstain from sexual immorality;* ⁴ *that each of you should know how to possess his own vessel in sanctification and honor,* ⁵ *not in passion of lust*, like the Gentiles who do not know God; ⁶ that no one should take advantage of and defraud his brother in this matter, because the Lord is the avenger of all such, as we also forewarned you and testified. ⁷ For *God did not call us to uncleanness, but in holiness.* ⁸ Therefore *he who rejects this does not reject man, but God*, who has also given us His Holy Spirit.

We read in these verses that it is the will of God that Christians "abstain from sexual immorality," "passion of lust," and "uncleanness." It says that God calls us (it is His clear will that we engage in and reflect) "in holiness." It then says that if we choose not to do this, that we "reject... God." This clearly demonstrates that we have a choice to do the will of God, or to do something else. If you've been around for any length of time, chances are that you've known a Christian that has messed up in this area, and chosen not to live up to God's will and standard for them. This proves that God does not always get what He wants. Not because of any weakness on His part; but because of His beautiful will that we would be free beings that can choose to love Him genuinely. This brings us to the next example.

Perhaps the most obvious example of God's will *not* being done is concerning Salvation. What more central, seemingly obvious thing could we say is the will of God, but that all people would be saved?

1 Timothy 2:3-4
[3] ... *God our Savior,* [4] who *desires all men to be saved* and to come to the knowledge of the truth.

2 Peter 3:9
The Lord is not slack concerning His promise, as some count slackness, but is longsuffering toward us, *not willing that any should perish but that all should come to repentance.*

> Perhaps the most obvious example of God's will not being done is concerning Salvation.

These Scriptures clearly tell us that it is not God's will that any would perish, but that everyone would come to the knowledge of the truth, repent, and be saved. Hello? The whole centerpiece of human history is Jesus coming to the cross so that *all men* could be saved and reunited with God through His sacrificial work! I've seen people try to pick these verses apart and say basically that "not willing" doesn't really mean, "not willing." They'll say there is two ways to define what God's "will" is (the so-called "dual nature of God's will").

Although I understand that there are two meanings for "will" (one for something you don't necessarily "want" to do, and one for an actual "desire"), give me a Holy Ghost break! The point is made so clear throughout the Word, that the point is moot. God's will is salvation for all. God's will is healing for all. God paid the highest price that could ever be paid to make this available to all men, so that "*whoever* believes" could be saved, healed and delivered! God *wills, desires,* and *wants* with all of His heart for *all* men to be saved and set free from the devil's works, period.

John 3:16
For God so loved the world that He gave His only begotten Son, that *whoever* believes in Him should not perish but have everlasting life.

God's clear will is that *all the world* be saved; and yet, not all men will be saved. Every day, there are people dying who haven't accepted God's free gift of Salvation. So in the largest, most important issue there is—it is clear that God's will is not being done. Most people can recognize this clear example, and admit that even though it's God's will for everyone to be saved, not everyone gets saved. But even if they understand that, they'll go back to their old, failed logic when it comes to healing.

We must never judge God's will by our own experience.

"Well, I prayed for healing; but I'm still sick. So it must just be God's will. If God wanted to heal me, I'd be healed." Not so! We must never judge God's will by our own experience. We can go through the same Scriptural process with Healing that we did with Salvation:

3 John 2
Beloved, I pray that you may prosper in all things and be in health, just as your soul prospers.

If this is God's will for us, as expressed by the Holy Spirit, through the Apostle John, then it is clearly God's will that we "be in health," just as our soul prospers. God wants us to "be in health." That's a clear statement. Or, how about straight from the mouth of Jesus:

Matthew 8:2-3
[2] And behold, a leper came and worshiped Him, saying, "Lord, if You are willing, You can make me clean." [3] Then Jesus put out His hand and touched him, saying, "*I am willing,* be cleansed." Immediately his leprosy was cleansed.

64

Again, we see Jesus clearly saying here that He is willing. When Jesus said, "I am willing," He was saying that this is His will, His *desire*. It describes an unchanging attribute of His eternal good nature and love. It's just Who He is! And if we have any doubt about what "willing" means in this case, how does Jesus demonstrate what it means? His life clearly demonstrates what He means by "willing" in regards to healing. He *always* healed *everyone* that came. *Always*.

God also identifies Himself as Jehovah Rapha (The LORD Who Heals) in the Old Testament (Exodus 15:26b). It's His very Name. It's His Name, because again, it's His unchangeable Nature! God is a Healer. It's Who He is, so it's what He does. *Always*.

So, God is clearly "willing," or "desiring," for all to be well. And yet, some people are obviously still sick and dying—just as in the case of Salvation. Why? Because, again, God's will is not automatic. God Sovereignly chose to give man certain freedoms and responsibilities, and the authority to handle them. He gave His Word on it, and once He does that, it's law. His Word is the basis for our faith, our prayers, and our exercise of God-given authority. We can either believe and receive, or doubt and do without—that's just the bottom line!

> We can either believe and receive, or doubt and do without—that's just the bottom line!

Spouses, Slaves and Robots

If God foreknew Man's sin and fall, why did He still create us? The answer is…. LOVE. There is a famous saying, "If you love something, set it free. If it comes back to you, it is yours. If it does not, it never was." What do I mean? Let me explain. God created Man for one purpose: to have relationship with us. Loving relationship is God's big goal in creating humanity! In order to have a meaningful relationship with someone, it must be a two-way street. Both parties must freely choose the other, or it would not be a loving relationship—it would be slavery. God didn't want slaves, He wanted friends, He wanted a Bride. Some people think that God should have created a world where there was no possibility of man sinning. But there *had* to be the option to sin, or there could be no freedom to choose God from a pure heart of love for Him. *There is no true loving relationship if one has their freedom taken away!*

Control is rooted in fear. If someone has control issues in their relationship, it's because they are afraid of something. They're afraid you'll leave. They're afraid that once you really know them, you won't love them. They're afraid they'll be abandoned. They're afraid you'll like somebody else more. Listen, God is not insecure. He is 100% whole and confident in Who He is. He knows that if you ever really know Him, you'll love Him forever. He loves you and wants you to stay, but if you choose to leave, that's up to you.

1 John 4:18
18 There is no fear in love; but perfect love casts out fear, because fear involves torment. But he who fears has not been made perfect in love.

Let's say you are looking to get married. You want a spouse to share a lifelong, loving relationship with. Do you meet someone, get to know one another, and both freely decide to marry? I hope so—for that is the nature of love. These other options are scary:

Maybe you could buy a slave-spouse on the Internet somewhere. Sick! If you have any justice in your heart whatsoever, the idea makes your skin crawl! What joy could you possibly have, if your so-called "spouse" had to be chained to the bedroom wall in your absence; because they didn't love you, and only stayed around out of fear and control? Oh, they act nice enough when you're there; but you both know that if they were unlocked and free to decide, they'd be out of there in five seconds flat! Would you feel the love? Would they? Of course not!

66

Or, maybe you could buy a state-of-the-art robot that is at your beck and call. If someone thinks that God forces one to love Him (by only creating people with no option to do otherwise), then they are saying that God just wants a robot for a wife. Everything that God suggests, the robot just says, "Yes, awesome. Let's do that." How would that relationship be meaningful to God? He programs a human robot to say, "I love you, God." Would hearing that bring joy to His heart? Would He say in return, "You are the apple of my eye (Zechariah 2:8)"? Would He rejoice over that robot with singing (Zephaniah 3:17)? Would He say to this programmed robot-bride, "I'll send my Son to die so I can have you (John 3:16)"?

True Love = Freedom to Choose

On the other hand, what does a genuine, loving relationship look like? It's two individuals choosing to spend time together. The guy chooses the action movie, and the girl goes along with it one time. Next time, the girl chooses the chick flick, and the guy goes. Reciprocation. Honor. Putting others first. Learning to appreciate how that person is unique. Soon, we may find that we like some things that they like—things that may have seemed so foreign to us in the beginning. Appreciation. Growth. You call them one time; they call you the next. Balance. Love. They visit you, then you visit them. They cook dinner, and then you cook dinner. They choose the restaurant, then you choose the restaurant. Both parties take initiative to develop a real relationship—not just one.

Some of you can probably speak from experience, and say that if things don't work that way, you quickly sense the imbalance. If you're always doing what the other person wants to do, and they just blow off everything you suggest—the relationship will

> Thank God for free will—without it, there is no true love!

diminish in value to you. Or, if the other person is always doing what you want to do, (assuming you're not totally self-absorbed) you will find yourself saying, "Let's do something *you* want to do." If that person says, "I only want to do what *you want* to do," we'll think something is wrong with them. That would get weird very quickly. No—true, balanced, meaningful relationships, be they friendships, romances, or parent-child relationships— need two individuals who honor one another, share, and reciprocate love. It's no coincidence that God uses each of those human relationships as pictures of our relationship with Him. He wants us to choose Him. To choose Him, there must also be an alternative choice. That is why having the option to sin is necessary. Thank God for free will—without it, there is no true Love!

John 4:19
We love Him because He first loved us.

God loved us first. Because He truly loved us, He had to set us free. One is only free if one has options, choices. So God willed that there would be options available to us. Some will choose wisely, others won't. He gives us the freedom to make the choice. In the face of freedom, He desires that we choose Him. In the end, we love Him, because He loved us enough to set us free—and keep us that way!

Sin is not God's will; but the *freedom* to sin *is*.

Relationship is only genuine and meaningful if both individuals freely choose one another. Any time one party has no choice about being in the relationship, it is something other than love. So, the point is: God created a world, knowing in advance that Satan would tempt people to sin. Some would do it. But some, on the other hand, would choose God. God wants everyone to choose Him; but knows not all will. But the love of those that choose Him makes the whole drama worthwhile. God does not will for us to sin; but He does will for the option to be available! Sin is *not* God's will; but the freedom to sin *is*.

Joshua 24:15 (excerpts)
"... *choose for yourselves* this day whom you will serve...But as for me and my house, we will serve the LORD."

Deuteronomy 30:19
I call heaven and earth as witnesses today against you, that I have set before you life and death, blessing and cursing; *therefore choose life*, that both you and your descendants may live;

God loves us. He's not a control freak. He has created us with a free will to choose to love Him or not. He's clearly laid out the options. But He cares so much for us, He gives us a big hint about which choice to make! How would He command us to "choose for yourselves," knowing that we didn't have a choice at all, but were simply robots programmed to do whatever He had previously decided? Nonsense. That would be completely deceptive, or unjust at a minimum—neither of which are attributes that describe our Holy God.

But God does require that there are options available to us. This is a simple necessity of love. If we are to choose Him at all, then there must also be another option available. This is why he created the devil, knowing that in time, he would rebel and fall and tempt Mankind. Temptation=options. God does not approve of stealing; but He does approve of us having the option to steal. His will is that we would *not* steal. He does not approve of rape, incest, or murder; but He does want us to have the *option*. God hates these things, and His will is that we *do not* do them. And yet some people will. We can only love God meaningfully if we also have the option to do otherwise. God gave us options, because He loved us, and wanted us to love Him back—solely because we genuinely desired Him.

> We can only love God meaningfully if we also have the option to do otherwise.

Notes:

CHAPTER 4

DEVILS, THE CURSE, and FREE WILL

Why is the World Such a Mess?

So, people may ask, if God is so powerful and good, then why is the world such a mess? I'm glad you asked. This one question— and the average Christian's inability to answer it satisfactorily— has probably turned more people away from Christianity than any other thing. We need to know this stuff!

There are three primary answers to this question:
- The Devil and his angels (Spiritual)
- The Earth being under a curse, as a result of sin (Natural), and
- The choices of Mankind (Humans and their Free Will).

1) The Devil and His Angels

It's appropriate to again quote Ephesians on this subject:

Ephesians 6:12
For we do not wrestle against flesh and blood, but against principalities, against powers, against the rulers of the darkness of this age, against spiritual hosts of wickedness in the heavenly places.

This says that we have a battle with spiritual forces that oppose us. If devils oppose us, and God is for us, then that demonstrates that the devils are not doing the will of God. Some people think that the devil is just a pawn, or a tool that God uses to accomplish His Own will. Check out the chapter, "God is Good" for more on this subject. For now, it should be obvious that the devil's will and God's will are not one and the same.

1 Peter 5:8
Be sober, be vigilant; because your adversary the devil walks about like a roaring lion, seeking whom he may devour.

The devil is trying to devour people. But note that it says whom he "may" devour. So he can't devour just anybody. We are supposed to be on the lookout, and be prepared so that we can resist him and foil his attacks. We do have authority, but we need to use it.

James 4:7
Therefore submit to God. Resist the devil and he will flee from you.

Assuming we are submitted to God, if we'll resist the devil, he will flee. The devil knows that Christians have authority over him—better than most Christians do. That's one reason he hates us. He is a rebel, and we are authority figures. He is a criminal, and we are the cops! He rebelled against God in the beginning, and he's rebelling against those that stand in God's authority to this day. God loves people. The devil hates people; because he knows that we are the objects of God's affection. We've been made in God's image and likeness and have been exalted in Christ to a place the devil wanted for himself. He also knows that in hurting us, he can cause God pain.

> The devil knows that Christians have authority over him— better than most Christians do.

John 10:10
The thief does not come except to steal, and to kill, and to destroy. I have come that they may have life, and that they may have it more abundantly.

So it is clear that one reason the world is such a mess is that we have an enemy—Satan and his devils—who are opposed to us, fighting us, seeking to devour us, killing, stealing, and destroying. But if we're in authority over the devil because of what Jesus accomplished, then why is he still able to get away with murder—both figuratively and literally?

The Devil is a Law-Breaker

Even now that authority over the earth has been handed back over to Believers—The devil can still get away with a lot, even though he has been defeated and stripped of all authority. Why? Three main reasons:

- The devil is a *thief* (John 10:10). A thief knows that there are laws and authority, but he breaks the law anyway.

- He hasn't been properly *identified* as the culprit! When people who have been victimized by the devil get to look at the "lineup" of those who they can blame, most people see God there, and they blame *Him*! Then the cops (Believers) end up "booking" the wrong guy! So the devil walks out scot-free and continues his crimes against humanity!

- A few of us can accurately identify him as the bad guy, and catch him—but we're not always sure how to convict him, lock him up, and stop him from violating us! We just sit around and talk about it: "Boy, that dirty devil sure did me wrong!" But we haven't enforced the laws!

> If nobody is going to enforce the law, the devil figures, "Why not break it?!"

Most of us don't even know the laws! If nobody is going to enforce the laws, the devil figures, "Why not break 'em?!" Satan will bring sickness and disease on anyone he can, even though he knows it's not "legal," because he is a rebel, and most of the time nobody stops him. This is why people today don't have to sin or do anything wrong to get sick. If someone is sick, it just means the devil is a dirty old dog, that's all. Somebody doesn't need to sin or do anything wrong to "deserve" a sickness or disease. The devil will try to kill anybody he can, whether they "deserve" it or not, and whether they "left a door open" or not.

He will hate us and hurt us, good or bad, young or old, innocent or guilty. He's a no-good thief and a law-breaker, period.

Listen, let's say that you "left the door open" on your house, and some thief comes in and runs out with your TV. You find out, the cops catch him red-handed, and he comes before the judge at his trial. If he says, "Well, Your Honor, he left the door open," the judge isn't going to say, "What did you bring this poor, innocent man here for? The door was open. Case dismissed!"

> Sickness is sometimes a direct spiritual attack from the devil.

No, no, no. He's going to say, "So what? The house was not your property—you trespassed! Nor was the TV your property. You took it without permission—you stole! Period. Guilty as charged—Do not pass 'Go', do not collect $200—Go directly to Jail!!"

So I don't care if somebody "left a door open" for sickness to come in. That doesn't make it OK for Satan to steal, kill, and destroy. He's a thief and a killer and we need to put him under arrest and put him in jail.

Here are some Scriptures that show that sickness is *sometimes* a direct spiritual attack from the devil:

Mark 9:17-18, 25-27
[17] Then one of the crowd answered and said, "Teacher, I brought You *my son, who has a mute spirit.* [18] And wherever *it seizes him, it throws him down*; he foams at the mouth, gnashes his teeth, and becomes rigid. So I spoke to Your disciples, that they should cast it out, but they could not..."
[25] When Jesus saw that the people came running together, *He rebuked the unclean spirit, saying to it, "Deaf and dumb spirit, I command you, come out of him and enter him no more!"* [26] *Then the spirit cried out, convulsed him greatly, and came out of him.* And he became as one dead, so that many said, "He is dead." [27] But Jesus took him by the hand and lifted him up, and he arose.

The man said his son had a mute *spirit* that was causing his condition. Jesus agreed, cast it out, and the boy was healed.

Here's another one:

Luke 13:10-16

[10] Now He was teaching in one of the synagogues on the Sabbath. [11] And behold, there was a woman who had *a spirit of infirmity* eighteen years, and was bent over and could in no way raise herself up. [12] But when Jesus saw her, He called her to Him and said to her, "Woman, you are loosed from your infirmity." [13] And He laid His hands on her, and immediately she was made straight, and glorified God.

[14] But the ruler of the synagogue answered with indignation, because Jesus had healed on the Sabbath; and he said to the crowd, "There are six days on which men ought to work; therefore come and be healed on them, and not on the Sabbath day."

[15] The Lord then answered him and said, "Hypocrite! Does not each one of you on the Sabbath loose his ox or donkey from the stall, and lead it away to water it? [16] So ought not *this woman*, being a daughter of Abraham, *whom Satan has bound*—think of it—for eighteen years, be loosed from this bond on the Sabbath?" [17] And when He said these things, all His adversaries were put to shame; and all the multitude rejoiced for all the glorious things that were done by Him.

> Jesus blamed Satan for sickness.
> Simple enough, right?

These show a couple of clear examples of some sicknesses being *directly* caused by a demonic spirit. In the Luke 13 example, Jesus even calls the lady one "whom Satan has bound." Note that he didn't blame God! Jesus blamed Satan for sickness. Simple enough, right? So, obviously, the devil can directly cause destruction and mayhem; but he is not the only reason that the world is a mess...

2) The Earth is Under a Curse

Not only are we opposed by demonic, spiritual forces, there are actually "natural" forces that are out of line with God's will—that oppose God's will being done. What am I talking about? When you see a terrible storm that floods a city, and thousands die— did God do that? No. Did the devil? Well, yes, indirectly—by tempting Adam to sin and bring a curse on the earth. But ultimately, it's just that the Earth system is now messed up and out of line with God's authority. "Nature takes its course", and that course is no longer in the perfect order that God created it to be. Remember when God created the earth and said, "It is good" (Genesis 1:31)? After Adam sinned, it wasn't quite as good.

As a result of Man's fall, the earth came under a curse, right? "Cursed is the ground for your sake," God said in Genesis 3:17. When Adam gave authority to the devil, and the devil had his way, things got pretty out-of-whack! Nature, weather, animals, plants, genetics, ecology, you name it. Sin results in a downward spiral of destruction and death.

Some sickness, then, comes from Creation being under a curse— thrown off course by the sin of Mankind. It could be out-of-kilter body functions (decay, breakdown, cancer, deformity, chemical and hormone problems, etc). Or it might be out-of-order microscopic creatures (bacteria, viruses, etc) that had some positive, useful purpose prior to the Fall. This still ultimately makes *all* sickness the work of the devil, because he is the one that tempted Adam to fall into the sin that brought the Curse.

> Some sickness comes from Creation being under a curse—thrown off course by the sin of Mankind.

This is why we *must* start learning how to operate in the authority Jesus gave to us! The sick are waiting for us!! The lost, the lonely, the oppressed, the depressed, the enslaved, the sad, the greedy, the proud, the poor, the rich, the young, the old— they're all waiting! Even the *earth itself* ("nature") is waiting for us. Look at these powerful verses from Romans 8:

Romans 8:18-22

[18] For I consider that the sufferings of this present time are not worthy *to be compared* with the glory which shall be revealed in us. [19] For the earnest expectation of the *creation eagerly waits for the revealing of the sons of God*. [20] For the *creation was subjected to futility, not willingly,* but because of Him who subjected *it* in hope; [21] because the *creation itself also will be delivered*

from the bondage of corruption into the glorious liberty of the children of God. ²² For we know that the whole creation groans and labors with birth pangs together until now.

> All of Creation is crying out, "Please, sons of God, come into your place of authority and bring back the rule of God!"

The oceans and rivers, trees, tectonic plates, skies, animals, stars—all of them are groaning for the manifestation of the sons of God!!! All of creation is crying out, "Please, sons of God, come into your place of authority and bring back the rule of God!"

Where else can we find the concept of Nature being out of line with God's will in the Word? How about in the Word made Flesh—Jesus Himself? We see Jesus exercising authority over out-of-order nature at least twice in the Bible. First, let's look at the fig tree:

Matthew 21:18-22

¹⁸ Now in the morning, as He returned to the city, He was hungry. ¹⁹ And seeing a fig tree by the road, He came to it and found nothing on it but leaves, and said to it, "Let no fruit grow on you ever again." Immediately the fig tree withered away. ²⁰ And when the disciples saw it, they marveled, saying, "How did the fig tree wither away so soon?" ²¹ So Jesus answered and said to them, "Assuredly, I say to you, if you have faith and do not doubt, you will not only do what was done to the fig tree, but also if you say to this mountain, 'Be removed and be cast into the sea,' it will be done. ²² And whatever things you ask in prayer, believing, you will receive."

Jesus wanted (willed) to eat fruit from the tree. There was no fruit on the tree (against God's will). Jesus said to Nature (the tree) "You're out of whack, not doing what you're supposed to be doing. You're wasting space—Go away." Nature was operating out of the will of God. Jesus corrected it. We are supposed to be like Him.

Second, let's look at the storm:

Luke 8:22-25

²² Now it happened, on a certain day, that He got into a boat with His disciples. And He said to them, "Let us cross over to the other side of the

lake." And they launched out. [23] But as they sailed He fell asleep. And a windstorm came down on the lake, and they were filling *with water,* and were in jeopardy. [24] And they came to Him and awoke Him, saying, "Master, Master, we are perishing!" Then He arose and rebuked the wind and the raging of the water. And they ceased, and there was a calm. [25] But He said to them, "Where is your faith?" And they were afraid, and marveled, saying to one another, "Who can this be? For He commands even the winds and water, and they obey Him!"

> If the storm was God's will, then was Jesus fighting against the Father?

Here we again see Jesus exerting authority over nature that is not operating in accordance with God's will. And He's a bit disappointed that the disciples haven't yet learned how to do it themselves! But here's what I'd like us to ask ourselves: If the storm was God's will, then was Jesus fighting against the Father?

- If so, then Jesus is NOT "the image of the invisible God" (Col.1:15).
- If so, then Jesus is NOT Immanuel "God with us" (Is.7:14, Matt 1:23).
- If so, Jesus and the Father are NOT "One" (John 10:30).
- If so, then when we've seen Jesus, we have NOT "seen the Father" (John 14:9).
- If so, then Jesus did NOT only do the things He saw the Father doing (John 5:19-20). If God was causing the storm, then Jesus would have seen this and cooperated— He would not have rebuked the will of God from being done.
- If so, God has *two* wills, He is fighting against Himself, the House is divided—and "a house divided against itself will fall" (Luke 11:17). Will God Himself—the Trinity—fall? According to the "God controls everything, including the weather" interpretation of the storm story, He must.

In simpler terms, EITHER:
A) God willed/caused the storm, or B.) Jesus is God in the flesh. We can have one or the other; but we can't have both, because

78

they are mutually exclusive! I vote "B," in case you didn't know!

In both instances—the fig tree and the storm—Jesus found forces in nature that were contrary to God's will. One way or the other, He used His authority to correct the situation. These stories clearly show that there are things happening in Nature that are *not* God's will. This explains natural disasters of all kinds, from earthquakes to tsunamis, to hurricanes, tornadoes and floods... These bring pain, loss, death, and horrible misery to thousands—millions even. Is this the righteous hand of a loving God? No! All of these are a result of the earth being affected by the curse that came as a result of Adam's sin. Remember Romans 8:18-22! The Earth is crying out to be brought back into harmony with God's original design!

If Jesus is our example, then we must learn to operate in the authority over Nature that He has restored to us. All creation is subject to us as redeemed people that are seated at God's right hand in Christ. This includes storms and fig trees, but also includes bacteria, viruses, sicknesses and diseases. They are Creation, and as God's heirs, we are His stewards over Creation. We must enforce God's order on our watch! Not only do we see *Jesus* taking authority over Nature—He tells us to do the same thing!

> Not only do we see *Jesus* taking authority over Nature—He tells *us* to do the same thing!

Matthew 21:21
So Jesus answered and said to them, "Assuredly, I say to you, if you have faith and do not doubt, you will not only do what was done to the fig tree, but also if you say to this mountain, 'Be removed and be cast into the sea,' it will be done.

Luke 17:6
So the Lord said, "If you have faith as a mustard seed, you can say to this mulberry tree, 'Be pulled up by the roots and be planted in the sea,' and it would obey you.

Some would say, "Sure, Jesus said that; but He was just using figurative language." Well, I don't deny that it certainly can be applied figuratively. For instance, a "mountain" can be any problem in your life, you can command it to leave, and it will obey you if you do so in faith. However, Jesus said it plainly, and in Matthew 21:21, He directly connects it to what happened with the fig tree—a plainly literal application. We also saw in the story of Jesus rebuking the storm, that He plainly expected that the disciples would have already learned how to calm the storm without His assistance by then. We have command over Nature—are we using it?

3) The Biggest Problem – Mankind and Human Will

On top of spiritual/demonic forces that hate us and want to kill us, and natural forces that are under a curse and therefore out of order—we also have to factor in Mankind. In my opinion— Even more than devils or a curse-affected Earth—*We* are our own worst enemy. People have free will and make decisions— not all of them good. People choose to sin. Innocent people are victimized. Other times, they just don't do the smartest things. People make imperfect plans—plans that sometimes fail. Bad things can come about as a result. God has certain plans, but people have other plans that are *different* than God's will for their lives!

> Even more than devils or a curse-affected Earth— *We* are our own worst enemy.

Isaiah 30:1a
Woe to the rebellious children, says the Lord, who take counsel *and* carry out a plan, but not Mine...

So when these bad things happen to good people—whether it was "on purpose" or "by accident"—it isn't God's fault! God isn't judging someone for their sin and causing their kid to die in a car crash. Somebody made a bad judgment call—they drank and drove, or they drove tired, or they stepped on the gas instead of the brake—and the collision was a result of man's choice or neglect. Period. Maybe someone slipped and fell and broke their leg. The devil didn't do it directly. It's not nature's fault. AND there was no decision to sin involved. The ground was slippery, and the person slipped! "Stuff happens!" is a cliché for a reason!

Luke 13:1-5
[1] There were present at that season some who told Him about the Galileans whose blood Pilate had mingled with their sacrifices. [2] And Jesus answered and said to them, "Do you suppose that these Galileans were worse sinners than all *other* Galileans, because they suffered such things? [3] I tell you, no; but unless you repent you will all likewise perish. [4] Or those eighteen on whom the tower in Siloam fell and killed them, do you think that they were worse sinners than all *other* men who dwelt in Jerusalem? [5] I tell you, no; but unless you repent you will all likewise perish."

Jesus gave us quick examples of two of the mess-causers we have discussed—"Free Will" and "Stuff happens." The second case might also have involved some Free Will issues and/or Fallen Creation issues.

In the first, Pilate and his gang were involved in a deliberate choice to sin, probably killing these Galileans. In the second, a tower fell on some folks and they died. Jesus says essentially, "Look, neither of these situations have anything to do with the judgment of God on sin. Pilate made a decision and sinned in the first case. 'Stuff happened' in the second. People died. If you think that this is the judgment of God for their sin, be careful; because you'd be next in line, since all have sinned."

If bad stuff happened to people only because of their individual sin, then we'd all be doomed. We probably would never have lived long enough to get saved. Or do you think you're more righteous than the Christian brother who fell off of his ladder? Do you think you're more just than the innocent baby who dies in a car wreck? Or do you think God just loves you more than He does them? Are you judging? Are you serious? No, the fact is, we can be negatively affected by our own decisions, *and* by the decisions of others. This leaves God, the devil, and the curse completely out of the equation in some cases! Our decisions affect the world around us!

Romans 12:3b
"...God has dealt to every man the measure of faith."

He's given *every single person on earth* the necessary faith to believe and cooperate with Him. But he gives us the freedom—and responsibility—to make that choice for ourselves. Freedom to choose is the nature of real Love, remember? Love=Freedom=Choices. Don't we also see this principle in the story of the Prodigal son (Luke 15:11-32)?

Illustration: The Prodigal Son

The younger of two sons asked his Father for his inheritance, when the Father hadn't even died! Stranger still, the Father didn't say no—He freely gave the son all the resources he had coming to him, to use at his own discretion. He gave it to him, because He wanted the son to be free. Love gives freedom. Did the Father know that the son was making a bad decision? Yes. Did He still let him make that choice? Yes. Does that make the Father responsible for the son sinning and ending up in a pigpen? No way!

The son made bad decisions and wasted the freedom that was given him, ending up realizing that relationship with his Father was actually the best option. He returned to His Father, and His Father had been longing for his return. He wasn't mad or bitter that the son had left and chosen other things. He simply received Him back in love, and restored him completely to his position in the family, and throws him a huge "Welcome back" party.

The elder brother finds out about the party and gets upset. "Dad, I never left. I've worked every day for you, and I never even got a goat to eat with my friends." The Father tells him,

"Son, I love you. All that I have is yours, and you could have had it any time you wanted. Not because you earned it; but because you're family! Your younger brother knew he didn't earn or deserve it, but now he's enjoying it anyway; because love doesn't hold anything back!"

How does this relate to the subject of it being God's will that we have the option to sin? I'm glad you asked. Those that say God predestines certain individuals to choose Him, but others He predestines for Hell, often use this text from earlier in Romans 9 to prove their point:

Romans 9:14-24
[14] What shall we say then? Is there unrighteousness with God? Certainly not! [15] For He says to Moses, "I will have mercy on whomever I will have mercy, and I will have compassion on whomever I will have compassion." [16] So then it is not of him who wills, nor of him who runs, but of God who shows mercy. [17] For the Scripture says to the Pharaoh, "For this very purpose I have raised you up, that I may show My power in you, and that My name may be declared in all the earth." [18] Therefore He has mercy on whom He wills, and whom He wills He hardens. [19] You will say to me then, "Why does He still find fault? For who has resisted His will?" [20] But indeed, O man, who are you to reply against God? Will the thing formed say to him who formed it, "Why have you made me like this?" [21] Does not the potter have power over the clay, from the same lump to make one vessel for honor and another for dishonor? [22] What if God, wanting to show His wrath and to make His power known, endured with much longsuffering the vessels of wrath prepared for destruction, [23] and that He might make known the riches of His glory on the vessels of mercy, which He had prepared beforehand for glory, [24] even us whom He called, not of the Jews only, but also of the Gentiles?

First of all, this Scripture (and the other "predestination text" in Ephesians) is not even addressing the predestination of *individuals*. It's in the context of Paul explaining to a group of racist Jews that God has Sovereignly predestined for salvation to be available to the whole Gentile world! He basically says, "Now God has chosen to give mercy to *everybody*, and there's nothing you can do or say about it!" He's saying, "God has predestined that anybody and everybody can get saved. Deal with it!"

Additionally, this text is answering the question, "If God makes the option to sin available, and creates all people—knowing in advance that some will make the wrong choice—How can He later judge those individuals for making that wrong choice?" That's because if He looked into the future, saw who would choose Him and who would not, then only created the ones that would choose Him—then we'd essentially be back to the "robot" situation! He has to make both, even though it is against His will that people would not choose Him.

God Gives People What They Choose

This Scripture in Romans 9 also says that, "whom He wills He hardens." That sounds like God chooses to make people's hearts hard and unable to choose Him. But what is happening is that God is simply responding to the people's choice. If you will take the time to look at these Scriptures, you will see that God is just giving people what they choose. Pharaoh *first* made a choice to say no to Moses and God. He chose to harden his heart against God, so God let His heart get harder. Please read Exodus, chapters 4-14 with a fine-toothed comb, and you will note that in *every* instance, Pharaoh *first* makes a choice, and God *responds* by hardening Pharaoh's heart—giving him more of what he chose. God honors our choices, even when they are bad ones. Here's R.A. Torrey on the subject:

"This is God's universal method, not only as taught in the Bible, but as taught in experience, that He allows every man to choose either to listen to Him and know the truth, or to turn a deaf ear to Him and to be given over to strong delusion. If men will not receive 'the love of the truth, that they may be saved' (2 Thessalonians 2:10), then God gives them over to believe a lie (v.11)."[1]

God honors our choices, even when they are bad ones.

If a person chooses sin, God has chosen to give them that right. He honors our right to make bad

84

choices, and we can misuse our authority if we want to. We see this again in Romans 1.

Romans 1:21-28
[21] because, although they knew God, they did not glorify *Him* as God, nor were thankful, but became futile in their thoughts, and their foolish hearts were darkened. [22] Professing to be wise, they became fools, [23] and changed the glory of the incorruptible God into an image made like corruptible man—and birds and four-footed animals and creeping things.
[24] Therefore God also gave them up to uncleanness, in the lusts of their hearts, to dishonor their bodies among themselves, [25] who exchanged the truth of God for the lie, and worshiped and served the creature rather than the Creator, who is blessed forever. Amen.
[26] For this reason God gave them up to vile passions. For even their women exchanged the natural use for what is against nature. [27] Likewise also the men, leaving the natural use of the woman, burned in their lust for one another, men with men committing what is shameful, and receiving in themselves the penalty of their error which was due.
[28] And even as they did not like to retain God in *their* knowledge, God gave them over to a debased mind, to do those things which are not fitting;

Here's what I want us to see:

- "Although they knew God, they did not glorify Him as God...*Therefore* God also gave them up to uncleanness..."
- "(They) exchanged the truth of God for the lie... *For this reason* God gave them up to vile passions..."
- "They did not like to retain God in their knowledge, God gave them over...to do those things which are not fitting"

In each of those excerpts you can see it clearly: People made a choice, God responded according to their choice. Everything God did was in *response* to the people's decisions! This is exactly the case with Pharaoh and Israel in Romans 9, and with every person on the Earth! So rather than proving the point that it is God's will for people to sin, this text only further proves that God honors man's decisions, and responds accordingly—such is the nature of true love.

If God Loves Us, Why Doesn't He Do Something About This Mess?!

"If God wills for all to be saved, then why aren't they saved?" "If God wanted me to be healed, then I'd be healed." "Everything happens for a reason. It must not be God's will." All of these things we hear so commonly reflect an underlying belief that everything that happens is God's will. That plainly is not the case! There are devils that hate God and are in outright rebellion against God and His will. Some people choose to do the same. We make bad decisions, whether ignorantly or on purpose. Plus, due to Adam's sinful choice, Nature is now out-of-whack, and operates outside God's original good will and design.

> God's will is to have kids who love Him genuinely, and co-rule with Him forever.

God's will is to have kids who love Him genuinely, and co-rule with Him forever. This requires that we have free will. It also requires that we have something to rule over—Nature and the works of the enemy. Because God gave authority to Man for this season, His hands are tied. Yes, His hands are tied. You might say, "Now come on, how can the hands of the Almighty, Sovereign God be tied? That can't be right!" I know it sounds crazy—it might even sound sacrilegious or blasphemous to you; but it's true nonetheless.

Psalm 78:41-42
Yes, again and again *they* (Israel) tempted God, and *limited the Holy One of Israel*. [42] They did not remember His power...

Who "limited" God in this Scripture? The Israelites—people. How? Did they overpower God Almighty? Of course not. They simply functioned in the role of authority granted them by God, and made a bad choice: "They did not remember His power." If we don't remember, we don't expect. If we don't expect, we don't ask. If we don't ask and expect, He can't help.

If you can't believe that man can limit God, then you can at least believe that God chose to limit Himself. He is a God of His word, and He's Sovereignly ruled and declared that Man would have authority on the earth (for a season) as His managers. God has Sovereignly chosen to allow Mankind to make our own decisions, and to either welcome or limit His intervention. We can limit God's intervention by unbelief, or by not remembering His power.

Mark 6:5
Now He *could* do no mighty work there, except that He laid His hands on a few sick people and healed them. [6] *And He marveled because of their unbelief.*

Note that it doesn't just say that He (Jesus) "did not," but it says He "*could* not"—that one word is huge, because it describes ability, not desire. Of course Jesus had the power (physical force) necessary to do any mighty work He wanted to. However, He "could not" bring it to bear, in the sense that He honored His proclamation that Mankind would have dominion and choice. Why couldn't they access Jesus' assistance? "Because of their unbelief." I do want to briefly point out that He still healed the sick there, even in the face of their unbelief. We'll delve deeper into that in Chapter 11.

> God has Sovereignly chosen to allow Mankind to make our own choices, and to welcome or limit His intervention.

Summary:

When Man sinned, things were put out of line with God's design and authority. Hence, we have sickness and disease, natural disasters, wars and strife and trouble and sin at every turn. Not to mention the devil and his bunch trying to kill us, and then add on top of it other people exercising their own free will and sinning or just making bad decisions. And of course, let's not forget the "stuff happens" factor.

While God is powerful, He is also a God of impeccable integrity. Because He declared that Mankind would have authority on the earth for this season, He cannot go back on His Word. Because He desires a genuine relationship with us, He honors our decisions, whether good or bad. So He has limited His intervention by His Word. If we choose Him, He can respond and bring the blessing He intends. Otherwise, we're subject to devils, other people's choices, and fallen Creation.

As a natural illustration, we may have laws against crime, and a bunch of police to enforce them; but crime continues nonetheless. In spiritual reality, *we* are the police—It's *our* job to stop the chaos! Things aren't supposed to be like this; and all of creation—especially Man—knows it!

In the meantime, the Scriptures plainly teach that Man can limit God—in the ways God has Sovereignly determined. "But how can that be? God is All-Powerful." Yes, He is Supreme, Self-determining, and not dependent upon anyone to meet His needs. And God has Sovereignly decided to give Mankind the authority in the Earth. We can either welcome or limit God's intervention. We can rebel against Him, or we can love Him and cooperate with Him, co-laboring with Him to make His enemies His footstool. The choice is ours. Either way, God's will is *always* healing!

CHAPTER 5

SALVATION: THE OL' SWITCHEROO

The Law of Identification

How does Salvation work? Most people have heard that Jesus died to cleanse us of our sins; but how does *Jesus'* action 2,000 years ago accomplish anything for *us today*? This is the miracle of Salvation—He took our place, and we took His. This takes place through the "Law of Identification." What is this law? I've heard it stated like this: Everything God did in Christ, He set to your account as though you did it yourself.

You could also say that when we died in Christ, *our* account got closed altogether; and now we're joint account holders with Jesus! If it's in His account, it belongs to us (and if it's *not* in His account, it doesn't belong to us). When we go to make a withdrawal from our joint account, we show our ID and all it says on there is "Jesus!" Our picture even looks like Him! If we'll believe it, and receive this gift of Salvation by faith, we effectively switch places with Jesus! We get His record, just as He got ours on the Cross! We experience the life that He earned. He did it whether we believe it or not; but we get to experience the benefit of it, only when we believe.

> The Law of Identification: We show our ID and all it says on there is "Jesus!"

He identified with us, humbling Himself and becoming one of us. He overcame every temptation, and did it all without ever sinning—Not even once!

Philippians 2:8-9a
And being found in appearance as a man, He humbled Himself and became obedient to the point of death, even the death of the cross. [9] Therefore God also has highly exalted Him...

Hebrews 2:17
Therefore, in all things He had to be made like His brethren, that He might be a merciful and faithful High Priest in things pertaining to God, to make propitiation for the sins of the people.

Even though He never sinned, He received the full wages of sin on the cross. He got the whole "paycheck," and took it to the bank. He cashed it. He spent it—It is finished. No more wages left for us! But here's the fun part... When Christ died, so did you and I! All thanks to the Law of Identification! We need only believe to receive the benefit of it!

In Christ, We Died

As we humbly acknowledge our exalted position in Christ, while maintaining the heart of a servant to others, we can state right along with Paul:

Galatians 2:20
I have been crucified with Christ; it is no longer I who live, but Christ lives in me; and the life which I now live in the flesh I live by faith in the Son of God, who loved me and gave Himself for me.

> Through faith, we are united with Jesus and everything He earned becomes ours!

When Paul wrote this, someone might easily have said to him, "Now wait a minute Paul! You weren't on that cross! I saw Jesus die and you were not even there!! And even if you had been there, you certainly didn't die—you're right here writing this letter! You were not crucified and you are not dead!" Paul is talking about the Law of Identification here. What God did in Christ, He did on our behalf. We were there, in Him! Jesus not only died *for* us, He died *as* us. Jesus died as us, so we could live as Him! Through faith we are united with Jesus and everything He earned, becomes ours! I was crucified with Christ. You were crucified with Christ. We are dead men (as far as our old existence is concerned). Our sinful, old state got slaughtered!

Romans 6 (excerpts)

" ... How shall we who *died to sin* live any longer in it? Or do you not know that as many of us as were baptized into Christ Jesus were *baptized into His death*? ...*we were buried* with Him... *into death*... we have been united together in the likeness of His death... our *old man was crucified* with Him, that the body of sin might be done away with... For he who has *died* has been freed from sin. Now if *we died with Christ*... we shall also live with Him... having been raised from the dead... Death no longer has dominion... Likewise you also, *reckon yourselves to be dead* indeed *to sin, but alive to God* in Christ Jesus our Lord..."

In Christ, We Went to the Place of the Dead

Jesus went to the Old Testament equivalent of Hell... "Sheol"— the holding place of the dead—in our stead. For three days and three nights, Jesus experienced the consequences of all Mankind's sin.

Acts 2:22-32

[22] "Men of Israel, hear these words: Jesus of Nazareth... you have taken by lawless hands, have crucified, and put to death; [24] whom God raised up, having loosed the pains of death, because it was not possible that He should be held by it. [25] For David says concerning Him: '...*You will not leave my soul in Hades*, Nor will You allow Your Holy One to see corruption... the patriarch David... being a prophet... spoke concerning the resurrection of the Christ, that His soul was not *left in Hades*, nor did His flesh see corruption. [32] This Jesus God has raised up, of which we are all witnesses.

It says right here that Jesus wasn't "left" in Hades (the Greek word closest to the Hebrew "Sheol" from the Scripture Peter was quoting—Psalm 16:10—a prophetic Messianic Psalm). In order to be "left" somewhere you have to have been there in the first place, right? Yes, Jesus went there. Some people reject that part of the story; but oh well, there it is. And look, here it is again in Psalm 88, another Messianic Psalm—We see Jesus in the place of the dead, taking the harsh brunt of sin's wages, for all men:

Psalm 88: 6-17

[6] You have laid me in the lowest pit, In darkness, in the depths. [7] Your wrath lies heavy upon me, And You have afflicted me with all Your waves. Selah...

[10] Will You work wonders for the dead? Shall the dead arise and praise You? Selah

[11] Shall Your lovingkindness be declared in the grave? Or Your faithfulness in the place of destruction?... I suffer Your terrors; I am distraught... [16] Your fierce wrath has gone over me; Your terrors have cut me off. [17] They came around me all day long like water; They engulfed me altogether...

When the wages of all Mankind's sin (death in all its forms) were fully experienced by Jesus, God raised Him from the dead, and He was declared to be the "firstborn" Son of God.

Acts 13:30-34

[30] But God raised Him from the dead... God has fulfilled this for us their children, in that He has raised up Jesus. As it is also written in the second Psalm: *You are My Son, Today I have begotten You.'* [34] And that He raised Him from the dead...

We see this exact quote repeated in Hebrews 1:5 and 5:5—It must be important. "Begotten" means born. God says that "Today", that is, on the day Jesus was raised from the dead, He was born... again.

In Christ, We Were Raised Up, and Born Again

You may be wondering if that means what it sounds like... Was Jesus "born again"? This is another concept that some folks get all nervous about; because they think it means we are saying that Jesus must have had a "sin nature" in order to need to be born again. Or, they think it questions Jesus' Purity and Holiness. "Why would Jesus need to be born again, unless He sinned," they ask.

But there is a misunderstanding. Saying that Jesus was "born again" questions *none* of these basic Biblical teachings. They simply do not understand the lengths that Jesus went to, in order to fully identify with the condition of Man—which was necessary to secure our salvation. They are simply not recognizing that *the Law of Identification works both ways*. In order for us to be able to identify with Christ, He first had to identify with us.

Let me reassure you: Jesus was—and is—God in the flesh. Further, let's state unequivocally that Jesus was—and always will be—the holy, pure, spotless Lamb of God. He had *zero* sin *of His own* to die for. This is confirmed in Hebrews 4:15—Jesus never sinned!

> In order for us to be able to identify with Christ, He first had to identify with us.

Hebrews 4:15
For we do not have a High Priest who cannot sympathize with our weaknesses, but was in all points tempted as we are, yet without sin.

Jesus was tempted with every sin that anyone has ever been tempted with. Yes, *every* sin! Jesus was tempted with lying, cheating and stealing. Jesus was tempted with fornication and adultery. Jesus was tempted with idolatry. Jesus was tempted with drunkenness, homosexuality, and even Satan worship (We even have Scriptural record of that one)! These facts might rub you the wrong way; but they're true nonetheless. The Bible says, "in all points tempted as we are," and "all points" means "all points." Here's the thing to remember: It's not a sin to be tempted! Jesus never *yielded* to these temptations; and so He never, ever sinned! He forever remained the spotless, sinless Lamb of God—the only one qualified to take away the sins of the whole world! What strength! What courage! What faithfulness! What love! What a Man! What a God!

So if Jesus never sinned, and was One with the Father—why on earth would He need to be born again? In the wonderful work that is Salvation, Jesus took *our* place. He didn't just take our sins on Himself like a huge, fat backpack full of muck—

93

something separate that He just "carried." No, He literally *became* sin. God made Jesus to *be* sin for us.

2 Corinthians 5:21
For *He made Him who knew no sin to be sin for us*, that we might become the righteousness of God in Him.

This verse describes some of what we call "The Great Exchange." Jesus *became* our sin, and we *became* His righteousness. He identified fully with our condition so that we could identify fully with His! It's funny, some people are ready to become the righteousness that Jesus earned—and receive all its effects; but they won't acknowledge what Jesus did to make it available! He did the exact opposite. He became the unrighteousness that *we* earned—and received all *its* effects!

Romans 8:3-4
[3] For what the law could not do in that it was weak through the flesh, *God did by sending His own Son in the likeness of sinful flesh, on account of sin*: He condemned sin in the flesh, [4] *that the righteous requirement of the law might be fulfilled in us* who do not walk according to the flesh but according to the Spirit.

What are the effects of sin? Sin results in death. Not instant physical death, but instant spiritual death. God warned Adam of this fact in Genesis:

Genesis 2:17
"but of the tree of the knowledge of good and evil you shall not eat, for in the day that you eat of it you shall surely die."

Since we know Adam lived for many years after the day he sinned, we know that God didn't mean physical death. He meant spiritual death. What is spiritual death? For now, let's say it's a separation from the experience or awareness of the life of God. You might define it differently; but whatever it is, it's definitely the automatic result of sin.

Ezekiel 18:4, 20a
The soul who sins shall die...

94

Romans 6:23
[23] For *the wages of sin is death*, but the gift of God is eternal life in Christ Jesus our Lord.

Remember, 2 Corinthians 5:21 says that Jesus literally *became* sin for us. Jesus had to experience the full state of fallen humanity, or He never identified with us! If Jesus never identified with us, then we *cannot* identify with Him. There must be full exchange—This is the very nature of Covenant. If that is the case, then He had to have experienced the results of sin—spiritual death. That is why He had to go to Sheol/Hades! That is why He had to become sin, experiencing spiritual death on our behalf. Remember His cry on the cross?

Matthew 27:46
And about the ninth hour Jesus cried out with a loud voice, saying, "Eli, Eli, lama sabachthani?" that is, "My God, My God, why have You forsaken Me?"

Here He echoed the words of the prophetic, Messianic Psalm 22. Why did Jesus cry out that God had "forsaken" Him? He did this because He had become sin, and entered spiritual death for us. For the first time in His eternal existence, He had no perception, experience, or conscious awareness of God's presence! He entered into the experience of sinful Man! If Jesus didn't *fully* identify with our condition (sin and death), and didn't pay *everything* that our sins would have cost us—spiritual death (separation from the awareness or experience of the life of God)—then guess what? He didn't pay the price, and we still owe it!

> If Jesus didn't pay *everything* that our sins would have cost us... we still owe it!

But no, Jesus *did* identify fully with us. He did not sin; but He *became* sin. He experienced the wages of spiritual death. He received the full effect of sin on behalf of all humanity. The Church tells people every day that if they stay in their sin, they will remain spiritually dead, and go to a place of misery called hell where they will not perceive or experience the presence of

95

God. But then when someone says that Jesus actually *paid* this required price *for* us—and that's why His coming did us any good—they get mad. I don't get it! Isn't that the central message of the gospel? Jesus paid what we owed, and we get what He earned! Jesus died as us, and we live as Him—The Son of God died as Man, so Man could live as sons of God!

After paying the full price for our sin, Jesus was *born again*—from the dead—just as we are when we receive what He did for us. Just to confirm this, Jesus is called the "Firstborn from the dead" at least twice in Scripture:

Colossians 1:18
And He is the head of the body, the church, who is the beginning, *the firstborn from the dead*, that in all things He may have the preeminence.

Revelation 1:5
and from Jesus Christ, the faithful witness, the *firstborn from the dead*, and the ruler over the kings of the earth. To Him who loved us and washed us from our sins in His own blood,

Some say that this only means Jesus was born from among the physically dead. But this can't be right for at least two reasons:

First, Jesus is called the "Firstborn from the dead"; but that can't mean the "physically dead;" because He wasn't the *first* person to come back from being *physically* dead. Remember Lazarus, or the widow of Nain's son, or Jairus' daughter, or the boy that Elisha raised up… need we go on?

Second, and most importantly in this context, *physical death does not pay the price for sins!* If physical death was enough to pay the price for our sins, then we could all reach our natural, physical death, breathe our last breath, and our own physical death would pay the price for our sins. If this were the case, Jesus would have never needed to come! No, no, no! *Spiritual death is the wage that sin earns us!* And Jesus paid it all for us!

So if He became the Firstborn when He was raised from the dead—from a condition of spiritual death—that means He was "born again." First, He was born physically through Mary. Because He lived a sinless life, He was not tainted with the stain of sin left through Adam. But because He so fully yielded to taking our place on the cross, He became sin for us, experienced spiritual death, and went into the place of the dead on our behalf. Then, He was "born again," back from a position of spiritual death, into eternal "zoe" life through His glorious resurrection.

John 3:3
[3] Jesus answered and said to him, "Most assuredly, I say to you, unless one is born again, he cannot see the kingdom of God."

Remember, Jesus said we couldn't see the Kingdom of God unless we are born again. We must be born again. And because we can't accomplish this feat on our own, that means that Jesus accomplished it for us! Jesus was born again. The difference between Jesus' experience and ours— Please hear me—is that *our own sin earned us our spiritual death.* But Jesus received His spiritual death by *becoming sin on our behalf—identifying fully with our lost condition, as a vicarious act* of Divine Love. Thank You, Jesus!

> Our own sin earned us *our* spiritual death. But Jesus received *His* spiritual death by becoming sin *on our behalf*.

This does not deny His Holiness or Deity. This does not take away from Jesus! Quite the contrary, it gives us further appreciation of all that He did for us! It enriches our understanding of the greatness of Salvation. It deepens our revelation of His amazing love for us! It gives Him greater glory! Jesus, we rejoice in Your awesome love that drove You to such lengths to save us fully and completely!!

In Christ, We Are Children of God

Now, I hate to state the obvious; but if there is a "*Firstborn* from the dead", then that automatically implies that there were *others* born from the dead after that—a second-born, a third-born, etc. That would be all Believers that become sons and daughters of God through being "born again." If we are the second born, third born, and so on, then we came out of the *same womb* Jesus did—not Mary's; but the "womb" of spiritual death—and in the *same way* that Jesus was—by being "born again," "born of the spirit," or "born of God" (1 Peter 1:23; John 3:6, 8; 1 John 5:1, 4).

This isn't as difficult as some try to make it. Because we have the same Father, and were born of the same womb, we are now brothers and sisters with Jesus—children of God!

1 John 3:1
Behold what manner of love the Father has bestowed on us, that we should be called children of God!

Romans 8:29
For whom He foreknew, He also predestined to be conformed to the image of His Son, that He might be the *firstborn among many brethren.*

We weren't just "adopted" like we tend to think of adoption in human terms. When God adopts us, He re-creates us! We are re-Fathered and re-gene-rated (that means we have new "genes"). We are a new people, a new creation, a species of being that has never before existed! If Jesus is the Firstborn, and we are second and following, then we are the younger brothers and sisters of Jesus. He was the "firstborn among many brethren." We see this exact point yet again in Hebrews 2:

Hebrews 2:11
For both He who sanctifies and those who are being sanctified are all of one, for which reason *He is not ashamed to call them brethren,*

Jesus is not ashamed to call us His brothers and sisters. Let's not be ashamed to call ourselves His brothers and sisters either. And let's not be so falsely humble as to not receive this honor He has bestowed. And let us not be so religious and uptight that we won't recognize that Jesus came from the same womb we did—the womb of spiritual death.

In Christ, We Ascended and Now Sit at God's Right Hand

We discuss the ramifications of this truth in much greater detail in the chapters on the Believer's Authority and God's Sovereignty; but here are some Scriptures that discuss our resurrection, our ascension with Christ, and our being seated with Him in Heaven.

Colossians 2:11-15
[11] *In Him you were* ... [12] *buried with Him* in baptism, in which *you also were raised with Him* through faith in the working of God, who raised Him from the dead. [13] And *you... He has made alive together with Him*, having forgiven you all trespasses...

Ephesians 2:1-6
[1] And you He made alive, who *were* dead in trespasses and sins, [2] in which you *once walked* ...[3] among whom also we all *once conducted* ourselves in the lusts of our flesh...and *were* by nature children of wrath, just as the others. [4] But God, who is rich in mercy, because of His great love with which He loved us, [5] even when we *were* dead in trespasses, *made us alive* together with Christ (by grace you *have been saved*), [6] and *raised us up* together, and *made us sit* together in the heavenly places in Christ Jesus...

Many people like to acknowledge that they were crucified with Christ; but then they won't acknowledge that they were also raised with Him—and forget being seated in authority at the right hand of God. Don't worry, it's not something to be proud or arrogant about—we did nothing to achieve it. Rather, let us humbly thank God for the fullness of His grace towards us! So let's hear it again in Colossians:

99

Colossians 3:1-3

[1] If then you *were raised* with Christ, seek those things which are above, where Christ is, sitting at the right hand of God. [2] Set your mind on things above, not on things on the earth. [3] For you *died*, and your life *is hidden* with Christ in God.

In the context of a book on Healing, there are some questions begging to be asked here: Is there sickness where we are—seated on the throne with Jesus at the right hand of God? Of course not. If we are hidden with Christ in God, is there sickness hidden in Him too? Let's not be silly! If that is where the Bible says we are, and that we ought to set our minds on things there, and not on things of the earth, and commands us to pray that it would be on Earth as it is in Heaven (Matthew 6:10)... Does sickness have any place in God's will for our lives? None whatsoever!

> Is there sickness where we are— seated on the throne with Jesus at the right hand of God?

Put On the New Man—Put On Christ

Our identification with Christ is complete. We are in Him, and He is in us. He took our place, and we took His. We are united with Him completely through salvation, and enjoy a new life in Him— His life.

Colossians 2:6

As you therefore have received Christ Jesus the Lord, so *walk in Him,*

Acts 17:28

for *in Him we live and move and have our being...*

Our new reality, as the Distilled Bible puts it:

Galatians 2:20 (Distilled Bible)

I consider myself as having died and now enjoying a second existence which is simply *Jesus using my body.*

Many of us are so aware of the visible "old reality" that we lose sight of the invisible "new reality," or "second existence," as the Distilled Bible puts it. There is an old, dead "you" and there is a new, alive "you" in Christ. So how do we begin to experience the reality of our new man? Like everything else in the Kingdom of God—We enter into it by Grace, through Faith, resting in His already finished work.

Ephesians 4:21-24

[21] if indeed you have heard Him and have been taught by Him, as the truth is in Jesus: [22] that you *put off*, concerning your former conduct*, the old man* which grows corrupt according to the deceitful lusts, [23] and *be renewed in the spirit of your mind*, [24] and that you *put on the new man* which was created according to God, in true righteousness and holiness.

So what does our "new man" look like? What does he talk like? What does he act like? What is his nature? He looks, talks, and acts just like Jesus. As a matter of fact, two other Scriptures—instead of telling us to put on the "new man" and leaving us asking these very questions—tell us plainly to put on Christ:

Romans 13:14

But *put on the Lord Jesus Christ*, and make no provision for the flesh, to fulfill its lusts.

Galatians 3:27

For as many of you as were baptized into Christ *have put on Christ*.

Our "new man" is Christ! Each day, you put Him on (in your mind) like a coat. Galatians just said you've *already* put him on! You're one spirit with Him, after all (1 Corinthians 6:17). Slide right into your new outfit! Button up and partake of your new nature—His Divine Nature (2 Peter 1:4).

> Our "new man" is Christ!

Romans 8:12-14

[12] Therefore *do not let* sin reign in your mortal body, that you should obey it in its lusts. [13] And *do not present* your members as instruments of unrighteousness to sin, *but present yourselves to God* as being alive from the dead, *and your members as instruments of righteousness* to God. [14] For sin shall not have dominion over you, for you are not under law but under grace.

Romans 6:16, 19

[16] Do you not know that to whom you *present yourselves slaves to obey*, you are that one's slaves whom you obey, whether of sin leading to death, or of obedience leading to righteousness? ... [19] I speak in human terms because of the weakness of your flesh. For just as you presented your members as slaves of uncleanness, and of lawlessness leading to more lawlessness, so *now present your members as slaves of righteousness for holiness.*

Our bodies are inhabited by God (1 Corinthians 6:19). It's not even us that lives there anymore—it's Christ living through us (Galatians 2:20). It's in Him that we live, and move, and have our very being (Acts 17:28). So just stay aware of your own death in Christ, and let Him live through you! This is what it means for us to "take up our cross daily (Luke 9:23)." This is what it means to "mortify deeds of the flesh (Romans 8:13)." It doesn't mean continual striving and self-effort. In fact, the Bible actually says that we've *already* put on the new man in the image of Christ:

Colossians 3:9-11

[9] Do not lie to one another, *since you have put off the old man* with his deeds, [10] *and have put on the new man who is renewed in knowledge according to the image of Him who created him...* Christ is all and in all.

> Who will I let use my body today—That old dead man, or Jesus?

It already took place—we have already put on Christ (see also Galatians 3:27 again). It's really just a matter of simple choices each day: "Who will I let use my body today—That old dead man, or Jesus?" Who will I identify with—myself, or Jesus? Who will I obey? Who and what will I yield myself to? Am I dead to sin and alive to God, or vice versa? If we believe the gospel, then there really is no choice left to make—it's just a matter of trusting Him to live through us. Believing and receiving. I suggest that we stay dead, and let Jesus use our bodies. Jesus purchased us, right? If so, then He possesses us. So let's be "possessed" by Jesus!

Remember, according to 2 Corinthians 5:21, old things have passed away, and all things have become new. According to Galatians 5:22-23, the fruit of the new us is love, joy, peace, patience, kindness, goodness, gentleness, faithfulness, and self-control. This is our new nature. We need only receive it. How? Like everything else in the Kingdom: by Grace through Faith. Believe it. Receive it. Rest in it. *Be* it!

The Great Exchange – The Ol' Switcheroo

All of this talk of the Law of Identification is a description of how many describe salvation: "The Great Exchange." I like to call it, "The Ol' Switcheroo." In a nutshell: He got what we deserve, so we could get what He deserved. He became what we were, so we would become what He is! We earned wages for our sin, and He got to experience it. He earned perfect relationship and right standing with the Father—we get to experience it. He earned holiness and perfection, overcoming every temptation without sinning—and we get to be right with God—as if we ourselves had never sinned. We earned hell, but He experienced it. He earned Heaven, but we live there. He became the curse and experienced all its effects, while we become the blessing and experience all the effects of God's favor. All that Jesus did is already put in our account. We receive all of this very simply—By grace through faith—Our simple trust in God's gift.

Ephesians 2:8-9
For *by grace you have been saved through faith*, and that not of yourselves; it is the gift of God, not of works, lest anyone should boast.

This is Salvation Basics! Jesus took our place, and we get to have His! We can't earn it; we don't deserve it. We can't work for it, we can't improve on it, we can't maintain it—We only need believe it. And here's the kicker—the faith required to believe it was a free gift too! It's all God's doing, and it is marvelous in our eyes! In His place, there are certain benefits. We receive the benefits in our account as a free gift, simply by faith:

103

Romans 4:3
For what does the Scripture say? "Abraham *believed* God, *and it was accounted* to him for righteousness."

In this Great Exchange, Jesus experienced the full effect of the curse that came because of Adam's sin. He not only experienced the curse, He *became* the curse.

Galatians 3:13
Christ has redeemed us from the curse of the law, *having become a curse* for us (for it is written, "Cursed is everyone who hangs on a tree")

What were the full effects of the curse? There are many curses spoken of in the Bible; but in the context of Galatians 3, it is referring to the Law itself being a curse. Why was the Law a curse? Until there was Law, there was no knowledge of sin. Once we knew the Law, we were guilty of sin. The Law magnified our sin. Sin brought death in all its forms, including sickness. There are different takes on exactly how it happened; but any way you slice it, Jesus became the curse and took its effects—which include sickness—so that you don't have to. In The Ol' Switcheroo, Jesus became sin and died spiritually; but we become righteousness and are made spiritually alive:

> Jesus became the curse and took its effects—which include sickness—so that you don't have to.

2 Corinthians 5:21
For He made Him who knew no sin to be sin for us, that *we might become the righteousness of God* in Him.

In The Ol' Switcheroo, Jesus became sickness and died physically; but we receive/become health, healing and physical life:

Romans 8:11
But if the Spirit of Him who raised Jesus from the dead dwells in you, *He who raised Christ from the dead will also give life to your mortal bodies* through His Spirit who dwells in you.

If the Holy Spirit lives in you, He gives "life to your mortal bodies." Obviously that means that the physical bodies of Believers are meant to experience some benefit that is not experienced by the unbeliever. Why? Because we are now "free from the law of sin and death."

Romans 8:2
For the law of the Spirit of life in Christ Jesus has made me *free from the law of sin and death*.

What is the law of sin and death? Sin comes and results in death. What is sickness and disease, except death in an immature, "seed" form? If we let it grow up, it will kill us. Sickness is death! Decay and breakdown is death! We are freed from this cycle that Adam and Eve started! Jesus changed everything! And the simplest truth regarding healing in this Great Exchange: We were healed—past tense, done deal—by the stripes that Jesus took on His back at the whipping post.

1 Peter 2:24
Who Himself bore our sins in His own body on the tree, that we, having died to sins, might live for righteousness—*by whose stripes you were healed*.

We cover this in greater depth in the chapter on Salvation: A Benefits Package; but it's already clear that Jesus paid the full price to set us free from sin, death, and sickness—He's freed us from every effect of the curse of the law. He's freed us from every curse that came

> Jesus paid the full price to set us free from sin, death and sickness.

as a result of sin. Let's rejoice in that freedom! Let's identify fully with Christ. Let's purpose in our hearts to receive all the benefits that Jesus earned and deserves—including healing; because in The Ol' Switcheroo, we are joint heirs and it all belongs to us too! God's will is *always* healing!

Notes:

CHAPTER 6

SALVATION—A DONE DEAL

Our Great Salvation is a Done Deal

I'm so glad I'm saved. Aren't you? "Saved"—There's a lot of truth wrapped in that one little word! Even without getting in too deep, one thing I'd like us to notice is that it's a past tense verb. It's also an adjective that describes a state of being. I have *been* saved, so now I *am* saved. Yes! What is the power in that, you ask?

A lot of people spend a lot of time begging God to do things He's already done. Others talk about what He's going to do some time in the future, when again, it's already done. God is not "about to" or "getting ready to" or "someday going to" do anything about things He's already taken care of in Christ! Nor will He do something He's told us, the Church, to do!

The truth is, God has already finished all the work He needed to do! He accomplished it all in Christ, and left nothing undone. This is known as the "past tense of the Gospel." It's a finished work! Jesus did it all!! As we discuss Salvation in this chapter, note the tenses of the verbs in the Scriptures—basically anything describing our salvation is past tense! No more need to beg and plead, and no more pushing it all sometime into the future! No, no, no... It's done! Our part is to believe, receive, and give thanks!

> God has already finished all the work He needed to do!

The Power of Past Tense

As we read the following Scriptures, please note the fully completed nature of what God has done for us. I've emphasized some key past tense verbs and other words that drive the point home for us.

Galatians 3:13
Christ *has redeemed* us from the curse of the law, *having become* a curse for us...

Note that He "has redeemed us," *not* "will someday redeem us." It's done.

1 Peter 2:24-25
²⁴ who Himself *bore* our sins in His own body on the tree, that we, *having died* to sins, might live for righteousness—by whose stripes you *were healed*. ²⁵ For you *were* like sheep going astray, *but have now returned* to the Shepherd and Overseer of your souls.

He *bore* our sins. We *have died* to sins. By His stripes we *were healed*. Though you *were* like sheep going astray, you've *already returned* to the Lord. It's all done already.

Colossians 1:13
He *has delivered us* from the power of darkness *and conveyed us* into the kingdom of the Son of His love,

Don't tell me the devil has power over you! You've been *delivered* already! You're no longer under the power of darkness. You've already *been conveyed* into the Kingdom of God.

Romans 8:29-30
²⁹ For whom He *foreknew*, He also *predestined to be conformed to the image of His Son*, that He might be the firstborn among many brethren. ³⁰ Moreover whom He *predestined*, these He also called; whom He *called*, these He also *justified*; and whom He justified, these He also *glorified*.

You might be thinking, "How can that be? When was I glorified?" At the same time you were justified. When did that happen? It happened when Jesus paid the price for our sins. Remember The

108

Ol' Switcheroo? Jesus has been exalted and glorified, and we were in Him when it happened. If you are "in Christ," then you were there with Jesus—*in* Jesus—when it happened.

Ephesians 1:3
Blessed be the God and Father of our Lord Jesus Christ, who *has blessed us* with every spiritual blessing in the heavenly places in Christ,

This one says that God "has blessed us" with every spiritual blessing. Not "might bless you if you pray just right, and get your act together, and press in hard enough." No, it says that it's already done. Is healing one of these blessings provided for us in Christ? You betcha. So that means He's already blessed us with it. It's already done. Paid for. Finished. Here's another one:

2 Peter 1:3-4
[3] as His divine power *has given* to us all things that pertain to life and godliness, through the knowledge of Him who called us by glory and virtue, [4] by which *have been given* to us exceedingly great and precious promises, that through these you may be partakers of the divine nature, *having escaped* the corruption that is in the world through lust.

"*Has* given." Past tense. Has given to whom? "To *us*." To you and I. Has given us what? "*All* things." How many things? Which things? He's given (already) to us all things "That pertain to life *and* godliness." Everything for both this life and the life to come... He has given—past tense. Already done. You have all you need to go out and get the job done. Amazing!

> You have all you need to go out and get the job done.

What is it that makes us always want to believe we need something else before we do the will of God? More knowledge, more wisdom, more information, more teaching and training, more anointing, more character, more love, more power, more authority, more impartation... We already have everything we need! Listen to this exhortation from Paul:

Colossians 2:8-3:4 (excerpts)
Beware lest anyone cheat you... *you are complete in Him*... In Him you *were* also circumcised... by the circumcision of Christ, *buried* with Him in baptism,

109

in which you also *were raised* with Him through faith in the working of God... And you... He *has made alive* together with Him, *having forgiven you* all trespasses, *having wiped out* the handwriting of requirements that *was* against us, which *was* contrary to us. And He *has taken* it out of the way, *having nailed it* to the cross. *Having disarmed* principalities and powers, He *made* a public spectacle of them, *triumphing over them* in it. So let no one judge you... Let no one cheat you of your reward... you *died* with Christ... If then *you were raised* with Christ, seek those things which are above, where Christ is, sitting at the right hand of God. Set your mind on things above, not on things on the earth. For *you died*, and your life *is hidden* with Christ in God. When Christ who is our life appears, then you also will appear with Him in glory.

Twice Paul warns us not to let anyone cheat us of the reality of all that was done in Christ—the fact that we are complete in Him and have all we need to do the job assigned to us. Anybody that tells you that you're not yet ready to share about God's goodness is cheating you. Anybody that tells you not to pray for the sick is cheating you. Anybody that tells you to wait until you get more anointing, more gifting, or anything else before you represent Jesus is cheating you! Then he elaborates further, saying that we have no more requirements to meet. We are now qualified. We are hidden with Christ in God, above all the works of a defeated devil.

God is Done Working

Note all the past tense verbs, folks! Salvation is an already-accomplished fact! We could find another hundred verses that demonstrate this point; but I think these are sufficient. The point is clear: Our great salvation has *already* been accomplished! The enemy has *already* been disarmed, defeated, dethroned, and stripped of any authority! We have *already* been cleansed, redeemed, sanctified, justified, and glorified—seated in authority at the right hand of God in Christ. Jesus is *already* exalted above every sin, above every sickness and disease, and above every principality and power. His Name is above every other name. Salvation is a finished work!

Hebrews 4:10

For he who has entered His rest has himself also ceased from his works *as God did from His*.

What is the power in understanding that Salvation is an already-accomplished work? If God has ceased from His works (as the above Scripture states), then God doesn't need to lift another finger for the whole Earth to be saved, healed, delivered, and set free. It is now up to us to believe, receive, and tell everyone else the good news about what He's already done—to be the ministers of the New Covenant of reconciliation (2 Corinthians 3:6; 5:18-19). The provision for everyone to enjoy the Kingdom has been made! We need only receive it by faith.

> God doesn't need to lift another finger for the whole Earth to be saved, healed, delivered, and set free.

As we saw in the chapters on The Believer's Authority and God's Sovereignty—God created the world, and let Man manage it. Man messed it all up, and God sent Jesus to fix it. Jesus did His job, and did everything necessary to restore Man to God's original plan for us. Now we can be blessed, healthy, holy, happy lovers of God in open, unhindered relationship with our Father. Then He handed the earth back over to redeemed people and said, "Enforce what I accomplished." Jesus was enough! His blood is all-sufficient! The whole deal is signed, sealed, and delivered! We just need to trust Him, and walk out what He has already accomplished on our behalf.

Healing is Already Accomplished

How does the subject of "Salvation is a Finished Work" relate to Healing? Salvation is done—and healing is part of the salvation package! We cover this more in depth in the next chapter; but we'll assume for now that we already understand that physical healing has been provided through the work of Jesus. Salvation contains so much—and it's not only a spiritual provision. It also

111

impacts us here and now on Earth—where the rubber meets the road.

God has provided for our total salvation—spirit, soul, and body. God is concerned about our life here on Earth, not just about us "getting to Heaven." Actually He is more interested in us bringing "Heaven to Earth!!!" Remember the Lord's Prayer: "Your Kingdom come, Your will be done, on Earth as it is in Heaven..." (Luke 11:2). Is there sickness in Heaven? No! Then it is plain that if God is telling us to ask for it to be "here" like it is "there," then it is His will that there be no sickness here on Earth. And not just "someday." The Bible says that "*Now* is the day of salvation!"

2 Corinthians 6:2
For He says: "In an acceptable time I have heard you, And in the day of salvation I have helped you." Behold, now is the accepted time; behold, now is the day of salvation.

God is *not* "going to" heal you—You were healed 2,000 years ago!

So if Salvation is a completed work, and healing is included, then we are already healed—it's a done deal! Many think they have to "wait for God's timing" to be healed. Nope! It's a finished work. *Now* is the day of salvation. *Now* is the day of healing. God is *not* "going to" heal you—You were healed 2,000 years ago! Many think that God is sitting in heaven, deciding who He will or won't heal—person-by-person, situation-by-situation, case-by-case. Garbage! Jesus' stripes have already paid the price for *all* to be healed. 1 Peter 2:24 says His stripes did the job—past tense, and it's a done deal! The price is paid, the provision is made, healing is the Children's bread. It's ours—it already belongs to us. The covenant has been signed in the blood of Jesus Christ. He did it all!

Many Christians think that they need more anointing before they can minister healing to others. Nope! All you need is the Name of Jesus and faith in the name—and if you're saved, you have it.

112

Many think you need to have the "gifts of healings" (1 Corinthians 12:9) to operate in healing. Nope. You are one with Christ, and He has the Spirit without measure. The Holy Spirit lives in you, and His gifts are resident in you. Some think they need to get some additional knowledge to receive their healing, or to minister healing. Nope! As these Scriptures say, you already have everything you need! You are complete in Him (Colossians 2:8-10), and you have every spiritual blessing (spiritual power, authority, gifts, etc) that you need (Ephesians 1:3)—this includes the power to be healed, and to minister healing to others. In other words, because of the finished nature of Salvation, all there is left to do is *receive* our benefits by faith.

> The price is paid, the provision is made, Healing is the Children's bread!

Healing is Your Inheritance

So what all is contained in our inheritance, our great salvation? To answer that, ask yourself, "What is available in Heaven?" If it's there in Heaven, it's our inheritance in Christ, and it is available in salvation's "benefit package." There is no sickness there—only health. There is no lack there—only abundance. There is no turmoil there—only peace that passes understanding. There is no depression there—only joy unspeakable and full of glory. If it belongs to God, it belongs to us as His kids. Remember, you are a son or daughter of God, and you have an inheritance. Everything God has is yours. Everything available to Jesus is available to you—you're joint heirs! It's *yours!*

Let's consider again—in this context—the Parable of the Prodigal Son, found in Luke 15:11-31. Some think that we should wait until later (maybe in Heaven) to receive your inheritance. Remember the younger brother? He asked for His inheritance early (before the Father even died!), and the Father let Him have it. He held nothing back. But perhaps you envision yourself as a "wiser, more faithful," elder brother. He stayed with the Father, and continued to work in the fields every day.

Then when the younger son came back, after having blown his inheritance in sin, the elder brother got mad. The Father totally restored the younger brother to his position as son, killed the fatted calf, and threw him a big party. When the older brother came back in from the field, he was livid! He said, "Dad, you gave that dirtbag the fatted calf?! I've been a good son, and you never gave me even a goat to eat with my friends!" But remember what the Father told the elder brother: "You could have had a fatted calf any time you wanted to. *You are always with me and everything that I have is yours.*" That is the Father speaking to us! We are always with Him, and everything He has is ours!! Whether you identify more with the younger brother, or the older brother, God never held anything back from *either* of them!! Kill your fatted calf, my friend! Everything the Father has is already yours—Have a party!

> Kill your fatted calf, my friend! Everything the Father has is already yours—Have a party!

We are joint heirs with Jesus (Romans 8:17). And we are one spirit with Jesus Christ (1 Corinthians 6:17). That being the case, here's the good news: Whatever Jesus has, you have. What is available in Him, where He is, seated at the right hand of God? Anything and everything you'll ever need, and then some! You have everything you need. I'll repeat this verse:

Colossians 2:9-10
[9]For in Him all the fullness of Deity dwells in bodily form, [10]and *in Him you have been made complete*, and He is the head over all rule and authority;

Hebrews 10:14 (AMP)
For by a single offering He has forever completely cleansed and perfected those who are consecrated and made holy.

If we are in Him, we lack nothing. We have all the authority, all the power, and all the anointing we need. We have all the

114

wisdom and knowledge we need. We have all the love we need; all the joy we need; all the peace we need—you get the picture.

2 Peter 1:3
as His divine power *has given to us all things that pertain to life and godliness, through the knowledge of Him* who called us by glory and virtue,

If you need it for life or godliness (that covers all the bases—spiritual or natural), He's already given it. It's yours. Listen, salvation is more complete and more amazing than our brains have allowed for. This verse says it comes "through the knowledge of Him." Here's the importance of "renewing the mind" again. This is pretty much the key to the whole deal. We can't make sense of it in the natural—So let's just believe it, continue to let our minds be renewed by His Word, and live in the joy of it!

Faith and Invisible Reality

These are all well-known realities in the heavenly realm. God certainly knows them—He saw it coming a mile away (Isaiah 46:10). Jesus knows them—He finished the work (John 19:30). The angels of God know them—they helped, and watched the whole thing go down (1 Peter 1:12). The demons believe, and tremble (James 2:19)! The devil still has Jesus' sandal-print on his face, and he was dragged around in front of Jesus' victory parade (Colossians 2:15), so you can bet that he knows this stuff first hand. One day we will see the devil with our own two eyes and be amazed that so many people had him made out to be such a powerful being—when in reality, he is far from that.

Isaiah 14:16-17
[16] "Those who see you (Lucifer/Satan) will gaze at you, And consider you, saying: 'Is this the man who made the earth tremble, Who shook kingdoms, [17] Who made the world as a wilderness And destroyed its cities, Who did not open the house of his prisoners?'

> Most Believers do not know the reality of what is already done in the invisible, spiritual realm.

Most Believers, on the other hand, do not know the reality of what is already done—established truth—in the invisible, spiritual realm. The devil is so glad about this, because then he can go on pretending to be the god of this world, and most of the time nobody stops him. This is why we must learn to "set our minds on things above," and "look... at the things which are not seen."

Colossians 3:1-2
[1] If then you were raised with Christ, *seek those things which are above*, where Christ is, sitting at the right hand of God. [2] *Set your mind on things above*, not on things on the earth.

2 Corinthians 4:18
while *we* do not *look at* the things which are seen, but *at the things which are not seen*. For the things which are seen are temporary, but *the things which are not seen are eternal*.

Hebrews 11:1
Now faith is the substance of things hoped for, the evidence of *things not seen*.

We are supposed to keep our eyes on the invisible truths we find in the Bible, until faith makes them visible. The second we truly believe and trust the invisible more than the visible, it becomes visible. Faith is the substance (physical material) of things hoped for, the (visible) evidence of things in the invisible realm (Hebrews 11:1, paraphrased). So if it's all finished and settled there, then why do we not see it reflected in our reality on Earth yet? Remember, we do not have because we do not ask. We must ask, and trust that we have received the realities of the invisible Kingdom—this force of faith drags them into this natural realm.

Matthew 11:12 (NIV)
From the days of John the Baptist until now, the kingdom of heaven has been forcefully advancing, and *forceful men lay hold of it*.

Growing Into What is Already Ours

Some might also be wondering, "Well, if it's all mine already—if I'm already like Christ, if all my needs are met, if I have everything that God has—then is there still a 'maturing' or 'growth' process?" The answer is yes; but it might not be as you think of it. Let me explain. Here's a simple flowchart:

Salvation is ours → We *believe* → We *discover* who we are and what we have → We *experience* more of what's already ours!

All that God has accomplished is done in the invisible realm. We as humans tend to be more aware of the natural, visible realm. Once we are born again, beginning to live out what's real in the invisible realm takes some re-training! We have the mind of Christ (1 Corinthians 2:16), now we need to learn how to use it—if we want to have the will of God in our lives.

Romans 12:1-2
[1] I beseech you therefore, brethren, by the mercies of God, that you present your bodies a living sacrifice, holy, acceptable to God, which is your reasonable service. [2] And do not be conformed to this world, *but be transformed by the renewing of your mind, that you may prove what is that good and acceptable and perfect will of God.*

The renewing of our minds is the *only way* that the Bible gives us to transform our lives. There is *nothing* else we can do to be visibly and outwardly transformed into the image of Christ. There is *nothing* else we can do to have God's will proved out in our lives. We've got to change the way we think, also known as "repentance"—a turn, a change. This is the process of training ourselves in no longer looking at/living by the things that are seen (natural, sense-ruled, limited view), but by the things which are unseen (spiritual, faith-ruled, supernatural reality).

> The renewing of our minds is the *only* way that the Bible gives us to transform our lives.

2 Peter 1:2-4

[2] Grace and peace be multiplied to you *in the knowledge of God and of Jesus our Lord,* [3] as *His divine power has given to us all things that pertain to life and godliness, through the knowledge of Him* who called us by glory and virtue, [4] *by which have been given to us exceedingly great and precious promises, that through these you may be partakers of the divine nature,* having escaped the corruption that is in the world through lust.

Peter tells us clearly that we receive "all things that pertain to life and godliness" through the knowledge of Him. Again, the renewing of the mind creates faith in the unseen, which brings it to us. Or, as this verse says, the knowledge of His promises makes us partakers. He said that God "has given" us everything we need. Then in the following verses, he goes on to describe the growth process along the way of receiving what He's provided.

2 Peter 1:5-8

[5] But also for this very reason, giving all diligence, add to your faith virtue, to virtue knowledge, [6] to knowledge self-control, to self-control perseverance, to perseverance godliness, [7] to godliness brotherly kindness, and to brotherly kindness love. [8] *For if these things are yours and abound, you will be neither barren nor unfruitful in the knowledge of our Lord Jesus Christ.*

He says basically, "be diligent in growing your knowledge and faith. This produces the character and perseverance you'll need to wait for the fruit (the results, the manifestation of the promises) to come to you. Our knowledge (and hence our faith) grows by hearing the word of God.

Romans 10:17

So then faith comes by hearing, and hearing by the word of God.

The more we hear it, the more we know it. The more we know it, the more we think it. The more we think it, the more we speak it. The more we speak it, the more we believe it. The more we believe it, the more we live it. The more we live by unseen spiritual realities, the more real they become. It's not complicated. Look at God's thoughts in the Bible and agree with them. Think about them. Believe them. Agree with them. Act like they're true, and you'll have them. It's actually quite natural for the Believer. That's why we're called "Believers"—because we believe. It's what we do. It's what we were born into. It's in our new spiritual DNA. Let's give ourselves to it!

Accessing Invisible Reality Through Prayer

Some might be wondering, "OK, If God's already done all He's going to do, and He says yes to everything He's promised, then why pray? Why would I need to ask, if He's already done all He's going to do?" Great question! Most Believers know that we are supposed to pray for things that are the will of God, right?

1 John 5:14
Now this is the confidence that we have in Him, that *if we ask anything according to His will*, He hears us. [15] And if we know that He hears us, whatever we ask, *we know that we have the petitions* that we have asked of Him.

New Testament prayer is such a joy! It's already accomplished and belongs to us, so all we have to do now is say thank you! Most New Testament prayer is a Thanksgiving party! It's not so much asking for anything as it is just thanking God for what He's already done to take care of our needs and requests!

> New Testament prayer is a Thanksgiving party!

Philippians 4:6
Be anxious for nothing, but in everything by prayer and supplication, with thanksgiving, let your requests be made known to God;

You don't have to beg or plead. You don't have to doubt and wonder. God's will is clear and simple and good. If it was included in our Salvation—He's already done it—all that is left to do is receive it all with thanksgiving!

Colossians 4:2
Continue earnestly in prayer, being vigilant in it with thanksgiving;

"Vigilant with thanksgiving." I love that. What an expression. This is what the prayer of faith sounds like: "Thank you God that you have accomplished (blank) for me already! I believe it, I receive it, Amen!" Thanksgiving is an expression of faith in God's promises. This kind of faith unlocks it and drags it from the invisible to the visible. We've got to know that God has already done it for us! This is what most New Testament prayer should look like.

Why would we "ask" for something that's already been given to us? God is not holding back on us, brothers and sisters! He paid a dear price for our Salvation—which includes healing for our bodies, and the bodies of people we minister to—and so much more. If God was going to hold back *anything* from us, surely it would have been His Son!! But He didn't hold Jesus back from us! If God didn't hold back Jesus, do we honestly think He's going to hold back some healing? Or some money, or some other need we have? No, no, no! He wanted us so badly that He gave us the very best—the most valuable, prized and precious thing He had to give! We cost Him His precious Son! And in paying that great price, everything else in the salvation package was included and purchased for us!

Romans 8:32
He who did not spare His own Son, but delivered Him up for us all, how shall He not *with Him* also *freely give us all things*?

He freely gives us all things—with Him. When did God give "Him?" 2,000 years ago, friends. If He gave us "all things" "with Him," then when did He give us "all things?" Does it get any simpler than that? Let's remove the question from our minds about whether or not God is going to come through on His promises. He wants us to experience all that He provided even worse than we do! He's freely given His Own Son; and because of that, we know He's not keeping anything else back. And He's

120

not unpredictable. If He promises something, it's because He wants us to have it. And His Word is His bond (Numbers 23:19).

2 Corinthians 1:19-20
[19] For the Son of God, *Jesus Christ*, who was preached among you by us—by me, Silvanus, and Timothy—*was not Yes and No, but in Him was Yes.* [20] *For all the promises of God in Him are Yes, and in Him Amen*, to the glory of God through us.

If God promised it, and we're in Christ, then God's answer is already "Yes," and "So be it!" He's not stingy, He's not hoarding benefits in Heaven, waiting for us to earn or deserve them. If we deserved them, they would be a reward, not a gift. Jesus deserved them, and once we've identified with Him, we are joint heirs and they are ours too! God not only *wants* us to have the benefits He's provided, it brings Him *pleasure*!!!

Luke 12:32
Do not fear, little flock, *for it is your Father's good pleasure to give you the kingdom.*

Let's not deny the Father the pleasure He gets when we receive all He's purchased for us! Receive all He's made available to you. Enjoy what Jesus paid for. Trust God's Word. Give thanks. Receive it. Rest in it. Sink into it. Let the goodness of God overtake you! God's will is *always* healing!

Notes:

CHAPTER 7

SALVATION – A BENEFITS PACKAGE

Whole-Being Salvation

One of the most commonly misunderstood things about Salvation is that it includes more than going to Heaven when we die. It is so much more than that. Jesus accomplished full salvation for every part of our being—spirit, soul, and body! He destroyed the works of the devil! He took us out of the kingdom of darkness, and put us in His Own kingdom! He regained all authority, and restored it to redeemed mankind! Salvation touches every area of human existence!

The Greek word translated as "saved" is "sozo." In the Dictionary/Word Search portion of www.blueletterbible.org, we can see that there is a lot contained within the definition of "saved":

"to save, keep safe and sound, to rescue from danger or destruction... to save a suffering one (from perishing), i.e. one suffering from disease, to make well, heal, restore to health... to preserve..." [1]

In other words, to be "saved" means that we have been rescued, and enjoy safety, soundness (wholeness), deliverance (from devils, troubles, etc), preservation (from any harm), and healing (from every sickness and disease). "Sozo" is a little

> When we get "saved," we get more than "Heaven when we die someday."

word that contains big blessing! Aside from being sometimes translated as "saved," many other times in the New Testament it is translated as "healed." Other times it's "be whole" or "make whole." Of all the times this word is used in the New Testament, at least 18 instances deal directly with physical healing, and several others could be interpreted that way. So when we get "saved," we get more than "Heaven when we die some day." This is a "whole being" Salvation—spirit, soul, body, family, relationships, finances, health, character, emotions, thoughts, destiny—He's covered everything!

Salvation = A Benefits Package

As we discussed in the book's Introduction, there are many benefits that come as a result of being in relationship with God—and He loads us with these benefits every single day. Healing is clearly listed as one of these.

Psalm 68:19
Blessed be the Lord, Who daily loads us with benefits, the God of our salvation! Selah

Psalm 103:1-5
[1] Bless the LORD, O my soul; and all that is within me, bless His holy name! [2] Bless the LORD, O my soul, and forget not all His benefits: [3] *Who forgives all your iniquities, Who heals all your diseases,* [4] Who redeems your life from destruction, Who crowns you with lovingkindness and tender mercies, [5] Who satisfies your mouth with good things, so that your youth is renewed like the eagle's.

If healing is included in the benefits package as this Scripture clearly states, it's quite obvious it's for us to enjoy *here on earth*; because we certainly won't need it in Heaven—there's no sickness there! Healing is for right here, right now.

Think of Salvation like the benefits package at your job. When you got hired, the Human Resources person probably sat you down in an office and told you about this whole long list of benefits that were suddenly yours. Health, dental, vision insurance; 401k retirement plans; life insurance; employee stock share programs; employee discounts; paid vacations; paid sick days; partnerships with other companies; discounts on rental cars, hotels, and Disneyland tickets; etc, etc, etc—it was probably a bit overwhelming to hear it all!

Now, I'll bet that most of us can't remember half of the benefits available to us through our job—and it's no different with our Christianity! That's why Psalm 103 shows King David

> If we *for*-get, we don't *get*!

reminding himself, "Forget not all His benefits!" David knew there was a lot in the package, and it could be easy to forget something! If God's benefits were automatic, it wouldn't matter if we remember them or not! Reality is: If we *for*-get, we don't *get!* Many believers have either forgotten—or have never heard, learned, or believed the benefits that became ours at Salvation! If we heard it, some of it probably just slipped past us because it was all so overwhelming—almost too good to be true! But I say, "If the gospel you're believing isn't too good to be true, then it probably isn't."

"OK," someone might be saying, "If my salvation includes my healing, then why am I still sick?" Because we must receive healing just like we did the forgiveness of sin—by grace, through faith! And that's just not generally possible if you didn't know, remember, or believe it. We can't have faith for something until we know it's God's will. I'm sorry nobody told you it was a package deal when you got saved. And even if they did, who's to say if you'd have cared, understood, or believed them? Rather than wondering why nobody told you, just receive it now if you need it. Don't be like the older brother! Now you've heard, now you know, and now you can take advantage of it! Just say, "I'm so happy! All that the Father has is mine!"

> We must receive healing just like we did the forgiveness of sin—by grace, through faith!

What is the Atonement?

Many argue about whether or not physical healing is specifically included in the Atonement. First, for those that don't know what

125

"Atonement" means, Strong's Concordance defines the Hebrew word for atonement ("kaphar") as follows:

"cleanse...forgive...pardon...purge...reconcile..." [2]

For our modern understanding of how we're using it in this context, www.dictionary.com says:

"The doctrine concerning the reconciliation of God and humankind, especially as accomplished through the life, suffering, and death of Christ." [3]

In other words, we're talking about the suffering of Jesus and what it did for us. So, is physical healing specifically included in that package or not? Did Jesus pay a price specifically for our physical healing or not? While I will cover the reasons why I personally believe that He did, I ultimately want to discuss why I don't think it really matters whether you agree or not! We can look at the things *every Christian* believes about sin, sickness, and the Atonement—and *still* come up with the same conclusion—God's will is always Healing!

Jesus Bore Our Physical Illnesses

We've already seen that physical healing is included in the very definition of the Greek word for "saved." But just in case that wasn't enough for someone, we will now take a look at the primary Scriptures dealing directly with the issue of Healing in the Atonement. The first comes from Isaiah 53, which is a prophecy about Jesus, written about 700 years before He came to Earth. This chapter is considered by most to be the clearest Old Testament passage that deals directly with what Jesus would accomplish for us when He came:

Isaiah 53:4-5
[4] Surely He has borne our griefs and carried our sorrows; Yet we esteemed Him stricken, smitten by God, and afflicted. [5] But He was wounded for our transgressions, He was bruised for our iniquities; the chastisement for our peace was upon Him, and by His stripes we are healed.

126

First, we need to know that the Hebrew words translated as "griefs" (choliy) and "sorrows" (mak'ob) are mistranslated in several English Bibles. The correct translation is "diseases"[4] and "pains,"[5] respectively. Many translations actually do render the verse as meaning physical sicknesses, diseases, and pains. See, for instance, the Amplified Bible, Common English Bible, Holman Christian Standard Bible, The Message, the Wycliffe Bible, or Young's Literal Translation. Even a decent study Bible in King James, New King James, etc, will note this fact in the margin. If yours doesn't, feel free to look it up in the Strong's Concordance, or your favorite Hebrew lexicon. So we can read this verse as it was intended, let's see this same passage in the HCSB:

Isaiah 53:4-5 (Holman Christian Standard Bible)[6]

[4] Yet He Himself bore our sicknesses, and He carried our pains; but we in turn regarded Him stricken, struck down by God, and afflicted. [5] But He was pierced because of our transgressions, crushed because of our iniquities; punishment for our peace was on Him, and we are healed by His wounds.

I don't know about you; but whenever someone has to reach into the Hebrew and Greek and change the English translation of a word to make their point, I can sometimes question the weight of their argument. In this case, thankfully, not only do we have multiple Bible translations that agree; but we can be doubly sure of the correct translation of "diseases" and "pains," because the Bible itself confirms it! This verse is quoted by Matthew in the New Testament, translated this way, *and* is applied directly to a context where physical illness is the subject at hand. Let's look at it:

Matthew 8:16-17

[16] When evening had come, they brought to Him many who were demon-possessed. And He cast out the spirits with a word, and healed all who were sick, [17] that it might be fulfilled which was spoken by Isaiah the prophet, saying: *"He Himself took our infirmities and bore our sicknesses."*

Second, Matthew correctly translates the Hebrew words, "choliy" and "mak'ob" into the Greek words, "astheneia" and "nosos."

These words are clearly translated into English as "infirmities" [7] and "sicknesses." [8] Thank you very much for clarifying that, sir.

Third, lest the skeptics say, "This just means 'spiritual sickness' (sin, etc)" (as they seem to be fond of doing). While the word "astheneia" can mean either physical sickness, or weakness in another sense, the context is always the guide. Please see the appendix in the back of this book for its New Testament usage. Thankfully though, Matthew gets us over that hump too. All we need to do is look at the context! He very clearly quotes Isaiah 53:4 and applies it directly to a situation where Jesus was healing *physical* illnesses. So obviously that is what was meant in the Isaiah text, or Matthew would be misinterpreting and misapplying the Scripture. If you believe that Matthew was inspired by the Holy Spirit to record this (as I do), then a misinterpretation and/or misapplication on his part is not possible. Physical illness is the subject of Isaiah 53:4—period.

> Physical illness is the subject of Isaiah 53:4—period.

Whatever Jesus Did With Sin, He Also Did With Sickness

So, in describing Christ's work of Salvation for us, what does Isaiah 53 say that He *did*, exactly, *with* our diseases and pains? Verse 4 says that He has "borne" our diseases. This Hebrew word, "nasa'," means that He lifted, carried, and took them away. [9] It also says that He "carried" our pains. This Hebrew word, "cabal," means that He "bore the load of" them (like a loaded-down donkey), "carried" them (literally) away, or "receive(d) the penalties which another has deserved." [10]

What does this mean to us? Jesus carried our sicknesses, illnesses and diseases away—now we should no longer carry them. He bore the load of our pain, so that we wouldn't have to.

He received the penalty of the diseases that we "deserved"—and because "double jeopardy" is illegal, we cannot be forced to take that penalty when it's already been paid for! Whether we got a sickness, disease, or injury through sin, sowing and reaping, or outright attack from the enemy—It doesn't matter! Jesus took it all, carried it away, and took the brunt of it Himself! We do not have to do it again! Let us look at two more verses in the same chapter that use these same exact Hebrew verbs in regard to what Jesus did with our *sin*:

Isaiah 53:11-12
[11] He shall see the labor of His soul, and be satisfied. By His knowledge My righteous Servant shall justify many, for *He shall bear their iniquities*. [12] Therefore I will divide Him a portion with the great, and He shall divide the spoil with the strong, because He poured out His soul unto death, and He was numbered with the transgressors, and *He bore the sin of many*, and made intercession for the transgressors.

Verse 11 says that Jesus would "bear" our iniquities. This is the same Hebrew word "cabal" from verse 4, which we have already seen describing what Jesus did with our pains. Verse 12 says that He "bore" the sin of many. This is the same Hebrew word "nasa'," which we also saw in verse 4 describing what Jesus did with our *diseases*.

What does all this mean? It means that you can look at Isaiah 53:4, see clearly that it deals with sickness, and say that "borne" and "carried" mean whatever you want them to. However, if you are honest and consistent in your interpretation ethic, you must admit (according to Isaiah 53:11-12) that "Whatever Jesus did with our sins, He did the same exact thing with our physical sicknesses, diseases, and pains!"

> Whatever Jesus did with our sins, He also did with our sickness and diseases.

If Jesus Paid For Our Diseases, Why Am I Still Sick?

"Whatever Jesus did with our sins, He also did with our sickness and disease." This has massive ramifications! Some say that Jesus only put a temporary band-aid on sickness that ended some time in the past. But if they are consistent—according to Isaiah 53, then they must also say that He only put a temporary band-aid on sin, and forgiveness is no longer available today!

However, if someone says that Jesus has destroyed the power of sin—then they must also say that He has destroyed the power of disease. If someone says that Jesus set us free from sin, and we no longer live under its power—then they must also say that Jesus has set us free from sickness, and we no longer live under its power! If someone says that we have authority over sin, and can choose not to give sin a place in our lives—then they must also admit that we have authority over disease, and can choose not to give sickness a place in our lives! Why? Because "Whatever Jesus did with our sins, He also did with our sicknesses!"

> If Jesus paid for your sins, then why do you still sin?

This also answers the most common question I hear when I teach that Jesus paid the price for our healing: "If Jesus paid for my sickness, then why am I sick?" Since we know now that Jesus did the same thing with both sin and sickness—I would answer that question with the question, "If Jesus paid for your sins, then why do you still sin?" It's the same exact issue! Whatever answer you give for the second question, is also your answer to the first!

What do I mean? Is it true that Jesus has made enough grace available to us that we can be free from sin, and in time grow up into the fullness of Christ? Yes! Jesus has forever destroyed the power of sin, and has set us free. We are no longer captives and slaves of Satan and sin. But if you only believe that you have been "partially" set free, then you will live only "partially" free from sin. If you believe that you are still a sinner, then you will keep right on sinning—only now you'll feel bad about it! But if you will receive the righteousness of God by faith and live accordingly, you can experience the full freedom Jesus paid for! Because Jesus has broken sin's power, all it takes for us to not commit a particular sin is to believe we are righteous and respond accordingly. If we stay consistent in our trusting what God has accomplished in us by His Grace, we see the results— the sin has no more place in our lives!

All of the above is also true of sickness! If we believe that we have only been "partially" set free from sickness, then we will only live partially free. If we believe that Jesus didn't really accomplish healing in a way that genuinely affects our lives today, then we'll keep right on being sick, and fail to enjoy the full freedom He provided! Jesus set us free from the power of diseases and pains. We must believe it, recognize that it's a done deal, and follow through with corresponding action. If we are consistent and firm in our stand, we will see the results—sickness has to bow to the finished works of Christ, when enforced by a believing Believer!

> Sickness has to bow to the finished works of Christ, when enforced by a believing Believer!

What Does "Fulfilled" Mean?

This also eliminates a more modern objection to healing's inclusion in the atoning work of Christ. Some modern opponents of Divine healing have simply said that this healing can't apply to us today; because in the Matthew 8:17 reference, it says that Jesus "fulfilled" Isaiah 53:4 on that actual day when He healed the sick in that crowd. "So," they say, "if it was 'fulfilled' that day, there is no more fulfillment available for us today."

It is true that Jesus fulfilled Isaiah 53:4 on that particular day— the Scriptures tell us that very clearly. However, He fulfilled that

Scripture *many* times. He fulfilled it in every town He visited. Wherever there was a sick crowd, He was there, taking away their diseases, and carrying off their pains. He fulfilled it—in the richest sense—yet again when He was beaten on the whipping post—accomplishing it once and for all; and He fulfills this Scripture again and again every time someone receives by faith the healing His stripes provided!

Some prophecies are fulfilled once, and *only* once; others are fulfilled multiple times, and/or on multiple levels. This is common Biblical understanding. Jesus fulfilled Isaiah 53:11-12 on multiple occasions as well. He fulfilled it every time He forgave sins on earth (Matthew 9:5, Luke 7:49, Luke 23:34, John 8:11, etc). He fulfilled it again through His death, burial, and resurrection— making forgiveness available to all. These verses are fulfilled yet again every time one of us today believes the gospel and receives by faith the forgiveness that His blood made available! Say it again, "Whatever Jesus did with our sins, He did the same exact thing with our physical sicknesses, diseases, and pains!"

> Some prophecies are fulfilled only once; while others are fulfilled multiple times.

If "fulfilled" meant "once and no more," then we could no longer receive the forgiveness of sin, as described in Isaiah 53:11-12 where He carried off our sins. How can I say this? Because—We must not forget this—"Whatever Jesus did with our sins, He did the same exact thing with our physical sicknesses, diseases, and pains." Additionally, if "fulfilled" meant "once and no more," then we would read lots of Scriptures in a new, *incorrect* light. For instance:

James 2:23
And the Scripture was fulfilled which says, "Abraham believed God, and it was accounted to him for righteousness." And he was called the friend of God.

Well, I guess we can't obtain righteousness by faith anymore; because Abraham fulfilled it. We're out of luck! Oh no! Hahaha!

No! James spends a great deal of time telling us that we must do exactly that!

What about Acts 2, where Peter talks about the occurrences on the Day of Pentecost fulfilling the prophecies of Joel 2? He said, "This (what is happening right here, right now) is that which was spoken of by the prophet Joel." If that one day fulfilled Joel's prophecy, then there is no more gift of the Holy Spirit for us today! Ridiculous!

One of the Strong's Concordance definitions for this word "plēroō" (translated in English as "fulfilled") is "to carry into effect." [11] In other words, Jesus brought all of Isaiah 53 into effect for us. He cracked it open and made its repeated and continuous fulfillment readily accessible for all of us!

> Jesus brought all of Isaiah 53 into effect for us. He cracked it open and made its repeated and continuous fulfillment readily accessible for all of us!

As further confirmation of this interpretation of "fulfilled", we see this same Greek word used at least twice in the New Testament in precisely this manner. For the sake of brevity I will summarize them here; but please do investigate them in depth if you are so inclined.

First, in Matthew 12:17-21, Jesus fulfills the prophecy of Isaiah 42:1-4, which describes the Gentiles coming to trust in Him (among other things). This—although "fulfilled" in Matthew 12— did not come to realization until after His ascension to Heaven. Even today, it has yet to be accomplished in its fullest sense, when the "fullness of the Gentiles has come in (Romans 11:25)!"

And second, in Luke 4:17-21, where Jesus quotes Isaiah 61 as His Own "Mission Statement," the Bible says that after He read it, He sat down and Himself declared that "Today this Scripture is fulfilled..." Jesus again was saying basically, "Today this thing is opened up and made readily available on into the future."

Obviously, even today, Jesus is still actively engaged in the work He describes in quoting Isaiah: freeing captives, opening blind eyes, healing the brokenhearted, etc. I don't know any Christian that would argue that He isn't.

Again, for a third time, we have seen that this Greek word for "fulfilled" does not always mean, "once and no more." On the contrary, it is also used to describe events that are seen as groundbreaking, pioneering, foundational occurrences that open up new territory and make provisions freely accessible and available. In each case, Jesus continued to do the activities prophesied, even after the day they were proclaimed to be fulfilled; and He continues to fulfill them today—through His Body, the Church. It's exactly the same thing in the case of Isaiah 53:4-5, Matthew 8:17, 1 Peter 2:24 and physical healing.

Jesus Paid a Price for Our Healing

So exactly what price did Jesus ultimately pay (in the context of the Atonement) to set us free from sickness and disease? Again, we turn to Isaiah 53, the prophecy given about what Jesus would accomplish in the process of the suffering in our place.

Isaiah 53:5
5 But He was wounded for our transgressions, He was bruised for our iniquities; the chastisement for our peace was upon Him, and by His stripes we are healed.

The answer: "By His stripes!" The price for our healing was the stripes He bore on His body at the whipping post. How does that work? I don't know; but that's what the Word says, so like it or not, that's just the bottom line. Some say that this refers to spiritual healing only; but as we've already seen, there is no question that verse 4 dealt with physical sickness, disease and pain. Verse 5 moves on and tells that He also paid for our sins, then reminded us again about the physical healing aspect. Isaiah simply elaborated on that theme, telling us "how" He would ultimately bear and carry our diseases away—so we'd know it when it happened. Note that Isaiah spoke of Christ paying the price for our healing in the present tense ("are" healed, not "will be" healed). This is important. Why? Again—this verse is also referred to in the New Testament and gives us additional insight into the verse and answers this question.

1 Peter 2:24
who Himself bore our sins in His own body on the tree, that we, having died to sins, might live for righteousness—by whose stripes you were healed.

First, how do we know Peter is referencing Isaiah 53? Because he directly quotes Isaiah 53:9 two verses earlier (verse 22). Next, in verse 24, he has changed one word in the quote from Isaiah 53:5, and this one word helps us understand the meaning of the quote. He has changed "are" (healed) to "were" (healed). Why did he change it to past tense? Did he make a mistake? No! Was he taking "artistic license?" No! The reason Peter changed it to past tense is because at the time of his writing, the work had already taken place! It was now a finished work! When Isaiah wrote it, it was off in the future, although he saw and wrote it as present tense. When Peter quoted it, it was now in the past.

What happened between Isaiah and Peter that changed the verb tense? Jesus had now taken the stripes on His back—when He was beaten by the Romans at the whipping post. He had therefore fulfilled Isaiah's prophecy, and completed the payment for our healing. The price for our physical healing was quite separate from the price He paid for our sins— His blood. We will discuss this more in the section on Communion.

> The price for our physical healing was quite separate from the price He paid for our sins.

Some say that Peter is talking about spiritual healing, because he mostly addresses the sin issue in the context. However, since we already saw that without question Isaiah 53:4 is dealing with physical sickness, we know that Peter also means it this way. Otherwise, he would be misapplying the prophecy he's quoting.

As in the case of Matthew, I don't believe Peter can do this and still be inspired of the Holy Spirit. So Peter was talking specifically about physical sickness and disease. "By His stripes we were healed." Jesus accomplished it on the whipping post— It's now a finished work, a done deal.

Old Testament:
Passover Confirms Healing in the Atonement

The greatest Old Testament symbol ("type" or "shadow") of the vicarious work of Christ—is the Passover. Not just the annual celebration; but the original event, when the Israelites were delivered from Egypt.

As a brief reminder, the Hebrews were slaves in Egypt for 430 years. Moses was sent by God to deliver them from their bondage. In the course of "convincing" the Pharaoh to let them go, the Egyptians got pounded with several plagues and calamities. Nine had passed, and there was only one plague left to come—the death of every firstborn son in Egypt. A spirit of death would pass through Egypt and kill the firstborn son in every house, unless they communicated to that spirit that they were God's people. The sign that God gave for the Israelites to communicate this was that they should kill a lamb, cook and eat it (along with some unleavened bread, etc), and put the lamb's blood around the outside of their doorposts. The spirit of death would see the blood and pass over that house without harming the firstborn (hence the term, "Passover").

In Psalm 105, David reviews much of this story, and gives us an important detail we missed in the Exodus account:

Psalm 105:23-38
[23] Israel also came into Egypt... [26] He sent Moses His servant, and Aaron whom He had chosen. [27] They performed His signs among them, and wonders in the land... darkness... waters into blood... frogs... flies... lice... hail... flaming fire... struck their vines... locusts... [36] He also destroyed all the

firstborn in their land, the first of all their strength. [37] He also brought them out with silver and gold, and *there was none feeble among His tribes.* [38] Egypt was glad when they departed, for the fear of them had fallen upon them.

Did you catch the tail end of that? During the original Passover, "there was none feeble among His tribes!" Not even one of those 2-million-plus Israelites was sick or diseased when they were set free from Egypt. This is impossible in the natural, and if you've ever been to a developing country, you know that you can scarcely get 50 people together without somebody having sickness or pain to minister to. And that's in *today's* world. In Israel's case, not only are we talking thousands of years ago, they were also slaves—the lowest of the low, the poorest of the poor—oppressed and mistreated like none else. There is no way, naturally speaking, for there to be none feeble among a group like that, without a miracle of God. This was an awesome wonder, as David says in verse 38, "the fear of them (the Israelites) had fallen upon them (the Egyptians)." The Egyptians gave them their silver and gold and said, "Get out of here—Y'all freak us out!!"

We can confirm David's Psalm 105 report of this fact in Moses' Exodus 15 version. Immediately after the Israelites left Egypt, they ran up against the Red Sea. Pharaoh and his army pursued them there. Moses split the sea open by

> The very first thing God said to the newly-freed Israelites was, "I'm the God Who Heals You."

the power of God and the Israelites passed through to the other side safely. Pharaoh's army attempted to follow them; but the sea closed and killed them all, securing Israel's deliverance from Egypt. This is recorded in Exodus 14. Then, get this: *the very first thing* God says to them after delivering them is recorded in verse 26, (paraphrased) "Obey me. By the way, I'm the God Who Heals You."

Now, without understanding the miracle David described, God's *very first* statement to His newly-delivered people would seem completely random! "Yay! You're free. I'm the God Who Heals You." Huh? Why would he have to say that unless they were wondering about how they had all gotten healed? They had to have been curious about the miraculous healing and restoration of their health. God was simply answering the question on the tip of their tongue, "How did we all get healed?" The Israelites received salvation (deliverance from Egypt via crossing the Red Sea), and simultaneously received healing (deliverance from sickness via the very nature of God—Jehovah Rapha—the God Who Heals). This all happened in the original Passover—the *strongest* Old Testament type and shadow of the saving work of Christ Himself.

New Testament:
Communion Confirms Healing in the Atonement

The only New Testament equivalent to the Passover—the only memorial feast (if you will)—is Communion, a.k.a. The Eucharist, or the Lord's Supper. Jesus celebrated the Passover Feast with His disciples, just before being arrested and accomplishing Salvation for us.

Luke 22:19-20
[19] And He took bread, gave thanks and broke it, and gave it to them, saying, "This is My body which is given for you; do this in remembrance of Me." [20] Likewise He also took the cup after supper, saying, "This cup is the new covenant in My blood, which is shed for you.

Depending on your view of this ordinance/sacrament, the elements can be considered as symbols of the blood and body of the Lord, as the literal body and blood of the Lord, or somewhere in between. That issue is for another discussion. But whichever view we hold, we can all agree that Communion is a memorial declaration of what Jesus accomplished in the Atonement. As Jesus said, "Do this in remembrance of Me."

1 Corinthians 11:23-26

[23] For I received from the Lord that which I also delivered to you: that the Lord Jesus on the same night in which He was betrayed took bread; [24] and when He had given thanks, He broke it and said, "Take, eat; this is My body which is broken for you; do this in remembrance of Me." [25] In the same manner He also took the cup after supper, saying, "This cup is the new covenant in My blood. This do, as often as you drink it, in remembrance of Me." [26] For as often as you eat this bread and drink this cup, you proclaim the Lord's death till He comes.

Here's the thing to remember, folks. There are *two* elements in the Communion, not just one. The bread is the body, and the wine is the blood. According to the Bible, what is the price of getting forgiveness? What is it that can atone for a soul/spirit problem (sin)? Only blood!

> There are *two* elements taken in Communion, not just one!

Leviticus 17:11

For the life of the flesh is in the blood, and I have given it to you upon the altar to make atonement for your souls; for *it is the blood that makes atonement for the soul.'*

Hebrews 9:22

And according to the law almost all things are purified with blood, and *without shedding of blood there is no remission.*

Matthew 26:28

For this is *My blood* of the new covenant, which is *shed for many for the remission of sins*.

Jesus' blood (the wine in communion) paid the price for our sins. However, if all that was paid for at Salvation was the forgiveness of our sins, then what is the purpose of the bread/body? Jesus didn't give us two elements in Communion to meet some kind of heavenly food pyramid guidelines, folks! Each element is there on purpose, and for a specific reason. If all Communion does is commemorate the washing away of our sins, then we would only need to drink the cup. There would be no need to eat the bread.

So, what is the purpose of the bread/body of Christ in Communion? Jesus didn't tell us directly in any of the four gospels, like He did with the blood. Thankfully, Paul received additional revelation from Jesus on this, and shared it with us in 1 Corinthians! Yay, Paul!

1 Corinthians 11:27-30

[27] Therefore whoever eats this bread or drinks this cup of the Lord in an unworthy manner will be guilty of the body and blood of the Lord. [28] But let a man examine himself, and so let him eat of the bread and drink of the cup. [29] For he who eats and drinks in an unworthy manner eats and drinks judgment to himself, not discerning the Lord's body. [30] For this reason many are weak and sick among you, and many sleep.

Paul says that many people are "weak and sick" or "sleep" (die prematurely) "for this reason"—What reason?—"Not discerning the Lord's body." What is he talking about? What in the world is the connection between celebrating the Lord's Table and getting sick? He says that "not discerning the Lord's body" is partaking of the Eucharist in "an unworthy manner." In other words, if someone doesn't recognize the specific value of the body of Christ—the bread—and what it secured for us, they are rendering themselves unable to receive its benefit. What benefit are we talking about? Healing, of course! "By His stripes, we are healed!"

Why would this make us unable to receive the healing available in celebrating Communion? Every benefit God provides for the Believer must be believed and received by grace, through faith, with thanksgiving. If we do not discern the high price Jesus paid for our healing (His Own Body), it's our loss—we can go without. If we don't know the benefit is there, we can't receive it. If we say, "My physical healing isn't that important," we devalue the price that Christ paid for our healing; and we don't benefit from

> All Believers have discerned the Blood, but not all Believers have yet discerned the Body.

it. Paul says that if we would discern/value the bread/body the same way we do the wine/blood, we would be able to receive the benefits of both, and we would not become "weak and sick" or "sleep" before our time!

140

All Believers have discerned the Blood and what it accomplished (at least to some degree)—that's how we all became Christians in the first place! If you don't discern the Blood, you don't receive the forgiveness available in Jesus. In the same way, if you don't discern the Body, you probably won't receive the healing available in Jesus. All Believers discern the Blood, but not all Believers have yet discerned the Body. This is why many are sick and die before their time. They haven't yet seen what was made available through the stripes Jesus took on His Body. My people perish for lack of knowledge!

Communion—the greatest New Covenant picture of all that Christ accomplished for us—clearly demonstrates and confirms that Healing is included as a specific provision in the Atoning sacrifice of Christ. Since we know that the Blood/wine alone was enough to cleanse us from sin once and for all time, we must recognize that the bread/Body must accomplish something else. It is not a superfluous, non-essential. It's there for a reason, and Scripture tells us that it's there to memorialize the fact that the breaking of the Body of Christ accomplished our healing in exactly the same way that the shedding of His blood accomplished the cleansing of our sins! His Blood paid for our sins, but His Body took a beating for our physical healing. If we don't believe that Christ's Body paid for something beyond what His blood paid for, we may as well skip the bread next time we celebrate Communion!

> If we don't believe that Healing is in the Atonement, we may as well skip the bread!

Old Testament:
Bronze Serpent Confirms Healing in the Atonement

In Numbers 21, the Israelites were grumbling and complaining against God and Moses (once again). Out of the wilderness came a bunch of poisonous snakes, and the Israelites were getting bitten and dying. They repented and asked Moses to pray for God to protect and heal them, and Moses prayed...

Numbers 21:8-9
[8] Then the LORD said to Moses, "Make a fiery serpent, and set it on a pole; and it shall be that everyone who is bitten, when he looks at it, shall live." [9] So Moses made a bronze serpent, and put it on a pole; and so it was, if a serpent had bitten anyone, when he looked at the bronze serpent, he lived.

Now, you might say, "What does this have to do with healing and the atonement?" Well, the Israelites were healed of snakebites when they looked at the bronze snake that Moses lifted up on the pole, right? That snake was a type or shadow of Jesus Christ. I'm not just being creative in making the connection—Jesus confirms this for us very clearly in John's gospel, while talking with Nicodemus:

John 3:14
And as Moses lifted up the serpent in the wilderness, even so must the Son of Man be lifted up, [15] that whoever believes in Him should not perish but have eternal life. [16] For God so loved the world that He gave His only begotten Son, that whoever believes in Him should not perish but have everlasting life.

Jesus drew a direct parallel between the snake on the pole, and Himself on the cross making Atonement for us. If healing was available in the Old Testament symbol (the snake on the pole), then healing is also available in the New Testament fulfillment (Christ on the cross)! Many people don't know that also

> Jesus drew a direct parallel between the snake on the pole, and Himself on the Cross.

contained in the context surrounding the most well-known verse of all time (John 3:16) is the truth that healing was also provided in the saving work of Christ!

Additional Confirmations

There are additional Scriptural confirmations of the fact that physical healing is included in the atonement. First, in Leviticus 14, we have a ritual prescribed for one being declared healed of

142

leprosy. As part of the long process (thank God Jesus fulfilled all of these rituals!), the person was to offer both a lamb (Blood/wine) and a grain offering (bread/Body) as part of his offering.

Additionally, on multiple occasions we see a connection made between the atonement for sin, and a corresponding protection or healing from various plagues. For instance, in Numbers 25:6-13, Phinehas makes "atonement" for the Israelites (according to God's account of it in verse 12), and in so doing, stops a plague in Israel (verse 8). See also:

Numbers 8:19
[19] And I have given the Levites as a gift to Aaron and his sons from among the children of Israel, to do the work for the children of Israel in the tabernacle of meeting, and *to make atonement* for the children of Israel, *that there be no plague* among the children of Israel when the children of Israel come near the sanctuary."

Numbers 16:47-48
[47] Then Aaron took it as Moses commanded, and ran into the midst of the assembly; and already the plague had begun among the people. So he put in the incense and *made atonement for the people.* [48] And he stood between the dead and the living; *so the plague was stopped.*

The bottom line from these additional references is this: When sin is atoned for, healing takes place. This is

> When sin is atoned for, healing takes place.

certainly no less true in the ultimate Atonement—that of Jesus Christ suffering for the sins and sicknesses of all humanity!

Let's summarize: We have reviewed the story of the bronze serpent, the original Passover, the Communion feast, and additional Scriptural parallels. It's clear that both in Old Testament pre-views, and New Testament re-views of the Atoning work of Christ, we see that physical healing was included with the payment Jesus made for our sins.

Healing is in the Atonement—it's paid for, signed, sealed, and delivered. It's just as readily available to us as the forgiveness of sin is. Just like forgiveness, we need only believe it and receive it. Otherwise, we can doubt it and do without it! It's here I'll conclude the argument that physical healing is definitely included *in* the Atonement. Now let's talk about why it shouldn't really matter whether or not healing was specifically paid for in the Atonement or not!

Symptoms vs. Problems

We discuss this idea in greater detail elsewhere in the book; but let us summarize the point again here, briefly. Before Adam and Eve's sin, there was no sickness. After they sinned and "fell," they became subject to the "curse," which came by handing their authority over to Satan. Part of this curse was sickness, disease, and death. "The wages of sin is death" (Romans 6:23), and disease is death in seed form. So, in short, *sickness is ultimately a result of sin, and therefore a work of the devil.* Please understand that when I say sickness is a result of "sin," I mean the sin *principle*, as in, the curse from Adam and Eve's sin—general sin in the world—NOT any individual's sin). An individual today does not have to ever sin to get attacked with sickness, disease or pain—we live in a sin-cursed mess, and that's the only reason sickness got into our world. That said, let us move on to the point of our current discussion...

We can restate the previous paragraph like this: "Sin is the actual problem; and disease is merely a manifestation, a symptom, or a result of the real problem." Whenever I teach on healing, often someone will say something like, "Why all this emphasis on healing? God is much more concerned about salvation. Sin is a bigger problem than sickness." Another way this belief comes out is when people say to me, "I am more than content with just being saved. I'm not really that concerned about getting healed." All of these statements reflect one core belief: The spirit man is more important than the physical body, sin is more important than disease, and forgiveness is more important than healing.

While these statements may be true in some sense, my first argument would be this: Who told us that we must only pick *one* of the two? NO! *Both* are provided, and *both* belong to us in Christ. God is not asking you to prioritize and pick only one benefit to the exclusion of the others. Jesus gave His blood for our forgiveness; but He also took an inconceivable beating for our healing. Let's not let His pain be all for nothing! Let's receive the healing He earned for us!

I'll say it again—if healing isn't important to you, skip the bread at your next Communion service! Let's not forget—there are two elements in communion, so let's not dare neglect to partake of the bread of Christ's body! Interestingly, the belief that sin is the core problem, and sickness is of secondary importance actually bolsters the argument I am making right now. My point is this: Sickness is merely a result of sin. So if the sin problem is eliminated, then the sickness no longer has a basis to remain!

> Sickness is merely a result of sin. So if the sin problem is eliminated, then the sickness no longer has a basis to remain!

Holistic Medicine

In Western medicine, our Greek mindsets have divided the human being up into pieces and parts. If we get a headache, we take an aspirin to mask the pain. But the pain isn't the actual problem—it's merely an indicator that something is wrong. If we get a runny nose, sore throat, and cough—we take a medicine that will dry out our mucous membranes, mask the pain in our throat, and relax the muscles that reflexively help us to cough. But those things are symptoms. The problem is that we have a bacteria or virus that needs to be killed!

This approach is completely opposed to the Eastern view of viewing a person as one whole being. If you go to an eastern doctor with a cold, they will ask you about how things are going at your job. If you go in with back pain, they might ask you how your marriage is doing. Why? Because they recognize that a person is a complex being, with many parts of their life all integrated into one. Because our parts are all intricately and inextricably connected, a problem in any one part can produce ramifications or indicators in any other area of the person's life. So when the eastern-view doctor sees an indicator (like pain, etc), she will explore the patient's whole life to determine the actual cause—the root problem. Once the root problem is discovered and addressed, the indicator will resolve itself without even being directly addressed. For example, if we "fix the marriage, the back pain fades away to nothing." Remove the root problem, and the attention-getting, distracting symptom will disappear.

Check Engine

If you can't relate to the eastern vs. western medicine analogy, here's one most of us can understand. While most people may not know much about the inner workings of an automobile engine, we generally know one thing—If the "Check Engine" indicator lights up on our dashboard, there's a problem that needs fixing! It might feel like the car is doing fine; but that light is sure bothersome, isn't it? So we must do *something*. We could approach this problem in a couple of ways. First, we can eliminate the annoying light so we can stop worrying. Or second, we can find out why it turned on, and fix the real problem.

If we take the "western medicine," or Greek mindset approach, we could take the little dashboard light bulb out, remove the fuse, cut the wire, or just put some duct tape over the light. There we go, problem solved, right? No!

What is the smart approach? We take the car to a mechanic. He hooks a diagnostic machine up to the car and tells us why the computer turned the "Check Engine" indicator on in the first place. Then he fixes the actual problem in the engine. Once the root problem is fixed, there is no reason for the symptom to continue! Sometimes the light will turn off automatically. However, in some cases—even after the problem is fixed—the mechanic still has to take additional steps to get the "Check Engine" light to turn off.

I asked my mechanic why sometimes it turns off automatically and other times it doesn't. Do you know what he said? "I don't know; that's just how it is. It depends on the car, and it depends on the problem." That's good enough for me; because here's the bottom line: If we address the problem and the light doesn't go off by itself, all we need to do is address the light directly and we won't be bothered by it again! We can then get back on the road with no worries. Let's get our engines fixed—AND if necessary, let's also get our "Check Engine" alarm cleared so we can enjoy our journey, folks! Whether it turns off automatically or not—either way, there is no more reason for it to continue annoying us. Let him who has ears to hear, hear!

> Once the root problem is fixed, there is no reason for the symptom to continue!

The spirit man is our engine, if you will. Sickness, disease, and pain, are simply the warning lights on the dash. We can take our "car" to the designer, engineer, master mechanic Jesus, and let Him fix the problem in the engine. Once the engine is fixed, sometimes the "check engine" light goes off automatically. However, other times—even though there is no more legitimate reason for the light to be on—we must let the mechanic take the additional step to turn it off!

Because of the sin of man, we were disconnected—at the very least, in our own minds—from full, unhindered, intimate relationship with God. We cut ourselves off from the source of life, blessing, and every good gift—*that* was the true "engine problem." When we come into relationship with Jesus and receive the forgiveness of sins, we are able to enjoy living, breathing connection and unity with the Father.

Sometimes when this happens, the results of the former disconnection (like sickness or anything else that came in the Fall of Man) are immediately and automatically alleviated. Our engine light will turn off, so to speak. I've seen multiple occasions where people get saved and physically healed all in one fell swoop, for instance.

Other times, the engine problem gets fixed—the person gets reconnected to the Father, and yet the "dash light" is still lit up like a Christmas tree—the sickness remains. If we have been forgiven and restored to relationship with God through Jesus, there is no legitimate reason for us to still be sick—our engine's been fixed! In these cases, we must simply have the mechanic take the extra step of turning the light off! We need only receive the benefit of His skill and expertise—by grace, through faith.

Summary

I believe that Jesus paid a very specific price that purchased our healing—His Body. We have seen clearly in the Scriptures that whatever Christ did with sin, He also did with sickness. This is evidenced in the Old Testament types and shadows—the bronze serpent, the Passover, etc; and in the New Covenant celebration of the Atonement—Holy Communion. You may not believe this. However, all Believers must be able to agree on some basic facts: First, sickness came as a fruit of the sin problem. If Christ solved the sin problem, then the results of the sin problem (including sickness and disease) have no right to continue enslaving those that have been set free.

Any way you slice it, physical healing has been made readily and continually available to the Christian as a result of the finished works of Christ. Someone's failure to receive the fullness of this benefit is not evidence of its nonexistence. Just like someone's failure to receive the full benefit of forgiveness and restored relationship with the Father does not disprove the reality of Salvation provided by Jesus' blood.

Whether someone wants to say that physical healing is "in" the Atonement, or that it "comes right along with" the Atonement might not ultimately be worth arguing. One way or the other—sin, sickness, and death were dealt a death blow by the works of Jesus. It's all a finished work, and ours for the taking. Jesus really did "destroy the works of the devil!" God's will is *always* healing!

> One way or another— sin, sickness, and death were dealt a death blow by the works of Jesus!

Notes:

CHAPTER 8

UNION WITH CHRIST: The Words

The Truth That Trumps All Other Truth

The Church throughout history has accepted the idea of being *servants* of God. A slightly smaller group has really accepted what it means to be *sons and daughters* of God. Fewer still relate to being the *Bride* of Christ. Only very few have even scratched the surface of the revelation of being *One with Jesus*.

I believe that this new reality was the whole goal God had in mind before Creation, and His whole aim in accomplishing our great Salvation. If Christians truly knew, believed, assimilated, and experientially walked in this one Truth, the rest of this book would not be necessary. All arguments against Divine Healing would go out the window.

I have only caught a glimpse of this Truth, and this glimpse is all I can share. I pray that you and I both grow in this revelation! Some great men have recommended a study to me in times past. I've done it a couple of times and it's changed my life. I recommend the same to you. Because we receive salvation through identification with Jesus—all He is, and all He has done—the Bible now calls us "in Christ." If we will research a few phrases, we will get some idea of who we really are in Him. Look up every instance in the New Testament of "in Christ," "by Christ," "in Him," "by Him," "in Whom," "by Whom," "with Christ," "with Him," "with Whom," and other similar phrases. These phrases are used nearly 200 times in the New Testament. You will see some of what God has accomplished for us, and who we are now in Him. This is our true spiritual identity. Try it, you'll like it!

> Any lesser truth that comes our way must bow to this one central Truth—We are now one with Jesus Christ.

Being "in Christ" – A.J. Gordon called this Truth "the seal and signature of the Gospel." [1] The Apostle Paul simply referred to it as a "great mystery" (Ephesians 5:32). I will just say that this is the Supreme Truth—the Truth that trumps all other truth. Any lesser truth that comes our way must bow to this one central Truth—*We are now one with Jesus Christ*, the eternal Son of God!

We Are One With Jesus

There is a lot of power in Jesus' "High Priestly Prayer" in the book of John. This prayer is recorded for us in more detail than most any prayer we see Jesus pray. It's one of the last significant times of prayer for Jesus, before He went to the cross. We see Jesus place a significant focus on praying for Believers and our union with Him:

John 17:20-23
[20] "I do not pray for these alone, but also for those who will believe in Me through their word; [21] that they all may be one, as You, Father, are in Me, and I in You; *that they also may be one in Us*, that the world may believe that You sent Me. [22] And the glory which You gave Me I have given them, that they may be one just as We are one: [23] I in them, and You in Me; *that they may be made perfect in one*, and that the world may know that You have sent Me, and have loved them as You have loved Me.

Do you believe that Jesus prayed the will of God? I do! It is the will of God, then, that we be one in God—Christ in us, and God in Christ, made perfect (mature) in One. Since Jesus always prayed the will of God, we know that God always heard Him (John 11:22, 42, 1 John 5:14-15). Therefore, He received the answers to His requests. "But," someone might say, "We haven't been made One with Him yet. That happens later." Unfortunately for them, the Bible tells us it has already happened—past tense!

Disciples=Jesus

At the conversion of Saul, Jesus confronted him in a blinding supernatural encounter. Paul was on his way to persecute some Christians in Damascus, locking them up in chains, putting them in prison, and even supporting their execution (Acts 7:58). Saul never even met Jesus in person, and yet when Jesus confronts him, He asks, "Why are you persecuting *Me*?" He identifies the believers as Himself!

Acts 22:4-8

[4] I persecuted this Way to the death, binding and delivering into prisons both men and women, [5] as also the high priest bears me witness, and all the council of the elders, from whom I also received letters to the brethren, and went to Damascus to bring in chains even those who were there to Jerusalem to be punished. [6] "Now it happened, as I journeyed and came near Damascus at about noon, suddenly a great light from heaven shone around me. [7] And I fell to the ground and heard a voice saying to me, 'Saul, Saul, *why are you persecuting Me*?' [8] So I answered, 'Who are You, Lord?' And He said to me, '*I am Jesus of Nazareth, whom you are persecuting.*'

In case we didn't get it the first time, He repeats it for us, "I am Jesus of Nazareth, Whom you are persecuting." Paul could have said, "Wait, Jesus, I'm not persecuting *you*, I'm persecuting these followers of yours." But Jesus made it clear, "They are one with Me. If you're persecuting them, you're persecuting Me!" Jesus took it personally when the "bone of His bones, and flesh of His flesh" was being persecuted! This was shortly after the completed work of our great Salvation, and Jesus is already saying, "My prayer has already been answered— Believers are now One with God in the flesh!"

> Jesus made it clear, "They are one with Me. If you're persecuting them, you're persecuting Me!"

Believers=Christ

2 Corinthians 6:14-15

[14] Do not be unequally yoked together with unbelievers. For what fellowship has *righteousness* with lawlessness? And what communion has *light* with darkness? [15] And what accord has *Christ* with Belial? Or what part has a *believer* with an unbeliever?

This Scripture very clearly identifies Believers on one half of each statement. It puts us in the place of "believer," "righteousness," "light," and "Christ." It puts unbelievers in the place of "unbeliever," "lawlessness," "darkness," and "Belial." We are very clearly identified in Christ here. We are One with Him! This same equation (Believers=Christ) is seen again here:

Matthew 25:34-40

[34] Then the King will say to those on His right hand, 'Come, you blessed of My Father, inherit the kingdom prepared for you from the foundation of the world: [35] for I was hungry and *you gave Me food*; I was thirsty and you gave Me drink; I was a stranger and *you took Me in*; [36] I was naked and *you clothed Me*; I was sick and *you visited Me*; I was in prison and *you came to Me.*' [37] "Then the righteous will answer Him, saying, 'Lord, when did we see You hungry and feed You, or thirsty and give You drink? [38] When did we see You a stranger and take You in, or naked and clothe You? [39] Or when did we see You sick, or in prison, and come to You?' [40] And the King will answer and say to them, '*Assuredly, I say to you, inasmuch as you did it to one of the least of these My brethren, you did it to Me.*'

Jesus is saying here the same thing He said to Paul at His conversion, "If you did it to them, you did it to Me." You can also prove this with the other parallels. Take "light" for instance. Jesus is the Light of the world, and so are Believers:

John 9:5

As long as I am in the world, *I* am the light of the world.

Matthew 5:14

You are the light of the world...

Jesus was the light of the world while He was on Earth. When He left and we received Him, we became one with that light, so now *we* are the light of the world. Or, take "righteousness." The Bible says we *are* righteousness. Not that we *have* or *do* righteousness, or just that we are *righteous*; but that we actually *are* righteousness.

2 Corinthians 5:21
For He made Him who knew no sin to *be* sin for us, that we might *become* the righteousness of God in Him.

How did we become His righteousness? The same way we became the light of the world—Through our identification and union with Him—the Great Exchange! Jesus became sin. Why? Because *we were sin*. I know that sounds harsh, but there it is. If He *became* sin for us, then that means we *were* sin. He had to fully identify with the condition of lost Humanity—becoming sin—in order for us to later be fully identified as the very righteousness of God!

1 Corinthians 1:30
But of Him you are *in Christ Jesus*, who *became for us* wisdom from God— and *righteousness* and sanctification and redemption—

He became wisdom, sanctification and redemption for us. He did it all. By grace, through faith, we receive the benefit of His work. We have died, we have been buried, we have ascended, and we are seated at the right hand of God. We can neither add to, nor take away anything from what He already did. We need only identify with Him and receive the benefit.

As He Is, So Are We

At the moment of salvation, we are identified with Him. We are *completely* united to Him. From that point on, this is our spiritual reality: "As He is, so are we in the world."

1 John 4:17
Love has been perfected among us in this: that we may have boldness in the day of judgment; because *as He is, so are we in this world.*

We are one with Jesus! Some say, "That's when we go to heaven." Nope! It says, "in *this* world." The invisible reality is—

> The invisible reality is— We are just like He is, here and now.

We are just like He is, here and now. Not even like He *was* while He was on earth, but like He *is*—right now, seated at the right hand of God—Righteous, holy, justified, glorified!

Romans 8:30
Moreover whom He predestined, these He also called; whom He called, these He also justified; and whom He justified, these He also glorified.

Does it bother you to say that we are glorified? In Jesus' High Priestly prayer we discussed earlier (John 17:22), didn't Jesus also pray for this very thing? If it was answered, and if Romans 8:30 is also true, then we *are* glorified. When we received Christ, we were born of God—recreated in Him, and reflecting His heavenly likeness. This is not cause for pride; this is cause for humility. It only highlights the splendor of God's love that raised us to such a place of honor, from the depths in which He found us!

You Are United to Jesus in Body and Spirit

When we were born again, we became new creatures.

2 Corinthians 5:17
Therefore, if anyone is in Christ, he is a new creation; old things have passed away; behold, all things have become new.

Some say that this only means your spirit man is new. But the verse says "all things"—not just your spirit man. So there's a discrepancy—"all things" means *all* things. Once you receive salvation, you belong to God; and He paid for the whole package, not just your spirit man!

1 Corinthians 6:20

For you were bought at a price; therefore glorify God *in your body and in your spirit*, which are God's.

You were bought with a price. You belong to Him—*all* of you. He didn't just buy your spirit man. He bought your body, mind, emotions—everything—the whole package! Every part of you is now united to Jesus Christ. This is why Paul encourages us to let every part of us be set apart to be used by God:

> Once you receive salvation, you belong to God; and He paid for the whole package, not just your spirit man!

1 Thessalonians 5:23

Now may the God of peace Himself sanctify you *completely; and may your whole spirit, soul, and body* be preserved blameless at the coming of our Lord Jesus Christ.

Some say, "But the 'body' part only comes later." We'll cover this a bit more in Chapter 17. However, I do believe that there is implication in the Scriptures of much more belonging to us than we have begun to fathom. How we can begin to have faith for it and access it all is a whole new can of worms! But for now, let's keep it simple. Your body belongs to Jesus. Not only does it belong to Him, like some separate possession. Most Believers know that their body is the temple of the Holy Spirit. But beyond that, our body belongs to Him, as in, it's *His* Body. We died. Jesus moved in, and now it's Him living in our old house. It's Jesus living in our body. Even our flesh-and-blood body is united to Him!

1 Corinthians 6:15-17

[15] Do you not know that *your bodies are members of Christ*? Shall I then take the members of Christ and make them members of a harlot? Certainly not! [16] Or do you not know that he who is joined to a harlot is one body with her?

157

For "the two," He says, "shall become one flesh." [17] But *he who is joined to the Lord is one spirit with Him.*

This Scripture tells us that our *bodies* are members of Christ. He makes it clear that it's our physical body by saying the same thing can happen if we have sex with a harlot! What are all the ramifications of our body belonging to Him? I'm not sure; but one Scripture that perhaps gives us a little hint is in Romans:

Romans 8:11
But if the Spirit of Him who raised Jesus from the dead dwells in you, He who raised Christ from the dead will also give life to your mortal bodies through His Spirit who dwells in you.

Some say that this simply means, "Because of the Holy Spirit you are alive." But if that were all it meant, then how would an unbeliever be alive—since they are not yet the Holy Spirit's temples? I also see that the Scriptures teach that "the outward man is perishing," that our body is "corruptible," and that we wait for the ultimate "redemption of our bodies" (2 Corinthians 4:16, 1 Corinthians 15:35-58, Romans 8:23—See "Small Potatoes" for more on this too). But at the same time, Paul is obviously talking to Believers and saying that because the Holy Spirit now lives in us, our bodies should experience some level of regeneration and/or preservation and/or extended life because of His indwelling Presence. Of course it includes healing for all disease and injury; but does it include extended life on earth? I think it does. How far can it be extended? Where is the limit? I'm not answering these questions, I'm only asking them. It might be worth our praying into this and finding out for ourselves! For now I'll simply say, "According to our faith, be it unto us!"

The main thing I want us to notice in this verse is that not only does it say that our bodies are members of Christ; but we are also *one spirit with Jesus Himself.* I don't know of any more shocking revelation in the Scripture. Let's read it again in its simplicity:

1 Corinthians 6:17
But he who is joined to the Lord is one spirit with Him.

We already showed in the Scriptures that your body is one with Him. Now we see also that you are *one spirit* with Him. Your identity is now inextricably intertwined with Christ. You cannot be separated from Him. We are all mixed together with Him, and He with us. This is so true that we can't be distinguished from Him—We are hidden inside Him!

Colossians 3:3
For you died, and your life is hidden with Christ in God.

Some might say, "I don't look hidden to me! I still see a lot of myself in there!" The key—according to this verse—is that "you died." We must *consciously acknowledge that our old man is dead*, and out of that revelation, Jesus lives through us.

> Your identity is inextricably intertwined with Christ. You cannot be separated from Him.

You Are United to Jesus in Mind and in Nature

1 Corinthians 2:16
For "who has known the mind of the LORD that he may instruct Him?" But *we have the mind of Christ.*

We have *already* been given the mind of Christ. Do we always make our decisions based on the thoughts that come from His mind? No. But we *can* choose His thoughts over some other thoughts. We have the mind of Christ. We need only to agree and cooperate with it! When we yield our thinking to the Word of God, our minds are renewed, and our lives are transformed. Romans 12 tells us how our (outer, visible) lives can be transformed into the image of Christ, who we are in union with:

Romans 12:1-2
[1] I beseech you therefore, brethren, by the mercies of God, that you *present your bodies a living sacrifice*, holy, acceptable to God, which is your

159

reasonable service. [2] And do not be conformed to this world, but *be transformed by the renewing of your mind*, that you may prove what is that good and acceptable and perfect will of God.

Renewing our minds according to the Word of God is the only way our lives are transformed to reflect God's will. His will doesn't happen automatically, as we discussed earlier. The devil is defeated, and Jesus is exalted. We are now united to Him in body, mind and spirit; and One with Him in nature and authority. These are our new creation realities.

> Renewing our minds is the only way to be transformed.

We must renew our minds to be transformed into who God says we are in His Word. We must trust the Word enough so that our thinking changes to line up with what He says is the invisible truth. "OK," we might say, "I want to think in agreement with what God says about me!" It's easy to say that... until we find something the Bible says about us that we can't wrap our heads around! Here, we'll take a simple test:

1) Looking at Matthew 5:14, does it bother you to say that *you are* the light of the world?
2) In view of 2 Corinthians 5:21, does it bother you to say that *you are* the righteousness of God?
3) Remembering 1 John 4:17, does it bother you to say *you are* just like Jesus is?
4) Reading 1 Corinthians 6:17, does it bother you to say that *you are* one spirit with Jesus?

If so, we need to recognize that we are not thinking like God does. We are not thinking in line with His will. We are not agreeing with spiritual truth. That is why our minds need to be renewed. If we already thought like He wants us to, there would be no need to renew our minds with the Word. We must believe what God says—regardless of how we feel about it—

> We must simply believe what God says—regardless of how we feel about it—and act like it's true.

160

and act like it's true.

For one more test, another part of the mind of Christ is described to us here, and we are directly commanded to think like He thinks in this regard:

Philippians 2:5-6
⁵ *Let this mind be in you which was also in Christ Jesus,* ⁶ *who*, being in the form of God, *did not consider it robbery to be equal with God,*

Paul said essentially, "Hey, think like Jesus did. Think like this: 'It's not a crime to be equal with God (in Christ)'." That is a command of God recorded in the Bible. People can choose to obey it, or they can let it make them uncomfortable and pretend it isn't there. All of this "One with Christ" talk makes a lot of people nervous. But that's OK. God is OK with making us a little nervous. Sometimes His Truth can be a bit of a shock to our system! God is telling us to think of ourselves as His equal, because all that He has is ours. He says "Don't worry, you're not taking anything away from Me by agreeing that I've made you one with Me." He's made us heirs of all things. If it's God's, it's ours.

Not only that, but He's given us His nature, His mind, and because of the Law of Identification, we are One with Jesus Christ Himself. As a matter of fact, it's not even us living anymore—we've died—it's Christ living through us. Oh my! He has commanded us to

> It's only when we—in our *minds*—separate ourselves from Christ, that equality with God becomes unreasonable, arrogant or heretical.

think this way. It is here that we find equality with God—not in *us*, but *in Christ—our new identity.* As individual humans—fallen short of the glory of God—we have died. We are now clean, innocent, righteous, justified, glorified, and united with Jesus Christ, God in the flesh. It's not *us*, it's Christ *in* us. Our lives are hidden with Christ in God. This is our new existence. It's only when we—in our minds—separate ourselves from Christ, that equality with God becomes unreasonable, arrogant, or heretical.

161

OK, now to calm our nerves, we must also consider the next verses:

Philippians 2:7-8
[7] but *made Himself of no reputation, taking the form of a bondservant,* and coming in the likeness of men. [8] And being found in appearance as a man, *He humbled Himself* and became obedient to the point of death, even the death of the cross.

So here is the flip side of this revelation coin. Being legal equals with God—united with Christ, sons and daughters authorized to conduct His affairs, those with full authority to act on God's behalf—we must remember to do so exactly like the Jesus we're One with. We must maintain a humble servant's heart—dying to selfish motives and desires that are not His, and putting others first. We must reflect our union with Christ not only in His glory and authority, but also in His servanthood and humility!

This is the character and nature of Jesus. And the Bible says that we not only have the mind of Christ, we are also partakers of His very Nature!

2 Peter 1:1-4
[1] ... to those who have obtained like precious faith with us by the righteousness of our God and Savior Jesus Christ: [2] Grace and peace be multiplied to *you in the knowledge of God and of Jesus our Lord,* [3] as His divine power has given to us all things that pertain to life and godliness, *through the knowledge of Him* who called us by glory and virtue, [4] *by which have been given to us exceedingly great and precious promises, that through these you may be partakers of the divine nature,* having escaped the corruption that is in the world through lust.

Through the knowledge of God—the renewing of our minds—we receive the promises of God and partake of His very nature.

Peter says here that through the *knowledge* of God, we are given *promises;* and through these promises, we can partake of God's Divine Nature. What does that mean? We can walk in the fruit (character and results) of the spirit. Love, Joy,

162

Peace, Patience, Kindness, Goodness, Gentleness, Faithfulness, and Self-Control. This is a huge part of the transformation we're looking for by the renewing of our minds! Through the knowledge of God—the renewing of our minds—we receive the promises of God and partake of His very nature.

Galatians 5:22-25
[22] But the fruit of the Spirit is love, joy, peace, longsuffering, kindness, goodness, faithfulness, [23] gentleness, self-control. Against such there is no law. [24] And those who are Christ's have crucified the flesh with its passions and desires. [25] If we live in the Spirit, let us also walk in the Spirit.

The Great Mystery—Jesus in Your Shoes

I don't know about you, but looking at it in the natural—it's a mystery to me why God would choose someone as goofy and messed up as I was (and sometimes still seem to be) to live in, become one with, and touch others through. But we find one answer in 1 Corinthians:

1 Corinthians 1:25-29
[25] Because the foolishness of God is wiser than men, and the weakness of God is stronger than men. [26] For you see your calling, brethren, that not many wise according to the flesh, not many mighty, not many noble, are called. [27] But *God has chosen the foolish* things of the world to put to shame the wise, and *God has chosen the weak* things of the world to put to shame the things which are mighty; [28] *and the base* things of the world *and the things which are despised God has chosen*, and the things which are not, to bring to nothing the things that are, [29] *that no flesh should glory in His presence.*

He chose me *precisely because* I was such a mess! He wanted it to be *obvious* that anything good that came through me—was really Him! He gets *all* the glory! But in the larger sense, why on earth would God want to live in any person, no matter how awesome they may be? While we are created in His Image and Likeness, we must admit that it would be quite a step down for Him to dwell in any finite, limited human being. This is perhaps one reason why Jesus and Paul referred to our Salvation and union with Christ as a "great mystery" (Ephesians 5:32).

Mark 4:11
And He said to them, "To you it has been given to know the mystery of the kingdom of God; but to those who are outside, all things come in parables,

Ephesians 5:30-32
[30] For we are members of His body, of His flesh and of His bones. [31] *"For this reason a man shall leave his father and mother and be joined to his wife, and the two shall become one flesh."* [32] This is a great mystery, but I speak concerning Christ and the church.

He also calls it a mystery because even though God planned our salvation from before time, none of the Old Testament saints had a clear view of how it would all take place. Even the greatest prophets who heard God speak by audible voice, were caught up in whirlwinds, split the Red Sea, and performed other great miracles, had no clue about how Salvation would work. God kept it a secret so nobody could mess it all up!

Matthew 13:17
for assuredly, I say to you that many prophets and righteous men desired to see what you see, and did not see it, and to hear what you hear, and did not hear it.

Ephesians 3:1-6
[1] For this reason I, Paul... by revelation He made known to me the mystery... [5] which in other ages was not made known to the sons of men, as it has now been revealed by the Spirit to His holy apostles and prophets: [6] that the Gentiles should be fellow heirs, of the same body, and partakers of His promise in Christ through the gospel...

What is this great mystery? Christ in YOU. Christ in ME. God in Man. Jesus in your shoes. All of us made One with God in Christ. We now carry the glorious presence of the Almighty God around in our little bodies made of dirt. This is a great mystery.

Colossians 1:26-27

[26] *the mystery* which has been hidden from ages and from generations, but *now has been revealed to His saints.* [27] To them God willed to make known what are the riches of the glory of *this mystery* among the Gentiles: which is *Christ in you*, the hope of glory.

2 Corinthians 4:7

[7] But we have this *treasure in earthen vessels*, that the excellence of the power may be of God and not of us.

And contained in this great mystery of "Christ in you" is the hope of glory. Any glory God receives in the earth is because of Christ in us! In "Christ in you" is salvation for the masses of lost humanity. In it is healing for their bodies. In it is deliverance for their minds and emotions. In it is restoration to friendship and union with the God Who made us. In this mystery— "Christ in you"—is God's purpose for creating the world, and patiently enduring thousands of years of goofed-up human history.

> What is this great mystery? Christ in YOU. Christ in ME. God in MAN. Jesus in your shoes.

Summary:

If we are in Christ, we have the mind of Christ (1 Corinthians 2:16)—we can think His thoughts. We are one spirit with Him (1 Corinthians 6:17). We have been made partakers of His Divine Nature (2 Peter 1:4)! God views us exactly as He views Jesus; because we are in union with Him (1 John 4:17). We are hidden with Christ in God (Colossians 3:3). We are loved, favored, justified, exalted and glorified in Him (Romans 8:30). In Him we live, move, and have our being (Acts 17:28). It's not even us living any more—it's Christ living in us, and using our bodies (Galatians 2:20)! So He trusts that we will use His authority and Name to do exactly what He would do in our shoes! Because— He IS!!!

165

Have you ever read a book that must back up nearly every sentence with this much Scripture? I realize I have to do this with this subject in particular, or someone would accuse me of saying something wild and crazy, something perhaps "too good to be true." Even with all this Scripture, I know there are some who will *still* say that. They'll think it's so good that it must be a lie—a heresy! To say that we are the righteousness of God, that we are holy, that we are one spirit with Jesus, that we are glorified, that we are seated at the right hand of God—the seeming audacity! The scandal! But the Scriptures I'm simply repeating couldn't be any more clear, so the bottom line is: If the idea of being One with Jesus rubs us the wrong way, it only shows that our minds are not yet renewed by the Word of God concerning our identity in Christ! All of us must simply get in the Bible, and let God work on our thinking! When we find something in the Scriptures that differs from carnal reasoning and feelings, we must simply acknowledge, "God is right, and I have been wrong. I choose to agree with God."

> If the idea of being One with Jesus rubs us the wrong way, it only shows us that our minds are not yet renewed by the Word of God concerning our identity in Christ!

Our life is to be an extension of the earthly life of Jesus—Jesus using your body. Period. Jesus at your job. Jesus in your house. Jesus at your favorite grocery store. Again, Jesus in your shoes. You are in Him, He is in you, and you are one spirit with Him! Everything Jesus is and has is ours in Him. His inheritance is our inheritance. We exist only in Him, at the right hand of God; and here, there is NO sickness or disease allowed. It is vaporized. God's will is *always* healing!

CHAPTER 9

Union With Christ: The Pictures

The Scriptures we discussed in "Union With Christ: The Words" plainly tell us of our union with Christ. But they can be considered largely theological, or philosophical ideas that can be hard to wrap our heads around. Thankfully, God is a big fan of using metaphors, parables, and pictures to help us to unpack and understand truth. The truth of our union with Christ is so vital and central to God's relationship with us, and to us being who He made us to be. Because of this, He has provided several analogies to help us receive the revelation of our union with Jesus: Father-Son relationships, Husband-Wife relationships, and the relationship of a Head to the Body.

Sons are Legal Equals with their Father

Because of our westernized culture, we have lost some of the common Hebraic understanding of the Father-Son relationship. In Jesus' time, once a son passed into adulthood, the father took him to the town gates where all the leaders hung out, and declared his son to be a man. He did this publicly, acknowledging the son's privilege to now do business in the name of his father—to act on his behalf with his full authorization and authority. He was saying essentially, "See my son? If you see him, you see me. If he says it, I said it. His word is my word. As far as you're concerned, He is now Me." This is exactly what happened at Jesus' baptism, when we see God acknowledging His son publicly, with a voice from the sky:

Matthew 3:16-17
[16] When He had been baptized, Jesus came up immediately from the water; and behold, the heavens were opened to Him, and He saw the Spirit of God descending like a dove and alighting upon Him. [17] And suddenly a voice came from heaven, saying, "This is My beloved Son, in whom I am well pleased."

167

And again, on the Mount of Transfiguration:

Luke 9:35
And a voice came out of the cloud, saying, "This is My beloved Son. Hear Him!"

The Father's public "stamp of approval" on Jesus officially recognized and authorized Him to handle business for the family. We can understand being authorized to do business for our father, but in that time and culture, it was much more. Once a son became an adult, the son and the father were viewed as *equals*. This gave the Pharisees yet another reason to hate Jesus—He went around calling God His Father.

John 5:17-18
[17] But Jesus answered them, "My Father has been working until now, and I have been working." [18] Therefore the Jews sought all the more to kill Him, because He not only broke the Sabbath, but also *said that God was His Father, making Himself equal with God*.

Jesus said He was a Son, which makes Him *equal* with the Father. Now we'll read the rest of that conversation, and see Jesus doing just that:

John 5:19-37
[19] Then Jesus answered and said to them, "Most assuredly, I say to you, the Son can do nothing of Himself, but what He sees the Father do... [20] For the Father loves the Son, and shows Him all things that He Himself does; and He will show Him greater works than these, that you may marvel... [22] For the Father judges no one, but has *committed all judgment to the Son*, [23] that *all should honor the Son just as they honor the Father. He who does not honor the Son does not honor the Father* who sent Him...[26] For as the Father has life in Himself, so He has granted the Son to have life in Himself, [27] and *has given Him authority to execute judgment* also, because He is the Son of Man. [28] Do not marvel at this... [30] I can of Myself do nothing. As I hear, I judge; and My judgment is righteous, because *I do not seek My own will but the will of the Father who sent Me*. [31] "If I bear witness of Myself, My witness is not true. [32] There is another who bears witness of Me, and I know that the witness which He witnesses of Me is true... [36] But I have a greater witness than John's; for the works which the Father has given Me to finish—*the very works that I do—bear witness of Me, that the Father has sent Me*. [37] And the Father Himself, who sent Me, has testified of Me...

More goodies on the equality of Sonship, from the Gospel of John:

John 14:7-24

[7] "If you had known Me, you would have known My Father also; and from now *on you know Him and have seen Him." ... He who has seen Me has seen the Father,* so how can you say, 'Show us the Father'? [10] Do you not believe *that I am in the Father, and the Father in Me?* The words that I speak to you I do not speak on My own authority; but the Father who dwells in Me does the works. [11] *Believe Me that I am in the Father and the Father in Me...*[13] And whatever you ask in My name, that I will do, that the Father may be glorified in the Son. [14] If you ask anything in My name, I will do it...[24] He who does not love Me does not keep My words; and *the word which you hear is not Mine but the Father's who sent Me.*

John 10:30-39

[30] *I and My Father are one."* [31] Then the Jews took up stones again to stone Him. [32] Jesus answered them, "Many good works I have shown you from My Father. For which of those works do you stone Me?" [33] The Jews answered Him, saying, "For a good work we do not stone You, but for blasphemy, and because *You, being a Man, make Yourself God."* [36] do you say of Him whom the Father sanctified and sent into the world, 'You are *blaspheming,'* because *I said, 'I am the Son of God'?* [37] If I do not do the works of My Father, do not believe Me... [39] Therefore they sought again to seize Him, but He escaped out of their hand.

I'll say it again: To be a Son, was considered to be "legally" *equal* with the Father. If the Son promised something in the family name, the Father delivered it. If the Son committed, the Father backed him up. You might say, "Yeah, but that was Jesus!" You're right. But look at this command again to us as Believers:

Philippians 2:5-6

[5] *Let this mind be in you which was also in Christ Jesus,* [6] *who,* being in the form of God, *did not consider it robbery to be equal with God,*

We discussed this in the last chapter. As a reminder, we are sons and daughters of God, and therefore, in God's thoughts, we are legally "equal" in our authority to do business in His Name.

Galatians 3:26-4:7
[26] For *you are all sons of God through faith* in Christ Jesus... [29] And *if you are Christ's, then you are... heirs* according to the promise... [1] Now I say that *the heir, as long as he is a child, does not differ at all from a slave, though he is master of all...* [4] But when the fullness of the time had come, God sent forth His Son... that *we* might receive the adoption as sons... [7] Therefore *you are no longer a slave but a son*, and if a son, then *an heir of God through Christ.*

If you are a son or daughter, then you are an heir. If you are an heir, you are master (put in charge of, as a legal equal) of all. When Jesus died, the "probate court of Heaven" read His will, and it said, "You get *everything.*" Then when Jesus raised up from the dead, He said, "Don't worry, you *both* get everything. You're *joint heirs.*" God didn't have to split the inheritance down the middle and say "Here, Jesus, You get this half; and the rest of you can fight over the other half." No! Jesus, you, me—we all get the whole kit and kaboodle!

> When Jesus died, the "probate court of Heaven" read His will; and it said, "You get everything."

Romans 8:16-17
[16] The Spirit Himself bears witness with our spirit that *we are children of God,* [17] and *if children, then heirs—heirs of God and joint heirs with Christ,* if indeed we suffer with Him, that we may also be glorified together.

Some might say, "Sure, but we haven't been 'glorified' yet, so that must be in the future." They think it means when we die and get our new bodies. Nope! Jesus prayed in John 17:22, "And the glory which You gave Me I *have given* them" (Past tense). He's already given us His glory.

Then later in Romans 8, we see this confirmed again:

Romans 8:29-30

[29] For whom He *foreknew*, He also *predestined to be conformed to the image of His Son*, that He might be the firstborn among many brethren. [30] Moreover whom He *predestine*d, these He also called; whom He *called*, these He also *justified*; and whom He justified, these He also *glorified*.

As it is with anything regarding our salvation and its benefits, it's already been accomplished—past tense—in Christ. If we are "in Christ," then everything that happened to Him happened to us too! It's in our account as if we did it ourselves! This is because of the Law of Identification: What Jesus accomplished goes into our account as if we did it ourselves—we need only receive it by faith.

Suffice it to say that as sons and daughters of God, we are legal equals with God, and receive all the benefits that Jesus Himself enjoys right now, at the right hand of God. All that God has belongs to us—as much as it does to Jesus.

> All that God has belongs to us— as much as it does to Jesus.

1 Corinthians 3:21-22

[21] Therefore let no one boast in men. For *all things are yours*. [22] ... the world or life or death, or things present or things to come—*all are yours*.

We have a great inheritance in Christ. Everything that Christ has, we share in! If He has it, so do we! We are Joint Heirs! Jesus does not experience any sickness as He sits there at the right hand of God. Neither should we. We are one with Jesus Himself—Who is God in the flesh, God with us. Because we are "in Christ," we are on equal footing before the Father! We are just as loved as Jesus is! We have all Jesus has, and all He is! We are One with Him!

If you can't relate well to the Biblical Father-Son picture of our union with Christ, perhaps you can receive the same revelation through understanding what it means to be the Bride of Christ.

The Bride is One with the Husband

God has given us another picture of this beautiful union with Christ, which He accomplished through redemption. He has called us the Bride of Christ.

Revelation 21:9
Then one of the seven angels who had the seven bowls filled with the seven last plagues came to me and talked with me, saying, "Come, I will show you the bride, the Lamb's wife."

Then the angel shows John all the Believers in Heaven. *We* are the Bride of Christ. He has always longed for us in this way.

Isaiah 62:5b
"...as the bridegroom rejoices over the bride, So shall your God rejoice over you."

Hosea 2:16
" And it shall be*, in that day*," Says the LORD, " That *you will call Me 'My Husband*,' And no longer call Me 'My Master,'

Isaiah 54:5
For *your Maker is your husband*, The LORD of hosts is His name; And your Redeemer is the Holy One of Israel; He is called the God of the whole earth.

Men sometimes have a hard time relating to this picture of being a Bride; but God likes it, so let's roll with it. There is a rich revelation here if we'll keep looking at the Scriptures. One of the main reasons that earthly marriage exists is to give us a picture of our oneness with Christ! We see this when God presides over the first union of husband of wife—that of Adam and Eve:

> Marriage is designed to be a picture of our union with Christ.

Genesis 2:21-25
[21] And the LORD God caused a deep sleep to fall on Adam, and he slept; and He took one of his ribs, and closed up the flesh in its place. [22] Then the rib which the LORD God had taken from man He made into a woman, and He brought her to the man. [23] And Adam said: "This is now bone of my bones and flesh of my flesh; She shall be called Woman, because she was taken out

of Man." [24] Therefore a man shall leave his father and mother and be joined to his wife, and *they shall become one flesh.* [25] And they were both naked, the man and his wife, and were not ashamed.

He says that when a man and his wife are joined in marriage, they become *one flesh.* As precious as this is, even in the natural, marriage is designed to be a picture of something even greater—our union with Christ. Because God planned salvation from "before the foundation of the world" (Ephesians 1:4, Revelation 13:8), He built into creation pictures of our union with Him, which would be accomplished through Christ.

We see this picture more clearly in Ephesians. Paul gives all of these instructions to husbands and wives about how to love and honor one another. He says that a husband should love his wife like he loves his own body. Then he says, "He who loves his wife loves himself." The husband and the bride are *one.*

Ephesians 5:28-33
[28] So husbands ought to love their own wives as their own bodies; he who loves his wife loves himself. [29] For no one ever hated his own flesh, but nourishes and cherishes it, just as the Lord does the church. [30] For we are members of His body, of His flesh and of His bones. [31] "For this reason a man shall leave his father and mother and be joined to his wife, and the two shall become one flesh." [32] This is a great mystery, but I speak concerning Christ and the church. [33] Nevertheless let each one of you in particular so love his own wife as himself, and let the wife see that she respects her husband.

Then he kind of casually throws in, "By the way, I'm not really even talking about husbands and wives. I'm talking about us and Jesus!" Jesus loves us, and in so doing loves Himself! Why? Because we are *one.* In our marriage to the Lord, we become *one* with Him! I know this sounds too good to be true—to be one with the Lord Jesus Himself. Wow! But the Scriptures teach this very plainly:

1 Corinthians 6:15-17
[15] Do you not know that *your bodies are members of Christ?* Shall I then take the members of Christ and make them members of a harlot? Certainly not! [16] Or do you not know that he who is joined to a harlot is one body with her?

173

For "the two," He says, "shall become one flesh." [17] But *he who is joined to the Lord is one spirit with Him.*

If you are a born-again Believer, you are one spirit with Jesus Christ.

If you are a born-again Believer, *you are one spirit with Jesus Christ!!* What all does that entail? What is involved in being one with Jesus? What are the benefits? What are the responsibilities? What is available? These are questions we should be exploring; because this is the "great mystery" that Jesus died to accomplish—Our sins being washed away by His blood, so that we could be reconciled to God and made one with Him. Immanuel—God with us, or God in us—God dwelling in man. Loving relationship and union with our Maker, our Husband. God desires this more than anything else!

Jesus Himself speaks of the phenomena of a man and woman becoming one in marriage:

Matthew 19:4-6
[4] And He answered and said to them, "Have you not read that He who made them at the beginning 'made them male and female,' [5] and said, 'For this reason a man shall leave his father and mother and be joined to his wife, and the two shall become one flesh'? [6] So then, they are no longer two but one flesh. Therefore *what God has joined together, let not man separate.*"

Of course the analogy of marriage holds true here in the words of Jesus, and this is actually the most important thing to remember when considering our union with Him: "What God has joined together, let not man separate." If we are one spirit with Jesus Christ, and we are seated together with Him in the heavenly places (and we are)—we must not "separate" ourselves from Him in our theology and expectation. We must recognize that we are united to Him. Never, ever, separate yourself from

Anything you believe about yourself that isn't true of Jesus is a lie!

Jesus! Anything less than what Jesus Himself is, has, or experiences—is *not* for us! Anything you believe about yourself that isn't true of Jesus is a lie—a false existence!

174

Listen, if Jesus sits at the right hand of God—completely victorious over sin, sickness and disease, and all the other effects of the curse—then so do we. Any idea that contradicts this reality is a lie. From now on whenever anyone tells you to expect something less than what Jesus is, has, or does... Think to yourself: "What God has joined together, let not man separate!"

Because our earthly marriages are sometimes not exactly reflective of their Heavenly design and purpose, some of us miss the power of this picture of our union with Christ. So God gave us another picture—one that anyone can relate to on some level...

> What God has joined together, let not man separate!

The Body is One with the Head

We are the Body of Christ. There are, of course two ways to emphasize this truth, and both are valuable. One way uses the "Body" idea to emphasize our need for unity with the rest of the Body (the Church), and how we are to be united in purpose together under Jesus' Headship.

Romans 12:5
so *we*, being many, *are one body in Christ*, and individually members of one another.

1 Corinthians 12:12
For as *the body is one* and has many members, but all the members of that one body, being many, are one body, *so also is Christ*.

That is an awesome truth of course. But the second way to emphasize the "Body" picture, is to focus on how this analogy speaks of our unity with the Head, Jesus Himself. This, of course, is the point of this chapter so we will be focusing on this angle.

Ephesians 5:30
For we are members of His body, of His flesh and of His bones.

This Scripture from Ephesians is great because it connects the two analogies of us being both the Bride of Christ, and also His Body. This quote hearkens back to the Scripture in Genesis 2:23 where Adam called Eve "bone of my bones and flesh of my flesh." In exactly the same way, we are Jesus' Body—bone of His bones, and flesh of His flesh.

Naturally speaking, your head and your body create *one* being. Your head is not named Sue, and your body named Joe. The body and the head are *one*, and have only one *identity*. If you separate the body from the head, you have death. The head—smart as it may be—would be unable to do anything whatsoever to communicate, act, or impact the world around it in any way without the body. In the same way, if the body is disconnected from the head, it can do nothing of itself. As 1 Corinthians 12:12 said, "So also is Christ."

Ephesians 1:20-23
[20] which He worked in Christ when He raised Him from the dead and seated Him at His right hand in the heavenly places, [21] far above all principality and power and might and dominion, and every name that is named, not only in this age but also in that which is to come. [22] And He put all things under His feet, and gave Him to be head over all things to the church, [23] which is His body, the fullness of Him who fills all in all.

If we are in Christ, we are also—past tense, completed, right NOW—seated at the right hand of God. We are—right NOW—in a place of completely restored authority. "All things" are under us—right NOW, as we are submitted to the Father in our union with Jesus!

> The Body and the Head are one, and have only one identity.

This Scripture simultaneously underscores Christ's supremacy: Jesus is the "Head *over* all things to the church, which is His

176

Body." But it also reiterates our place of identity in Him: "the church...the fullness of Him." The Bible calls us the fullness of Christ! My body is just as much "me" as my head is! My body still enjoys the same benefits that my head does. If the Head lives in a nice house, protected from bad weather—so does the Body. If the Head has a great job and cool friends, so does the Body. If the Head eats a great meal, the Body gets the same benefit. "So also is Christ!" Let him who has ears to hear, hear.

Your Head is Huge!

We are one with Jesus. This truth starts to make some people nervous. They think that because we are identifying ourselves as one with Jesus, that we are somehow being in danger of pride, or self-exaltation. The reality is, we are simply receiving who the Bible says we are. In fact, it is actually true humility to accept what an invisible God says is true, in the face of facts we see with our own two eyes! The Grace and Goodness of God is the most humbling thing ever! We are One with Jesus! There is actually nothing more humbling than seeing what an amazing place of blessing and influence God has set us in, knowing we did nothing to deserve it. Oh, the magnificent Grace of God!!

Colossians 1:18
And *He is the head of the body, the church*, who is the beginning, the firstborn from the dead, that *in all things He may have the preeminence*.

To stay with the Head-Body analogy, even as the head on a physical body is the one that gets recognized, makes the decisions, and tells the body what to do—"So also is Christ!" In all things He has "the preeminence." He is the Head! He is first and foremost! He calls the shots! All glory belongs to Jesus for anything that is accomplished through His Body. At the same time, let the Body not be too timid to recognize that we are One with Him Who is above all else.

Ephesians 4:14-15
[14] that we should no longer be children, tossed to and fro and carried about with every wind of doctrine, by the trickery of men, in the cunning craftiness of deceitful plotting, [15] but, speaking the truth in love, may *grow up in all things into Him who is the head—Christ—*

The only real argument people have against our Union with Christ comes when they look around (in the natural) at the state of the Church and say—"It sure doesn't look like we're One with Christ!" There is a "growing up" that we need to cooperate with! We have already been recreated, and we are exactly like Jesus on the inside. The growing I'm talking about is in our thinking—in our revelation of what's already done. The more our revelation of it grows, the more it appears on the outside. Much of the Christian Lifestyle is this: Quit looking at what you *see!* Look at the invisible! As is typical of most anything God has promised us—We don't *see* it yet. It's invisible!

> Much of the Christian Lifestyle is this: Quit looking at what you see!

2 Corinthians 4:18
while we do not look at the things which are seen, but at the things which are not seen. For the things which are seen are temporary, but *the things which are not seen are eternal.*

That's exactly why His promises are necessary. That's why He gave us the Word—so we can look at the invisible/eternal Truth, compare it to the visible/temporary facts, and believe the invisible until it's visible. This is virtually the definition of faith.

Hebrews 11:1, 3
[1] Now faith is the substance of things hoped for, *the evidence of things not seen...* [3] By faith we understand that the worlds were framed by the word of God, so that the *things which are seen were not made of things which are visible.*

Our actions as a Church thus far (for the most part) have not evidenced the invisible spiritual realities God has made available and shown us in the Word. Right now, the Head is healthy and strong. Meanwhile, most of the Body of Christ looks totally disproportionate to the Head! It looks like an adult-sized Head stuck on a two-year-old's Body. Or as someone in a movie once said, "It looks like an orange on a wee toothpick!"[1] We've got to grow up, Church. Let's follow our instructions, and "grow up in all things into Him who is the Head."

> Most of the Body of Christ looks totally disproportionate to the Head!

We are to grow up into Christ! We already are One with Him in the Spirit. The goal of maturing in Christ is to look like Him in the natural too. It's the supreme Truth. Christ in us, the hope of glory! A new brand of existence—Jesus using our bodies! It's a spiritual reality—Let's get our minds renewed (yield to the mind of Christ you've already been given) and walk it out, folks! Let's *grow up into Christ* in all things—by Grace, through Faith, in Rest!!!

We're One With Christ—What Does That Have To Do With Healing?

You may be asking, "How do these two chapters on our union with Christ have anything to do with Divine Healing?" Here's how: Every theological objection to healing crumbles under the supreme Truth of our union with Christ, period. The central Truth of our union with Christ is one of the "trump cards"–a Greater Truth that conquers any argument against Healing. "In Christ" is a Higher Law. Is Jesus sick or diseased? No! We are One with Him, so neither should we be! Does Jesus have authority over every sickness and disease? Then so do we! Did Jesus heal the sick? Then so should we! How many sick did Jesus heal? All. So should we! What could stop Him? Nothing. Nothing should stop us either! Always remember: "What God has joined together, let not man separate!"

> Every theological objection to healing crumbles under the supreme Truth of our union with Christ.

Our union with Christ is a New Covenant reality. It is what God had in mind when He created Mankind—to become One with us. It was His whole goal in sending Jesus to redeem us. We are united to Christ—Who reigns victoriously on Heaven's throne. His name is higher than any sickness or disease or devil. Every sickness and devil is under His feet; and if we are His Body—One with the Head—they are under us too. Any other idea that seems to contradict the fact that "God's will is always healing," must bow to the reality of our union with Christ. God's will is *always* healing!

CHAPTER 10

GOD IS GOOD

Defining "Good"

Psalm 34:8
Oh, taste and see that the LORD is good; Blessed is the man who trusts in Him!

God is good. Many answer instinctively, "All the time." Not a lot of people disagree with the statement. However, the disagreements on this subject do arise sharply when we start to define what "good" means. It seems like it would be simple enough—"Good" means "good," right? Unfortunately, for some it's not that simple.

Before we get to the disagreements, let's check good ol' Dictionary.com. Because the definitions were so long, I've edited for clarity:

> "morally excellent; virtuous; righteous; pious; right; proper; well-behaved; kind, beneficent, or friendly; honorable or worthy; genuine; not counterfeit; reliable; dependable; responsible; healthful; beneficial; healthy; not spoiled or tainted; favorable; cheerful; optimistic; amiable; free of distress or pain; comfortable; agreeable; pleasant; close or intimate; warm; advantageous; competent or skillful; clever; fairly large or great; free from precipitation or cloudiness; loyal; favorably regarded" [1]

People who say "God is good," and then turn around and say that God causes, wills and allows sickness apparently haven't been on Dictionary.com. If someone broke your leg because they wanted to spend some quality time with you, would you call them "virtuous" or "right?" If they poked your eye out so you'd rely on them more, would you call them "honorable" or "morally

181

excellent?" If they injected you with the AIDS virus to teach you a lesson, would you call that "righteous" or "pleasant?" Or let's

say that they treat *you* nice, but they walk up to your *son* and stick a pencil in his ear—right through his eardrum—making him deaf. Would you say they were "advantageous" or "favorably regarded?" Or what if one day they are all smiles and hugs, then the next day they run over you with a car on purpose. Oh, and they also happen to be the doctor that fixes you up. Then, once you've recovered, they push you off a cliff. Would you call them "reliable" or "dependable?" No, no, and no.

And yet, people twist their definition of the simple word "good" to accommodate this kind of view of God all the time! For instance, some people believe that God gives us sickness, or allows it, or wills it, or approves of it—for various reasons. Any normal person who understands what "good" and "bad" mean, would say that sickness is bad. But these other folks would say that our saying, "Sickness is bad" is a limited, shortsighted view, and that God can bring good out of it in the long run. Therefore, even though sickness may seem horrible to us, the end result is good; and we can still call God "good," even though He brought this terrible illness on someone. What a load of hooey! That is "the end justifies the means" in the worst kind of way!

> Any normal person who understands what "good" and "bad" mean, would say that sickness is bad.

Come on folks, "good" means "good!" This reminds me of when a certain U.S. President was in trouble a few years ago, and while defending himself he said, "It depends on what the definition of 'is' is." [2] Come on Mr. President, everybody knows what "is" means! And everybody knows what "good" means too! Do not tell me in one breath that, "God is good—All the time," and then tell me that He gave you cancer to teach you something. That depends on what the definition of "slow, horrible, excruciatingly torturous death" is, right? Let's not be ridiculous.

182

The Dividing Line

John 10:10
The thief does not come except to steal, and to kill, and to destroy. I have come that they may have life, and that they may have it more abundantly.

This verse is Jesus speaking. He says that the devil is a thief that is trying to steal from us, kill us, and to destroy us. First of all, how can He call the devil a "thief" if he actually has God's permission? Meanwhile, by contrast, Jesus tells us that He Himself came to give us life more abundantly. I don't think it takes an English major to see that those are two very different goals. And it doesn't take a mathematician to do the math! Good=God, Bad=Devil. God is good and wants to bless us. The devil is bad and wants to harm us. I've heard this verse called, "The Dividing Line of the Bible." I like that. It really helps in interpreting the Scriptures, and understanding the nature of God, the devil, and the battle we are in.

Whenever something happens in our lives, we have to ask ourselves, "Which category does this fall under? A) 'Steal, Kill & Destroy,' or B) 'Life More Abundantly'?" If the answer is "A," then it was the devil. If the answer was "B," then it was God.

1 John 3:8
He who sins is of the devil, for the devil has sinned from the beginning. For this purpose the Son of God was manifested, that He might destroy the works of the devil.

Jesus came to *destroy* the works of the devil. If the devil was actually doing God's will, what kind of sense would it make for Jesus to destroy his works? Was Jesus destroying the will of God, to bring some *other* will of God? If the devil is actually doing God's will, and Jesus came to destroy the works of the devil, then Jesus was undoing the will of God! If so, then Jesus was a rebellious Son! Let's get real. God's good will, and the devil's evil will, are in direct opposition to one another.

God is Good

James 1:16-17
[16] Do not be deceived, my beloved brethren. [17] Every *good* gift and every *perfect* gift is from above, and *comes down from the Father* of lights, with whom there is *no variation or shadow of turning*.

The problem with having different definitions of "good" is that it creates "gray areas." If something seemingly bad happens to us, we don't know whether to rejoice that God is working, or fight because the devil is. God is not that confusing. Notice this Scripture says that if we are convinced that God ever varies from giving good and perfect gifts, we are deceived! It's only "good and perfect" gifts that come from Papa God. And if defining "good" or "perfect" is still a difficult prospect, just ask the nearest child—"Is this thing good?" If they say "No," just take their word for it!

> If we are convinced that God ever varies from giving good and perfect gifts, we are deceived!

Here's a good general rule for us—We'll call it, "The Kid-Check Theology Test": If our theology is too difficult for a little child to understand, it's probably wrong!

Matthew 19:14
But Jesus said, "Let the *little children* come to Me, and do not forbid them; for *of such is the kingdom of heaven*."

Luke 10:21
In that hour Jesus rejoiced in the Spirit and said, "I thank You, Father, Lord of heaven and earth, that *You have hidden these things from the wise and prudent and revealed them to babes*. Even so, Father, for so it seemed good in Your sight.

Matthew 18:2-3
[2] Then Jesus called a little child to Him, set him in the midst of them, [3] and said, "Assuredly, I say to you, *unless you are converted and become as little children, you will by no means enter the kingdom of heaven*.

The Bible says that adults need to be more like children, not the other way around! Jesus said that unless we become like *little* children, we won't experience the Kingdom (and its benefits)! So let's keep things simple... Run your theology past your kids before you repeat it publicly. If they don't get it, keep it to yourself, and rework it until they do.

James 1:16 says that every good and perfect gift come from our Father. This means that nothing good or perfect comes from anywhere else. Then verse 17 says that there's no variation in that fact—which means that nothing *other than* good or perfect gifts come from Him. Good + perfect= from God. Other-than-Good-and-Perfect = Not God. There's not even a hint or shadow of something different that could possibly come from Him. Speaking of shadows:

> Run your theology past your kids before you repeat it publicly.

1 John 1:5
God is light, and in Him there is *no darkness at all*.

God's character and ways are black and white. There is no gray area. If it's gray, that means there's some darkness there. That means it can't come from Him, because "in Him there is no darkness *at all*." If every time somebody gets sick, you have to wonder if it's from God or the devil, or whether it's His will or not, then that's become a gray area—As such, you can say clearly that it's not God. In Him is no darkness at all. "But," some are asking, "What about (some Scripture in the Old Testament) where it says that God made someone sick, or brought calamity, or created evil, or...?" We'll get to that in Chapter 12; but for now, just continue on the journey with us—and stay out of the shadows!

Luke 11:35
Therefore take heed that the light which is in you is not darkness.

1 John 1:7
... *walk in the light as He is in the light...*

185

THE DEVIL IS BAD

The devil is an independent entity with a will. He makes choices. Typically not good ones—I'm just saying. We know that Satan was once in the presence of God, and that he got into pride, rebelled, and ultimately got kicked out of heaven—taking 1/3 of the angels with him. The very fact that he rebelled makes it clear that his will is not the same as God's. Rebellion, by definition, is when one being chooses to go against the will of one in authority. In other words, unless you have two contradictory wills, you cannot have rebellion. If everything that happens is God's will, then there was no rebellion, and the devil ought to get a reward for his obedience, right? Wrong!

John 8:44
You are of your father the devil, and the desires of your father you want to do. He was a murderer from the beginning, and does not stand in the truth, because there is no truth in him. When he speaks a lie, he speaks from his own resources, for he is a liar and the father of it.

> If everything that happens is God's will, then there was no rebellion; and the devil ought to get a reward for his obedience.

This verse says that when the devil lies, he does it "from his own resources." Notice it doesn't say, "He follows the will of God." No, it says "He comes up with lies on his own." It says he is "the father of it." The Scriptures say that God—on the other hand—*is* truth (John 14:6, 17). He does not produce lies—The devil does.

Remember the Dividing Line (John 10:10). Satan is a thief. He comes to steal, to kill, and to destroy. There is no way one can justify his behavior and call it the will of God. To do so would be blaming God for all sin. Rubbish!

Is Satan an Agent God Uses to Accomplish His Will?

The "everything that happens is the will of God" people say that God just uses the devil as a pawn, a tool, an agent to do His will. "Satan is just a dog on God's leash"...or he's "God's messenger boy," some say. It seems to me that God is perfectly capable of bringing about His will without using the one whose character, nature and will is the exact opposite of His. Plus, since God rewards those who do His will, are they suggesting the devil should get the top prize?

Case in point: Some will point out that in Acts, it says that God has determined beforehand that people would kill Jesus.

Acts 2:23
Him, being delivered by the determined purpose and foreknowledge of God, you have taken by lawless hands, have crucified, and put to death;

Acts 4:27-28
[27] "For truly against Your holy Servant Jesus, whom You anointed, both Herod and Pontius Pilate, with the Gentiles and the people of Israel, were gathered together [28] to do whatever Your hand and Your purpose determined before to be done.

Listen, God simply sees the future, and responds in advance. In God's mind, Jesus has always been "the Lamb slain from the foundation of the world" (Revelation 13:8). The devil very stupidly tempted men to kill Jesus, and those men chose to yield and sin. But their sinning was not the will of God. God did not use the devil as a tool to tempt these people to sin by killing Jesus. How can I say that?

> God simply sees the future, and responds in advance.

James 1:13 (emphasis mine)
Let no one say when he is tempted, "I am tempted by God"; for God cannot be tempted by evil, *nor does He Himself tempt anyone*.

If God *willed* for the devil to tempt man to sin, then God is *responsible* for man being tempted. But James 1:13 says that

187

this cannot be the case. God certainly foreknew what the devil would do, and how man would respond, and He took the situation and turned it around for the salvation of all Mankind. But was the devil doing God's will? If so, should we honor him as a participant in bringing our salvation? No, he was a thief simply out to steal, kill and destroy. The Bible is very clear that God and the devil have two different wills and purposes.

James 4:7
Therefore submit to God. Resist the devil and he will flee from you.

Notice it doesn't say, "Submit to the devil, thereby submitting to God's will." It says submit to God, and resist the devil. It is clear that the devil is out to do things that are not God's will. Otherwise it would say, "Cooperate with the devil, because He's God's agent, who is doing the will of God." If the devil is doing God's work, then let's cooperate! Let's be thankful to the devil for helping God accomplish His will in our lives, right? Since he's modeling the will of God for us, let's do what he's doing so we can be in line with God's will, right? Ridiculous!

Matthew 7:18
A good tree cannot bear bad fruit, nor can a bad tree bear good fruit.

God is good, and His will is "good and... perfect (Romans 12:2, James 1:17)." If good fruit can only come from a good tree, then the devil must be a good tree if he's doing God's will, right? Hahaha. Come on! The devil is not a good tree. If these confusing theologies are wearying to you, you are in Good Company! This calling good, "evil," and evil, "good" wears the Lord out too!

> If good fruit can only come from a good tree, then the devil must be a good tree if he's doing God's will, right?

Malachi 2:17
You have wearied the LORD with your words; Yet you say, "In what way have we wearied Him?" In that you say, "*Everyone who does evil is good in the sight of the LORD*, And He delights in them,"...

The "devil is doing God's will" folks like to say that God's will is for the devil to do his own devilish will, in order to actually be accomplishing God's good will. But would their argument hold up in the life of Jesus? That would be the devil doing his own will against God, to bring about God's will in God's life, right? Yes, that is in fact as confusing as it sounds. It takes a theologian to come up with this stuff; because the Bible is not nearly as complicated as some like to make it.

Does God Will the Bad to Bring the Good?

Another favorite approach of the Hyper-Sovereignty ("Everything that happens is God's will") fans is to say that it's God's will for bad or evil situations to come so that He can bring good out of them. They'll even attempt to quote Scripture: "All things work together for good," they say. Well, the problem is, they've totally removed this verse from its context:

Romans 8:26-28
[26] Likewise the Spirit also helps in our weaknesses. For we do not know what we should pray for as we ought, but the Spirit Himself makes intercession for us with groanings which cannot be uttered. [27] Now He who searches the hearts knows what the mind of the Spirit is, because He makes intercession for the saints according to the will of God. [28] And we know that all things work together for good to those who love God, to those who are the called according to His purpose.

This Scripture is talking about praying in the Holy Spirit (God-empowered prayer in other tongues). It says that when we don't know how to pray about a certain situation, the Holy Spirit helps us by enabling us to pray the will of God. When we do, God then brings about His will in that situation. He takes the mess the devil (or people) created, and turns it all around for our benefit.

Even if you want to ignore the full context of praying in the spirit, it still only means that God takes a situation that is *not* His will, and changes it into one that *is!* The bad situation was *not* God's will, or He would *not* want to reverse it. Hello? Bad

189

situations are created by fallen creations. If a person invites God in faith to change the situation so it lines up with His (good) will, then He does it. If we'll invite God into our mess, He'll turn it around. That is what the verse means.

> If we'll invite God into our mess, He'll turn it around.

A Parable: Hero or Criminal?

Again, the confusion lies in a problematic understanding of God's Sovereignty. Hyper-Sovereignty folks say that God just uses the devil to do evil works, to bring about situations that God can ultimately reverse and get glory for. For instance, they say He uses the devil to make someone sick, so that Jesus could heal them and get God glory. Because God is so insecure that He needs to hurt the people He loves so He can get credit for healing them, right? Does God need recognition and glory from people that badly? We'll examine this idea further in Chapter 11.

For now, let's look at an analogy to clarify what this looks like in the natural:

Let's say you're watching the 11 o'clock news. They show a scene in a local neighborhood, with some fire trucks and ambulances outside a smoking pile of rubble. They are interviewing a man that just ran into his neighbor's burning house at his own peril. He rushed in and rescued a family from their beds, and carried them all, one-by-one, to safety. A couple of days later, he receives a key to the city from the mayor for his bravery and exemplary behavior. His picture is on the newspaper's front page. He gets free coffee for life at the local diner. He is a hero!

A week later you turn on the news and you see him there again—Only now it's been discovered that he paid some transient $50 to set the neighbor's house on fire in the first place! Whoops! Guess what—No more free coffee for him!!

There goes all his "glory!" "But," some people say, "because of the news story of the rescue, suddenly others were inspired to be heroes too; and a burst of heroic interventions occurred in the following week—isn't that a great outcome? Doesn't that outweigh his crime? So isn't the man still a hero after all?" Are you seriously suggesting that we should celebrate that goofball for paying someone to burn his neighbor's house to the ground? Is he a hero or a criminal? Come on folks, it's not a trick question. If you don't know the answer, ask the nearest child!

If someone has the idea that God "Sovereignly" uses the devil as pawn to do His will, then the goofball in this story is the God they believe in! God is the Man who rescued the family; but He also paid the devil to set the fire? Is God a hero, or a criminal in that view? Who would give God glory for that kind of behavior? Let's re-think this, shall we?

> Is God a Hero or a Criminal?

Matthew 12:33
Either make the tree good and its fruit good, or else make the tree bad and its fruit bad; for a tree is known by its fruit.

God is good, and so is everything He does; because He's a good tree. The devil is bad, and so is everything He does; because he's a bad tree. Any time we ascribe bad fruit (sin, temptation, sickness and disease, etc) to God, or good fruit (doing God's will) to the devil, we have violated this very simple rule: "A tree is known by its fruit."

Sickness is of the Devil

Remember the Dividing Line of the Bible (John 10:10)? "Steal, kill, and destroy" = works of the devil. Sickness is the devil stealing our health, slowly killing, gradually destroying. Any sickness, however small or insignificant, will kill a person if given the right conditions. For instance, a person whose immune system is compromised enough (with AIDS, for instance) can die of a common cold. Sickness is death in seed form. By the criteria of this simple Dividing Line, sickness is already easily identifiable as coming from the devil.

Not good enough? We see multiple occasions in the Scriptures where a demonic spirit brings sickness or disease on people. Deaf spirits, mute spirits, spirits of infirmity that deform people, spirits of epilepsy, spirits that cause "mental illness" and more (See Matthew 9:32-34, Luke 11:14, Luke 13:10-17, Matthew 17:14-21 and Mark 5:1-20 for some examples). In these cases, the condition is clearly stated in the text to be a *direct* work of the devil. Another Scripture about Jesus' life and ministry that clearly defines sickness as a work of the devil, is found when Peter is preaching in Acts:

Acts 10:38
how God anointed Jesus of Nazareth with the Holy Spirit and with power, who went about doing good and *healing all who were oppressed by the devil*, for God was with Him.

This plainly tells us that *all* of the people that Jesus healed were oppressed by the devil. It' doesn't get much plainer than that. Jesus healed everything from Peter's mother-in-law's fever to blindness and deafness, epilepsy, leprosy, and even raised the dead. According to Acts 10:38, *every single case* was an oppression of the devil!

Still, someone might be wondering, "So, you're saying that every sickness, disease, and pain is a work of the devil. What about my broken leg? I just fell off my bike. Are you telling me the devil pushed me off the bike?" Well, no. But I am telling you that your broken leg is still a work of the devil. How can that be? Sometimes he causes these things directly, as we discussed above. The rest of the time, he is still at fault; because he caused sickness and pain indirectly. How?

Remember that when God created man and put him in the Garden, there was no sickness, disease, or pain there; and God said that it was "Good." The devil got man to sin; and sickness, disease and pain came as part of the curse of sin. So every sickness is ultimately a work of the devil. Whether directly or indirectly—every sickness, disease, pain, and physical malfunction is a work of the devil. As such, they are not the will of God for us, His children. Therefore, we are not to accept them. We must renew our minds to the Word of God, grow up into Christ, and enforce His victory over all the works of Satan. So, in the case of someone falling off of a bike and breaking their leg—I believe that there was no injury or pain possible in the Garden. Since the fall and the resulting curse, however, the "laws of nature" work in a way that can cause harm to the human body when we act contrary to them.

Sickness is a curse. Anywhere you see sickness, disease, or pain mentioned in the Bible, it's a curse. It's not a blessing. It's not good—whether it's a natural result of sin's effects on the world (or sowing and reaping), or if it's an outright demonic attack. But it's *never* good, and it's not a part of what God considers a blessing. Nowhere in the Bible can you find a list of blessings God is proclaiming over someone where He includes "sickness and disease" in the list. As much as folks nowadays say that their sickness is such a blessing, it's funny—I can't find one single place in the whole Bible where *God* called sickness a blessing. It takes religion to come up with that one. On the other hand, He does promise healing and health—multiple times—as one of the blessings of being in relationship and covenant with Him.

> Whether directly or indirectly—every sickness, disease, pain, and physical malfunction is a work of the devil.

So, whether a person's sickness, disease or pain comes from a demonic spirit directly causing it, or from creation being out of order from the Fall and the Curse that resulted from Satan's tempting man to sin—it is always a work of the devil, and thus, it is *always* God's will to heal.

The Definition of Blasphemy

Matthew 12:22-32
[22] Then one was brought to Him who was demon-possessed, blind and mute; and He healed him, so that the blind and mute man both spoke and saw. [23] And all the multitudes were amazed and said, "Could this be the Son of David?"
[24] Now when the Pharisees heard it they said, "This fellow does not cast out demons except by Beelzebub, the ruler of the demons." [25] But Jesus knew their thoughts, and said to them: "Every kingdom divided against itself is brought to desolation, and every city or house divided against itself will not stand. [26] If Satan casts out Satan, he is divided against himself. How then will his kingdom stand? [27] And if I cast out demons by Beelzebub, by whom do your sons cast them out? Therefore they shall be your judges. [28] But if I cast out demons by the Spirit of God, surely the kingdom of God has come upon you. [29] Or how can one enter a strong man's house and plunder his goods, unless he first binds the strong man? And then he will plunder his house. [30] He who is not with Me is against Me, and he who does not gather with Me scatters abroad.
[31] "Therefore I say to you, every sin and blasphemy will be forgiven men, but the blasphemy against the Spirit will not be forgiven men. [32] Anyone who speaks a word against the Son of Man, it will be forgiven him; but whoever speaks against the Holy Spirit, it will not be forgiven him, either in this age or in the age to come.

Jesus clearly says that there are two kingdoms at work, with two different goals. But if you say that they are operating under the same kingdom, then that kingdom would be "divided against itself," will be "brought to desolation," and will not stand. Obviously the devil is *not* doing the work of God's kingdom, and Jesus was *not* working for the devil's kingdom by casting out devils. Jesus is the purest manifestation of God's kingdom, tearing down the devil's kingdom. These two kingdoms are not working in tandem; they are at enemies at war!

But what I really want to point out in this passage is that Jesus issues a strong warning to the Pharisees: "Whoever speaks against the Holy Spirit, it will not be forgiven him..." What caused Him to issue this warning? The Pharisees saw Jesus doing God's work, and said it was the devil's work. They were giving the devil credit for God's goodness. This sounds like the Hyper-sovereignty teaching to me. Jesus says this is the very definition of blasphemy! He says in today's English, "Blasphemy = Giving the devil credit for doing God's will (and vice versa)!"

> Blasphemy =
> Giving the devil credit
> for doing God's will
> (and vice versa)!.

Isaiah 5:20
Woe to those who call evil good, and good evil; Who put darkness for light, and light for darkness; Who put bitter for sweet, and sweet for bitter!

I want to also look at the flip side of this, and say that when we look at the devil's work, and give God credit (blame) for it, it's the same thing: Blasphemy! When we see "killing, stealing, and destroying" (the devil's work), and blame God for it, this is blasphemy. This brings confusion to people and dirties the reputation of God among men.

Folks, the bottom line is God is good. *Every* good and perfect gift comes from Him. *Only* good and perfect gifts come from Him. He has no variableness or shadow of turning from this: God is good, all the time; All the time, God is good. Not some loose, creative, "end-justifies-the-means-in-the-long-run-'good'." God, His will, and His works are "dictionary good." Keep it simple. All good, all the time, period.

The Fruit of Preaching an Inconsistent God

Let's face it, much of the time Christians describe God like this: "God is good and loving; but He is also in control of everything that happens, and therefore responsible for all of the bad too—He's good, but He's also bad—in a good way." If it was the First Church of Forrest Gump, they might say that *God* "is like a box of chocolates—You never know what you're gonna get!"[3] This is

195

so inconsistent! I believe that this simple, core inconsistency has been the cause of more people rejecting Christ than anything else. I believe that the world is supposed to see the goodness of God in our lives, and be provoked to want what we have.

Psalm 126:1-3
[1] When the LORD brought back the captivity of Zion, we were like those that dream. [2] Then our mouth was filled with laughter, and our tongue with singing. *Then they said among the nations, "The LORD has done great things for them."* [3] The LORD has done great things for us [And] we are glad.

Isaiah 60:1-4
[1] "Arise, shine, for your light has come, and *the glory of the LORD rises upon you.* [2] See, darkness covers the earth and thick darkness is over the peoples, but the LORD rises upon you and *his glory appears over you.* [3] *Nations will come to your light,* and kings to the brightness of your dawn.

However—because of the misunderstanding that God chooses to cause or allow sickness and other evils—many unbelievers have actually been turned *away* from faith in the gospel, rather than towards it. The unbeliever sees the horrors in the world, hears the Christian saying that God controls it all (and yet is somehow altogether good), and says, "If your 'loving' God did these horrible things, I don't want anything to do with Him." That is the opposite effect of the world being jealous at the goodness of God. God's goodness is displayed in healing, not in sickness. And it is the *goodness* or *kindness* of God that leads people to repentance!

> God's goodness is displayed in healing, not sickness.

Romans 2:4
Or do you despise the riches of His goodness, forbearance, and longsuffering, not knowing that *the goodness of God leads you to repentance*?

Hosea 3:5b (New Living Translation)
...In the last days, they will tremble in awe of the LORD and of his goodness.

Sure, one could preach judgement and hell and get a few people saved out of fear. But if Christianity is really a "relationship," as we say it is, then what quality of relationship can someone have with Jesus when it's based mostly on fear? How long will that fear motivate them? It will ultimately result in performance orientation, slavery and law-keeping without love! As the Scripture above states, "the *goodness* (or 'kindness') of God leads you to repentance!"

When people find out all that God has done for them: the huge price He paid for them even while they were in a mess of sin and rebellion, the benefits and inheritance He's freely given them, the magnificent gift of His unconditional love and acceptance... If they truly "get it," that kind of goodness can only humble them and draw them into a love relationship with the Savior that will last for eternity.

Preaching an inconsistent, mysterious God not only has a negative effect on unbelievers and evangelism; but it can also severely limit Believers. If we think God controls everything, and uses the evil devil to accomplish His will—we are on a shaky foundation. If we think God puts sickness in our lives for some higher purpose, we won't be free to confidently pursue healing—for us or anyone else. If we're unsure of the unshakable, uncomplicated, pure goodness of God—and His will, and His acts—we will be like a leaf blowing in the wind. If we label the devil's works as God's will, we won't fight, we won't grow, and we won't advance into the fullness of God's inheritance and destiny for our lives.

> If we think God puts sickness in our lives for some higher purpose, we won't be free to confidently pursue healing.

Sure God is Good, But What About...?

For whatever reason, there are always a few holdouts that really, really want to believe that God wants to make people sick. I know they wouldn't put it like that necessarily. I believe that they honestly love God and honor His Word. The problem is, that because of religious traditions and wrong interpretations

197

of that precious Word, they are defending something the Word doesn't actually teach. Some people can't name three of God's promises for healing; but they can name for you ten obscure Scriptures that can be twisted to say that God is in the business of making people sick and miserable. Of course, 99% of those Scriptures are in the Old Testament, and the New Testament is a *whole different world*. God has a *whole different relationship* with mankind now; but they most often fail to acknowledge that one H-U-G-E... Glaring... Fact! We'll address some of those Scriptures more specifically in Chapter 12. In the meantime, I think that this is a perfect opportunity to address this issue in a more general sense.

These folks ask lots of questions... What about God's judgment? What about natural disasters? What about the fact that God created the devil in the first place? Did God create evil? Does God send evil, lying spirits to people? Does God choose to harden people's hearts? These questions have confused many sincere Christians for 2,000 years. We try to touch some of these in this book; but each of those questions is worthy of a book in itself. There are already books that are written just to answer those individual questions. Let me assure you, there are good answers to them. For one good one that gives brief answers to several of them, I recommend Difficulties in the Bible, by R.A. Torrey. [4] These questions, at first glance, can appear to have very little to do with healing. However, they definitely impact our understanding of God, His nature, and our relationship with Him—all of which can have tremendously negative impact on faith for healing.

Many of these questions are answered by understanding the difference between the Old and New Covenants. Some others are clarified by understanding the role that God created man to have on the Earth, and the authority He gave us. More questions are answered by understanding the Fall of Man, and the resulting curse that we yielded Creation to. Still others are answered by understanding Hebrew and Greek language issues.

However, because this book is on healing, we'll have to try to stick to the subject a bit, without exploring all of those questions in depth. For now, we'll just trust that if those questions are nagging us, we'll do the necessary research to answer them to our own satisfaction.

It is my hope, however—that through this book—a few more Believers will understand these "trump cards," "pillars of truth," or the unarguable, larger truths of God's Word. That way, they can confidently know (and share with others) that God is always good, and the devil is always bad; that sickness is of the devil, and God's will is always healing. We can hold on to the simple facts that God gave us free will so that we could have loving relationship with Him; and that He gave us authority to run the Earth; that the New Covenant is worlds apart from the Old; that we are one with Christ and it's Him living through us; that our salvation is a package deal and it's already accomplished; that Jesus perfectly represented the will and character of God; and that we are God's children and joint heirs with Christ. Then, when these random questions and doubts come, we will be able to hold securely to the pillars, stay on course, and accurately experience and represent the Kingdom of God.

> God is always good, and the devil is always bad; sickness is of the devil, and God's will is always healing.

Heaven and the Garden Show the Will of God

How do we, as ambassadors of Christ, represent God as we journey through our time on earth? How do we know what God wants us to enforce as ambassadors in this foreign land? We have to look to our model—our homeland, where God does things His way. How do things look in Heaven?

We see God's will for man—the way He wills things to be—in two places: In the Garden, and in Heaven. If sickness is God's will, then why wasn't it in the Garden when He created it for us? When He made the Garden, the whole earth and all its creatures, He said, "It is very good." But if sickness was a part of God's will for our lives, He would have looked around and said, "Something's missing. Ah yes, a little cancer ought to do the trick!" No, no, no!

How did we get sickness on the earth? Man sinned and fell short of the glory. We gave the keys of authority to the devil and he became the god of this world. All of creation fell under the curse of his authority and became twisted from what God had designed and willed for us. Sickness, pain, struggle, poverty, strife, hatred, murder, death and everything that is not God's will came in. The devil tempted man and man sinned. *Sickness came as a result of sin. Sin is not God's will, and neither are its fruits. Sickness is not the will of God!*

If sickness is a part of the will of God, then why isn't there sickness in Heaven when we go there? Because it's *not* the will of God—it's a curse! Both the Garden and Heaven plainly display the will of God. God's will is being done in Heaven. There is no sickness there. Whenever God gets His way, there is no sickness allowed! Sickness is *not* the will of God!

> Whenever God gets His way, there is no sickness allowed!

Jesus commanded us to pray for His Kingdom to come, and His will to be done, "on earth as (exactly like) it is in Heaven" (Luke 11:2). Why would He commission us to pray for something that He had no intention of fulfilling? He wouldn't. He wants earth to look like Heaven! We should be praying very simply, "Lord, let there be no sickness here on earth, just like there isn't any in Heaven." But if God's will included sickness, then God would reply, "Sorry, sometimes I want sickness on earth, so this is an exception to that prayer. Don't pray for the Kingdom to come in regard to healing. Don't pray for Heaven on Earth in that case." That would be ridiculous and inconsistent. No. God wants it on earth, exactly like it is in Heaven. This is what Jesus commanded us to pray for, and it is the clear will of God. He's already paid the price for it to happen, and now it's our job to pray for it and enforce His way of doing things.

God is consistent. He never changes. He is always faithful. He always does what He says He will do. His Word is His bond. He has complete and utter integrity—which means He is exactly the same in thought and desire, intent and will, word and deed. It also means that once He says something, it creates a vacuum. If necessary, all of Creation will re-align itself to reflect His words; because His integrity is so airtight! What you see is what you get, so to speak. He has no hidden agendas, and no dark or mysterious intentions. He can be known; and once He is known, you might even say He's predictable in a way. He is no respecter of persons, and if He did it for one, He'll do it for another. God gives only good and perfect gifts, and there is no shadow of turning, no shade of variation in this. God is life, and in Him is no sickness at all. God is light, and in Him is no darkness at all. God is black and white. God's will is *always* healing!

Notes:

CHAPTER 11

Jesus – Our Standard

This chapter is of the utmost importance for us to "get" as Believers, for two main reasons: First, we as Christians are meant to look like Jesus. If this is to be the case, we need to know what He looks like, what His will is, and how He operates. This is because to be a Christian means to be *like* Christ. That's how Christians got their name, after all. The aim of Christian growth is Christlikeness—to be like Him in every way. We are His ambassadors, and as such, we are to re-present Him faithfully. We are supposed to do what *He* would do in *our* situation, because it's Him living through us.

Second, we as Christians ought to know God our Father, and Jesus is the most accurate picture we have of God. Anything we think we know about God's character or will that comes from somewhere outside of the Bible's picture of Jesus must bow to the clearer image that Jesus presents.

Christians Ought to Look Like Jesus

Ephesians 4:11-15
[11] And He Himself gave some to be apostles, some prophets, some evangelists, and some pastors and teachers, [12] for the equipping of the saints for the work of ministry, for the edifying of the body of Christ, [13] *till we all come* to the unity of the faith and of the knowledge of the Son of God, *to a perfect man, to the measure of the stature of the fullness of Christ;* [14] *that we should* no longer be children... [15] but... may *grow up in all things into Him who is the head—Christ*

Becoming Christlike means that we are to become "a perfect (mature) man" which looks like "the fullness of Christ." We are to "grow up in all things into...Christ." It's clear then—Jesus is our standard of expectation. Remember, as we've discussed many times: We are dead, and He lives through us. In Him we live, and move, and have our being. We have His mind. We are one spirit with Him, and we are partakers of His Divine Nature. We have "put on Christ." If He is the "new man" living through us, our lives should look like His. No lesser standard is to be expected or settled for.

1 John 4:17b
As He is, so are we in the world.

If we are ambassadors, called to represent (re-present, present again) Jesus Christ, then our mission is the same as His. We should be doing what He would do if He were standing in our shoes, because He *is*, remember? So what was His mission? Of course He came primarily to save us from our sins. He finished *that* job, so we don't need to repeat His work there. But what else did He come to do during His time on earth?

1 John 3:8b
... For this purpose the Son of God was manifested, that He might destroy the works of the devil.

Mission Description #1: Destroy the work of the devil. Of course, sin is a work of the devil, and all other works of the devil came about as a result of sin. This of course includes sickness, pain and disease. So when Jesus destroyed sin, He also destroyed sin's rotten fruit—including sickness. How did He do this? Peter tells us in his 6-verse gospel synopsis in Acts Chapter 10:

> When Jesus destroyed sin, He also destroyed sin's rotten fruit.

Acts 10:38
how God anointed Jesus of Nazareth with the Holy Spirit and with power, who went about doing good and healing all who were oppressed by the devil, for God was with Him.

Peter says that Jesus was anointed with the Holy Spirit and with power. We must be empowered to do the mission if we are to achieve the desired results!

Mission Description #2: Doing good and healing all who were oppressed of the devil. If Jesus healed them, they were oppressed of the devil. The bottom line is sickness is an oppression of the devil, and Jesus came to set the oppressed free and destroy the devil's works. We see this again, when He tells us His mission statement first hand in Luke 4, as He reads from Isaiah:

Luke 4:17-21
[17] And He was handed the book of the prophet Isaiah. And when He had opened the book, He found the place where it was written: [18] " The Spirit of the LORD is upon Me, because He has anointed Me to preach the gospel to the poor; He has sent Me to heal the brokenhearted, to proclaim liberty to the captives and recovery of sight to the blind, to set at liberty those who are oppressed; [19] To proclaim the acceptable year of the LORD." [20] Then He closed the book, and gave it back to the attendant and sat down. And the eyes of all who were in the synagogue were fixed on Him. [21] And He began to say to them, "Today this Scripture is fulfilled in your hearing."

Mission Description #3. There are multiple activities listed here, but we will focus on two of them. Jesus was anointed to "proclaim liberty to the captives," and to "set at liberty those who are oppressed" (by the devil).

Hebrews 13:8
Jesus Christ is the same yesterday, today, and forever.

Jesus' mission has not changed. He is still doing the same things that He did 2,000 years ago. If He healed then, He heals today. But somebody said, "Sure, but that was Jesus! We're not Jesus!" Right, but we're one with Him. We are crucified, resurrected, ascended and glorified with Christ; and it's no longer us that live, it's Christ living through us (Galatians 2:20), and "As He is, so are we in the world" (1 John 4:17b). Jesus is still doing the same stuff—the only difference is, now He does it through His new Body—and that's us! We are called to duplicate the works that Jesus did by letting Him express His Own life through us. Jesus said it Himself!

John 14:12
"Most assuredly, I say to you, he who believes in Me, the works that I do he will do also; and greater works than these he will do, because I go to My Father.

We should be doing the same works that Jesus did—and "greater works" than these! There's always been a lot of debate about how to interpret the "greater works;" but for now, let's at least do the *same* works He did. We'll cross the "greater works" bridge when we get to it. His job description is our job description. Remember, He is the Head, we are the Body. We are One with Him. We are ambassadors for Christ. That means we are called to do what He would do if He were on the scene; because we are one spirit with Him, so He *is* on the scene.

> For now, let's at least do the *same* works Jesus did. We'll cross the "greater works" bridge when we get to it.

Jesus Perfectly Reveals the Father

The other reason this chapter is of such central importance to us, is because Jesus is the most accurate picture we have of the Father! Anything we are supposed to know about God, we see most clearly in Jesus.

Colossians 1:15a, 19, 2:9
He is the image of the invisible God... [19] For it pleased the Father that in Him all the fullness should dwell... [9] For in Him dwells all the fullness of the Godhead bodily

John 14:7-9
[7] "If you had known Me, you would have known My Father also; and from now on you know Him and have seen Him." [8] Philip said to Him, "Lord, show us the Father, and it is sufficient for us." [9] Jesus said to him, "Have I been with you so long, and yet you have not known Me, Philip? He who has seen Me has seen the Father; so how can you say, 'Show us the Father'?

John 10:30
I and *My* Father are one.

Jesus is an *exact* picture of God the Father. That's because He's not a only a picture—He's also the original! He's a perfect window into the heart, mind and will of God. If we want to know the will of God on a given subject, we must always look to Jesus as the clearest Demonstrator of it. When He speaks, He speaks the words of the Father. When He acts He does the will and works of the Father.

John 5:19
[19] Then Jesus answered and said to them, "Most assuredly, I say to you, *the Son can do nothing of Himself, but what He sees the Father do*; for whatever He does, the Son also does in like manner.

If some area of our life and experience doesn't match what Jesus experienced and demonstrated, then we must not create an explanation (man-made doctrine) as to why that is the case. Rather, we must believe and expect our level of experience to rise to match the picture He displayed. Any area of our lives that does not look like what we see in the life and ministry of Jesus Christ has some growing to do. In order to be like Him, we must *know* Him—His words, His deeds, His character, His heart. If we are to have our minds renewed to think in alignment with the mind of Christ—and act out of our union with Him, we cannot do so without continually looking at Jesus. Any mindset in us that is not reflected in Jesus is something we need to abandon. That is the goal of this chapter—specifically in regards to Healing.

> Any mindset in us that is not reflected in Jesus is something we need to abandon.

One of the things I've often heard Pastor Bill Johnson say that expresses this idea is the following (paraphrased):

"If we have any (mis-)understanding of God that comes from somewhere *other than* Jesus' life and ministry, and it conflicts with or contradicts what we see *in* Jesus' life and ministry—then that understanding must at least be called into question and re-examined; because 'Jesus is perfect theology,' and He is the perfect picture of the Father." [1]

Thank you, Pastor Bill! This one revelation can destroy numerous Scriptural misunderstandings that run rampant in the Body of Christ. Our standard is not Job, we shouldn't expect the experience of Abraham, David, Elijah, or some other Old Testament saint. We should not set our bar of expectation by the experiences of the disciples, or even the Apostle Paul. Jesus gives a clearer picture of God the Father than the whole Old Testament. Jesus gives a clearer picture of the Father than anything in the Epistles. Jesus is simply God Himself in human form! Jesus is the absolute, acid test of any theology. Jesus made exactly this point to the Pharisees of His Own time:

John 5:39-40
You diligently study the Scriptures because you think that by them you possess eternal life. These are the Scriptures that testify about me, yet you refuse to come to me to have life.

Jesus says, "Look, guys, you know the Scriptures, and that's great. However, the whole point of the Scriptures is to introduce you to God—and here I am! Yet you reject Me because I don't match the image you made out of the words." A lot of people in the Church today have that same problem! They read the Bible and get a picture of God based on the way they read it. But as Jesus said, He Himself is the truest image of the Father. If the way we interpret the Scriptures creates a picture of God that isn't mirrored by Jesus, then we've mis-read the Book!

> If the way we interpret the Scriptures creates a picture of God that isn't mirrored by Jesus, then we've mis-read the Book!

We can't look at our own lack of experiencing God's will, and build our faith on our own experience. Jesus is the one whose image we are created in. Jesus is the one we are united to, one spirit with, and members of. We are called to grow up into *Him* in all things. We must take any idea we have about healing, and compare it to Jesus' example before we make a home for it in our heads and hearts. Jesus perfectly presents God, and Jesus perfectly models a Man in union with God. So let's take a look at

Jesus' life and ministry, and examine common objections and misunderstandings about Divine Healing. Along the way, let's be sure to see two things regarding sickness, pain, disease, and death: What is God's will, and what is our standard of expectation for ministry to the sick.

OBJECTION: God Heals Some, But Doesn't Heal Others

Yes, I've heard the arguments before. Some say that Jesus didn't heal everyone; and they typically cite two potential "examples."

First, they cite the man at the temple's gate that Peter and John ministered to in Acts 3. The Scripture says in verse 2, "And a certain man lame from his mother's womb was carried, whom they laid daily at the gate of the temple which is called Beautiful." From this, they argue that since Jesus often went to this temple, He must have chosen to purposely ignore this man, making a conscious decision of His will to *not* heal him.

This man may have been laid "daily" there, but it doesn't say for how long. Maybe he had another favorite begging spot during Jesus' ministry. Maybe he was there, but Jesus preferred a different gate. Maybe he was there, and Jesus used that gate; but missed seeing him because of the crowds that often accompanied or "thronged" Him everywhere. Remember Zaccheus climbing a tree to see him? Remember blind Bartimaeus having to cry out louder and louder until he could even get Jesus' attention? Remember the woman who had to press through a bunch of people just to touch Jesus' clothes and get healed—and Jesus *still* didn't even know who it was that had touched Him?! It is beyond plausible that Jesus never even saw this man at the Gate Beautiful. In any case, the Scripture doesn't say. That is what is called "making an argument from silence"— and as such, is not a valid argument.

The second example that people use to try and say that Jesus didn't heal everyone is the Pool of Bethesda, which is found in John 5. Many of you know the story. There's this pool called Bethesda. On occasion, an angel stirs the water in the pool, and the first one in the water gets healed. The Bible says there was "a great multitude of sick people, blind, lame, paralyzed, waiting for the moving of the water." Jesus passes by there on the Sabbath, sees a man who's been crippled for 38 years lying there, talks to him, heals him by telling him to take up his bed and walk, and then leaves. So the argument goes, "If Jesus wants everyone healed, why didn't He heal all those other people? He only healed the one guy!" I'm so glad you asked! The answer is right there in the text, if we'll just read it!

John 5:8-16
[8] Jesus said to him, "Rise, take up your bed and walk." [9] And immediately the man was made well, took up his bed, and walked. And that day was the Sabbath. [10] The Jews therefore said to him who was cured, "It is the Sabbath; it is not lawful for you to carry your bed."
[11] He answered them, "He who made me well said to me, 'Take up your bed and walk.'"
[12] Then they asked him, "Who is the Man who said to you, 'Take up your bed and walk'?" [13] But the one who was healed did not know who it was, for Jesus had withdrawn, a multitude being in *that* place. [14] Afterward Jesus found him in the temple, and said to him, "See, you have been made well. Sin no more, lest a worse thing come upon you."
[15] The man departed and told the Jews that it was Jesus who had made him well. [16] For this reason the Jews persecuted Jesus, and sought to kill Him, because He had done these things on the Sabbath.

"Jesus had withdrawn, a multitude being in that place... For this reason the Jews persecuted Jesus, and sought to kill Him, because He had done these things on the Sabbath." The guy got healed, instantly there was a ruckus with all the religious folks mad at the guy for carrying his bed on the Sabbath. They were upset because that was considered labor, and was therefore against their understanding of God's commandment to rest on the Sabbath. They were mad, asking what happened, looking for who to blame. Jesus had seen this before, and it wasn't time for Him to be crucified yet, so He had to split. Obviously, He didn't have time to hang around healing everybody while the Pharisees wanted to kill Him!

The Scriptures plainly tell us why Jesus had to leave; but some people haven't seen it there; because, frankly, it's just easier to believe that Jesus leaves some people sick. This allows us to feel OK when we are sick, or when we pray and someone is not healed. I don't know about you, but I don't *want* to feel OK when I pray and someone is not healed, because it's *not* OK! And I certainly don't want to make up a reason why they weren't healed, so my lack of results becomes acceptable. Let's keep the bar where Jesus set it, and grow in the experience of our union with Christ until we manifest Him perfectly! Jesus healed everyone!

> Let's keep the bar where Jesus set it, and grow in the experience of our union with Christ until we manifest Him perfectly!

OBJECTION: "We prayed and nothing happened... Therefore, it must not be God's will"

This is probably the root of most people's denial of the fact that it's God's will to heal everyone, all the time. "Oh no. I prayed for my dad when He got sick. He was a strong believer and so was I. We believed God for healing, and Dad still died. It must have been God's will to take him." This story, or any variation of it is the reason for most bad theology on healing. Somebody tried to believe God for healing, didn't receive, so they put it back on God and said it must not have been His will. They are simply pitting their own personal experience against the Word of God that says healing is the children's bread, and was already accomplished by the stripes of Jesus. But we must choose to believe the Word over our own experience. Let's watch Jesus in action:

Mark 9:14-27
[14] And when He came to the disciples, He saw a great multitude around them, and scribes disputing with them. [15] Immediately, when they saw Him, all the

people were greatly amazed, and running to Him, greeted Him. [16] And He asked the scribes, "What are you discussing with them?" [17] Then one of the crowd answered and said, "Teacher, I brought You my son, who has a mute spirit. [18] And wherever it seizes him, it throws him down; he foams at the mouth, gnashes his teeth, and becomes rigid. So I spoke to Your disciples, that they should cast it out, but they could not." [19] He answered him and said, "O faithless generation, how long shall I be with you? How long shall I bear with you? Bring him to Me." [20] Then they brought him to Him... He rebuked the unclean spirit, saying to it, "Deaf and dumb spirit, I command you, come out of him and enter him no more!" [26] Then the spirit cried out, convulsed him greatly, and came out of him... Jesus took him by the hand and lifted him up, and he arose.

Notice that when Jesus first came to the disciples, they were in an argument with the religious folks. My guess is, they were arguing about whether or not it was God's will to heal the boy, or maybe about some "hindrance to healing!" Now, let's not forget that these disciples were the experts on healing at that time—they were doing this stuff day in and day out, and had seen most every kind of healing by this point. So when they ministered to this boy and nothing happened, you can bet that

Our own failure to get the promised results is not a reflection of the will of God.

the Pharisees didn't miss their chance to deny the supernatural power of God and/or God's will to heal the boy! It's the same thing today.

Here's the bottom line: Even though the best "healing evangelists" of the time couldn't get the job done—What happened when Jesus showed up on the scene? He perfectly reflected the will of the Father—by bringing healing to the boy! That was, and is, God's will—every time! "Hindrance" or no hindrance, Jesus got the job done! Our own failure to get the promised results is not a reflection of the will of God!

OBJECTION: Unbelief Stops God's Healing Power

So after this episode, the disciples talk to Jesus privately and ask, "Lord, what's the deal? If it was God's will to deliver and heal the boy, why wasn't it done when we ministered to him?"

Matthew 17:20
So Jesus said to them, "Because of your unbelief; for assuredly, I say to you, if you have faith as a mustard seed, you will say to this mountain, 'Move from here to there,' and it will move; and nothing will be impossible for you.

Jesus makes it simple and clear: "Because of your unbelief." End of story. Yes, I realize that in Matthew 17:21 and in Mark 9:29 it says they should have prayed and fasted; but those verses aren't in the oldest manuscripts. Most Bibles will even tell you that in the footnotes. Feel free to check it out.

In any case, we need to point out something very important about unbelief here: Jesus never gets down on anybody that *needs healing* for *their* unbelief. He only gives a hard time to the ones who are supposed to be *ministering* the healing—for *their* unbelief! It's the *minister's* unbelief that's most often the problem. As representatives and ambassadors of Jesus Christ, and those united to Him, unbelief doesn't fit our new man. Jesus has given *us* the authority and power, and has commissioned and instructed *us* to heal the sick. If He gives instruction, He also gives the necessary provision and supply. He's given *us* everything necessary to do the job! He's given *us* His Word that He'd be there with us, and it's impossible for Him to lie. Unbelief has no hold in our hearts—I mean, we're called "Believers" for a reason, right? "But," some of you are thinking, "What about the time when Jesus was in Nazareth? Unbelief even stopped *Jesus* from healing there!" OK, well, let's just look at the text:

Mark 6:1-6
[1] Then He went out from there and came to His own country, and His disciples followed Him. [2] ... He began to teach in the synagogue. And many hearing Him were astonished, saying, "Where did this Man get these things? And what wisdom is this which is given to Him, that such mighty works are performed by His hands! [3] Is this not the carpenter, the Son of Mary...So they were offended at Him... [5] Now *He could do no mighty work there, except that He laid His hands on a few sick people and healed them.* [6] And He marveled because of their unbelief. Then He went about... teaching.

First, the people admitted that Jesus did mighty works! And it also says, "He laid His hands on a few sick people and healed

213

them." However, it does say, "He could do no mighty work there;" but it doesn't say exactly *what* mighty work He couldn't do. The people's unbelief limited what miracles He was able to perform. However, He still healed the sick! So their *unbelief had zero effect on Jesus' ability to heal the sick.* Why not? Because Jesus has authority over sickness, whether people believe it or not.

> Unbelief had *zero effect* on Jesus' ability to heal the sick.

Sickness is a separate entity from the afflicted person. Whether it is caused by a devil, or is totally natural, it is not a part of the *person*. Therefore, if we exercise authority over sickness, pain, or malfunction, the person's will or unbelief need not be a barrier; because we are not imposing our will on another person—we're destroying the works of the devil! Therefore, healing doesn't have to be limited by someone's unbelief! Wow!

This could be a paradigm-shaker, I realize; but Jesus demonstrated it! We can exercise authority over sickness with or without the sick person's faith. After reading the passage in this light, it seems that unbelief only hinders healing if we believe it does. According to our faith, be it unto us. Jesus lives through us, and not once did someone's unbelief ever stop Him when it came to healing. If Jesus could heal the sick in spite of their unbelief (while He walked the earth), then He can do it through us too.

OBJECTION: What About Demons?

It is clear in the gospels that in many cases, sickness is caused by a demon directly afflicting the person. When the demon was cast out of the person, the sickness left with it. If Jesus did it, so should we—So if there is a demon causing a sickness or pain, we have authority to cast it out.

Luke 10:19
Behold, I give you the authority to trample on serpents and scorpions, and over all the power of the enemy, and nothing shall by any means hurt you.

Mark 16:17a
And these signs will follow those who believe: In My name they will cast out demons...

Casting out demons is a Christian duty, responsibility, privilege, and honor; and let's face it—it's fun to get people set free by the power of God! A lot of people say, "Well, you can't just go casting out demons whenever you want to. If the person wants to keep the demon, then you can't override the person's will." I would agree that we shouldn't override the free will of another human being. I'd also agree that in some cases it may not be the best idea to set someone free who doesn't want to be free, because they can actually end up worse off than before (Luke 11:24-26). However, I'd like to repeat a statement I made in the last paragraph, except I'll substitute the word "demon" for the word "sickness": "The *demon* is a separate entity from the afflicted person, so Jesus is not imposing His will on someone by commanding a *demon* to leave—He's destroying the works of the devil!" He's imposing His will on the *devil*.

> Our job is simply to set captives free—Unlock the gates and kick out the jailers!

This also applies to a demon that is afflicting a person. Do you think that if a person could see the unseen, know the truth about God, Jesus, the devil, and demons—that they would freely choose the demon? Of course not. Someone that "wants" a devil has simply believed the lies they've been told—they are deceived. They've been tricked, punked, robbed, hoodwinked, bound and kidnapped! They are "captives;" and just as Jesus was anointed to "proclaim liberty to the captives" and "set at liberty those who are oppressed" (Luke 4), so are we. Our job is simply to set captives free—Unlock the gates and kick out the jailers! What the former captive does with their freedom at that

215

point is up to them. This is why discipleship is important! But that is another subject. The point is, no demon ever stopped Jesus from bringing healing, and no demon should stop us either.

OBJECTION: What About Sin Hindering Healing?

Can an individual's sin result in sickness and pain? It does happen. For instance, if someone is sexually immoral, they can get a Sexually Transmitted Disease. Or, if they abuse their body with alcohol and drugs, they can end up with cirrhosis of the liver, lung cancer, emphysema, ruined kidneys, etc. Someone can live a life of anger and violence and get injured in a fight. This is all simple sowing and reaping—If someone sins, they *can* have the natural result of it. Perhaps this is why we see Jesus say to a man He had just healed, "Sin no more, lest a worse thing come upon you" (John 5:14). But of course, most sickness just comes from the sin principle—sin's existence in the earth in general—and Nature being thrown off course as a result.

However, the question some ask is: Should sin in someone's life ever be allowed to hinder their healing? No! We can see this clearly in the life of Jesus. *Every single person* that Jesus ministered healing to during His earthly life was a sinner! *None* of these people were born again or had their sins washed away, because the price for their forgiveness had not yet been paid! Jesus hadn't gone to the cross yet! Sin *never* stopped Jesus from healing anybody!

Sin never stopped Jesus from healing anybody!

Further, Jesus also ministered to a Roman centurion's servant, and a Syro-Phoenician woman's daughter, and I'm sure others who were not Jews—and therefore they were also without any righteousness under the law, and without any covenant right to healing whatsoever. He also ministered to prostitutes, drunks, tax collectors, thieves and who knows who else. He ministered to crowds and crowds of people and always healed their sick. Surely a massive number of them were not in right relationship with God—and never is there any indication that sin ever once hindered Jesus from getting anyone healed or delivered. He healed them *all*.

Romans 5:20
...But where sin abounded, grace abounded much more,

If sin and/or its fruit (which includes sickness) is on the scene, there is always a larger, more powerful force of grace available to overcome it! Sin is a very small force, when seen standing next to God's Grace! As the Message Translation puts it, "When it's sin versus grace, grace wins hands down."[2] If sin could stop God's grace for healing, then that would mean that sin is more powerful than God. No! God is stronger than the devil. Grace is stronger than sin. Simple math.

> God is stronger than the devil.
> Grace is stronger than sin.
> Simple math.

OBJECTION: What About God's Judgment Against Sin?

While we're on the subject of sin, let's address the "judgment of God," question—as we see it in Jesus' life. Do we find *any* instance in the life of Jesus where He said that sickness was the judgment of God on them for their individual sin? Absolutely not! We should never, ever, assume someone is in sin when they are sick. That is a ridiculous assumption, and we'd be making ourselves judges—which we are not qualified to be. I dare say that *most* sickness and pain has *nothing whatsoever* to do with that person's sin; but it has *everything* to do with the ugly ol' devil and his illegal violence against humanity. We do, however, have an incident that deals with this "judgment" issue that people ask about, so let's see what Jesus does with it:

John 9:1-4

[1] Now as Jesus passed by, He saw a man who was blind from birth. [2] And His disciples asked Him, saying, "Rabbi, who sinned, this man or his parents, that he was born blind?" [3] Jesus answered, "Neither this man nor his parents sinned, but that the works of God should be revealed in him. [4] I must work the works of Him who sent Me while it is day; the night is coming when no one can work.

The disciples were saying the same thing some people today do: "Somebody must've done something wrong for this man to deserve this." And some people take Jesus' response to mean that God set this man up with a lifetime of blindness, just so one day Jesus could come walking along, heal him, and get God a little more glory. How cruel and narcissistic do we have to believe God is to get that interpretation? Does God need glory from people so much that He'd be willing to give someone a lifetime of misery to get it? If you still think that's what Jesus was saying, I'd recommend re-reading this entire book, especially the chapter, "God is good!" (For a more in-depth treatment of this text in John 9, see Chapter 17).

Jesus was simply saying, "Look guys, this isn't about a blame game. It doesn't matter how the man got this way. What we have here is an opportunity to bring God glory!" Then Jesus healed the guy, and he received his sight! Jesus calls healing, "the works of Him Who sent Me (God)!" Jesus made it clear that God is glorified through healing and deliverance, not through sickness and disease. With that, we'll move on, as the subject of judgment (determining who deserves what and why) is covered more in the chapter on "Old vs. New."

> Jesus made it clear that God is glorified through healing and deliverance, *not* through sickness and disease.

Matthew 10:8

Heal the sick, cleanse the lepers, raise the dead, cast out demons. *Freely you have received, freely give.*

We are not qualified or instructed to discern someone's spiritual state, or how they got in their condition, or whether or not they "deserve" it before we bring them healing and freedom. We aren't called to be judges; we're a liberating army! If someone is in a cell, our job is to bust open the door, break off the shackles, and tell them they're free to go—Every single one of them. It's not our place to determine who is, or who is not, "worthy" or "deserving" of healing. God gave us the power and authority freely; *we are commanded to give it away freely and without prejudice to anyone and everyone who needs it.*

If it was ever possible to be wrong in bringing someone freedom—Let's err on the side of mercy and compassion, err on the side of love—minister to everyone! Better to heal too many, than to risk withholding the goodness of God from anyone. Let's do unto others as we would have them do unto us. If you were sick, would you want someone with the power of God in their hands to pray for you? So also Jesus has commanded us, "Freely you have received, freely give." Let's give Jesus' love and power freely to *everyone that needs it!*

> We aren't called to be judges, we're a liberating army!

OBJECTION: What if it isn't God's Timing for My Healing?

Many times when the Church is attempting to minister healing, but not getting the results we're after, we're tempted to give the excuse, "Today might not be your moment. Maybe it's not God's perfect timing for your healing. Come back tomorrow, maybe it'll be your day!" For us today, this is a totally unacceptable response because as we discussed in Chapter 6, our healing in the New Covenant is already a finished work. Jesus paid for it 2,000 years ago. But since there are other issues that can be associated with "timing", I thought we'd examine the issue of timing in the ministry of Jesus. Even though the New Covenant in His blood was not even fully available yet while He ministered,

219

we can still learn some valuable lessons from our Master.

Again, there is no incident recorded in Scripture in which Jesus ever told someone it wasn't their time to be healed. Quite the contrary, Jesus ministered to everyone who asked, and He *always* got the desired results. The only real issue regarding timing was this—How long would it take from the time He ministered until the full manifestation of the healing? Believe it or not, the length of time actually varied from person to person!

> Jesus ministered to everyone who asked, and He always got the desired results.

Instantaneous Healing

Instantaneous miracles are, of course, everyone's favorite. Many of us figure, "If God is doing the healing, and He's Almighty, then of course He's going to do it instantly and completely." Unfortunately, the Bible doesn't agree with that reasoning. We see Jesus do things in a variety of ways. Of course it's true that sometimes, the person was instantly healed on the spot. There are multiple stories like this in all four gospels:

Matthew 20:34
So Jesus had compassion and touched their eyes. And *immediately* their eyes received sight, and they followed Him.

Mark 7:35
Immediately his ears were opened, and the impediment of his tongue was loosed, and he spoke plainly.

Luke 13:13
And He laid His hands on her, and *immediately* she was made straight, and glorified God.

John 5:9
And *immediately* the man was made well, took up his bed, and walked. And that day was the Sabbath.

Instantaneous healings were common in Jesus' ministry, to be sure. My wife and I have also seen many, many instant miracles in people's bodies. But many people mistakenly assume that if God is going to heal them, then someone will pray one simple prayer, and they will be instantly well. If they don't see it immediately, sometimes they let their disappointment throw their faith under the bus and cancel out what might have taken place. However, if we examine the Scriptures, we can see some other interesting ways people were healed under Jesus' ministry.

Healing After Repeated Ministry

Sometimes, the sick person might not experience the full manifestation of the healing the first time we pray. We might have to pray two or three times! Say it isn't so! Haha. But seriously, this even happened to Jesus Himself!

Mark 8:22-26
[22] Then He came to Bethsaida; and they brought a blind man to Him, and begged Him to touch him. [23] So He took the blind man by the hand and led him out of the town. And *when He had spit on his eyes and put His hands on him, He asked him if he saw anything.*
[24] And he looked up and said, "I see men like trees, walking."
[25] *Then He put His hands on his eyes again* and made him look up. *And he was restored and saw everyone clearly.* [26] Then He sent him away to his house, saying, "Neither go into the town, nor tell anyone in the town."

Jesus laid hands on this blind man (we'll try not to get sidetracked by the fact that Jesus *spit on his eyes*!!). Then, Jesus asked if He saw anything. First, why would Jesus ask him "if" he saw anything, if He always got the full manifestation of the healing on the first attempt? That *already* tells us that Jesus didn't always see immediate results with the first prayer. But let's continue... The man answered that he saw "men like trees, walking." So his eyes had been opened to a measure, but everything was still blurry. Verse 25 says that Jesus "put His hands on his eyes *again*!" After this second attempt, *then* the man was restored completely and saw clearly. Oh thank you,

221

Jesus, You didn't give up when You didn't see an instant miracle on the first prayer... and now we won't either!!

One time myself and a group of four or five teenagers ministered to a woman that was completely blind in her right eye. We prayed for her for almost an hour; and she gradually went from seeing nothing but blackness, to seeing light, to seeing fuzzy forms, to identifying colors, and finally to seeing our faces clearly! Sure, we might have prayed 10 or 20 times; but what difference does that make? She went away seeing!

How many times will we pray before we quit? Once? Ten times? Fifty times? A hundred? A thousand? Why do we sometimes get instant results with the first attempt, and on other occasions have to minister multiple times to get the results? Who knows? And ultimately, who cares? But one thing is sure: God's word is true. When we pray, the life of God is released into the person, and one way or another, they can be healed. So, as long as they're willing to let us pray again— Let's pray again!

> How many times will we pray before we quit? Pray again!

Gradual Healing

Again, it is a frequent misunderstanding that if God is going to heal, that it must be instant. God does it in a variety of ways; but one thing is sure—His will is always healing! Sometimes when Jesus ministered to people, they were healed gradually, rather than instantly. My favorite example is when He ministered to the ten lepers:

Luke 17:11-18
[11] Now it happened as He went to Jerusalem that He passed through the midst of Samaria and Galilee. [12] Then as He entered a certain village, there met Him ten men who were lepers, who stood afar off. [13] And they lifted up their voices and said, "Jesus, Master, have mercy on us!"
[14] So when He saw them, He said to them, "Go, show yourselves to the priests." And so it was that as they went, they were cleansed. [15] And one of

them, when he saw that he was healed, returned, and with a loud voice glorified God, [16] and fell down on his face at His feet, giving Him thanks. And he was a Samaritan. [17] So Jesus answered and said, "Were there not ten cleansed? But where are the nine? [18] Were there not any found who returned to give glory to God except this foreigner?" [19] And He said to him, "Arise, go your way. Your faith has made you well."

Jesus didn't pray for these guys at all, He didn't lay hands on them or anything. He just said to these ten lepers, "Go show yourselves to the priests." I love Jesus. He throws out all of our religious ideas of what healing ministry should look like! Sure, for some He prays, and lays hands on them. But other times He just declares them to be well, or commands them to get up and walk or stretch out their hand, or go visit the priest! Still other times, He spits on people, grabs their tongues, puts fingers in their ears, or makes mud and puts it on their faces! Please don't try to put God in a box when it comes to healing—He'll be sure to break it down!

> Jesus throws out all of our religious ideas of what healing ministry should look like.

Anyway, something very important to notice is that those ten lepers showed no sign of any change whatsoever while Jesus was there with them. How do we know? The Bible says, "*as they went*, they were cleansed." Not "*before* they went," but "*as* they went." Jesus told them to go have the priests check out their healing, before there was any physical sign of it taking place!

I'm told that it was a 3-day journey from this area to where the priests were. I don't know that first-hand—I'm not a geography expert. However, one thing I do know, because the Bible says so: These guys were not healed instantly, they were cleansed of their leprosy "as they went." Did it take an hour, a day, two days, or three? We don't know; but it did *not* happen right when Jesus prayed. It also says that when the one man saw that he was healed, he "returned" to thank Jesus. If he had to "return," then that obviously demonstrates that some time had passed and he had traveled some distance already. We also see other instances where Jesus ministered to people and they were healed "that same hour," or "from that hour," which could imply that the healing began at the time Jesus ministered, and continued until its gradual completion. See, for instance:

Matthew 8:13
Then Jesus said to the centurion, "Go your way; and as you have believed, so let it be done for you." And his servant was healed *that same hour*.

Matthew 15:28
Then Jesus answered and said to her, "O woman, great is your faith! Let it be to you as you desire." And her daughter was healed *from* that very hour.

The tiny word, "from," is important here. It's the Greek word "apo." Vine's Dictionary says that "'apo' suggests a starting point." [3] In other words, the daughter's healing "started" when Jesus said it, and continued to its full completion later.

This ought to encourage us. We must *not* look at the natural results when we pray, and get discouraged if we don't see an instant miracle. God is faithful. He's clearly said and demonstrated that His will is always healing. So when we pray, we must believe that He's answering—one way or the other. Instant, gradual, one prayer, or 100 prayers—Sickness and the human body must respond to the God-given authority of His sons and daughters!

> We must not look at the natural results when we pray.

BOTTOM LINE: Jesus Healed Everyone, So Should We

We've hit the major objections that the Church falls back on when attempting to say that God's will is *not* always to heal. There are also other ones out there; but if we hold *any* of these excuses up to the life of Jesus, we see that *none* of them hold any water.

Can anyone show us one instance where someone came to Jesus for healing, and He said to them, "I'm sorry, but in your

224

case, it's God's will for you to be sick?" How about, "Today must not be your day?" Or maybe, "We need to dig into your past sins and family history to get out all the roots that your sickness may stem from first." What about, "Come back when you have more faith?" Oh my goodness, Jesus never said anything like any of these statements, and yet we hear them in the Church all the time! Instead, what we see in the life of Jesus, is that He healed *every single person* that ever came to Him for healing.

Matthew 4:24
Then His fame went throughout all Syria; and they brought to Him *all sick people* who were afflicted with various diseases and torments, and those who were demon-possessed, epileptics, and paralytics; and *He healed them.*

Luke 4:40
When the sun was setting, all those who had *any that were sick* with various diseases brought them to Him; and *He laid His hands on every one of them and healed* them.

Matthew 9:35
Then Jesus went about all the cities and villages, teaching in their synagogues, preaching the gospel of the kingdom, and healing *every sickness and every disease* among the people.

Luke 9:11
But when the multitudes knew it, they followed Him; and He received them and spoke to them about the kingdom of God, and *healed those who had need of healing.*

No devil, no "open door," no curse, no unanswered prayer, no unbelief, no stronghold, no "mysterious purpose" of the Father, no *nothing* could ever stop Jesus from bringing the necessary healing. He ministered using many different methods. Sometimes they were healed instantly, sometimes they required repeated prayer, and sometimes they were healed gradually. But this is the simple truth: Every single time someone that needed healing came to Jesus, He healed them. *That's right—without exception—every single one!* There is *zero* record of Jesus ever failing to heal someone who needed it and came to Him to get it—*for any reason whatsoever*!!

225

Summary:

Job is not our standard of expectation; the Old Testament is not our standard. The disciples are not our standard, nor is the Apostle Paul. Perhaps most significantly, *our own past experiences are not our standard.* Jesus alone is the model for what we really look like in Him, how it looks when He lives through us, and what it looks like when He ministers healing through our hands. Any other expectation is sub-standard. Jesus never failed to heal anyone. Do we fail to reflect that standard much of the time? Yes! But will we create some garbage excuse for our immaturity in fully manifesting Christ? No! Any theology that allows for anything less is a man-made tradition that makes the word of God of no effect in our lives.

> Every single time someone that needed healing came to Jesus, He healed them-- without exception!

Man-made traditions make us satisfied with less than Jesus purchased. Man-made traditions relegate us to our "old man" and make it impossible to "put on Christ." Man-made traditions say we can never walk as Jesus walked, and make us comfortable in our lack. Man-made traditions are excuses. The bottom line is that if Jesus modeled and taught it, then He will live and teach it through us too—if we'll let Him. We are not going to be ashamed, or guilty, or condemned in our lack, failures and misunderstandings; but instead, we will get up, dust ourselves off, and continue to press on for the mark of the prize of the high call of God that is in Christ Jesus! God's will is *always* healing!

CHAPTER 12

OLD vs. NEW

Many of the misunderstandings about God's will concerning healing come from a failure to "rightly divide" the Word. Different parts of the Bible apply to specific people, in specific circumstances. Different parts of the Bible describe how God deals with people based on different covenants and different types of relationship with Him. Some aspects never change, some do; but in general, the Old Covenant and the New Covenant are worlds apart! It is vitally important that we be able to see the things that were eliminated or forever altered by the Cross of Christ, and adjust our thinking accordingly.

Many places in the Old Testament, we read about people being struck with curses, sickness, diseases and pain as a result of their sins. They get boils, tumors, leprosy, and all kinds of

> The Old Covenant and the New Covenant are worlds apart!

disasters come on them. Many fail to constantly remember that the Old and New Covenants are two very different worlds. So, when we read about things that happened in the Old Testament, and think we should expect the same things in the New Testament, we are failing to rightly divide the Word. This can lead to all sorts of wrong ideas about God, His Nature, His ways, and what we can expect of Him as His children. This chapter is an attempt to help us understand why certain things happened in the Old Testament that are not on today's New Covenant agenda. This should clear up a few of the most common theological misconceptions that hinder Believers from receiving healing.

Old Covenant Justice: Sin and Death

Perhaps the biggest, most obvious difference between the Old and New Covenants is that of Law versus Grace. The difference revolves around the issue of performance. Whose performance will you rely on—Jesus' or yours?

The Old Covenant was one of Law: getting what you "deserve"; reaping what you sow; crime and punishment; sin, guilt, judgment and death. It demonstrated the power of sin to defile and enslave. The world was bound by the letter of these laws— an eye for an eye, a tooth for a tooth, a life for a life. If one planted sin, they reaped death. The soul who sins shall die.

Deuteronomy 19:21
Your eye shall not pity: life shall be for life, eye for eye, tooth for tooth, hand for hand, foot for foot.

Ezekiel 18:20
The soul who sins shall die. The son shall not bear the guilt of the father, nor the father bear the guilt of the son. The righteousness of the righteous shall be upon himself, and the wickedness of the wicked shall be upon himself.

Under the Old Covenant, one could only experience the blessings of God if they obeyed the rules laid down in the Law. One could basically only experience God's goodness if they performed up to the standard of His perfection. The converse was also true: If someone didn't meet the standard, then they reaped the curse that exists in the realm of sin. That meant *everyone*!

This kind of "If you do __(blank)__, then I will __(blank)__," and "If you don't do __(blank)__, then __(blank)__," agreement is seen in many Old Testament Scriptures:

Deuteronomy 28:1-2, 15
[1] "Now it shall come to pass, *if you diligently obey* the voice of the LORD your God, *to observe carefully all His commandments* which I command you today, that the LORD your God will set you high above all nations of the earth. [2] And *all these blessings shall come upon you* and overtake you, *because you obey* the voice of the LORD your God...

[15] "But it shall come to pass, *if you do not obey the voice of the LORD your God, to observe carefully all His commandments and His statutes* which I command you today, that *all these curses will come upon you and overtake you...*

(See also Exodus 19:5, 1 Samuel 12:15, 1 Kings 6:12, Jeremiah 18:9-10, Mark 11:26, etc)

Guess what? Mankind couldn't meet the standards! When Old Covenant people fell short of the standard (sinned), they received the natural result: Death—in all its stages and forms.

Romans 6:23
For the wages of sin is death, but the gift of God is eternal life in Christ Jesus our Lord.

Sickness and disease—if left unchecked—are simply the early stages of death. Without our immune systems, even a common cold would kill us. Most victims of AIDS die of common illnesses; because their immune systems are too weak to kill these little viruses. Think of sickness as an evil being that will grow up to be death when it matures. So sin results in sickness, disease and death, if there is no system in place to get rid of the sin while it's immature! Thank God for the New Covenant "immune system!" The works of Jesus can "kill" sin, sickness, disease, and even full-grown death!

> When OT people fell short of the standard (sinned), they received the natural result: Death—in all its forms.

Old Covenant Justice: Perfect Performance Required

But in the Old Covenant, sin resulted in death. It didn't matter if you got most of it right, most of the time. There was no such thing as "close enough." There were no scales in Heaven, with all of one's good deeds on one side, and sins on the other, and if your good deeds outweighed your bad deeds, then you were OK (That's religion!) No, if God is perfect, and someone wants to be reconciled to Him (brought into a love relationship), they've got

229

to be perfect too! If they ever broke even one of the laws, in comparison to God's beauty and perfection, they were seen as guilty of the whole thing!

James 2:10
For whoever shall keep the whole law, and yet stumble in one point, he is guilty of all.

Someone might think that this sounds kind of rough—impossible even! They're right! Living 100% perfect before God in natural, human strength is not possible. Through the Law, sin gained power, because if we couldn't keep it all, we became guilty of it all. What a mess! In Romans 7, Paul recalls what it was like to be someone bound up under knowledge of the Law, but powerless to meet its standards:

Romans 7:7-13
[7] What shall we say then? Is the law sin? Certainly not! On the contrary, I would not have known sin except through the law. For I would not have known covetousness unless the law had said, "You shall not covet." [8] But sin, taking opportunity by the commandment, produced in me all manner of evil desire. For apart from the law sin was dead. [9] I was alive once without the law, but when the commandment came, sin revived and I died. [10] And the commandment, which was to bring life, I found to bring death. [11] For sin, taking occasion by the commandment, deceived me, and by it killed me. [12] Therefore the law is holy, and the commandment holy and just and good. [13] Has then what is good become death to me? Certainly not! But sin, that it might appear sin, was producing death in me through what is good, so that sin through the commandment might become exceedingly sinful.

Once we knew something was wrong, we were held accountable to the system of sin and death. If we failed in one point, we were guilty of all of it. People were hopelessly unable to perform to this standard of perfection, so it seemed that sin was more powerful in us than God was!

Romans 7:15, 19, 22-25
[15] For what I am doing, I do not understand. For what I will to do, that I do not practice; but what I hate, that I do... [19] For the good that I will *to do,* I do not do; but the evil I will not *to do,* that I practice... [22] For I delight in the law of God according to the inward man. [23] But I see another law in my

members, warring against the law of my mind, and bringing me into captivity to the law of sin which is in my members. [24] O wretched man that I am! Who will deliver me from this body of death? [25] I thank God—through Jesus Christ our Lord!

Before we were "in Christ" as believers, we lacked the raw power necessary to consistently do the right thing! Man was continually at war—with himself! That's why the Law, although glorious to a degree, was ultimately a curse. Failure was guaranteed! This was the whole need for Jesus and a New Covenant! Thank God, Jesus came and became this curse for us, and set us free from that cycle of hopelessness! He rescued us from the system of sin and death, restoring us to holiness and blessing!

Galatians 3:13-14
[13] Christ has redeemed us from the curse of the law, having become a curse for us (for it is written, "Cursed is everyone who hangs on a tree"), [14] that the blessing of Abraham might come upon the Gentiles in Christ Jesus, that we might receive the promise of the Spirit through faith.

This verse very clearly points to the fact that in the New Covenant in the blood of Jesus, we are no longer stuck in the curse of the Law! More on that coming up...

Old Covenant Justice: Sowing and Reaping

When God made the earth, He created the law called sowing and reaping, or seedtime and harvest. Some call it karma, some call it "What goes around comes around;" and some say, "You made your bed, now lie in it." If someone sinned, they were subject to judgment without mercy! This was just raw, natural law.

Genesis 8:22
"While the earth remains, Seedtime and harvest, Cold and heat, Winter and summer, And day and night Shall not cease."

Of course this law has many applications; but right now we're talking about the Old Testament, and sin. So in this case, think of sin as a seed. The sin seed will ultimately grow up and produce a fruit called death. Along the way, there are the leaves and branches of sickness, poverty, sadness, depression, grief, sorrow, shame, turmoil, and everything else less-than-Heavenly.

James 1:15b
... sin, when it is full-grown, brings forth death.

God set up this system of sowing and reaping, which also applies to sin and death. Because of this, much of the Old Testament points to God as the executor of judgments (death, sickness, etc) on people's actions. However, in most (if not all) cases they were simply receiving the natural fruit of the seeds they sowed.

Old Covenant Justice: Judgment and Punishment

In other cases, God *may have* rendered just judgment to those that committed the sins. If so, He really had *no option* but to do so. He made laws with prescribed consequences and people could choose to obey or not. So, whether it was simple sowing and reaping, or getting punished for sins, one of these explanations clarifies the Scriptures where it says God gave Miriam leprosy, sent plagues on Egypt, sent disease on Israel, gave the Philistines tumors, sent sickness on individuals, and so on. There are many more examples of this, and I encourage you to look them all up, then continue reading. Please see the following chart of some of the more obvious instances.

Scripture Reference	What happened?
Exodus 7-12	Plagues sent on Egypt
Exodus 32:35	Plague sent on Israelites for idol worship
Numbers 12:1-16	Miriam gets leprosy for rebellion/pride

232

Deuteronomy 28:21-22; Deuteronomy 28:59-61; Deuteronomy 29:22	Sickness declared as one of the curses on disobedience
Numbers 11:33	Plague on Israelites for complaining
Numbers 14:37	Plague & Death of Israel's unbelieving spies
Numbers 16:41-50	Plague on Israelites for complaining (again)
1 Samuel 5-6	Plague sent on the Philistines
2 Samuel 12:14-19	David's son gets sick and dies due to David's sin
2 Samuel 24:10-25; 1 Chronicles 21:1-30	Plague on Israel due to David's disobedience
2 Kings 15:5	King Azariah struck with leprosy
2 Chronicles 13:20	The Lord struck Jeroboam and he died
2 Chronicles 21:14-15	Jehoram and family struck with disease
2 Chronicles 26:16-23	Uzziah struck with leprosy due to pride
Zechariah 14:12	A prophecy of plague being sent on Israel's enemy

If these Scriptures aren't rightly divided, someone reading them today might think that if they don't behave and keep God's rules, He might "smite" them with some crazy illness. Many people actually do believe this--but that isn't the case! We must keep the Old Testament where it belongs—in the Old Testament!

Some say that the Hebrew language makes God look active in situations, even if He wasn't. That would certainly explain a lot; but I can't confirm or deny this, as I'm not an Ancient Hebrew scholar. We

> Old Testament people simply received the natural results of their sin.

also have to recognize that the Old Testament Hebrews had very little understanding of the devil, if any. Many of them even

233

thought he was a spirit that worked for God, and this belief often came through in the way they described events. Even writing under the inspiration of the Holy Spirit, sometimes their incomplete understanding can come through in their phrasing. However, whether God was active or passive in the process, Old Testament people simply received the natural results of their sin. There was no way around this! Sin had natural consequences, and somebody had to receive the harvest from the seed they sowed!

Hebrews 9:22
And according to the law almost all things are purified with blood, and without shedding of blood there is no remission.

The price for covering sin is blood. Why? Because the "life is in the blood" (Leviticus 17:11). And remember, "the wages of sin is death" (Romans 6:23). Hence, blood equals the pouring out of life, which equates to a kind of death (the wages of sin). So, in the Old Testament, animals were sacrificed, and their death temporarily substituted for the death that the people would have naturally experienced as a result of their sin.

The Israelites had a system of sacrifices in place that would allow the people to experience some brief respite from the harshness of this system of sin and death; but it only lasted until their next sin. It was a constantly repeating cycle of sin, guilt, condemnation, fear of judgment, sacrifice. More sin, more guilt, more sacrifice. This was not God's best. All of Old Covenant history demonstrates one fact: Mankind on his own is utterly incapable of keeping the rules. Natural man will sow sin and reap death.

> Mankind on his own is utterly incapable of keeping the rules. Natural man will sow sin and reap death.

Hebrews 10:1-4
[1] For the law, having a shadow of the good things to come, and not the very image of the things, can never with these same sacrifices, which they offer continually year by year, make those who approach perfect. [2] For then would they not have ceased to be offered? For the worshipers, once purified, would

234

have had no more consciousness of sins. [3] But in those sacrifices there is a reminder of sins every year. [4] For it is not possible that the blood of bulls and goats could take away sins.

The Old Covenant: A Jobless Tutor

The Bible says that the Old Covenant was simply a tutor that would teach us our need for Christ and His sacrifice. The tutor taught us some valuable lessons. But after Jesus' work on our behalf, we get His grades and report card; and we pass the course with flying colors! Now the tutor is out of a job!

Galatians 3:23-25
[23] But before faith came, we were kept under guard by the law, kept for the faith which would afterward be revealed. [24] Therefore the law was our tutor to bring us to Christ, that we might be justified by faith. [25] But after faith has come, we are no longer under a tutor.

The Old Covenant was an imperfect system. If it had been perfect, there would have been no need for a new one, right?

Hebrews 8:7-13
[7] For if that first covenant had been faultless, then no place would have been sought for a second. [8] Because finding fault ... He says: "Behold, the days are coming, says the LORD, when I will make a new covenant ... [9] not according to the covenant that I made with their fathers...; because they did not continue in My covenant... [10] For this is the covenant that I will make ... I will put My laws in their mind and write them on their hearts; and I will be their God, and they shall be My people... all shall know Me... [12] For I will be merciful to their unrighteousness, and their sins and their lawless deeds I will remember no more." [13] In that He says, "A new covenant, " He has made the first obsolete. Now what is becoming obsolete and growing old is ready to vanish away.

He's basically saying, "If the Old one would have cut it, I wouldn't have made a new one." The Old Covenant is now "obsolete"—it doesn't apply to us anymore.

The Old Covenant is obsolete!

The Law was glorious in its own right. Through the Law, men could see the perfection of a Glorious and Holy God! But the glory of God visible in the New Covenant makes the Old Covenant glory look like no glory at all by comparison!

2 Corinthians 3:7-11

[7] But if the ministry of death, written and engraved on stones, was glorious, so that the children of Israel could not look steadily at the face of Moses because of the glory of his countenance, which glory was passing away, [8] how will the ministry of the Spirit not be more glorious? [9] For if the ministry of condemnation had glory, the ministry of righteousness exceeds much more in glory. [10] For even what was made glorious had no glory in this respect, because of the glory that excels. [11] For if what is passing away was glorious, what remains is much more glorious.

Paul said here that "The Old was good, but had to pass away to make room for the New, and the New is much more glorious!" Remember the "If you do __(blank)__, then I will __(blank)__," performance-oriented nature of the Old Covenant? The Old (Mosaic) Covenant was between God and men. The problem was, men couldn't hold up their end of the bargain, so the Old Covenant was weak because flesh (carnal, natural man) was involved.

Because man couldn't hold up his "If" end of the covenant, it was continually broken, and God almost never got to do His "Then" end of the bargain. But He loves people and wanted us to be able to enjoy His goodness, and the benefits of right standing and relationship with Himself. So, before the foundation of the world, He planned that Jesus would fix man's whole performance problem. However, without the lessons of the Old Testament, we wouldn't have seen our *need* to receive Jesus, so that had to come first.

Again—the Law was our tutor—just as planned from the beginning, in God's great wisdom. Now that we have Christ Himself, we don't have a need for the tutor anymore. We are in right relationship with God by faith in Jesus'

The tutor is out of a job!

236

performance for us! That Old Covenant of self-works is no longer! It's been done away with! But someone's thinking, "That can't be. What about Matthew 5:18?"

Matthew 5:18
For assuredly, I say to you, till heaven and earth pass away, one jot or one tittle will by no means pass from the law till all is fulfilled.

Jesus said the Law wouldn't pass away until all was fulfilled. Then, Jesus Himself fulfilled the whole Law, so now it has passed away. In Jesus' own words as He hung on the Cross, "It is finished!"

John 19:28, 30
[28] After this, Jesus, knowing that *all things were now accomplished*, that the Scripture might be fulfilled, said, "I thirst!" [30] So when Jesus had received the sour wine, He said, "*It is finished*!" And bowing His head, He gave up His spirit.

Thank God, we have been "delivered from" and have "died to" the Old Covenant (Romans 7:6). It's been "annulled" (Hebrews 7:18). It is "abolished" (Ephesians 2:15). I don't know how many ways God can say it, but let's try to get it through our heads—it's no longer for us!

The Old Covenant "If... Then" contract said, " 'IF' you perform to an unreachably perfect standard, 'THEN' God can bless you; but 'IF' you don't, 'THEN' too bad, so sad for you!" This is virtually the exact opposite of the New Covenant. The New Covenant says, " 'IF' you try to perform, 'THEN' you're on your own; but 'IF' you rest in Jesus' performance *for* you, 'THEN' you're perfectly right with God!"

> If you rest in Jesus' performance *for* you, then you're perfectly right with God!

Romans 11:6
And if by grace, then it is no longer of works; otherwise grace is no longer grace. But if it is of works, it is no longer grace; otherwise work is no longer work.

In the Old Covenant, people had to clean up their act externally through self-effort. This is called "works." But again, "works" didn't work! They were trying to change their behavior, while all the while having a heart that was selfish and carnal. The New Covenant gave us a heart transplant! No longer do we try to clean up our outside; and no longer does God have to deal with us from the outside! He's given us a new heart, united us to Himself, taken up residence inside of us. Our new nature is intertwined with God's, and this new nature flows to the outside, conquering our old, natural, carnal habits and thinking along the way. And nothing we do can add to it or take away from it. Jesus did it all. We simply receive it by faith, and all the external good works flow out of union with Him (He lives through us).

New Covenant Justice:
A Contract Between God and Perfect Man

What was God's ultimate plan? Eliminate natural, fleshly man's awful performance from the terms of the covenant! God decided He'd just substitute in for us, come as a Man, fulfill both ends of the agreement Himself, conquer the devil, sin, and death—and let "whosoever" enjoy the benefits of the eternally sealed and guaranteed deal! Brilliant!

Romans 8:3-4
[3] For what the law could not do in that it was weak through the flesh, God did by sending His own Son in the likeness of sinful flesh, on account of sin: He condemned sin in the flesh, [4] that the righteous requirement of the law might be fulfilled in us who do not walk according to the flesh but according to the Spirit.

> We can't break a covenant between Jesus and the Father—it's not our contract to break!

Jesus performed perfectly. He fulfilled all of the righteous requirements of the law, never once sinning. He did this as Man, as *you* and as *me*. God as Man, yes; but Man nonetheless. A Perfect Man--One who could follow through on our end of the contract! If we enter into Christ through faith by the Law of Identification, we get the credit, and become perfect in Him! Not only that, but we will never pay the natural penalty for sin; because our failure to meet the standards of perfection can't affect the fact that Jesus met them for us! We can't break a covenant between Jesus and the Father—it's not our contract to break! We are not separate from Christ, so let's stop thinking of ourselves as separate! We are in Him, and He sealed the deal. We are set!

Colossians 2:13-14
[13] And you, being dead in your trespasses and the uncircumcision of your flesh, He has made alive together with Him, having forgiven you all trespasses, [14] having wiped out the handwriting of requirements that was against us, which was contrary to us. And He has taken it out of the way, having nailed it to the cross.

Jesus did it all for us, and this New Covenant is one of perfection that is received by faith, not by performance! So we have been freed from the Law and from its curse.

Romans 7:4-6
[4] Therefore, my brethren, you also have become dead to the law through the body of Christ, that you may be married to another—to Him who was raised from the dead, that we should bear fruit to God. [5] For when we were in the flesh, the sinful passions which were aroused by the law were at work in our members to bear fruit to death. [6] But now we have been delivered from the law, having died to what we were held by, so that we should serve in the newness of the Spirit and not in the oldness of the letter.

New Covenant Justice: Crop Failure

Through faith in the vicarious (us-included) work of Jesus, we get to enjoy all that He earned—all the benefits that come as a result of unbroken, right relationship with God! Sin is no longer an issue for the Believer! It's been removed, done away with, forgotten, and wiped away! We are totally clean and right with God; and we get to enjoy the full benefits of Heavenly citizenship as sons and daughters of God Himself! This is really where the rubber meets the road when it comes to overcoming Old Covenant roadblocks to Divine Healing.

The Law of Sowing and Reaping is no longer a limitation to the Believer in Christ! We can still use that law to our benefit (or detriment) if we choose to, or we can also access a higher law called Grace! Under the Law of Grace, we are not bound to reap the negative results of our own sowing. We can receive a crop failure for all the bad seeds we've sown! If we enter in to Jesus by faith, we get to reap the harvest that *He* sowed!

> If we enter in to Jesus by faith, we get to reap the harvest that He sowed!

For instance, if an unbeliever sows smoking, the natural harvest could be lung cancer, emphysema, or other conditions. If an unbeliever sows sexual immorality, the natural harvest can be AIDS or other STDs. But under the New Covenant, there is now Grace available to cancel the curse, get healed, and minister that same healing to others!

Romans 8:2
For the law of the Spirit of life in Christ Jesus has made me free from the law of sin and death.

The Law of Sin and Death is no longer binding to us. If we (in Christ) haven't sinned, then we have no death coming to us. There is no sin on our records once we are forgiven. The Law of Sin and Death can't dish out any consequences to us; because in Christ we no longer have sin to be punished for! We are tapped into a higher law called the Law of the Spirit of Life in Christ Jesus! "Life in Christ Jesus" is a whole different world from life under "Sin and Death"!!!

Romans 10:4
For Christ is the end of the law for righteousness to everyone who believes.

What does this mean? Under the Old Covenant, they planted the seed called sin, and reaped the fruit called death (in its many forms). Under the New Covenant, when/if we sin, we've received forgiveness through the blood of Christ, and the harvest of death is cancelled and reversed! If we sin, instead of death and sickness, we just receive more Grace!

New Covenant Justice: Abounding Grace

Romans 5:20b-21
[20] ...But where sin abounded, grace abounded much more, [21] so that as sin reigned in death, even so grace might reign through righteousness to eternal life through Jesus Christ our Lord.

The more one sins, the deeper they go into it—Rather than reaping the deserved harvest of poverty, sickness and death, they get more Grace than ever!!! The Grace of God forgives, and restores to perfection, wiping out any record of the wrong. This sounds ridiculous to the natural mind. "That's not fair!" our logic screams. "Where is the justice in that?" our sense of reason begs to know. God's justice looks a lot different than ours does—Thank God!!! Of course this naturally brings up a question. Thankfully, Paul answers it in the following verses, as he continues his discourse:

> God's justice looks a lot different than ours does!

Romans 6:1-4
[1] What shall we say then? Shall we continue in sin that grace may abound? [2] Certainly not! How shall we who died to sin live any longer in it? [3] Or do you not know that as many of us as were baptized into Christ Jesus were baptized into His death? [4] Therefore we were buried with Him through baptism into death, that just as Christ was raised from the dead by the glory of the Father, even so we also should walk in newness of life.

The question was: "OK, since the more I sin, the more Grace I get—Why don't I just keep on sinning then?" The answer: "Don't be ridiculous! You are dead to sin. It's no longer your nature—You've got a totally new one! Now sin is just a bad habit you need to re-think and change through practice (repent of)." This involves the renewing of the mind to think like the mind of Christ

241

you now have. Then we live out of the thoughts that come from His mind, rather than the old patterns we're used to. Grace isn't freedom *to* sin, it's freedom *from* sin! It's God's enabling power to live free from sin! Thank you, Lord, sin no longer has any grip on us! If we're in Christ, we're a new breed of perfect men! All things have been made new!

New Covenant Justice: Perfect and Being Perfected

I can hear the arguments in advance: "Come on, nobody's perfect!" Well, God says that we are. He's made us completely new creations in Christ; and as such, we are perfect (mature) and complete according to the Scriptures.

2 Corinthians 5:17
[17] Therefore, if anyone is in Christ, he is a new creation; old things have passed away; behold, all things have become new.

Hebrews 10:14
For by one offering He has perfected forever those who are being sanctified.

Colossians 2:10
and you are complete in Him, who is the head of all principality and power.

It's an already-accomplished reality in the invisible realm. Over time, we better reflect the invisible realm—here in the visible realm. That is why, even though we just read Scriptures that say we are already perfect and complete, we can read others which talk about there being a process of this perfection and maturity showing up more consistently on the outside.

Philippians 3:12
Not that I have already attained, or am already perfected; but I press on, that I may lay hold of that for which Christ Jesus has also laid hold of me.

2 Corinthians 13:9
For we are glad when we are weak and you are strong. And this also we pray, that you may be made complete

James 1:4
But let patience have its perfect work, that you may be perfect and complete, lacking nothing.

These Scriptures talk about the "process" or "growth" involved in walking out our new identity. The progress shows up as we increase in the knowledge of what we already are, and what we already have. As we increase in the knowledge, our thinking changes—we believe what God says He did for us in Christ, and it is reflected in our works. In other words, we learn what the invisible reality is (in the Scriptures), if we believe it, we naturally act like it's true. Our thoughts and actions change in accordance with the truths we trust in. Gradually, we look (visibly) more and more like our (invisible) new-creation selves. We simply live the invisible reality of what God accomplished in us in Christ. But God sees it as being done already, and proclaims the end from the beginning, calling those things which are not, as though they were.

> "Christian Growth:" As we increase in knowledge, our thinking changes... and it is reflected in our works.

Isaiah 46:10
Declaring the end from the beginning, And from ancient times things that are not yet done, Saying, 'My counsel shall stand, And I will do all My pleasure,'

Romans 4:17b
God, who gives life to the dead and *calls those things which do not exist as though they did*;

So if God calls us perfect and complete in Christ, who are we to argue? Let God be found true, and every man a liar! Let's believe the report of the Lord. In Christ, we are now (invisibly) perfect, and are being (visibly and outwardly) perfected as we yield to the mind of Christ that is now ours—and godly life is the (super-) natural result. It's done—so let's walk it out!

New Covenant Justice: Disqualified From Punishment

In Christ, we are holy, perfect, accepted, worthy, and qualified for every blessing He has provided. Conversely, we have been disqualified for judgment and made undeserving of any punishment. Jesus took care of that once and for all on our behalf. Not only do the Laws of Sowing and Reaping, and Sin and Death, no longer apply to us—Now, as perfected people in Christ, the Laws of Judgment and Punishment no longer apply to us either!

> Jesus satisfied the impossible demands of the Law... No more paying the piper—the piper's been paid.

Romans 8:1
There is therefore now no condemnation to those who are in Christ Jesus, who do not walk according to the flesh, but according to the Spirit.

We are free from any and all judgment! For the New Testament Believer, there is no smiting, striking, curses or judgments. Jesus satisfied the impossible demands of the Law. The Law was a tough taskmaster; but now there is no more "paying the piper" for us—the piper's been paid. And in case there was any confusion, even God said, "I'm not interested in being the Judge. Jesus, you take over the job."

John 5:22
22 For *the Father judges no one*, but has committed all judgment to the Son,

Jesus says, "Well, I don't want to judge anybody either. I want to save them! Isn't that why I came in the first place—to set the people free from their sin and its results?"

John 12:47
And if anyone hears My words and does not believe, I do not judge him; for I did not come to judge the world but to save the world.

John 8:11, 15
11 ...And Jesus said to her, "*Neither do I condemn you*; go and sin no more."
15 You judge according to the flesh; *I judge no one*.

So now—during this age of Grace—neither God the Father, nor God the Son want to judge anybody. That doesn't mean they can't receive the penalty or results of their sin if they want to. This Scripture in Romans seems to indicate that if people ignore the gift and Grace of God, they can continue under "sowing and reaping, sin and death" if they so choose.

Romans 1:27
...committing what is shameful, and receiving in themselves the penalty of their error which was due.

But Jesus is not sitting in Heaven, looking at individuals and saying, "You there, you sinned, here's your punishment!" No, He's already established judgment for everyone. Jesus has basically said, "OK, I've told you how to receive righteousness, and I've also told you what behaviors will result in death. My words stand forever. If you listen and believe Me, you'll get the rewards. If you don't, you choose your own fate. The judgment you receive is determined by your own response to what I've already spoken."

John 12:48
He who rejects Me, and does not receive My words, has that which judges him—*the word that I have spoken will judge him in* the last day.

I'm sure someone's asking, "But what about the Great White Throne Judgment? Isn't Jesus the Righteous Judge there?" Yes, there is coming *one* day (singular—as in, one... single... day!) in the future, where Jesus will judge men according to their deeds. Believers will only get rewards, because there is no record of their sins! Unbelievers will be judged by the words of Jesus and how they responded, receiving their chosen end. But guess what? That "Judgment Day" hasn't yet arrived yet! Today is a time for mercy, grace, forgiveness and God is not passing judgment, or doling out punishment on *any individual, group, or nation!* He's already rendered judgment on the matter for this

> "Jesus reaped the harvest for every sin ever planted." *That's* the judgment of God!

245

whole age. Do you want the judgment of God? Here it is: "Jesus reaped the harvest for every sin ever planted. Everyone else gets the harvest Jesus earned." That's the judgment of God for this age of Grace.

2 Corinthians 5:18-20
[18] Now all things are of God, who has reconciled us to Himself through Jesus Christ, and has given us the ministry of reconciliation, [19] that is, that God was in Christ reconciling the world to Himself, not imputing their trespasses to them, and has committed to us the word of reconciliation. [20] Now then, we are ambassadors for Christ, as though God were pleading through us: we implore you on Christ's behalf, be reconciled to God.

God has done everything necessary for the whole world to be reconciled to Himself. How has He done this? "Not imputing their trespasses to them." And then He gave us the job of spreading this "word of reconciliation." This is how He describes the job of being an "ambassador for Christ." So, if God reconciled people to Himself by not imputing their sins to them, then guess how *we're* supposed to continue this ministry of reconciliation—*the same way!* "Hey world, because of what Christ did for you, you're free from the consequences of sin; and you're free to enjoy unbroken relationship with Him forever. It's a gift—Here, take it!" This is the proclamation of the simple, pure gospel!

Summary

God does not send sickness, injury, pain or death to punish people for sin and failure.

Some people think that if someone is sick, maybe it could be the judgment of God on them. But as we've discovered, today is not Judgment Day. This mistaken idea came from looking back at Old Testament Scriptures, where people received sickness as either reaping from their sowing, or as a result of their sins. That was unavoidable in the Old Covenant; but we can't bring that paradigm over here into the New Covenant. The New Covenant is a whole new world, a whole new ballgame! The old rules don't apply anymore.

In God's great gift of Salvation, He doesn't remember our sins anymore—any of them. They are gone! They've been washed away in the blood of Jesus, forever eliminated from the record. We stand in the righteousness of Jesus Christ Himself, and that's exactly how God sees us if we are in Him! Therefore, there is no judgment coming to us as Believers. In this New Covenant world—this age of Grace, God does not send sickness, injury, malfunction, pain or death to punish people for sin and failure. Because of what Christ did, we are undeserving of punishment!

We also no longer need to be bound to the natural laws of Sowing and Reaping, or Sin and Death. Higher laws are now freely accessible to us—the Law of Grace, the Law of Identification, the Law of the Spirit of Life in Christ Jesus. We do not have to get the results of our old sins. Jesus entered into our humanity and reaped the harvest of death for us—He got what we had earned! Now we get what *Jesus* deserved! Praise the Lord!

Because of the finished work of Christ, we reap the harvest that He planted. We receive the benefits of the New Covenant contract that Jesus fulfilled on our behalf! Healing is one of those benefits—It's the Children's Bread! It's in the Communion with the body of our Lord! It's in His Stripes! It's in His Name! It's in our union with Him! God's will is *always* healing!

Notes:

CHAPTER 13

WHAT ABOUT PAUL'S THORN?

A common objection to the idea that "God's will is always healing," is: "What about Paul's 'thorn in the flesh'?" People bring this up because they have been taught the *false tradition* that Paul's "thorn" was some kind of sickness. This idea has been passed from teacher to teacher, for *centuries*. Once someone has heard it, the idea floats around in their head until it's replaced with the truth of the Word. We cannot allow the idea that Paul's thorn was a sickness to rest in our minds as Believers. As a man of God used to say, "You can't stop a bird from landing on your head; but you can stop it from making a nest in your hair!" We've got to kick false traditions and lies out of our head as soon as they "land!"

I can't overemphasize how important it is for us as Believers to take the time to read and interpret the Scripture for ourselves. Don't just swallow everything you hear from everybody. Read the Bible slowly, read it carefully and consider each and every word. *Think* about what you are reading. Look at the context. What *does* it say? What does it *not* say? Then read it again with an understanding of the *bigger picture*. Think about it in light of the *New Covenant*—what Jesus accomplished for us on the cross. Consider God's *character* as seen in Jesus Christ. If you have questions about it, *ask* the Lord. *Wait* for answers. Folks, If we'll take the time to read the Bible deliberately and with the Holy Spirit's help, we will find *lots* of things that don't match what we've heard from pulpits over the years! We will avoid a lot of well-intentioned deception, and stay *free* in the truth of the gospel!

In any case, many people read 2 Corinthians 12 with the misunderstanding that Paul's thorn is sickness. Then, looking through that "dirty lens," it looks like God is willing (or allowing) Paul to just stay sick and suffer. So what is the ultimate "message" that people who believe this want to proclaim to us? They are saying, "God left Paul sick and wouldn't heal him, so we can expect the same." By this point in the book, we should have enough pillars of truth in place in our hearts that a lie this blatant sets off our "Hooey" alarm! But it's not enough to know something *is* hooey. We need to be able to articulate *why*.

First of all, the thorn is not sickness in the first place—but we'll get to that later! Second, even if we didn't know what the thorn was, we ought to already know some central Biblical truths: Healing is the children's bread. We are one with Christ (and He certainly isn't sick), seated in heavenly places (where the will of God is being done perfectly), and we are hidden with Christ in God (where there is no sickness allowed)! God is *good*, and the devil is *bad*! He is Jehovah Rapha, the Lord Who Heals. Jesus is the perfect representation of the Father, and He *never* left *anyone* sick that asked to be healed. Jesus paid a specific price for our healing—the stripes on His Own back. It's included in our package-deal salvation, which is an already finished work we can't do anything to earn or deserve! But if you or someone you are ministering to has ever been taught this idea about Paul's thorn being a sickness, it can create an unnecessary roadblock to receiving healing from God.

> We should have enough pillars of truth in place in our hearts that a lie this blatant sets off our "Hooey" alarm!

Of course we must also dive in to look at 2 Corinthians 12 at some point to deal with that text specifically. But first, I would like to address one word upon which some of the wrong interpretation of 2 Corinthians 12 is founded. Throughout this chapter, we'll expose the cracked foundations, and eventually see that there is no basis on which the "Paul's thorn was sickness" interpretation can stand.

250

1. What Does "Infirmity" Mean?

Before we dive into the text of 2 Corinthians 12, first we need to address one little Greek word that leads to a lot of the misinterpretation about Paul and his life. That word is "infirmity." Because in English, we are likely to think of "infirmity" as sickness, it's easy to see why many people read these various Scriptures and automatically think "sickness." Nothing else in the context of these verses would lead us to that idea. The Greek word for "infirmities" here is "astheneia."[1] *Sometimes* it is used to refer to physical illness; however, it refers to non-physical "weaknesses" a *majority* of the times it is found in the New Testament (See Appendix B). We will also see through the rest of this study that in this case "sickness" does not fit in the text of 2 Corinthians 12 if we try to plug it in there.

I generally like the New King James pretty well; but with this word, they certainly could have interpreted more precisely. Please don't be unaware that translators have also been exposed to bad teaching and tradition—and have a corresponding slant on the way they translate! I'm sure they think they're doing us a favor; but often they are actually giving the text a meaning it wasn't intended to carry. Because this one word is open to some interpretation, we must look at the larger context, and some other issues, to find which translation would be best in this case. As a "for instance," King James translates it in 2 Corinthians 12:10 as "infirmities," whereas the ASV, CEB, Darby, ERV, ESV, GW, GNT, HCSB, Phillips, LEB, NASB, NCV, NIRV, NIV, NLV, NLT, TNIV, WE, and many others all avoid the word "infirmity" here, and instead opt for "weakness" as the more precise meaning in this context. We will see why this would have been a clearer, more appropriate choice as we go on.

So with that introduction, let's look at the primary text in question:

2 Corinthians 12:7-10

[7] And lest I should be exalted above measure by the abundance of the revelations, a thorn in the flesh was given to me, a messenger of Satan to buffet me, lest I be exalted above measure. [8] Concerning this thing I pleaded with the Lord three times that it might depart from me. [9] And He said to me, "My grace is sufficient for you, for My strength is made perfect in weakness." Therefore most gladly I will rather boast in my infirmities, that the power of Christ may rest upon me. [10] Therefore I take pleasure in infirmities, in reproaches, in needs, in persecutions, in distresses, for Christ's sake. For when I am weak, then I am strong.

Some things in these Scriptures can be easily misinterpreted if we only look on the surface, with false traditions ringing in our ears. For a few minutes, let's put all of that aside. Yes, the Scripture says God didn't take away the "thorn"—but until you know what the "thorn" is, it is fruitless to go into God's response to Paul's prayer. We'll discover together that this "thorn" is not sickness—it's actually defined for us very clearly in the Bible. Once we clear up that central issue, the rest of the text gets much, much simpler. So first, let's satisfy the most important question...

> Some things in Scripture can be easily misinterpreted if we only look on the surface, with false traditions ringing in our ears.

2. Paul's "Thorn in the Flesh": What Was It?

If we are to understand why God answered Paul's prayer the way He did, we first have to understand that the "thorn" is not sickness. So what is it? Many people say that no one can know for sure; but I think it's only people that believe "the thorn is sickness" that think we can't know what it was. The Bible tells us the answer repeatedly. We see it clearly defined in the immediate context of 2 Corinthians 12, and elsewhere in the Scriptures.

• Paul Himself Defines the "Thorn"

We must lean on Hermeneutics 101—CONTEXT, CONTEXT, CONTEXT! This is probably the first and most obvious rule of Bible interpretation: When interpreting Scripture, look at a verse or passage in its *context!* The first place we look for the answers is the surrounding text. In many cases, the answer is right there! In this case, Paul is discussing the thorn in the flesh in verses 7-10. In verse 10, he gives the description of what the "thorn", or "weakness" is--

2 Corinthians 12:10
Therefore I take pleasure in infirmities, in reproaches, in needs, in persecutions, in distresses, for Christ's sake. For when I am weak, then I am strong.

Here is a basic synopsis of these verses: A "thorn in the flesh" was given to Paul. The thorn was "a messenger of Satan." It was given to him to prevent him from becoming "exalted above measure." Paul asked God repeatedly to take this thorn away. God answered, referring to the thorn as "weakness." Paul says, "OK, then I'll boast in this weakness." Then *Paul himself defines the "weakness"* that He and God are discussing! "infirmities.. reproaches.. needs.. persecutions.. distresses for Christ's sake!"

> The first place we look for the answers is in the surrounding text. In many cases, the answer is right there!

Yet another fact of Bible translation is that since there is no *punctuation* in the original Greek, it is totally up to the translators on where to put it, and what to put there. How much clearer might this text have been if they had used "weakness" and punctuated it differently? How about this (my own alteration to the NKJV):

- "Therefore I take pleasure in weakness (in reproaches, in needs, in persecutions, in distresses), for Christ's sake..." ..or..
- "Therefore I take pleasure in weakness—in reproaches, in needs, in persecutions, in distresses—for Christ's sake..."

253

Just use "weakness," and add some parentheses or a dash and it would be so much clearer and more consistent with the context! Again, read for yourself! Look at the original text! Look at the context! Look at the cross! Look at the character of God! I believe that Paul was *defining* the "weakness" or the "thorn" for us right there: "Reproaches... Needs... Persecutions... Distresses"—There you have it from the immediate context! The definition of Paul's "thorn in the flesh" was right there all the time!!

Remember this also—the chapter breaks aren't in the original text either! Just like capitalization and punctuation, they're added by translators. Ignoring the chapter break then, what is

> Look at the original text! Look at the context! Look at the cross! Look at the character of God!

Paul talking about *right before* he mentions the thorn in chapter 12? What is the subject at hand? In the previous chapter (the pretext of the passage we are examining in this chapter), Paul *again* described to us his "thorn," in even more detail:

2 Cor 11:23-28
Are they ministers of Christ?—I speak as a fool—I am more: in *labors* more abundant, in *stripes* above measure, in *prisons* more frequently, in *deaths* often. [24] From the Jews five times I received forty *stripes* minus one. [25] Three times I was *beaten* with rods; once I was *stoned*; three times I was *shipwrecked*; a night and a day I have been *in the deep*; [26] in *journeys* often, in *perils of waters*, in perils of *robbers*, in perils of my own *countrymen*, in perils of the *Gentiles*, in perils in the *city*, in perils in the *wilderness*, in perils in the *sea*, in perils among *false brethren*; [27] in *weariness and toil*, in *sleeplessness* often, in *hunger and thirst*, in *fastings* often, in *cold and nakedness*— [28] besides the other things, what comes upon me daily: my *deep concern* for all the churches.

Whew! That is a long list! It sounds like Paul named every challenge he could think of that he faced as a Christian. Here's an obvious question I'd like to ask: Where was "sickness" on the list? It seems to me that if some sickness was such a plague to

Paul that he repeatedly pleaded with God to take it away—but it just continued on unendingly—it would have at least made this list... but it didn't! Paul was *not* some sickly guy, plagued with a chronic illness. We'll discuss that more later. The important thing to notice here right now is the *context*.

For these two chapters, Paul is discussing tribulations, challenges and persecution. He says that this is a place of utter human weakness, where he must rely fully on God's strength. He rejoices in his human efforts becoming worthless, so he can simply receive the grace of God—which is enough for every situation! But nothing in this context has anything to do with sickness!

God said, "my strength is made perfect in weakness." Paul says, "Then I love being in a place of weakness (reproach, need, persecution, and distress for Christ's sake)! In these situations, His strength and delivering power is displayed in my life!" People often quote this text, saying "His strength is made perfect in weakness." Isn't it funny how nobody ever quotes Paul by saying, "God's strength is made perfect in sickness," but they plug "sickness" into the rest of this text when they already know instinctively that it doesn't belong there!

We have discovered together that the definition of Paul's thorn is right there in verse 10 in Paul's own words. It's also in the context of the discussion at hand, both before and after the verses in question. But let's not stop there--We can also see it clearly in the Old Testament—in a common Hebrew figure of speech!

- **The Old Testament Defines The "Thorn"**

The issue of Paul's thorn again takes us back to yet another helpful rule of correct Bible interpretation. In this case, it's the "Law of First Mention." This means that in order to gain an accurate understanding of what something means, we look for the first time (or times) it was mentioned in the Bible, and use that as a guide. If we'll do this, we can find the Biblical, Hebraic understanding of the *figure of speech*, "thorn in the flesh." Hint: looking up the Greek words will not help you!

Paul's first language was Hebrew; but he wrote to the Corinthians in Greek. He is simply translating a common Hebrew figure of speech, "thorn in (one's) *side*" into Greek. Then we translate the Greek into English and come up with "thorn in the flesh." Because "thorn in the flesh" is a Hebrew figure of speech, its proper definition must be discovered in the Old Testament Scriptures. Let us look up every instance of this phrase in the Bible. When we do, the definition of the thorn becomes even clearer.

> Because "thorn in the flesh" is a Hebrew figure of speech, its proper definition must be discovered in the Old Testament Scriptures.

Numbers 33:55
But if you do not drive out the inhabitants of the land from before you, then it shall be that those whom you let remain *shall be* irritants in your eyes and thorns in your sides, and they shall harass you in the land where you dwell.

Judges 2:3
Therefore I also said, 'I will not drive them out before you; but they shall be *thorns* in your side, and their gods shall be a snare to you.'"

And here's a third reference. Although it's not exactly phrased word-for-word the same; the obviously similar language conveys the exact same message and intention. Especially note the similarities to the Numbers 33:55 reference above:

Joshua 23:13
Know for certain that the LORD your God will no longer drive out these nations from before you. But they shall be snares and traps to you, and scourges on your sides and thorns in your eyes, until you perish from this good land which the LORD your God has given you.

Let's look at those Scriptures in their context and see if we can decipher from the context what that Hebrew figure of speech means. God was repeatedly telling Israel as they were moving in to the Promised Land, "If you don't get these other people out of there, they will be 'thorns' to you." We can see clearly that the "thorn in the side" or "thorn in the flesh"—as translated from Hebrew, to Greek, to English—is referring to *irritation, opposition, persecution and trouble*!

Or, in today's common English: "Thorn in the flesh" = "Pain in the butt"!!! If we say that about someone, we don't mean it literally—Our gluteus maximus probably feels just fine. We simply mean that they are an irritation to us. This is exactly what the Hebrew "thorn in the side" means, and this is what Paul was talking about in 2 Corinthians 12—Irritation, opposition, persecution, and trouble. Let's say you wrote a letter to a church in English this week. You would probably use some common figures of speech in it. Now imagine that 2,000 years from now, someone was trying to translate your letter, word-for-word, into another language. What might you say that would confuse them or their readers? What if you said that the devil was a "pain in the neck," or that someone was "driving you up the wall?" What would those future readers think? Let's let figurative language stay figurative, especially when it's used that way multiple times in the Holy Scripture.

"Thorn in the flesh" = "Pain in the butt!"

Some may be reading this and saying, "But I've *always* heard that the thorn was sickness. How did you come up with this? Has anyone else in Christian history ever held the interpretation that the "thorn in the flesh" was persecution, or something besides sickness? Yes!

3. Who Agrees With This Interpretation?

So, first we examined the context to see how Paul himself defines his thorn. Then we took into account the Law of First Mention, and let "Scripture interpret Scripture." It is therefore the *only* hermeneutically correct interpretation that Paul's thorn was persecution and trouble. Am I alone in this interpretation? No sir! Even the great (albeit imperfect) reformer, Martin Luther, came to the same conclusion. Let's listen to him:

"Many teachers have explained Paul's thorn to be the temptations of the flesh. The Latin text is responsible for this interpretation; it reads, "stimulus carnis," ... Yet that rendering does not do justice to the words.... Paul Himself explains the nature of the... thorn. He calls it 'a messenger of Satan,' a devil, to 'buffet' him.. The explanation appeals to me that the persecutions and sufferings the Apostle recounts above constitute the devil's flaying. Thus his meaning would be: 'I have received great revelations, for which... the many dangers and misfortunes with which the devil buffets...'" [2]

Thank you, Mr. Luther. By the way, the "many teachers" he references who (mistakenly) explained Paul's thorn to be the temptations of the flesh based on the Latin Vulgate translation... included John Calvin. Obviously, Calvin's interpretation doesn't hold up; but I bring this up to say that *even John Calvin* didn't believe that the thorn was sickness. Thank you, Mr. Calvin.

Additionally, Chrysostom (whom I disagree with on other points) also agrees with Martin Luther and myself on the obviously Scriptural interpretation of Paul's thorn in the flesh:

"And so by the "messenger of Satan," he means...*those who contended with and fought against him, those that cast him into a prison, those that beat him, that led him away to death*); for they did Satan's business." [3]

Elsewhere, Chrysostom referred to the thorn as "*trials,*" [4] or "*dangers.*" [5] In his "Letter to Olympias I," he elaborates further:

"...(Paul) was buffeted by trials... which inflicted much physical pain. 'For there was given unto me' he says 'a thorn in the flesh, a messenger of Satan to buffet me,' meaning by this *the blows, the bonds, the chains, the imprisonments, the being dragged about, and maltreated, and tortured by the scourges of public executioners...*" [6]

Numerous other church fathers like Theophylact, Theodoret, Ecumenius, Ambrose, and Erasmus also believed that the thorn refers to *the persecutions Paul endured from his adversaries.* [7]

258

That being said, whether or not anyone agrees with me *just doesn't matter*. The Bible speaks for itself. So let's continue examining the text, now with the understanding that the thorn is *persecution*.

4. The "Thorn" Was a Messenger of Satan, Not of God.

Besides mistaking the thorn to be sickness, many also blame *God* for giving it to Paul. Let's get rid of that idea right here and now. The Scripture does say that the thorn "was given" to him. So we might be tempted to ask, "Who gave it to him?" Actually, this is a passive Greek phrase that just means Paul "had" a thorn in the flesh (as this same phrase is also used in Revelation 13:14-15).

But even without understanding the Greek, this question is *still* answered for us in the text. It plainly says that the "thorn" was a "messenger of *Satan*"—not a messenger of God; but still much of the Church blames God. I don't get it!! The Greek word translated as "messenger" is "aggelos," which is where we get our English word, "angel." This word is in the New Testament 186 times. In 179 of those cases, it is translated as "angel!" The other 7 times it's "messenger." [8] But whether you prefer to use "angel" or "messenger," the word *always*, one hundred percent of the time, refers to a *being*, an entity, a personality. It *never*—not even once—refers to something inanimate or impersonal (like sickness).

Some people blame a *specific* person or people as being the "messenger of Satan." But because this same issue plagued Paul from city to city everywhere he went, I tend to lean toward the "angel of Satan" or "demon" interpretation. Whether you think it was a demon or just individual people, it's crystal clear from the Scriptures: The

> The thorn in Paul's flesh was constant, Satan-inspired trouble and persecution—*not* sickness or disease!

259

thorn in Paul's flesh was constant, Satan-inspired trouble and persecution—*not* sickness or disease.

Some might ask, "Since the thorn was a messenger from Satan, and we have authority over devils, then why didn't Paul just rebuke this demon and command it to flee?" First, maybe Paul *did* try rebuking the messenger of Satan (without the desired results) before praying and asking God to do it. It doesn't say in the text that he didn't. We are all (even Paul) growing and learning how to operate more fully in the "grace" (which God recommends to Paul) and authority of the Kingdom. If we think Paul had it all figured out, that would be a mistake. Paul's failure to achieve his desired outcome does not in any way indicate that it wasn't an angel of Satan. Nor does it indicate that God wouldn't have approved of Paul's victory over it. As mature as he was, he was still growing and learning, just like we are (Philippians 3:12-15).

Second, even though it was demonic influence that continually dogged Paul's trail with persecution and opposition, Paul attempting to end the persecution by commanding and rebuking would not *necessarily* work. He probably tried that (to no avail), which is why we see here that he was repeatedly asking *God* to do something about it. But here's the thing—devils can inspire people to cause trouble; and we can certainly bind that devil. However—in the case of persecution—if a person (or group of people) simply gets *their own willpower* engaged in persecuting us, we can't take authority over humans and force them to stop it. "Binding" *people* doesn't work! Lastly, *we are not promised deliverance from persecution.* In fact, quite the contrary. If we were, then we would have legal right and authority to enforce God's promise in that regard.

We are *not* promised deliverance from persecution. In fact, quite the contrary.

We'll also discuss some possible interpretations of God's answer to Paul that are more Scripturally, logically, and historically consistent. Or maybe there was some other reason we don't know about; but one thing is sure: Paul's thorn was *not* sickness.

5. Persecution is a Promise

Some might ask, "Since this thorn was persecution, why wouldn't God remove it when Paul asked Him to?" Why did God allow this thorn to remain? The answers to all of these questions are the same.

God has promised—and paid for—our deliverance from sickness. It's included in our Salvation, so it's never a question if He is willing for us to be healed. This is one very simple reason (among many) we can know for certain that Paul's thorn was not sickness. By contrast, He has *not* promised us deliverance from persecution. Persecution is actually—perhaps to our dismay—a promise of God that will come whether we pursue it or not.

Matthew 5:11-12
Blessed are you when they revile and persecute you, and say all kinds of evil against you falsely for My sake. [12] Rejoice and be exceedingly glad, for great is your reward in heaven, for so they persecuted the prophets who were before you.

John 15:20
Remember the word that I said to you, 'A servant is not greater than his master.' If they persecuted Me, they will also persecute you. If they kept My word, they will keep yours also.

If we are like Jesus, we *will* be persecuted. That being said, How do people get the idea that God didn't answer Paul's prayer? He clearly did... Maybe just not in the way that Paul had hoped. Paul was asking, "Lord, take the opposition and persecution out of the way so I can preach the gospel freely," which sounds like a good, logical request.

We can certainly feel free to *ask* God for things He hasn't necessarily promised which we think *may* be available. This is the case with deliverance from persecution—we do see some cases in the Scripture where people are delivered from persecution. For instance, Peter gets delivered from jail by an angel (Acts 12:1-19); and Paul and Silas also got a supernatural jailbreak (Acts 16:16-31). Since we see that Paul himself was delivered from persecution there, and on other occasions, it would be reasonable to see why—even though we are not promised it—he would still ask.

However, we *are* to bind and loose, enforce Kingdom law, and exercise authority over the devil concerning things that *have* been promised and provided by Jesus—like healing! Do we have this all perfected? No. Are we growing in understanding in this regard? Yes. Would this discussion about Paul's thorn not being sickness—if held before the Church worldwide—be one small, beneficial step toward that end? I believe that it would.

6. Understanding God's Answer:
"My Grace is Sufficient for You"

Now that we've learned (from Paul, from the Hebrew Scriptures, from the context, from logic, and from history) that the thorn was persecution stirred up by the devil, we can understand God's response more clearly.

Paul was saying, "God get these hassles and hindrances, persecutions and opposition out of my way!" But God's response was, "My grace is sufficient for you..." What does this mean? It could be properly interpreted as either—or both—of these:

   A) God's grace can strengthen us *through persecution*
   B) God's grace can *break us through to deliverance*

Neither of these have anything to do with sickness, since—as we've already seen—that is not what Paul was even praying about. He was praying about being delivered from trouble and opposition. Since Paul was eventually executed (*not delivered* from his persecution), either of these interpretations of God's answer would be valid.

If it was "A", then God simply gave him the grace to go through his trials, imprisonments, beatings, rejections, and eventual execution. If it was "B," then Paul was perhaps unwilling to take advantage of the deliverance God made available to him. Maybe, like some of the saints we see described in Hebrews 11:35, he simply did not "*accept deliverance*, that (he) might obtain a better resurrection." Isn't this what Jesus Himself modeled for us? No man took His life—He laid it down willingly (John 10:18). Even at His arrest in Gethsemane, He had deliverance available to Him, which He chose to forsake:

Matthew 26:53
Or do you think that I cannot now pray to My Father, and He will provide Me with more than twelve legions of angels?

We know from Scripture that Paul did struggle with this decision—He really seemed to prefer the idea of martyrdom:

Philippians 1:21-26
[21] For to me, to live is Christ, and to die is gain. [22] But if I live on in the flesh, this will mean fruit from my labor; yet *what I shall choose I cannot tell.* [23] *For I am hard-pressed between the two, having a desire to depart and be with Christ, which is far better.* [24] Nevertheless to remain in the flesh is more needful for you. [25] And being confident of this, I know that I shall remain and continue with you all for your progress and joy of faith, [26] that your rejoicing for me may be more abundant in Jesus Christ by my coming to you again.

Later, Paul was also warned in many places, and specifically by the prophet Agabus that he would be imprisoned if he went to Jerusalem (Acts 20:23, 21:10-11), but he chose to go anyway. He went above

> Paul chose *not* to take the door of deliverance that God was offering.

263

and beyond the call of duty. Here was his decision:

Acts 21:12-14
[12] Now when we heard these things, both we and those from that place pleaded with him not to go up to Jerusalem. [13] Then Paul answered, "What do you mean by weeping and breaking my heart? For *I am ready not only to be bound, but also to die* at Jerusalem for the name of the Lord Jesus." [14] So when he would not be persuaded, we ceased, saying, "The will of the Lord be done."

Paul chose not to take the door of deliverance that God was offering. He chose instead to lay down his own life for the unique opportunities it would give him to preach the gospel.

Luke 21:12-13
...they will lay their hands on you and persecute you, delivering you up to the synagogues and prisons. You will be brought before kings and rulers for My name's sake. [13] But it will turn out for you as an occasion for testimony.

So we can see how God saying, "My grace is sufficient for you" makes perfect sense—Whether we understand it to mean, "I'll enable you to endure," or "I'll deliver you." God offers both, and Paul eventually made his choice to turn aside from deliverance and pursue his martyr's crown. And *none* of this has *anything* to do with sickness! His answer was not a "No," as it is traditionally interpreted. Quite the opposite, God's answer was exactly the answer Paul was seeking. God always provides the grace. What we choose to do with it is another question entirely.

> God always provides the Grace. What we choose to do with it is another question entirely.

On another note, it is quite possible that after God's answer, Paul realized that it was up to him to use the grace God made available to take authority over the demon inspiring the persecution. Maybe he did so at that time, thus removing his own thorn by God's grace. We read here from the last chapter of Acts:

264

Acts 28:30-31
Then Paul dwelt two whole years in his own rented house, and received all who came to him, preaching the kingdom of God and teaching the things which concern the Lord Jesus Christ with all confidence, no one forbidding him.

Apparently *something* had changed from the nonstop trouble and persecution he was experiencing previously!

7. "My Strength is Made Perfect in Weakness"

Back to the second half of God's reply: "My strength is made perfect in weakness." This gets a pretty consistent interpretation no matter which interpretation you choose for the first half: "You're in such a state of helplessness and weakness—unable to do anything about the persecution and opposition. The good news is that on the other side of it, one thing will be obvious: My Grace gave you superhuman endurance—or completely delivered you. This will force people to recognize that it was Me, not you."

How many times have you heard nearly that exact testimony from the captors, persecutors, torturers, or guards of various martyrs through history? "I saw the way that this person would not—could not—deny their faith, even in the face of the worst tortures. In fact, they seemed full of peace and joy in spite of it all. This forced me to look deeper, and in doing so, I came to Christ." In this case, can you not see that God's strength is made perfect and put on display in weakness?

Now, we can't apply this same principle to sickness... it won't work. In fact, sickness has the *opposite* effect on unbelievers! The world sees a Christian that believes God made them sick; and they come to the conclusion that either God is mean and cruel, or too weak and powerless to solve the problem.

More importantly, it *does not and cannot* apply to sickness, as Healing is something that was *paid for* by Jesus, *promised* to us,

265

and *accomplished* at Calvary (1 Pet 2:24, etc)! Healing is therefore a covenant privilege and provision for the Christian.

But we can't just say, "His grace is sufficient for me I guess—I'll just keep suffering," throw up our hands and surrender. No, "the Kingdom of Heaven suffers violence, and the violent take it by force." We are in a war. Granted, it's a war that's already won; but it's a war nonetheless. We battle against false ideas that contradict God's word, and we enforce Kingdom law over devils that want to break it every chance they get. Very often it takes making a stand (in rest, grace, trust and faith) to see God's provisions manifest in our lives on the earth. We must trust that God is true to His Word!

God's answer to Paul in verse 9 actually provides even more contextual proof that the thorn cannot be sickness. After reading God's answer, we can ask, "If someone *stays* sick or *dies* of illness, is *that* what God's "strength being made perfect" looks like? Is this what it looked like in Paul's life? Absolutely not! When God's strength is made perfect in someone who is sick, they are *healed!*

However, when God's strength is made perfect in someone who is being *persecuted,* what does it look like? Sometimes it looks like Peter being led out of jail by an angel. Other times it looks like Jesus on the cross:

Luke 23:34a
Then Jesus said, "Father, forgive them, for they do not know what they do."

Acts 7:59-60
[59] And they stoned Stephen as he was calling on God and saying, "Lord Jesus, receive my spirit." [60] Then he knelt down and cried out with a loud voice, "Lord, do not charge them with this sin." And when he had said this, he fell asleep.

That, my friends, is what it looks like when God's supernatural, Divine strength is perfected in the midst of our human frailty and weakness!

266

8. The Thorn Kept Paul from Being "Exalted Above Measure"

In order to completely examine the "thorn" issue in 2 Corinthians 12, we must also see that the Scripture says that this "thorn" was given to Paul "lest (he) be exalted above measure by the abundance of revelations given" to him. We must first ask the question, "What does 'exalted above measure' mean?" There are two likely answers to this question: First, it could mean that people might give him an undue place of "unhindered influence and favor." Or second, it could mean, "proud" or "arrogant." We'll explain these in more detail here; but neither one make any sense whatsoever if the thorn is sickness. Would being sick give us more favor and influence with people? No. Or would being healed create a risk of us becoming arrogant? Of course not. Yet again, sickness makes *zero* sense here if you plug it into the context. But let's look at the two interpretations, with the foundational understanding that the thorn is persecution.

- ### "Exalted Above Measure" = "Boundless Influence & Favor"

We see plainly in the text that the thorn was a messenger from Satan. Because of the great revelations Paul had, many were being saved by the simplicity and power of the gospel he preached in signs and wonders. Satan must have figured that if he allowed Paul to really put down roots anywhere, his influence would begin to spread unhindered—that he would be "exalted without measure/boundary." So the devil made it his primary aim to trouble Paul everywhere he went—to stop him or at least severely limit his impact. Paul usually only had a short time in a place, before he got run out of town by angry mobs. This limited Paul's immediate influence. Satan was trying to keep Paul from having any long-term impact. This makes perfect sense in the context; but the Greek word for "exalted above measure" more commonly has the "proud/arrogant" connotation, so let's try that one out...

- ### "Exalted Above Measure" = "Proud/Arrogant"

Most of the "thorn=sickness" people think that God gave a sickness to Paul to keep him from being proud and arrogant. First, we already know the thorn wasn't sickness, but persecution. Second, we see that it was *Satan* that gave the thorn of persecution to Paul, not God. Would *Satan* want to keep Paul out of pride? Of course not! Satan would love to have Paul fall into this deadly sin. However, while Satan did give Paul persecution to *stop* him, might God allow that persecution to continue, to keep Paul in a place of humble reliance on God's delivering strength? This is certainly more plausible. Although we are most often encouraged in the New Testament to humble *ourselves*, so God can *exalt* us (James 4:10, 1 Peter 5:6). That said, this is still a possible rendering of the Greek text that is congruent with the thorn being persecution.

> Would Satan want to keep Paul out of pride?

On the other hand, if you prefer the traditional misunderstanding of this text, does it make any sense to say that if *sickness* were removed from Paul, that he might become arrogant as a result? No! I've known *lots* of people who've been healed by God. I've *never* known one to get arrogant about it. Quite the contrary, people that are healed by God are humbled by the display of God's goodness. They obviously recognize that their healing has nothing to do with their own goodness or power. When someone is healed by God, the Lord is always the One Who comes out exalted, *not* the person who got healed. So by asking that question, it is further proven that the "thorn" is not sickness. It just makes no sense.

However, let's ask, "If *persecution* were removed from Paul, does it make sense that he might get proud or arrogant?" Because of the depth of Paul's revelations and experiences, he got great results when preaching and demonstrating the gospel. Could this thrust him into pride? Might people might see Paul's powerful ministry and give him a place of undue authority? Acts 28:3-6 illustrates that this is possible. Here, Paul healed all the sick on the island of Malta, and they proclaimed him to be a god at one point. We see this again in 1 Cor 3:1-7, when people were identifying more with Paul than they were with Jesus!

There is a saying that "Absolute power corrupts absolutely." It's possible that if Paul continually found himself in this position, he might eventually yield to pride. He might assume a role of authority that was "above measure"—not rightfully his—claiming glory that is God's alone. Paul was persecuted all the way to his death, so this never happened to him for us to see it in his case. However—on a larger scale—What happens to the Church when (officially sanctioned, widespread, large scale) persecution is removed?

The devil *finally* discovered that he was only helping the cause of Christ by persecuting Christians. First, we only got more staunch and determined in our faith. And second, as we fled persecution, the gospel spread even further around the globe (See Acts 8:1-4)! So the devil changed strategies—He removed our thorn in the flesh and let us get exalted above measure! When did that happen? Let's look at the time of the Emperor Constantine, when Christianity was sanctioned as the official religion of the Roman Empire. What were the historical results of *persecution* being removed from the Church?

First, we had a sudden influx of less-than-sincere Believers coming into the newly-in-vogue Roman "social club" known as Christianity. But here's the question: Were men "exalted above measure" when this persecution was removed? Unquestionably, yes.

We see it so clearly in the history of the post-Constantine church. The Church came into power, men were appointed as "exalted fathers" and they proclaimed themselves to have special rights and privileges. Priests claimed to be the only ones allowed to read and interpret the Scriptures. Later, it got so bad, that they would forgive sins if you paid them enough money (called "indulgences"). That sounds a lot like people being "exalted above measure" to me! Was the removal of the "thorn" of persecution the whole cause of the Dark Ages? Just maybe.

> What happens to the Church when persecution is removed?

Thank God for the Reformation—but even after that we see various men who started out good—then they were given an inappropriate place of influence in people's lives, and it eventually ruined them! In much of the western world today, we have found ourselves enjoying a Christianity without persecution for many years. Where has it gotten us? Have we seen some Christians (even leaders) become "exalted above measure?" I dare say yes. The state of the western Church today is a result of Satan removing persecution—the "thorn in the flesh." On the other hand, have you heard about the *thriving* persecuted Church in China, Africa, and other nations of the world, how they are rising in glory, in unity, in purity, in power? Me too!

Any of these possible interpretations make infinitely more sense (Scripturally, logically, and historically) than Paul getting arrogant about getting healed of a *sickness*. This is further proof that the thorn was not sickness; but let's get back to looking at the passage itself.

9. More Clues from the Context

- #### The Messenger Came to "Buffet" Paul

The text says that this angel of Satan came to "buffet" Paul. This word, "buffet" is the Greek word, "kolaphizo." It means,

> "Buffet" =
> "to strike; to beat"

"to strike with the fist, give one a blow with the fist," or "to maltreat, treat with violence and contumely"[9] According to the dictionary, "contumely" means "insulting speech or behavior" or "contemptuous or humiliating treatment." [10] In other words, by definition, to get "buffeted" is to get beaten in contempt and persecution! This word occurs only 4 other times in the New Testament (Matthew 26:67-68; Mark 14:65; 1 Corinthians 4:11; 1 Peter 2:20). In *every* case this word is used, it clearly means to be (externally) beaten, specifically in persecution for preaching the gospel and living as Christ—and has absolutely *zero* to do with sickness.

- #### The Power of Christ Rested on Paul

Paul said that in his "weakness," the power of Christ would rest upon him (v.9). If someone takes Paul to mean "sickness," then I must ask the obvious question, "What *always* (without exception) happens in the Scripture when the power of Christ rests upon one who was *sick?*" They were healed! Proof text? Matthew, Mark, Luke and John—for starters! Yet another reason that we know Paul's thorn wasn't sickness!

> What *always* happens in Scripture when the power of Christ rests upon one who is sick?

- #### The "Thorn" was "For Christ's Sake."

Let's also notice another very important point here: Paul says that these "infirmities" in which God's strength is made perfect and put on display, must be "for Christ's sake." Again, this is the

Greek word "astheneia," most often translated as "weakness." We know it can't be translated as "sickness" here either; because if it was to be translated as "sickness," then the context would also demand that we ask: If someone is *sick*, is it "for Christ's sake"?

How can *sickness* be for Christ's sake, when He paid a very specific price to deliver us from it? "Jesus, I know you already paid for this sickness; but I just love you so much that I'm going to ignore that you already paid for it and pay for it myself. I'm sick for you, Jesus!" Does that make *any* sense whatsoever in light of our redemption? No! On the other hand, can someone be persecuted, opposed, reproached, or put in distress or need "for Christ's sake"? Obviously, the answer to this is yes. We see this every day, all around the world!

> How can sickness be for Christ's sake, when He paid a very specific price to deliver us from it?

Crushing the "Support" Scriptures:

• Was Paul a Sickly Man?

Now that we've established beyond question that the thorn was persecution and trouble—not sickness—We need to at least briefly address the so-called "support texts" for the theory that Paul's thorn was sickness, lest we be accused of ignoring them. Yes, let's beat this dead horse and remove all doubt!

Some people want so badly for the "thorn" to be sickness. So they reach for random verses in other places, take them out of their context, and try to *force* them to support their theory about 2 Corinthians 12—but the bottom line is: they don't! Nothing about these texts by themselves would lead you to do so. So we'll just take them one by one:

272

[13] You know that because of *physical infirmity* I preached the gospel to you at the first. [14] And my *trial which was in my flesh* you did not despise or reject, but you received me as an angel of God, even as Christ Jesus. [15] What then was the blessing you enjoyed? For I bear you witness that, if possible, you would have plucked out your own eyes and given them to me.

Wow! Look! It says "physical infirmity." Yes, it does; but it still doesn't mean sickness or disease. Look at the Greek, and think "bodily weakness." Paul had just been stoned and left for dead (most scholars believe he was *actually* dead) in Lystra, which is in Galatia (See Acts 15:8, 19-20). The believers gathered around Paul, and he was raised from the dead (or at the *very* least raised from the "almost dead"). In any case, Paul was in rough shape. I'm sure he looked pretty battered for at least those first couple of days he was there preaching. He's saying, "Thanks for getting past the way I looked enough to listen to what I had to say to you."

Not only that; but Paul was apparently *healed* of his injuries. Look at the text: He says that the trial "*was*" (not "is") in his flesh. This means at the time of his writing 2 Corinthians, *he didn't have it any longer*. If Paul was tormented with some lifelong illness (as some say he was), then he couldn't have put that illness in the past tense!

- **Chronic Eye Problems?**

He then commends them for their generosity toward him, "You would have plucked out your eyes and given them to me," he says. Some people take this and twist it to say that Paul must have had some serious eye problem! But listen, if I said, "My friend would have given me his right arm," that doesn't imply that there is a *problem* with *my* right arm. If I say, "He would give me the shirt off his back", that doesn't mean anything is wrong with *my* shirt—it's just an expression describing generosity. Again folks, let's remember that every language has figures of speech, and learn to take them as they're meant. But then they'll turn to Galatians 6 for another random verse to support their theory...

Galatians 6:11
See with what large letters I have written to you with my own hand!

This may be the biggest stretch of all. "See, Paul had to write really big because of his eye problem," they say. No. The Greek word, "pelikos" translated here as "large" can mean either quantity or size. It can even mean "distinguished." [11] And the Greek word, "gramma" translated in the NKJV as "letters" can mean either "letter" as in "A, B, C" or it can mean "letter" as in, "epistle" or "writings," which is actually the more frequent NT translation.[12] The bottom line is that you can't make the case from the Greek one way or the other. So, once again, let's look at the *context* for clarification!

In the context of Galatians 6, Paul is comparing himself to others who don't really care for the Galatians but just want to brag about getting them to be circumcised. It's perfectly logical in this context for him to be saying, "I actually care about you—Look at this 'long letter' I'm writing you! Those other guys don't do this!" But what sense would it make in that context to suddenly say, "I really care about you—Look at my large printing!" Zero! Context prevails again! He's not saying, "Look at the massive "P-A-U-L" I wrote on the page." He's saying "I sure write some long letters." Kind of makes more sense, doesn't it? At least the original King James, and the Darby translations both got the verse right!

Galatians 6:11 (Darby)
See how long a letter I have written to you with my own hand.

• Boasting in Sickness?

Did Paul have any kind of "infirmity?" Yes. We've already proven that, in this context, the better translation of astheneia in all of these cases concerning Paul is "weakness." As evidence, try this:

274

If you plug "sickness" into those verses instead of "weakness," you can see that it is obviously *not correct*. For example, Paul's "infirmity" was something he liked to "boast" in.

2 Corinthians 11:30
If I must boast, I will boast in the things which concern my infirmity.

2 Corinthains 12:5b
...I will not boast, except in my infirmities.

Would it make any sense whatsoever for Paul to *boast* about a disease? "Look at me, I'm sick!" No. However, does it make sense for him to boast about his "weakness" (persecution, the resulting trouble, and the *humility* that Paul came in)? Yes. According to him in this very context and many others, these persecutions, beatings, *and* his humility (the "weakness" of not exalting himself or demanding money or special treatment) were the credentials that most clearly proved his apostleship to the Corinthian Believers. Please see also 2 Corinthians 1:12-14; 11:16-33; 12:1-6, 11-15 for further confirmation. Note also that these references are surrounding the whole "thorn in the flesh" passage! Ah, you've gotta love it: *context, context, context*!

> Would it make any sense whatsoever for Paul to *boast* about a disease?

Was Paul a sickly man? Heck no! Read 2 Corinthians 11:23-28 again. Read the book of Acts. Could Paul have done all this crazy travelling all over the known world in a state of unrelenting illness? Could he have endured the nakedness, fastings, deprivation, shipwrecks and being lost at sea while suffering some chronic disease? Could he have endured the beatings, stonings, whippings and persecutions if he had some incessant, nagging sickness? Let's not be ridiculous. Listen, if we are in some physical condition that prevents us from living as Paul lived, then what we have is *not* Paul's thorn in the flesh. Every time Paul listed the constant challenges he faced as a Believer, sickness was nowhere to be found.

Paul also "finished his course" (2 Timothy 4:7)! He accomplished his mission, and when he was done, he decided when he would go. If sickness, disease or injury is snatching your life away, sapping your strength and vision, and keeping you from what you've been called to do—then what you have is *not* Paul's thorn! Listen folks, Paul received healing for himself, and ministered healing to others as a part of our New Covenant inheritance in Christ! Paul knew that God's will is always healing.

Through this chapter, we have let Paul himself define what the "thorn in the flesh" is—"reproaches... needs... persecutions... distresses..." We also looked at how the Hebrew Old Testament defines this common figure of speech. Additionally, we've looked at the specific context, comparing "sickness" with "persecution" in each case—slaughtering the idea that the thorn could ever be sickness. Multiple church fathers agree. We have also used logical questions and Church history to confirm this interpretation. We have clarified the random texts used as support for the "sickness" theory, and utterly beat the dead horse. All of this evidence conclusively proves that PAUL'S THORN WAS NOT SICKNESS. So let's stop leaning on this as a reason to either stay sick, or to avoid ministering to the sick in Jesus' Name!

A Testimony

I saw this simple truth (that Paul's thorn was not sickness) get someone healed once. While in Ministry School, I was out ministering with a fellow student named Carmen. The Lord supernaturally directed us to a man walking with a cane and a severe limp through the mall food court—His name was Brett. After introducing ourselves and chatting, he told us that he is a Bible teacher. He had injured his back by falling from a truck 6 years prior. He then had a botched surgery that ruined nerve function down his left leg, which made it so he had little or no feeling in the leg, and very little control of movement. We asked him to demonstrate, and he couldn't even lift his knee an inch while standing there, leaning on his cane. He also had severe back pain that had resulted from the injury and the surgery.

We asked him if we could pray for him, and he asked, "What if this is like my 'thorn in the flesh'?" He said that his pastor had originally given him this idea. Lord, help us! Anyway, he received what we said about every instance of the "thorn in the side" in the Bible having NOTHING to do with sickness. I asked Him if he remembered that 2 Corinthians 12 also said that the thorn was a "messenger of Satan", and he said he did. I then asked, "Well, if the thorn is a messenger of Satan, why would you want one of those?" He agreed that if it was a "messenger of Satan", that he probably didn't want it, so he was open to prayer.

He jumped at least twice during the prayer like electricity was hitting him, saying, "Wow... I've never felt this before," and, "I feel tingling in my leg and foot." After praying, he said that all of the pain left his back; but he still couldn't move his leg even one inch. So we prayed for new nerve cells to be created and he immediately began moving his leg and he was shocked! Long story short—after just a few moments of prayer, he walked away without needing his cane! Thank the Lord!! The knowledge of truth will set us free! God's will is *always* healing!

Notes:

CHAPTER 14

WHAT ABOUT JOB?

One of the first things people sometimes say when I say, "God's will is always healing" is, "What about Job? Maybe I'm another Job, and God has sent me this time of suffering." They think that God brought sickness and all of those calamities on Job, because that's what someone told them. It's difficult to pursue healing when we think that God might have sent the sickness! So in this chapter, we'll look at the Scriptures to see what actually happened. But first, we need to recognize some very important, larger issues when looking at Job's situation.

Job was not a New Covenant Believer

The first and most important point to recognize is that Job was not a New Covenant Believer, and we are. This places us in two *entirely different* categories—two different worlds, really. New Testament Believers have authority, promises and benefits provided to us through the work of Jesus, that Job did not have.

Job is the oldest book of the Bible. As such, Job's life was likely before the Old (Mosaic) Covenant—and probably even before the Abrahamic Covenant. Either of those covenants pale in comparison to the New Covenant; but Job's situation may have been even *more* bleak.

> New Testament Believers have authority, promises and benefits that Job did not have.

Best-case scenario, Job was under the Old Covenant. Our Covenant with God is immeasurably better than the Old was. That is why God created a New one. If the Old one did the job, the New one wouldn't have been necessary. Hello? We covered some of these major differences in Chapter 12. Now let's get back to Job.

A Strange Introduction

I think it would be helpful to read the whole first chapter, because it contains some valuable insights that are often overlooked. I will include some brief comments along the way:

Job 1:1-3
[1] There was a man in the land of Uz, whose name *was* Job; and that man was blameless and upright, and one who feared God and shunned evil. [2] And seven sons and three daughters were born to him. [3] Also, his possessions were seven thousand sheep, three thousand camels, five hundred yoke of oxen, five hundred female donkeys, and a very large household, so that this man was the greatest of all the people of the East.

This is our introduction to the man Job. It tells us basically that Job was a good and righteous man, and he was rich and influential. The introduction continues:

Job 1:4-5
[4] And his sons would go and feast in their houses, each on his appointed day, and would send and invite their three sisters to eat and drink with them. [5] So it was, when the days of feasting had run their course, that Job would send and sanctify them, and he would rise early in the morning and offer burnt offerings according to the number of them all. For Job said, "It may be that my sons have sinned and cursed God in their hearts." Thus Job did regularly.

Now this tells us about his sons, and who makes dinner on what day, and about Job making daily offerings for them in case they sinned. This is a *very* strange bunch of details to include when introducing a person, don't you think? I believe that the oddity of including verses 4-5 in our introduction to Job is meant to call our attention to this section, and gives it a degree of importance that we need to recognize. There is a key here that I believe helps us to understand all that happened to Job.

God Protected Job and All He Had

In verses 6-12, we have a very important chunk of the story. This is the section that causes most of the misunderstanding regarding Job. Many people read this and come to the conclusion that God gives Satan permission to harm Job. That is not the case. First, let's look at verses 6-10:

Job 1:6-10
[6] Now there was a day when the sons of God came to present themselves before the LORD, and Satan also came among them. [7] And the LORD said to Satan, "From where do you come?"
So Satan answered the LORD and said, "From going to and fro on the earth, and from walking back and forth on it."
[8] Then the LORD said to Satan, "Have you considered My servant Job, that there is none like him on the earth, a blameless and upright man, one who fears God and shuns evil?"
[9] So Satan answered the LORD and said, "Does Job fear God for nothing? [10] Have You not made a hedge around him, around his household, and around all that he has on every side? You have blessed the work of his hands, and his possessions have increased in the land.

First, some people think that this is God setting Job up for failure, calling the devil's attention to Job and bragging on how awesome he is. I realize that this way of phrasing verse 8 can sound that way, so let's look at the literal Hebrew for what God actually said here:

> God protected Job!
> God is in the protection business, not the calamity business!

Job 1:8 (Young's Literal Translation)
And Jehovah saith unto the Adversary, "Hast thou set thy heart against My servant Job because there is none like him in the land, a man perfect and upright, fearing God, and turning aside from evil?"

Sounds a little different that way, doesn't it? Sounds more like "Do you have it in mind to hurt Job? He's one of my faves, so tread lightly, boy!" Then Satan says, "Of course he's one of your faves—You protect him and everything he's got, and you bless him on top of it." Satan admits that God placed a hedge of protection around Job's life that he hadn't been able to penetrate. Hello? God protected Job! God is in the protection business, not the calamity business. Now here's an important thing to recognize: During Job's lifetime, Satan was the one currently holding the authority on the Earth. God had no covenant with Job, and no real relational invitation from Job to justify the level of protection God had been providing. God just loved Job and protected him the best He legally could at the time.

"Behold" Means "Look"

Job 1:11-12
[11] But now, stretch out Your hand and touch all that he has, and he will surely curse You to Your face!" [12] And the LORD said to Satan, "Behold, all that he has is in your power; only do not lay a hand on his person." So Satan went out from the presence of the LORD.

This is the big problem right here. People think that God took the hedge down so Satan could get to him. Let's read again what God actually said: "*Behold*, all that he has is in your power." "Behold" just means "Look!" God just said, "Look! The hedge is down, dummy." The Bible just says that God made an observation, not that He took the hedge down. So if God didn't take it down, how did it get down? We'll explore that shortly.

> God just made an observation, He didn't take the hedge down.

Also note in verse 12 that God observes that "all (Job) has is in (Satan's) power. As New Covenant Believers, this is not the case for us. As a matter of fact, quite the contrary—Satan is in *our* power. We covered this in depth in the earlier chapters. Remember, the New Covenant is a whole new ballgame!

God Restrained Satan's Destructive Activity

An important thing to notice in these verses is that God actually placed a limit on Satan's destruction! God commanded Satan not to touch Job's person. God *generally* (perhaps always) only interacts in human affairs at their invitation, because He handed

282

authority over the earth to us in Genesis 1. This touches on issues of human authority and God's sovereignty, which we cover in greater depth in those chapters.

The key is that *somehow*—even without covenant as a "legal" basis, God was able to put this restraint on Satan's activity. This could have been in response to Job's faith, or someone else's. Perhaps Job had a promise from God that promised him a certain number of years. Perhaps Job had faith enough to believe for God to save his life, and that was all. Perhaps one of Job's family members or friends prayed that Job's life would be protected from harm. We don't know how God was able to limit Satan in this particular case. But in these verses we actually see God *protecting* Job, *not* giving Satan permission to *harm* him.

Back to the story. In verses 13-19, we see raiders and wind kill all of Job's ten children and many of his servants, and take away his belongings. Then we see Job's response:

Job 1:20-22
[20] Then Job arose, tore his robe, and shaved his head; and he fell to the ground and worshiped. [21] And he said: " Naked I came from my mother's womb, And naked shall I return there. The LORD gave, and the LORD has taken away; Blessed be the name of the LORD." [22] In all this Job did not sin nor charge God with wrong.

We see Job give this opinion again in Job 2:10, where he says to his wife, "Shall we indeed accept good from God, and shall we not accept adversity?" This is also a part of the cause of misunderstanding regarding Job. Job says that, "the LORD has taken away," and "this adversity comes from God," so people today read that and think that must be the truth.

People think that Job's statement must be true. But here's the thing—it is accurately *recorded* that Job made that statement; but *the statement itself* is not true!

The Scriptures *are* Inspired of God—
But are there Lies in the Bible?

There are many untrue statements, lies and inaccurate opinions that are faithfully and accurately *recorded* in the Bible. Did Job lie? Not willingly. The Bible says He did not sin in what he said (Job 1:22), and lying willingly would be sinning. But by "lie" I also mean "genuine, albeit mistaken opinions." These opinions originate from LIES of the enemy, brought to accuse God's character and nature. Even righteous people can believe lies, and re-tell them, with the best and most honest of intentions. Such is the case with Job; because an action must be intentional

Job was righteous, but wrong.

to be a sin (James 4:17). So Job was righteous, but wrong!

There are both unintentional lies (mistaken opinions) and intentional lies (sin) included in the Scriptures. Here are just a couple of examples:

- Sarah lied and said, "I did not laugh," when she did (Genesis 18:15).
- Abraham (the father of the faith) lied about his wife Sarah saying, "She is my sister" (Genesis 20:2).
- Ananias and Sapphira lied about the price of some property (Acts 5).
- People said that Jesus was a drunken glutton, had a demon, and worked miracles by demonic power (Luke 7:34, John 8:48, Mark 3:22 and Luke 11:15).
- Job's three "friends" –They say all kinds of inaccurate things about both Job and God throughout the book; and at the end, God says, "You guys don't know what you're talking about!"
- Many more...

However, if we had read any one of these statements and assumed it was a true statement since it's recorded in the Bible—We would end up with some wrong ideas! That is what people do with Job's mistaken opinion that "the Lord has taken away." That is not true! We saw very clearly in the Scriptures that it was *Satan* who took away, *not* God. We can't take Job's under-informed opinion, and expect that it will give us an accurate understanding of God.

> We can't take Job's under-informed opinion, and expect that it will give us an accurate understanding of God.

Let's put his opinion in contrast with a plain statement from the New Testament Epistles that tells us directly about God's character:

- Job says, "The Lord gave, and the Lord has taken away."
- James 1:17 says "Every good gift and every perfect gift is from above, and comes down from the Father of lights, with whom there is no variation or shadow of turning."

So, two conflicting statements are accurately (inerrantly) recorded; but which one is the TRUTH? If you said James 1:17, you are right. God gives good and perfect gifts, and He doesn't ever do anything even a shade different from that. Period. And *that* is the New Testament reality that we live under, thank God!

> Two conflicting statements are accurately (inerrantly) recorded; but which one is the TRUTH?

Job's Opinion was Well-Intentioned; but Wrong

We can see clearly that Job was giving his honest-but-incorrect opinion. He was not intentionally lying, and therefore was not sinning, even though his statement was incorrect. He was, however, ignorantly repeating a lie from the devil.

How can I say so surely that Job's opinion was wrong? Because the book of Job testifies to it—by God, by Elihu, and by Job himself!

Job 38:1-2 (God speaking)
Then the LORD spoke to Job out of the storm. He said: "Who is this that *obscures my plans with words without knowledge?*"

God essentially said, "You're painting a cloudy picture of my will with your ignorant statements!" Let's hear one of Job's friends:

Job 35:13-16 (Elihu speaking)
"Surely God will not listen to *empty talk,* Nor will the Almighty regard it. Although you say you do not see Him, Yet justice is before Him, and you must wait for Him. And now, because *He has not punished in His anger,* Nor *taken much notice of folly,* Therefore Job *opens his mouth in vain; He multiplies words without knowledge.*"

Elihu (the only one of Job's "friends" that God never corrected!) says that Job has spoken "without knowledge," with "empty talk," "in vain," and in "folly (foolishness)"—and he was right!!!

Job 42:3 (Job speaking)
"*I have uttered what I did not understand,* Things too wonderful for me, *which I did not know.*"

In other words, Job says, "You're right, God—I didn't know what I was talking about!" Everyone in the story agrees that Job said things that were empty, vain, foolish, without knowledge, and just plain wrong! His words were inerrantly recorded in the Bible, but they were ignorant and incorrect nonetheless!

Round Two

Let's continue with Job's story. In Chapter 2, we see Satan coming to talk to the Lord:

Job 2:1-7

[1] Again there was a day when the sons of God came to present themselves before the LORD, and Satan came also among them to present himself before the LORD. [2] And the LORD said to Satan, "From where do you come?" Satan answered the LORD and said, "From going to and fro on the earth, and from walking back and forth on it." [3] Then the LORD said to Satan, "Have you considered My servant Job, that *there is* none like him on the earth, a blameless and upright man, one who fears God and shuns evil? And still he holds fast to his integrity, although you incited Me against him, to destroy him without cause." [4] So Satan answered the LORD and said, "Skin for skin! Yes, all that a man has he will give for his life. [5] But stretch out Your hand now, and touch his bone and his flesh, and he will surely curse You to Your face!" [6] And the LORD said to Satan, "Behold, he *is* in your hand, but spare his life." [7] So Satan went out from the presence of the LORD, and struck Job with painful boils from the sole of his foot to the crown of his head.

God says, "Haha. Even though you 'incited' (urged, encouraged, tried to get) Me to destroy Job without a cause, he is still righteous." Satan says, "Come on, do it! Hurt him and he won't love you anymore." But God says, "Look dummy! He's in *your* hand... but don't you dare kill him." God simply makes the *observation* that Job's hedge is down—and therefore he's within Satan's reach—and again, somehow manages to place a limit on the damage Satan can do. Note especially verse 7 that—again—tells us plainly that it was *Satan* that struck Job, *not* God.

Even in the Old Covenant, the people had very little revelation about Satan. That revelation didn't come until much later, in the New Covenant. Job was even more unknowledgeable than that! Because of their ignorance of Satan during this time, virtually every event was seen as coming from God; and He got a lot of blame for things He didn't do. We see this again at the end of Job. After God restores Job, and doubles all that he lost, we see some ignorant folks who still don't know God:

Job 42:11

Then all his brothers, all his sisters, and all those who had been his acquaintances before, came to him and ate food with him in his house; and *they consoled him and comforted him for all the adversity that the LORD had brought upon him.* Each one gave him a piece of silver and each a ring of gold.

These folks came to Job and said, "Man, it's terrible that God did all this to you. Here's some money."

> It's such a shame that several thousand years later... People still haven't learned that it wasn't God Who was responsible for Job's calamities!

All of these incidents of people talking about God in the book of Job fall under the "sadly mistaken opinions" category. It's such a shame that several thousand years later—Even after Jesus, the Cross, the Resurrection, and the New Covenant—People still haven't learned that it wasn't God who was responsible for these events!!!

If God didn't do it, then how did the Hedge get down?

If God didn't take the "hedge of protection" down, then what happened to it? Where did it go? Job himself answers this question for us in Chapter 3:

Job 3:25
"For the thing I greatly feared has come upon me, and what I dreaded has happened to me."

Job opened the door to Satan through *fear*. What does that mean? How does that work? Faith and fear are opposite forces that work in the same way. People have authority in the earth (Genesis 1:26). Through faith, we can open the door for God to break in and do something good. In the same way, through fear, we can open the door for Satan to come in and do something bad. Faith and fear *both* grab a hold of things in the supernatural, invisible realm, and drag them into this physical, visible realm.

Job had been righteous for years. His faith in God had allowed God to build a hedge of protection around him (Job 1:10). If nothing else, Job sowed good seed and reaped a good harvest. However, as his kids got older, Job got into fear about them sinning. His fear tore down the hedge!

Job didn't just say he "feared" that this would happen, he said he "*greatly* feared" it (Job 3:25). To get up every day and give offerings to God, just in case your kids sinned? To specifically have a fear that raiders and storms are going to come and kill your family? Those are examples of *extreme* fear, friends!

Job opened the door to Satan through fear.

Remember at the beginning of this chapter, when we talked about the unusual introduction we are given to Job's life in Job 1:4-5? "Job was righteous, rich and influential. His sons had a dinner-making schedule, and Job made offerings for them every day because he feared they would get into sin." You must admit that this is a weird introduction. Again, I don't think it's any accident that this information is given to us in a seemingly awkward spot, right in the introduction to the man Job. God is getting our attention because this information is key to understanding the whole book.

The devil was used to seeing Job with the hedge up, so he couldn't do anything to harm him. Job's fear dismantled the hedge. Job used his authority to invite Satan's will into his world. He did it innocently and ignorantly; but "My people are destroyed for a lack of knowledge!"

So am I blaming Job? NO. I blame the devil! While Job had a measure of responsibility to watch over his life and stay in faith towards God—He only had so much information. He didn't have the Holy Spirit. He didn't have the anointing, or the blood, or the Name of Jesus. He most likely had zero covenant with God; and had no precedent for believing God for protection. Plus, the devil

289

is a deceiver. Job probably didn't know what he was doing by getting into fear. In his ignorance, the devil gained access to wreak havoc in his life. Again, Job also didn't have full authority restored to him as we do.

So, since we do have all of those advantages, would I blame someone *today* who is experiencing sickness, and say to them (like Job's friends did): "Well, you must have sinned or done something wrong to deserve this situation!" NO! Why not? Again, the devil is the culprit and he gets all the blame! There are forces arrayed against us, and sometimes we get attacked. Even with knowledge of God's will, sometimes we look at the "seen" instead of the "unseen" and get into worry and fear. Can fear make the devil's job easier? Sure; but God isn't into the condemnation blame game. He wants us healed and well and blessed, regardless of how we got where we are!

Happily Ever After

One of the most important things we should remember about Job's story is that it has a happy ending! Whatever we do, we mustn't forget this!

Job 42: 10 (AMP)
And the Lord turned the captivity of Job and restored his fortunes, when he prayed for his friends; also the Lord gave Job twice as much as he had before.

Job ended up with twice as much as he had started with! And here's another thought about the start of this verse: If God "turned the *captivity* of Job"—who was the *captor*? God, or the devil? If God was turning the captivity of someone that He Himself was responsible for capturing (through giving permission to the devil), what kind of sense would that make?

> If God "turned the captivity of Job"—Who was Job's captor? God or the devil?

Job 42:12-17 (AMP)
And the Lord blessed the latter days of Job more than his beginning... After this, Job lived 140 years, and saw his sons and his sons' sons, even to four generations. So Job died, an old man and full of days.

Just to play devil's advocate—One last challenge to those who want to identify with Job in his suffering: Have you experienced the same outcome that Job did? Job's whole ordeal—terrible as it was—*lasted less than a year*! At the end of it, God began restoring what the devil had stolen, and Job ended up with double.

Has your ordeal lasted longer than Job's few months? Has your captivity been turned? Have you received your double blessing yet? If you want to use Job as your pattern, then don't just settle with the mess—Trust God that you will end up with twice more than what has been taken away; because God is no respecter of persons! Even Job got his "happily ever after"— Receive yours!

Better still, *forget* using Job as a pattern, look at *Jesus* as our New Covenant example instead. Remember that we are one with Him, receive all things that pertain to life and godliness, and believe God for the already-accomplished victory over every attack of the devil!

> Even Job got his "happily ever after"— Receive yours!!

Keep the Big Picture in Mind

We can easily see how someone could read Job on the surface, and come up with the traditional interpretation—"God allowed Satan to ruin Job's life for a while to see if he *really* loved God." (Although I personally must admit that—even reading on a surface level—I wouldn't be comfortable seeing God as being that insecure and cruel.) However, after reading this chapter, I also hope it's reasonable to see that there is another, perfectly reasonable way to look at it when examining the text.

291

If you're not convinced by the point-by-point, verse-by-verse explanations of Job itself, it's OK. BUT remember the big picture. Remember the pillars of truth we established in the first half of this book. If you aren't convinced by the explication of an individual "question text" (like Job, for instance)—a chapter here, a verse there... The knockout punches are really in the major, clearer, central, major, unavoidable, undeniable Biblical truths. With these as our framework for Biblical interpretation, this (or some similar) interpretation of Job fits in without contradicting the consistent character and ways of God.

To maintain the "God willed/allowed Satan to Destroy Job's Life" interpretation, you have to ignore the following:

- God's nature, as clearly displayed in Jesus' life and ministry
- The fact that the devil had control of the earth at Job's time and could "legally" get away with a lot
- God's creation before the Fall had no sickness, Heaven has no sickness, and God's clearly expressed will is that we don't have it here on earth.
- God—through the Redemption accomplished by Jesus—redeemed us from sickness. This demonstrates that sickness is a curse and is not something God approves of.
- Even in the Old Covenant, God is called Jehovah Rapha "the Lord who heals," (Exodus 15:26) not "Jehovah Sicko—the God who makes His kids sick"
- Jesus paid a very specific price for our healing, which is now a done deal (Is.53:5, 1 Pet.2:24).
- In the New Covenant, Jesus is our standard—not Job. Jesus modeled what we should expect to walk in and look like, so Job's life is *not* to be our expectation.

Bible Interpretation Key #1: The Bible Interprets Itself

This is one of the major rules of Hermeneutics (Bible Interpretation): "When taken as a whole, the Bible interprets itself." What this means is that when you read and study the whole Bible, there are certain truths that are central, core, clear, and unarguable. These clear truths will clarify the verses or passages that aren't clear (or that seem to conflict).

There are passages and doctrines that are clear, and others that aren't so clear. There are also individual verses

> When taken as a whole, the Bible interprets itself.

and passages that seem to conflict with others when read on the surface. Folks, God is not inconsistent! So what do we do? If a few verses or passages seem to conflict with the major clear truths, then we are misinterpreting those verses. We've got to look at the bigger picture. We must see those verses in light of the whole counsel of Scripture, not just as an individual verse or passage. The way that cults form is that they take a verse or passage "for what it says" (isolated or out of context), and don't reconcile it with the rest of the Bible. So we don't want to do that, right? When we look at the big picture, one thing becomes clear: God's will is *always* healing!

Notes:

CHAPTER 15

SICKNESS IS NOT OUR TEACHER

Another common objection to the idea that healing is always God's will, is that God might be using the sickness to make a person humble, or Christ-like, or teaching them to slow down. Maybe He wants the person to learn to rely on God or others more, not being so proud and independent. Maybe He's using the sickness to mature their character. The whole idea in a nutshell is that maybe God is using sickness to teach the person.

There are multiple problems with this idea, some of which we will explore in this chapter. Because some people think their sickness might be from God to teach them something, often they won't fight against it at all. Or if they attempt to fight, they only do it half-heartedly, because—After all, if God wants to teach them, why would they want to stop Him? While their heart may be right, their thinking is all twisted up. This thinking holds some Believers back from enjoying the full freedom Jesus has provided for them. It also keeps us from confidently ministering healing to others, setting them free in Jesus' Name. So let's knock these ideas out of our brains with the Word of God...

Chastening is Not Child Abuse

Let's say you had a coworker that told you his 7-year old son had been acting up over the weekend. He says, "Yeah, that boy was just being rebellious, talking back and such. I decided I'd teach him a lesson, so I stuck him with a syringe full of the AIDS virus. Then I broke his legs." What would you do? Would you say, "Good job! That'll teach him?" No way! You'd be on the phone to the police, and you'd report that man for child abuse! Hello? There's not a country in the world that would say this was an acceptable method of training one's children.

And yet, some of God's kids think that He would treat *us* that way? How is it that we'd be righteously angry with a *person* that did this to their child, yet we'd call *God* wise and benevolent for doing the same exact thing? Nonsense! God is more loving, gentle and kind than you or I or any human parent could ever hope to be. So the idea that He would ever do anything like that is perverted and twisted. Plus, you'd be calling yourself a better parent than God is! That is pride, and this is a doctrine of devils!

> God is more loving, gentle and kind than you, or I, or any human parent could ever hope to be.

Now let's take a look at the Bible passage that deals specifically with the idea of God training and correcting, or "chastening," His children:

Hebrews 12:5-11

[5] And you have forgotten the exhortation which speaks to you as to sons: "My son, do not despise the chastening of the LORD, nor be discouraged when you are rebuked by Him; [6] For whom the LORD loves He chastens, And scourges every son whom He receives." [7] If you endure chastening, God deals with you as with sons; for what son is there whom a father does not chasten? [8] But if you are without chastening, of which all have become partakers, then you are illegitimate and not sons. [9] Furthermore, we have had human fathers who corrected us, and we paid them respect. Shall we not much more readily be in subjection to the Father of spirits and live? [10] For they indeed for a few days chastened us as seemed best to them, but He for our profit, that we may be partakers of His holiness. [11] Now no chastening seems to be joyful for the present, but painful; nevertheless, afterward it yields the peaceable fruit of righteousness to those who have been trained by it.

In this passage from Hebrews, we see that "chastening" is the loving correction of a Father toward His children. It does say that it's like being "scourged," and is "painful;" but makes no mention of serious injury, sickness, or disease. In fact, if we try to inject this idea into the story, it becomes clear that sickness cannot be included in the Biblical definition of "chastening," or this whole passage falls apart.

Chastening is for Sons, and it Profits Us.

Let's look again at the passage. It says that God chastens and corrects only those that are His "sons" (v.6). It says that every "son" gets chastened (v.7). Then it says that those that are "not sons" are not chastened (v.8). Now, here's a key: If sickness were the chastening of the Lord, then unbelievers (those that are "not sons") would never get sick, because those who are not sons are "without chastening."

Next, it says that God's chastening is "for our profit" (v.10). The discipline and correction of the Lord profits us. According to these verses, the profit is that it makes us "partakers of His holiness," and yields "the peaceable fruit of righteousness." In other words, we become more holy, and enjoy more of the benefits of right relationship with God when He corrects us. Again, this idea breaks down if we include sickness in the definition of chastening. If sickness were the chastening this passage is talking about, then everyone that gets sick and diseased would become more holy, and enjoy more of the benefits of right relationship with God during/after being sick. Ridiculous!

> Sickness and disease are not included in the Biblical understanding of the "chastening of the Lord."

It should be painfully obvious (no pun intended) by now that sickness and disease are not included in the Biblical understanding of the "chastening of the Lord." So what is, then? How is "chastening" defined?

Defining "Chastening"

Sometimes when we discuss the idea that God is not currently pouring out judgment on people, and does not use sickness and disease to correct, teach, or develop us, some ask, "What about the 'chastening' or 'discipline' of the Lord?" So let's define

297

"chastening," the way the Bible does. The Greek word, "paideia," which is translated as "chastening", means:

1) "the whole training and education of children..."
2) "whatever in adults also cultivates the soul, esp. by correcting mistakes and curbing passions..."[1]

The only other times the word is used outside the passage in Hebrews 12, it is translated as "nurture" (Ephesians 6:4), and "instruction" (2 Timothy 3:16). So the Greek word paideia, then, means "training... education... cultivation... correcting... curbing... " and "nurture... instruction"—as would apply to children. Please note that "violence," "cruelty," and "torture" were not found in the definition. We can't include sickness into the definition of chastening without ultimately accusing God of child abuse... So if sickness isn't the tool God uses to teach, cultivate, correct, nurture, and instruct us, then who or what is? How has He told us He will do these things?

> We can't include sickness into the definition of chastening, without ultimately accusing God of child abuse.

Who is Our Teacher?

The Bible tells us very clearly that *the Holy Spirit is our Teacher*—not sickness, disease or disaster. Do you think that God agrees when we say that sickness does a better job than the Holy Spirit does? No, He is the best Teacher there is! So when God has something He wants to teach us, He tells the Holy Spirit about it, and He teaches it to us.

John 16:13
However, when He, the Spirit of truth, has come, He will guide you into all truth; for He will not speak on His own authority, but whatever He hears He will speak; and He will tell you things to come.

Remember, a *huge* difference between the Old Testament and the New Testament is that now God lives *inside* the Believer! He doesn't have to bring all kinds of situations and tribulations and

298

external circumstances to try to get a message through our thick heads. He doesn't have to bring sickness or pain to our bodies. God doesn't have to get through to us from the outside! He has moved right into our hearts, become one spirit with us (1 Corinthians 6:19), gave us the mind of Christ (1 Corinthians 2:16), and now He just gives us reminders, bears witness with our hearts, and communicates with our inner man!

John 14:26
But the Helper, the Holy Spirit, whom the Father will send in My name, He will teach you all things, and *bring to your remembrance all things that I said to you.*

Romans 8:16
The Spirit Himself *bears witness with our spirit* that we are children of God,

Some will admit that maybe sickness is not sent to "teach" us; but then say that maybe God ordained it to "mature and perfect" us—to develop our character. Garbage! Sickness was not sent to perfect us, *Jesus* was—and He did it by reconciling us to God through His finished works!

> God doesn't have to get through to us from the outside! He has moved right into our hearts.

Hebrews 10:14
For *by one offering He has perfected* forever those who are being sanctified.

Hebrews 13:20-21
[20] Now *may* the *God* of peace ... *make you complete* in every good work to do His will, working in you what is well pleasing in His sight, *through Jesus Christ...*

Disease is not the developer of our faith. Jesus is! He requires no assistance from the works of the devil! God perfects us through Him. When I believe God enough to obey Him, my faith automatically grows and becomes effective.

Hebrews 12:2a
looking unto Jesus, the Author and Finisher of our faith...

Jesus created faith, gave it to us, and He alone perfects it. You might say, "Yes, but in order for faith to grow, we must have a challenge to face." True, but even if it is sickness that fills the role of "challenge," it is still the Holy Spirit that teaches us, never the sickness.

Disease may be a circumstance in which we find ourselves. We may need to exercise our faith to overcome the disease, and consequently our faith grows stronger through the victory. But *God* is the one to be credited for teaching us, and for giving us the tools to overcome. The *devil* is responsible for the sickness.

That would be like me, as a former soldier in the U.S. Army saying, "Man, that enemy army sure taught me how to use my M-16." No, the U.S. Army was my teacher. They trained me, and they gave me the tools. War with the enemy is just an opportunity to use what I have been taught. And the Army didn't need to go start a war to teach me. They just say, "Here's your weapon," then they teach you how to fire it on a practice range. They know that war will come on its own without them needing to start one. War is hell; it's not my teacher. I'm sure glad the Army prepared me for it and gave me the tools necessary to overcome and be victorious. God trains us and gives us weapons for a war that's already in progress! Let him who has ears, hear.

> God does not create the problems He wants to solve.

God does not create the problems He wants to solve. He does not create the challenges He equips us to conquer. In other words, God does not make someone sick, and simultaneously hand us the name of Jesus, faith in His name, the indwelling presence of the Holy Spirit, the anointing, the gifts of the Spirit, Kingdom authority, and a command to "heal the sick"... just so we can go conquer a problem that He Himself created.. Ridiculous!!

How Does God Teach, Correct and Develop Us?

God does not send or allow physical pain, sickness and disease to develop our faith, or to conform us to the image of Christ, He uses His Word! Remember when we looked up the Greek word for "chastening;" and one of the two times it was used outside of Hebrews 12, it was translated as "instruction?" That occasion shows us clearly that God teaches, corrects and develops us with His Word:

2 Timothy 3:16-17
[16] All Scripture is given by inspiration of God, and is profitable for doctrine, for reproof, for correction, for *instruction* in righteousness, [17] that the man of God may be complete, thoroughly equipped for every good work.

God uses His Word—not sickness—to teach us, chastise us, correct us, and instruct us about right relationship with Him. Sickness doesn't help us become more holy. The Holy Spirit uses the scrub brush of the Word of God to wash off all the junk the world piles on top of our new, Christ-like nature.

> God uses His Word —*not* sickness— to teach us, chastise us, correct us, and instruct us about right relationship with Him.

John 15:3
You are already clean because of the word which I have spoken to you.

Ephesians 5:25-27
[25] Husbands, love your wives, just as Christ also loved the church and gave Himself for her, [26] that He might sanctify and cleanse her with the washing of water by the word, [27] that He might present her to Himself a glorious church, not having spot or wrinkle or any such thing, but that she should be holy and without blemish.

It's the Word that does this, not sickness! And disease does not help us mature and look more like Jesus. The renewing of our mind by God's Word does:

Romans 12:2

And do not be conformed to this world, but *be transformed by the renewing of your mind*, that you may prove what is that good and acceptable and perfect will of God.

It's the study and meditation of the Word of God, which trains our thinking to line up with the mind of Christ. As our minds are renewed to think like God through the promises in His Word, we understand more of our new nature, and more and more we become partakers of Christ's nature in us.

2 Peter 1:4

by which have been given to us *exceedingly great and precious promises*, that *through these you may be partakers of the divine nature*

Sometimes, God uses other members of the body, leaders in the Church to deliver His Word in such a way that we are trained, developed and further matured into the character of Jesus.

Ephesians 4:11-15

[11] And He Himself gave some to be apostles, some prophets, some evangelists, and some pastors and teachers, [12] for the equipping of the saints for the work of ministry, for the edifying of the body of Christ, [13] till we all come to the unity of the faith and of the knowledge of the Son of God, to a perfect man, to the measure of the stature of the fullness of Christ; [14] that we should no longer be children, tossed to and fro and carried about with every wind of doctrine, by the trickery of men, in the cunning craftiness of deceitful plotting, [15] but, speaking the truth in love, may grow up in all things into Him who is the head—Christ—

> If we want to teach or correct our children, we don't poke their eyes out!

Yes, when God's Word comes to us—whether directly or through His Body, we grow up into Christ! God teaches and matures us with His *Words*! Just like we, as natural humans, teach our children using words. What if they won't listen? If we need to correct them, we may even go so far as to give them a spanking. But we aren't going to do it in a way that it causes any long-term harm or damage,

302

or puts them through some torturous misery. If we want to teach or correct our children, we don't poke their eyes out, or run them over with our car, or inject them with some deadly virus! Again—that's child abuse! God is not a child abuser. No, God is the best Father there is, and He uses words to teach us. We are created in His image, and we as godly, earthly parents also use words. We talk, we share, we communicate.

Can We Learn and Grow by Going Through Challenges?

When we teach our kids with our great words of advice and instruction, sometimes they listen, and sometimes they don't. Either way, occasionally a situation arises that serves as an object lesson that demonstrates more clearly the wisdom of our words. We don't have to create or "set up" the situation—Life just happens, and sometimes there are "teachable moments" that help drive a point home.

If you're still thinking that God sends sickness and disease to teach us, then this part is for you. Understanding this is the key to all the stories you're thinking of about how uncle so-and-so matured, grew up, got more Christ-like, strengthened in faith, or learned patience—through the process of illness, disease or pain.

We've all probably heard someone say, "This sickness has been such a blessing to me, really. I ended up on my back, and had to look up to God. I've grown so much closer to Him now." Or maybe God even took advantage of someone being sick, and they received salvation during that time. "Man, I never gave Jesus the time of day until I got laid up in the hospital. But laying in that hospital, I had time to think hard about my life. I received Jesus, and I probably never would have otherwise."

First of all, sickness is *never* a blessing. Everywhere in the Bible that talks about sickness describes it as a curse! Sickness is a work of the devil with one aim—to kill, steal, and destroy. With that said, it's probably true that getting broken down can cause someone's pride and self-reliance to take a big enough hit that they finally look to God. Or being stuck in a hospital bed can give someone time enough to slow down, think about life, and receive the Lord.

Yes, of course, God in His mercy will take awfully pitiful situations that we or the devil create, and turn them for our good. But guess what? It didn't have to be that way! All we have to do is listen to His words! God doesn't need sickness to get close to us! He doesn't need for someone to get injured to get them saved! As a matter of fact, pain and misery tend to turn people away from God—They wonder, "How can a God of love can 'let' such terrible things go on in the world?" No, the Bible teaches us exactly the opposite:

> Yes, of course, God in His mercy will take awfully pitiful situations that we or the devil create, and turn them for our good.

Romans 2:4
Or do you despise the riches of His goodness, forbearance, and longsuffering, not knowing that the goodness of God leads you to repentance?

It's not "sickness from God" that leads to repentance—it's the "goodness of God" that leads people to repentance. Jesus did all that was necessary for salvation, and then He put it in His Word and sends people to tell all about it. To develop a Christian's character, all He does is take up residence in us and speak His amazing words—which are spirit and life! We just need to choose to listen! Now, will He take some terrible situation as a teachable moment to show the wisdom of His Words? Sure He will, as any good father would!

A Fall or A Push?

I remember when my son was about two or three years old. We'd go shopping at the grocery store and I'd sit him in the child seat area of the shopping cart (this was before they had all those harnesses and seatbelts on there). Occasionally, his male daredevil tendencies would get a hold of him and he'd try to stand up in the top of the cart. I'd sit him back down and say "No, son, you need to sit down. It's very easy to accidentally fall down and hurt yourself. I love you and don't want that to happen, so stay seated on your butt!"

Two minutes later, I'd turn my back to grab something, turn back around, and there he was trying it again. I might even swat his behind now, and say, "Son, I told you to sit down and I meant it. I love you and I don't want you to hurt yourself." One time I went through this, and the next thing I knew I heard a "THUMP," and turned around to see my son on the hard tile floor bursting into tears. He smacked his head a good one and had an instant lump swelling up on his head. Like any loving father I swooped my son up and comforted him in his pain.

A little while later, however, I took advantage of this teachable moment and said, "Son, this is why I kept telling you not to stand up in the cart. I wasn't trying to take away your fun; I was trying to protect you from pain because I love you!" Guess what? I don't remember my son ever standing up in the cart again after that—he learned a great lesson that day. But I didn't need to create the situation; it just came along as a natural matter of course.

But, let's change the story now. Instead of just teaching my son with words in response to him falling on his own—What if I had just decided that I really wanted him to learn this lesson

> Was it a fall, or a push? It makes all the difference in the world!

well, and that I was willing to take it into my own hands to make sure he learned it quickly. So, I *pushed* him out of the cart myself. Then, as he whacks his head on the ground and begins to cry out in pain, I say, "Serves you right, dummy," and leave him there crying. Then once he stops crying, I say, "Told you so, I'll bet you'll listen next time, eh?" What would you think of me?

305

How long would it take you to call the police and report me for child abuse? One minute or two?

Was it a fall or a push? It makes all the difference in the world! If he just fell, then there's still a lesson to learn, but he's responsible for his own failure to listen to my words. On the other hand, if it was a push, then I'm a cruel parent, responsible for abusing my child. One is an accident; one is an intentional act of violence. And yet this is exactly what people are saying God is like when they say that God sends sickness, disease and pain on people to teach them something. Ridiculous! Twisted! God does not create pain, misery and death to teach us. There's enough of that going on in life without His needing to cause, send, or allow it. This takes us once again to Romans:

Romans 8:28
And we know that all things work together for good to those who love God, to those who are the called according to His purpose.

God takes the bad situations we find ourselves in and turns them around when we invite Him to do so. He doesn't create a problem, only to fix it. We must remember the other lessons in this book—fallen man, the curse on the earth from man's sin, things out of whack, not everything is God's will, man's authority, etc. Hahaha! Notice that it's called the "Fall of Man," not the "Push of God!" It's true that God will take a bad situation and turn it around for our good, or help us to see a lesson in challenges. But life is full of teachable moments, without God creating them for us.

Satan: Perfecter of the Church?

Always remember the dividing line of the Bible—elementary Christianity's Lesson number one: "God is *good*—All the time!"

John 10:10
The thief does not come except to steal, and to kill, and to destroy. I have come that they may have life, and that they may have it more abundantly.

God: good. Devil: bad. Elementary, my dear friends. God intends health and blessing for us (3 John 2). Satan, meanwhile, is the author of sickness and disease. Disease is a twisted curse that mankind only experiences as a result of Adam's sin. It didn't exist before that. It wasn't in the garden, and it doesn't exist in Heaven. Sickness is not the will of God—it's the work of the devil! By stating that sickness develops our character, matures us, or perfects us—We are calling Satan the perfecter of the Church! Not only is the very idea absurd in and of itself, as we've discussed elsewhere, giving Satan credit for the work of God is the Biblical definition of blasphemy (Matthew 12:22-32)! Satan doesn't trouble us to develop us into the image of Christ! He brings trouble to steal the Word of God out of our hearts!

Mark 4:14-19

The sower sows the word. [15] And these are the ones by the wayside where the word is sown. When they hear, *Satan comes immediately and takes away the word* that was sown in their hearts. [16] These likewise are the ones sown on stony ground who, when they hear the word, immediately receive it with gladness; [17] and they have no root in themselves, and so endure only for a time. Afterward, *when tribulation or persecution arises for the word's sake, immediately they stumble.* [18] Now these are the ones sown among thorns; they are the ones who hear the word, [19] and *the cares of this world, the deceitfulness of riches, and the desires for other things entering in choke the word, and it becomes unfruitful.*

Tribulation is not our teacher—it is sent by Satan to cause us to stumble! Troubles are designed and used by Satan to steal the Word of God out of

> Troubles are designed and used by Satan to... render us useless in advancing God's Kingdom.

our hearts and render us useless in advancing God's Kingdom. How does he do that? By stirring up a situation that forces us to either believe God's Word or ignore it. Will we listen to God's loving, wise, Fatherly advice and wisdom and act accordingly? If so, it produces fruit. If we ignore our Father's Word and do our own thing (much like my son did), we've rejected the seed that God sowed into us, and if we fall and hurt ourselves, that's nobody's fault but our own.

"But," someone said, "What about 'counting it all joy' when we fall into trials…? Doesn't it say that trials give us patience and faith?" No, not really. Let's look:

James 1:2-5
[2] My brethren, count it all joy when you fall into various trials, [3] knowing that the testing of your faith produces patience. [4] But let patience have its perfect work, that you may be perfect and complete, lacking nothing. [5] If any of you lacks wisdom, let him ask of God, who gives to all liberally and without reproach, and it will be given to him.

It's the "testing of (our) faith" that produces patience. Faith is tested by tough situations. What does a test look like? When God promises something to us, yet something comes our way that looks contrary to His promise. That is a test. A response of faith is believing what God said on the subject, and discounting any other version of the story.

Romans 3:4
"…Let God be true, but every man a liar…"

Simply put, we believe God; and we speak and act accordingly. Once we've acted in faith and drawn a line in the sand, we then apply patience. Patience is simply steady belief and trust—not backing down—until we see the promised results. Then we end up "perfect and complete, lacking nothing"—We get what God promised, and lack no good thing (Psalm 34:10, 84:11).

Hebrews 6:11-12
[11] And we desire that each one of you show the same diligence to the full assurance of hope until the end, [12] that you do not become sluggish, but imitate those who through faith and patience inherit the promises.

Faith + Action = Matured Faith, and…
Matured Faith + Patience = Fulfilled Promises!

As our minds are renewed to the Word of God—and we act on it in faith—then our faith and patience become complete and effective!

James 2:22
Do you see that faith was working together with his works, and *by works faith was made perfect?*

It is quite clear from all of the Scriptures in this chapter that God perfects, matures, grows and develops us through His Word— Written or in Person (Jesus), by the work of the Holy Spirit, as we cooperate with Him through renewing our minds and acting on our faith. Nowhere in the Scriptures is there any indication that God uses sickness to accomplish any of this in our lives. It's through faith we believe God for His promises. Through patience we receive them. Through victory over challenges, our faith is strengthened and we gradually look more on the outside like we do on the inside—like the victorious Christ!

> Through victory over challenges, our faith is strengthened; and we gradually look more on the outside like we do on the inside—like the victorious Christ!

Some Challenges

If you still think that maybe it's God sending sickness and disease to help develop and perfect us as Believers, let's think it through a little:

- If God needed to use sickness to get the attention of an unbeliever to get them saved, then what about all the people that went to hell without this Divine intervention? Wasn't God being a respecter of persons to go through all that effort for one, but not for another? Rubbish!

- If God needs sickness to get people saved, how can we cooperate with God in this method of evangelism? Hold an evangelistic service in which we expose the crowd to the deadly Ebola virus? Great plan! Ridiculous!

- The next time you get sick, do *not* call for the elders to pray for you so you can be healed (in violation of James 5:14-15)! Instead, enjoy your new and exciting season of advanced spiritual growth and development! Hogwash!

- If sickness is the tool He's using to grow your faith and character, then let Him use it for crying out loud! Don't you dare take medicine or go to the doctor! Why would you want to rob yourself of the blessing God is trying to bring you?! You don't want to fight against God, do you?! Absurd!

- If pain and injury helps develop us and make us more like Jesus, how about this: Let's go outside and I'll run you over with my car—I'll only charge you $1,000 for this new "Accelerated Course in Christ-likeness!" Ludicrous!

- If disease makes our faith grow, let's go drink from a filthy river in Africa, get malaria and hang out together in the dirty hospital thanking God for working in our lives! Preposterous!

- Speaking of hospitals, if sickness made us more like Jesus, hospitals would be the greatest revival centers in the world! Look at all the patients simultaneously maturing in faith and becoming more like Jesus! The hospital is absolutely heavenly! Nonsense!

- Who needs church? Who needs Bible schools and seminaries? Let's all get together, shoot up with some dirty needles so we can get AIDS and Hepatitis to do the job we won't trust the Holy Spirit and the Word to do! Poppycock!

Does this all sound utterly insane to you yet? I hope so; because these are actually clear, logical ramifications of believing that God sends sickness, disease, and pain to teach or develop our character and faith. But my guess is that something in you just knows better than this. Somewhere inside, everyone knows that sickness is not right, and it can't be the good will of a good God.

Summary:

God works on us *from the inside out—not from the outside* in (with physical pain); because this is the New Covenant, and He lives inside of us. He's one with us. He loves us. He's not mad at us. He's not judging us. He accepts us, He's cleaned and justified and perfected us. He communicates with us and gently instructs us with His wise words. He's a good father, not a child abuser. If we'll just listen, we can avoid learning things the hard way—in the school of hard knocks!

> Somewhere inside, everyone knows that sickness is wrong, and it can't be the good will of a good God.

Proverbs 1:32-33
[32] For the turning away of the simple will slay them, and the complacency of fools will destroy them; [33] But whoever listens to me will dwell safely, and will be secure, without fear of evil."

Proverbs 13:1
A wise son heeds his father's instruction, but a scoffer does not listen to rebuke.

Some think that God sends sickness, disease and pain to teach us, to correct or discipline us, to develop our faith or patience, or to make us more like Jesus. But, as we've clearly seen in the Scriptures, the Holy Spirit is our Teacher, He uses the Word of God as His teaching tool. The renewing of our mind on His Word causes us to partake of Christ's nature and reflect Him more and more accurately. Actually acting on what we believe is what perfects our patience and completes our faith—bringing God's promised answers and victory over all the works of the enemy. God's will is *always* healing!

Notes:

CHAPTER 16

CRUSHING CESSATIONISM

Introduction

When we read the pages of the Bible, it is jam-packed with stories of prophecies, healings, miracles, signs and wonders. However, when we look at a decent-sized portion of the Church today, there is a glaring lack of these things. Why? How did this happen? Why the disparity between God's activities in the Bible, and what we see in some of today's Church? Did God change? Did He "turn off the miracle faucet" at some point? Did He replace miracles with something else? How did we get here?

Cessationism is the belief that the charismata (the supernatural gifts of the Holy Spirit—things like the gift of prophecy, word of knowledge, gifts of healings, working of miracles, speaking in other tongues, etc) stopped, or "ceased" at some time in the past—typically, either with the passing of the last of the 12 Apostles, or with the closing of the canon of Scripture. Continuationism is the opposite of cessationism, and it says that the gifts "continue," even until today.

> Cessationism is the belief that the supernatural gifts of the Holy Spirit stopped, or "ceased."

Can we fully address the issue of cessationism in a few pages? No way. However, there are a lot of people out there that still cling to this idea (especially in evangelical, North American churches). This belief hinders them from receiving healing for themselves, and from ministering it to others as well. So, I felt it important to at least broach the subject and share enough from the Scripture to show that cessationism isn't Biblical. In the interest of space, we'll have to just touch on a few points and let the chips fall where they may, trusting God to make up the difference.

A Brief History of Cessationism

Early in Christianity, some Christian theologians (Justin, Origen) noted that the Jewish people no longer had miracles and prophecy as they had earlier in their history.[1] Unfortunately, they used this fact to say essentially, "The Jews no longer have miracles. Because we Christians do have them, that must mean that God is giving us His stamp of approval now. Our doctrine is right, and we are now His approved messengers." This idea is called evidentialism, which says that miracles exist *only as evidence*—to prove a message, or to accredit a messenger. In other words, if someone has miracles, it proves they are right. This mistaken understanding of the *purpose of miracles* and the other charismata is the root cause of cessationism. It is a huge error that carries down through history.

> Evidentialism says that miracles exist only to prove a message or to accredit a messenger.

Thomas Aquinas came along in the 13th century, and tried to solidify cessationism in his theology. He perpetuated the idea that the main function of miracles was to be a physical sign or testimony that God is the source of a message being proclaimed. He also said that Jesus and His disciples did enough miracles to prove the truth of Christianity, so after that miracles were not required. However, he also made two important exceptions. First, he said that *we can* still have miracles *if* they confirm the preaching of the Word. Second, he said that believers who were exceptionally holy (whatever *that* means in his view) could still do miracles. [2] Of course, because Aquinas was Catholic, this contributed to the problems of the canonization of saints, and the veneration of shrines and relics. Not to mention that both of his two exceptions totally contradict the idea of hard-line (principled) cessationism.

Another theologian that significantly impacted modern cessationism was John Calvin, from the Protestant Reformation in the 16th century. He developed his cessationist ideas primarily in response to two groups that he personally disagreed with: the Catholic Church, and the more radical arm of the Reformation movement (Anabaptists, etc). Both movements were basically saying, "We have miracles, so we must be right. You have no miracles, so you must be wrong." The problem was, Calvin could see that some of these groups were espousing some ideas that were against Scripture. Calvin also bought the mistaken idea that miracles only exist to accredit doctrine (evidentialism). Based on that foundational misunderstanding, he reasoned (my paraphrase), "Obviously these particular doctrines are wrong, so since true miracles of God only accredit true Scriptural doctrines, then the miracles experienced by these other people must be false miracles." [3] The problem with this is that if you believe in "false miracles," or "lying signs and wonders," then it's obvious that miracles can't be used as proof of anything, which in itself eliminates the validity of evidentialism.

Second, this coin also had a flip side that was necessary for Calvin's own defense. He had to explain why—if miracles confirm correct doctrine—he himself didn't have any miracles. "It is unreasonable to ask miracles–or to find them–where there is no new gospel," [4] he said to this challenge. In other words, he was basically saying, "We don't have miracles to accredit our doctrine; because all correct doctrine was already established early in Church history, and proven by miracles at that time." This echoes Thomas Aquinas. Interestingly, Calvin also echoed Aquinas' exception that miracles may still "revive" under certain conditions, "now and again... as the need of the times demands." [5] Again, allowing for this exception blatantly contradicts his assertion that the gifts had ceased.

> John Calvin had to explain why—if miracles confirm correct doctrine—he himself didn't have any miracles.

Later, during the "Enlightenment" or "Age of Reason" (18th century), many challenged the ideas of miracles having ever happened at all. This "Liberalism" in the Church obviously called into question much of the truth in Scripture. One of the great defenders of fundamental Christianity at the time was B.B. Warfield, a theologian and professor at Princeton's Seminary. He strongly defended the inerrancy of Scripture, and the miracles contained in it. However, he simultaneously denied the validity of miracles in the post-Biblical era. He wrote what is considered by many modern cessationists to be the best expression of cessationism, <u>Counterfeit Miracles</u>.

Warfield took the strongest cessationist position yet, eliminating the allowances made by Calvin and Aquinas—saying that miracles stopped with the death of the last of the 12 apostles, period, no exceptions.[6] He does this because, as he admits openly, once you allow any miracles past the lives of the original 12, you *must* allow the rest of them throughout Christian history—and they only become more abundant and better-evidenced as time goes on.[7]

> Once you allow any miracles past the lives of the original 12, you *must* allow the rest of them throughout Christian history.

Despite the many theological and historical inconsistencies with the arguments of cessationism, these ideas are still taught today in many conservative seminaries. Hence, cessationism has filtered into many evangelical churches—especially in the western world. Interestingly, most of these same denominations (Wesleyan, Methodist, Lutheran, Baptist, etc) *all* came out of revival movements that were full of signs, wonders, and miracles of their own! Over time, they lost sight of their history and settled for "good doctrine"—with little or no demonstration of God's power. As a result, today we have many well-intentioned Believers that go without the full package of supernatural, miraculous benefits that Christ provided for us in our great Salvation.

Does the Bible Say That Miracles Will Cease?

What is the main Scripture that the average cessationist leans on to say that the charismata have "ceased?" Without a doubt, it's 1 Corinthians 13:8.

1 Corinthians 13:8
Love never fails. But whether there are prophecies, they will fail; whether there are tongues, they will cease; whether there is knowledge, it will vanish away.

"See," they say, "it says that prophecies will run out, tongues will cease, and (revelation) knowledge will stop." Yes, they are right. It does say that they *will* all cease... and nobody is arguing that point. But if you read the next few verses, you'll understand the answer to the crucial question: *WHEN?*

1 Corinthians 13:9-12
[9] For we know in part and we prophesy in part. [10] But *when that which is perfect has come*, *then* that which is in part will be done away. [11] When I was a child, I spoke as a child, I understood as a child, I thought as a child; but when I became a man, I put away childish things. [12] For now we see in a mirror, dimly, but *then face to face*. Now I know in part, *but then I shall know just as I also am known*.

The answer seems plain enough in the text: "when that which is perfect has come," "then face to face," and "then I shall know just as I also am known." However, Cessationists generally say that the closed Canon (or the established Church) is "that which is perfect." If Christians no longer needed any guidance or revelation from God for anything in life, I might buy that; but we do! As such, our current level of revelation is incomplete, or "imperfect." But even if we accept that one, what about "face to face?" Face to face with what—the Bible? Face to face with what—the "mature," established Church of the 3rd century? The same Church that most cessationists also accuse of being immature and unreliable—*that* mature Church? Which is it—were they mature or not? Might want to think that one over! No, this

317

is talking about when we are face to face with *Jesus Himself* at His Second Coming (the "Parousia"). It's only *then* that we will know Him just as we are known.

1 John 3:2
Beloved, now we are children of God; and *it has not yet been revealed* what we shall be, but we know that *when He is revealed, we shall be like Him, for we shall see Him as He is.*

It is clear throughout the New Testament that there is a contrast between "now" and "then." Yes, we believe for the "then" to come into our "now" experience—this is the essence of faith, really—believing for the invisible, eternal truths to invade our visible, temporal reality. I believe that God's will is for us to experience all of the "then," right now. Those things are the will of God, that's why things are that way in Heaven—His will is being done there! "Your Kingdom come, Your will be done, on earth as it is in heaven" (Matthew 6:10), is to be our constant declaration, after all. For me, much of our earthly Christian life is about establishing that reality in the middle of this one.

That being said, we have *not yet seen* the full, "perfect" or complete *manifestation* of what we will be at the Parousia. We don't yet consistently walk in full revelation, and we don't fully know Jesus now like we will when we see Him "face to face." So, according to these Scriptures, it is

> It is only at the Parousia that the charismata will cease.

only at the Parousia that the charismata will cease.

In the early Church, this verse was clearly understood. They used it in the exact opposite way that cessationists use it now. There was a group called the Montanists who were moving in the supernatural. As commonly occurs, there were those within the movement that got into extremes and made mistakes, giving the movement a bad name. There was a Montanist woman named Maximilla who incorrectly prophesied, "After me there will be no more prophecy, but the end." [8] Eusebius records for us that Militiades corrected her using this very text (1 Cor. 13), saying, "It is necessary that the prophetic charisma be in all the Church *until the final coming*." [9] They actually used these verses like Paul did—to show that the gifts must continue until the Return of Christ!

Add the following names to the list of Church fathers that interpreted it this way: Eusebius, Didymus of Alexandria, Irenaeus, Origen, Methodius of Olympus, and Archelaus, and others. [10] Not to mention that one of cessationism's strongest proponents—John Calvin himself (in his commentary on 1 Corinthians)—agrees that the "perfect" in these verses refers to the "day of judgment," and said that it is "stupid" or "ignorant" to try and make it refer to any time before that. [11] He said it, I didn't! Calvin continues:

"The adverb *then* denotes the last day...although full vision will be deferred until the day of Christ, a nearer view of God will begin to be enjoyed immediately after death, when our souls... will have no more need of the outward ministry, or other inferior helps." [12]

In this verse, Paul actually makes the point that the gifts of the Spirit will continue until we have Jesus standing right in front of us. It is only then that we won't need them anymore. The charismata continue until the Parousia—the second coming of Christ—the full and complete manifestation of the Kingdom of God. It is at that time that the Church will have reached its full maturity—knowing Christ fully, and all the devils of hell will have bowed their knee to His authority. No more seeing in a glass dimly, no more sickness, pain or tears. God will meet all human needs, and have unhindered communion with His people. Then—and not one moment sooner—will the gifts become unnecessary and pass away.

> Paul actually makes the point that the gifts of the Spirit will continue until we have Jesus standing right in front of us.

Did the Charismata Fade Away or Get Replaced?

Some cessationists realize and admit that the Scripture teaches that the gifts must continue until the Second Coming of Christ. They then offer the opinion that maybe they didn't stop; but they must have been replaced or changed. This is referred to as the "transmuting" of the charismata. This means that the supernatural gifts of the Holy Spirit were phased out and swapped for natural, human gifts, abilities and knowledge.

For instance, some cessationists might argue, "We have medical science, so in fact, the gifts of healings and the working of miracles are *not* necessary today. We have the Bible, so we don't need the word of knowledge or the discerning of spirits. We have orderly preaching of the established Bible doctrines, so we no longer need the gift of prophecy or the word of wisdom. We *learn* foreign languages and preach the gospel in them—this is the modern equivalent of speaking in tongues."

This idea says that the Church needed miracles in the beginning until it was established (the first two or three centuries A.D.), then "the [miraculous] power ceased, and God left it to be maintained by ordinary ways." [13] They say that the charismata acted like scaffolding on a building (the Church) until it was built, then the scaffolding was unnecessary. Even Warfield said that this particular theory is "helpless..."

"...because *the reason which it gives for the continuance of miracles during the first three centuries, if valid at all, is equally valid for their continuance to the twentieth century*... If the usefulness of miracles in planting the church were sufficient reason for their occurrence in the Roman Empire in the third century, it is hard to deny that it may be sufficient reason for the repetition of them in, say, the Chinese Empire in the twentieth century. And why go to China? *Is not the church still essentially in the position of a missionary church everywhere in this world of unbelief?*" (emphasis mine) [14]

This is simple logic. Warfield is essentially saying, "If we needed the gifts to evangelize and proclaim the gospel of Jesus and to establish the Kingdom in the 1st-3rd centuries, then we need them now for that same purpose." This point is truer and more valid than I think he realized. The church today is every bit as much on a mission field as it was then. If the charismata were beneficial to evangelism and Christian ministry then, then they are just as beneficial now. That is a great logical and historical argument;

> If we needed the gifts to evangelize... in the 1st-3rd centuries, then we need them *now* for that same purpose.

but more importantly, what does the Bible say about the idea of God's supernatural power being replaced by human means?

Galatians 3:3
Are you so foolish? Having begun in the Spirit, are you now being made perfect by the flesh?

How did anyone get the idea that we could accomplish God's purposes better through natural human methods, than we could through the supernatural means of God's very own power? This is pride of the highest degree. In Galatians 3:1, Paul wonders if people who think this have been "bewitched!" Are human methods more advanced or superior to God's?

1 Corinthians 1:25, 3:18-21
Because the foolishness of God is wiser than men, and the weakness of God is stronger than men... Let no one deceive himself. If anyone among you seems to be wise in this age, let him become a fool that he may become wise. [19] For the wisdom of this world is foolishness with God... Therefore let no one boast in men.

Let's get this straight: Cessationists are saying that Jesus' ways are *inferior* to our "modern" methods. Jesus' healing power is less effective than a doctor's knife or a bottle of pills? Come on, let's get real, folks! Lest you think I'm exaggerating, I quote B.B. Warfield, "We ourselves *prefer*... the establishment of hospitals like the Presbyterian Hospitals in New York and Philadelphia, in which Christian charity provides the best medical

> Nothing man could ever accomplish in our own strength can improve on the way Jesus Christ did ministry!

service for human ills." [15] Yes, he said he *prefers* hospitals to the healing power of God! Listen, nothing man could ever accomplish in our own strength can begin to compare with God's ways. Man's organization, education, skill, ability, knowledge, science, medicine, technology—none of it can improve on the way Jesus Christ did ministry! He is always the Supreme Standard! We are called to minister in power just as He did.

Those that believe the "transmuting" theory say that the miraculous gifts gradually faded away. But the historical record doesn't back up this theory. Even cessationist extraordinaire B.B. Warfield admits that this can't be right:

"If the evidence is worth anything at all, instead of a regularly progressing decrease, there was a steadily growing increase of miracle working from the beginning on... there is a much greater abundance and precision of evidence, such as it is, for miracles in the fourth and the succeeding centuries, than for the preceding ones... the genuineness.. of the ecclesiastical miracles being once allowed, no stopping place can be found until the whole series of alleged miracles down to our own day be admitted..." [16]

"If we are to admit that the miracles of the first three centuries happened... we should in all reason go on and admit that the much more numerous and much better attested miracles of the fourth century happened too–and those of the fifth, and of the sixth and of every subsequent century down to our day... no doubt *the references increase in number and definiteness as the years pass... in the later period everybody appears to have witnessed any number of them, and the workers of them are not only named but prove to be the most famous missionaries and saints of the church...*

... They are... outstanding scholars, theologians, preachers, organizers of the age. It is Jerome, the leading biblical scholar of his day... Gregory of Nyssa... the incomparable Athanasius himself... the greatest preacher of the day, Chrysostom; the greatest ecclesiastic, Ambrose; the greatest thinker, Augustine,–*all describe for us miraculous occurrences of the most incredible kind as having taken place within their own knowledge.*" [17]

In other words, for a cessationist to be consistent, they must reject every miracle after the 12 apostles. Otherwise, they are left to the "abundance and precision" of evidence of a multitude of miracles which have only *increased* through Christian history to our day. One must either accept or reject post-biblical miracles on principle. And if it's on principle alone, then we must accept or reject them *all* in one whack. If we'll examine the "principle" that causes cessationists to reject miracles, we see that it ultimately doesn't hold water, and we'll all be free to enjoy the miracles that God has for us today. That root principle is called evidentialism, and we'll look at it in the following section.

The Purpose of the Gifts Determines Their Duration

What is the purpose of the charismata? This question is of central importance; because both sides of this debate agree upon one concept: The purpose of the charismata determines their duration. Knowing the *Biblical* answers to this one question will either confirm or destroy cessationism.

Cessationists say that God only does miracles during times of new revelation. They say that the purpose of the charismata was *solely* to prove the truth of the gospel message and to accredit its messengers until either the Scripture was written, or until the Church was "established." Therefore, once we had the Bible, or once the Church was established, they say that the miracles were no longer necessary—and therefore stopped—they had served their purpose. This core misunderstanding of the purpose of a miracle—"miracles exist only as evidence of new revelation"—is the principle that causes cessationism to reject the miracles of God today.

> What is the purpose of the charismata? Knowing the Biblical answers to this one question will either confirm or destroy cessationism.

Meanwhile, a *majority* of the Body of Christ says that there is much more to miracles than accrediting a message or its messengers. According to continuationists (and the Scriptures),

323

other purposes of miracles are to *express or communicate* the gospel, to *apply* the truth of the gospel, to *demonstrate* the character and nature of God, to *serve* humanity, and many other purposes that we examine below. Since these functions all continue until Christ's return, the gifts also remain until then.

So, who is right? What is the purpose of a miracle? Let's first look at the cessationist claims, in light of the Bible...

Evidentialism Mistake #1:
Miracles Exist to Accredit God's Messengers

Does God do miracles solely as credentials for His messengers? No. Admittedly, miracles *can* definitely have that effect (Mark 16:15-20; John 3:2, 6:2, 10:25, 37-38; Acts 2:22, 2 Cor.12:11-12, Heb 2:4). However, this is certainly not the *only* or even the *primary* Biblically-defined purpose of miracles. We will examine

Miracles and signs do not conclusively prove one's relationship with God.

the Biblical purposes of miracles later. In the meantime, we will show that miracles and signs *do not* conclusively prove one's relationship with God...

• The Nameless Exorcist

See Mark 9:38-40. This is an interesting case, because the man casting out devils in Jesus' Name "does not follow" with the disciples, and yet Jesus says he is "on our side." Jesus approves of the guy's work and allows him to continue in this case, saying, "Do not forbid him." Cessationism says that God only does miracles when He is communicating revelation and accrediting His messengers. However, this man worked miracles, but we don't even know his name, never mind what his revelation from God was.

324

- ## The "Lord, Lord" Crowd

See Matthew 7:21-23. In this case, obviously, Jesus does not approve of their work—calling it "lawlessness," and denying them access to His eternal presence. And yet, while they were on earth, these individuals still did real miracles. And the miracles were done in Jesus' Name; yet obviously they did not attest to the person's relationship with Jesus. He did not "know" them (intimately). There is power and authority in the Name of Jesus, regardless of who uses it—as long as they truly believe there is power in it. It's clear in Scripture that miracles do not necessarily prove someone's relationship with Jesus. Nor do they attest to one's spiritual maturity, as we see in the following instances...

- ## The Disciples

All 12 of Jesus' original disciples worked miracles, and yet they were goofballs most of the time. We see them wanting to call fire down on people, finagling over who will get to be Jesus' right hand man, arguing over which of them was the greatest, rebuking Jesus for saying He would go to the cross... Heck, one of these miracle-working disciples routinely stole money from their funds, and ultimately betrayed Jesus for 30 pieces of silver! These guys were obviously not the most spiritually mature bunch. In fact, at that point, they weren't even born again! And yet they worked miracles alongside Jesus, by the power of the same Holy Spirit! We also see interesting dynamics like this elsewhere in the Scriptures...

- ## The Apostle Peter

Even after the resurrection—even after receiving the indwelling Holy Spirit and His power—the twelve didn't always have it together. As a quick example, let's look at Peter in the book of Acts. Peter was a vessel for some amazing miracles. For instance, people were healed as Peter just walked by (Acts 5:12-

16)! These were great miracles by anyone's standard. And yet, Peter still had some character issues to work out.

In the midst of his miracle-working, we witness Peter being a total hypocrite (Galatians 2:11-13). He was acting free from the law around the Gentiles; but then acting like a racist, law-keeping Jew around some conservative Jewish guys who were visiting. Paul had to publicly correct him (v. 14-21)! It's obvious that Peter didn't have it all together—he hadn't made the transition to understanding Grace vs. Law. And yet, Peter also routinely worked miracles.

- **The Corinthian Christians**

This is demonstrated yet again in the Corinthian church. They are known for a constant use of the gifts of the Spirit. They were all showing up to church, speaking in tongues, prophesying, giving words of knowledge, etc. So much so, that Paul had to lay down some guidelines to keep it all in some kind of order (1 Corinthians 14:26-40). There was certainly no shortage of the charismata in Corinth. And yet, they were simultaneously marked by immaturity, carnality, and even unusually notable sin (See 1 Corinthians 3:1-3, 5:1)! God was not accrediting them as His special messengers! "These signs follow *those that believe*" (Mark 16). Any Christian can flow in the gifts of the Spirit, regardless of our level of spiritual maturity or development!

> Any Christian can flow in the gifts of the Spirit, regardless of our level of spiritual maturity or development!

Evidentialism Mistake #2:
Miracles Exist to Confirm Correct Doctrine

Cessationism claims an "inseparable connection" [18] between miracles and divine, canonical revelation. They say that God doesn't just *haphazardly* do miracles any old time; but that miracles only come during periods of new revelation (Moses, the prophets, Jesus and the disciples). [19] They must serve some grand, universal purpose. John Calvin said, "Their requiring miracles of us is altogether unreasonable; for we forge no new Gospel, but retain the very same whose truth was confirmed by all the miracles ever wrought by Christ and the Apostles." [20] In this view, God doesn't speak to us on an individual basis. Therefore, once the Bible was complete, there was no more revelation, and therefore no miracles necessary to confirm the message.

Do signs and wonders accredit someone's message as being from God? Again, "not necessarily." However, it is correct that signs and wonders *can* serve that purpose. We see this in several Scriptures (Mark 16:20, John 2:23; Acts 8:6-7, 14:3, 15:12, etc). Clearly, God *can* and does use the charismata to confirm a message. But we also see that this isn't always the case. Sometimes people (even mature Christians of integrity and character) haven't got *all* their doctrine straight, and yet still do miracles.

• The Apostles in Jerusalem

In Acts, we read about just such an occasion. The Apostles in Jerusalem (Apostles!) thought that the Jews were the only ones that God wanted to be in covenant relationship with. Jesus had commanded them to go into all the world and make disciples of all nations; but they either forgot, or disagreed with Jesus' assessment. Even Peter had to be convinced of it by receiving a repeated vision from heaven while in a trance, and hearing God's audible voice. He finally gave in, obeyed the Lord, and preached the gospel to Cornelius' household.

The apostles in Jerusalem heard about it; and they were upset with Peter for going into Cornelius' house and eating with Gentiles (See Acts 11:1-18). They still didn't even understand that God wanted the Gentiles saved. In other words, the

Apostles (again, not just anybody—the first Apostles!) thought that it was God's will that 95% of the world should go to hell—talk about some bad doctrine!! And yet, during the earlier chapters of Acts, we read about signs and wonders and miracles taking place through the hands of these Apostles in Jerusalem (See Acts 2:43, 5:12, etc). These were the very same apostles with this twisted doctrinal understanding, who were also being directly disobedient to Jesus' command to go into all the world! Mature? Right doctrine? "No" on all counts! And yet they moved consistently in signs and wonders.

- **John the Baptist**

Let's come at this false evidentialist concept from the opposite angle: Sometimes, God's Biblical prophets had their doctrine perfect—a message directly from the mouth of God—and yet did *no* confirming miracles. Think about John the Baptist. Jesus said that he was the *greatest prophet of all history* up to that point (Luke 7:28). He carried the *ultimate* message from God, "Behold the Lamb of God." In other words, "The One we've been waiting on for all of history, the One Who will change everything, He's right here, right now." And yet, the Scripture says that John the Baptist did *no* miracles (John 10:41)! The ultimate message had *zero* confirming signs... So much for the "inseparable connection" between miracles and revelation. We can have the right message, we can have miracles, we can have both, or we can have neither.

So what is the conclusion of this issue? Should we believe someone just because they work signs and wonders? Not necessarily—Even false religions have miracles. Should we believe someone that has their doctrine just right; but has no miracles? Again, not necessarily—Perfect doctrine with no tangible results is not an accurate representation of Jesus. I think Augustine had it right. He said, "Let us therefore believe those who *both* speak the truth *and* work miracles."[21] As Paul said, the gospel is both word and deed. We must both speak the message, and have signs and wonders. *Both* right doctrine, *and* signs and wonders are important—They complement one another. Anything else is less than the *full* preaching of the gospel. We'll talk about that more in the coming pages...

So we have seen that the charismata do not exist merely to accredit a messenger or confirm a message, just using the individual cases listed above. If miracles confirm or attest to anything, it's this: "God is good, He is full of love and mercy, and He is more powerful than the enemy!" There are some larger principles in the Scripture that doubly prove the point.

> If miracles confirm or attest to anything, it's this: "God is good, He is full of love and mercy, and He is more powerful than the enemy!"

Grace vs. Law, Faith vs. Works, Gift vs. Reward

A question comes to the minds of some: How can someone work legitimate miracles from God, and operate in the gifts of the Holy Spirit—while they are simultaneously carnal, immature, hypocritical and/or in blatant sin? Doesn't that prove that the miracles they do aren't the work of God? No, it doesn't! Ask the disciples, the Corinthians, or the Apostle Peter! Remember, Jesus *chose* to give legitimate, godly, miracle-working authority and the power of the Holy Spirit even to Judas—His own betrayer—in full knowledge that he was a snake!

But why would God use someone like *that?* If He did, wouldn't He be saying that their sin is no big deal? No, it's saying that, "Where sin abounds, grace abounds much more" (Romans 5:20)! If Jesus even used Judas, His betrayer, to do miracles through, certainly He will use His born again brothers and sisters—that's US! God uses flawed, immature vessels with un-renewed minds—jars of clay that carry His glory—we're the only ones He's got! And because God loves the person we're going to

329

minister to so much that He won't let our stupidity get in the way of Him blessing them!

Listen Church, God doesn't sit in heaven, withholding the gifts of the Spirit, healings, and miracles until we get our doctrine just right. He's not waiting until we get our behavior "holy enough" to "qualify" to be used. That is human works and effort, and it will never get us anything from God. God doesn't expect us to have all of our "I's dotted and T's crossed" before He can manage to use us to bless someone's life supernaturally. If the charismata were earned, deserved, or merited—then they would be the "rewards," "awards," or "brownie badges" of the Spirit; but they aren't. They are called the "*gifts*" of the spirit; because they are given freely—by grace, through faith. Paul made this quite clear in writing to the Galatians, who were getting caught up in trying to keep the Law perfectly:

Galatians 3:5
Therefore He who supplies the Spirit to you and works miracles among you, does He do it by the works of the law, or by the hearing of faith?

"Faith" is the obvious answer. He couldn't be much more blatant than this. Paul is saying, "God doesn't do miracles and dish out the gifts based on how 'good' you've been, or how 'right' you are. He does miracles for those—and through those—who will simply believe!" It's a simple matter of faith.

> God wants to help people; and He'll use whoever is available. That means you and me, with all of our imperfect doctrines and personalities.

Now, should we go ahead in sin, since He'll use us anyway? Let's not be ridiculous. Of course we shouldn't sin. Sin brings death and hurts people, and misrepresents the heart of God. But to think that God requires His kids to have perfect doctrine or mature character before He'll use them supernaturally is simply naive and unscriptural. That is an Old Testament Law-and-performance, tit-for-tat mentality. No, this New Covenant is a Covenant of Grace and Faith. God wants to help people, and He'll use whoever is available. That means you and me, with all our imperfect doctrines and personalities. I've seen people who just got saved pray for the sick and get miracles. They didn't earn it—they simply got born again, and became temples full of the Holy Spirit of God, and they believed enough to do what Jesus said to do. Go and do likewise!

Scriptural Purposes of the Charismata

We have examined the cessationist claims about the purpose of a miracle and have seen that they are not soundly Biblical. Cessationism says that since the whole truth of Jesus' death, burial, and resurrection has already come and been confirmed, there is no further need for miracles.

First of all, the idea that God stopped giving us revelation is ridiculous. I don't know a cessationist that feels like God has never told them—or "led" them individually by His Spirit—to do or say something. That, in and of itself, violates their arguments entirely. But even if we agree with Calvin's premise that all revelation is finished—Let's not confuse the *sufficiency* of the gospel message, with the *methods by which this good news is expressed and applied* to people's lives. As Dr. Jon Mark Ruthven points out in his book:

"Just as sound and inspired preaching *applies*, but does not change, the all-sufficient Scripture, so true gifts of prophecy, knowledge or wisdom reveal human needs, directing them to God's truth within the eternally-sealed limits of the biblical canon. Just as gifts of administration or hospitality tangibly *express* the gospel and *advance* the Kingdom of God, but do not alter its doctrinal content, so likewise gifts of healing and miracles." [22]

Ruthven also observes, "Just as a heartbeat sound may be used to prove someone is alive, proof is not the reason-for-being of the heartbeat." [23] Miracles *can* indeed prove the gospel; but that's not the reason they exist. The Bible clearly tells us otherwise.

So if signs, wonders, miracles, and healings don't exist only to attest to a message or a messenger, then why do they exist? If they don't *prove* anything, what good are they? I'm glad you asked! There are many purposes for the charismata, as taught in Scripture. Here is just a partial list:

> Miracles *can* indeed prove the gospel; but that's not the reason they exist.

- Signs Display God's Glory (John 2:11a; 11:4, 40-44)
- Supernatural Ministry Gives God Glory (1 Peter 4:11, Luke 5:26)
- Wonders Magnify Jesus (Acts 19:11-17)
- Miracles Provoke Praise to God (Luke 7:11-17, 19:37; Matt.14:33)
- Miracles Inspire the Fear of the Lord (Mark 4:41, 5:33; Luke 8:36-37; Acts 2:43, 19:17
- Tongues Edify the Individual Believer (1 Cor.14:4, 16-17; Jude 20)
- Tongues Enable Supernatural Prayer (1 Cor.14:14-15; Romans 8:26-27)
- Tongues Express Thanksgiving and Praise (1 Cor.14:15-17)
- Tongues are for a Sign to Unbelievers (1 Cor.14:22)
- Prophecy is also a Sign to Unbelievers (1 Cor.14:24-25)
- Prophecy Edifies, Exhorts and Comforts (1 Cor.14:3-5, 31)
- Miracles Benefit Us (1 Cor.12:7; Psalm 103:2-3)
- Miracles Meet Human Needs (Luke 9:11; Matthew 14:15-21; John 2:3-11)
- Healing Gets People's Attention (Acts 3:10, 4:16, 8:6, 15:12)
- Healing Destroys Satan's Work (Mark 3:20-27; Acts 10:38; 1 John 3:8)
- Healing is Part of Jesus' Ministry—Then and Now (Matt.4:23-24, 9:35, 15:30, 19:2; Luke 4:18; Acts 9:34)

- Healing is Our Commission as Believers (Mt.10:1; Lk.10:8-9; Mk 16:17-18)
- Healing Expresses God's Compassion and Mercy (Matt.9:36, 14:14, 20:34; Mark 1:41, 5:19; Luke 7:11-17
- Signs and wonders are part of the full proclamation of the gospel message (Romans 15:18-20; 1 Corinthians 2:4-5).

I wish we could show all these Scriptures and go over them individually; but space forbids. Please take the time to review all of the above Scriptures and see what the Bible defines as the purposes of the charismata! This is vital to destroying the foundation of the cessationism paradigm! If, as both cessationists and continuationists agree, "the Biblically-defined purposes of the gifts determine their duration," then the gifts must continue until these purposes are fulfilled. Dr. Jon Mark Ruthven agrees:

> If the Biblically-defined purposes of the gifts determine their duration, then the gifts must continue until these purposes are fulfilled.

...These are not signs "accrediting" the gospel, but the means by which aspects of the gospel are revealed and presented... As long as the gospel is to be preached and applied, *i.e.*, "to the end of the age" (Mt. 28:20), these functions of worship, prophetic guidance, encouragement, exhortation, edification and conviction will continue to have relevance, and, if function determines duration, sufficient relevance to continue to the *Parousia* of Christ... The summary statements about the function of charismata bypass entirely the notion of ... evidentialist accreditation of apostles or doctrine. [24]

Every single purpose on the above list is still valid for today. Therefore, the charismata by which God has supernaturally enabled His Church to accomplish these purposes are also still necessary and continue today.

As a final nail in the coffin of the cessationist concept of miracle-as-evidence:

Matthew 16:1, 4
Then the Pharisees and Sadducees came, and testing Him asked that He would show them a sign from heaven... A wicked and adulterous generation seeks after a sign, and no sign shall be given to it except the sign of the prophet Jonah...

Jesus specifically took issue with those that looked for *signs as evidence* of His message, *or as credentials* for Himself as God's messenger. He referred those people to the Scriptures and His coming death and resurrection. Nevertheless, for the multitudes, He consistently did signs and wonders *to minister* to those in need, *to express* the loving heart of God, *to bring praise* to the Father, and *to demonstrate* the supremacy of the Kingdom of God He proclaimed. Jesus taught, preached, and healed—the message and the miracles went hand in hand. That was Jesus' ministry in a nutshell.

> Jesus taught, preached, and healed—the message and the miracles went hand-in-hand.

The Show-and-Tell Gospel

Contrary to the cessationist view that a miracle exists as *evidence* for a message, the Bible shows us that miracles are a *part of the full proclamation* of the gospel message. This is not a gospel of "the wisdom of words" (1 Corinthians 1:17). This is a "show-and-tell" gospel. It has words to explain it, *and* actions to demonstrate and express it. The Apostle Paul expressed these ideas several times in Scripture:

1 Corinthians 2:4-5
[4] And my speech and my preaching *were* not with persuasive words of human wisdom, but in demonstration of the Spirit and of power, [5] that your faith should not be in the wisdom of men but in the power of God.

> This is a "show-and-tell" gospel. It has words to explain it, and actions to demonstrate and express it.

Paul says that although he did give some simple words to proclaim the gospel message, he didn't rely on

334

his words to inspire the people's faith. He relied on "demonstration of the Spirit and power." He would *tell* the good news, and then he would *demonstrate* how that good news applies to people's lives. "Jesus died on the cross for you, forgave your sins, and conquered the devil," Paul might say. The crowd responds, "Great. What does that mean to us? How does that affect real life in the here and now?" Paul would pull someone up there, get them healed, and say, "Look, it means God's Kingdom really is superior to the devil's kingdom. It means you really are redeemed from the curse of sin and death, and Jesus really did defeat the devil and set us free! It means that God really does love you!" The miracles were a demonstration of the Kingdom message.

Romans 15:18-19

[18] For I will not dare to speak of any of those things which Christ has not accomplished through me, in word and deed, to make the Gentiles obedient—[19] in mighty signs and wonders, by the power of the Spirit of God, so that from Jerusalem and round about to Illyricum I have fully preached the gospel of Christ.

Here Paul made the point of saying that he had "fully" preached the gospel "in word and deed... in mighty signs and wonders." His clear implication is that word without deed

> Miracles don't just *confirm* a message, they *are* a message!

(or vice versa) would only be a "partially" expressed gospel. Preaching a message without supernatural signs and wonders is only a half-message! In other words, miracles don't just *confirm* a message, they *are a* message! Even if I stayed *silent*, but ministered to someone and they were healed, I guarantee they'd hear the message "Jesus is real and He loves you." Of course I would take advantage of the situation and tell them the words so they would understand more fully; but the healing was already a message in itself! Some people use flannel boards, and some people use PowerPoint presentations; but miracles make the very best visual aids!

Scripture Blatantly Contradicts Cessationism

Most cessationists fail to recognize how their views impact and contradict the established, systematic Christian doctrines of Pneumatology (doctrine of the Holy Spirit and His miraculous, supernatural, and charismatic work), Christology (doctrine of Jesus Christ, and His ministry then and now), and the doctrine of the Kingdom of God (and its continual and progressive conquering of the enemy's kingdom by miracles and wonders done through His people).

We don't have the space here to elaborate on these numerous "large" fatal theological flaws in the cessationist arguments. If you'd like to learn more about these larger issues, problems with Warfield's book specifically (and cessationism in general), I highly recommend Dr. Jon Mark Ruthven's book, <u>On the Cessation of the Charismata: A Protestant Polemic on Post-Biblical Miracles</u>, available on the Internet. We will, however look at some "smaller scale" specific Scriptures that clearly contradict the cessationist viewpoint.

Mark 16:17-18
[17] And *these signs will follow those who believe*: In My name they will cast out demons; they will speak with new tongues; [18] they will take up serpents; and if they drink anything deadly, it will by no means hurt them; they will lay hands on the sick, and they will recover."

Signs, wonders, healings, and miracles ought to be a natural outflow from the lives of whoever believes. Believes what? These signs will follow anyone who believes that these signs will follow them! Yes, I know the authorship of these particular verses is questionable (although I personally believe them to be the Word of God), so we'll move along to some more...

> These signs will follow anyone who believes that these signs will follow them!

1 Corinthians 14:1
Pursue love, and *desire spiritual gifts,* but *especially that you may prophesy.*

336

If the charismata stopped, then it would make no sense for the Bible to tell us to desire them, right? But it *does* command us to desire spiritual gifts—and not just once; but *at least twice* in one chapter:

1 Corinthians 14:39
Therefore, brethren, *desire earnestly to prophesy*, and *do not forbid to speak with tongues*.

In case we didn't get it the first time, the Holy Spirit repeats the command to desire (earnestly!) to prophesy, and gives us another order immediately following it: "Do not forbid to speak with tongues." The Bible gives us a clear, direct order; and yet there are whole denominations that strictly enforce the exact opposite! Someone might say, "Well, the Bible may say not to 'forbid' it, but it doesn't necessarily encourage it either." Wrong again. While Paul is clear that it is preferable to prophesy in a language understandable to the listeners, he is by no means discouraging speaking in tongues.

1 Corinthians 14:5a
I wish you all spoke with tongues, but even more that you prophesied...

The Spirit of God (through Paul) tells us that He wishes we'd *all* speak in other tongues—*and prophesy!* If He wants it, that's good enough for me! But just in case we thought this particular desire of his might not apply to every Believer, Paul clarifies the point:

1 Corinthians 14:31
For *you can all prophesy* one by one, that all may learn and all may be encouraged.

And lest we think that these promises are only for the Corinthians, or only for the first generation of Believers, let's turn to Acts 2, when the Holy Spirit was first poured out to the Church:

Acts 2:38-39

[38] Then Peter said to them, "Repent, and let every one of you be baptized in the name of Jesus Christ for the remission of sins; and you shall receive the gift of the Holy Spirit. [39] For *the promise is to you and to your children, and to all who are afar off, as many as the Lord our God will call."*

Peter is talking about the gift of the Holy Spirit, specifically in the context of the disciples speaking in tongues. He says that this gift is for *all* Believers, for *all time*. What more do we need?

1 Thessalonians 5:19-20

[19] *Do not quench the Spirit.* [20] *Do not despise prophecies.*

If we took the "do not" out of these two verses, you might have a couple of points on the "Statement of Beliefs" of some modern denominations! The Scripture commands us to let the Holy Spirit move how He wants to, and not to hate or reject it when He does. That is so clear! We could go on and on telling obvious Scriptures that command us to do what much of the western Church forbids or frowns on; but the point is made.

> The Scripture *commands* us to let the Holy Spirit move however He wants to, and not to hate or reject it when He does.

Back to the Standard

Some try to find Scriptures we can misinterpret or take out of their context to weasel out of the uncomfortable responsibility of cooperating with the Holy Spirit in doing the impossible. They aren't seeing the forest, for all the trees. Instead, let's step back and once again look at the big picture—our clear example and standard—the Lord Jesus Christ! It is Jesus Christ alone that we are called to emulate and represent. We are to do ministry the way He did it. How did He do it?

Acts 10:38

how God anointed Jesus of Nazareth *with the Holy Spirit and with power*, who went about *doing good and healing all* who were oppressed by the devil, for God was with Him.

Yes—Again, it's back to this: Jesus is our standard. Is the cessationist philosophy of the gifts being unavailable, or being replaced by natural talents and abilities reflected in the life of Jesus? No. Jesus did ministry "with the Holy Spirit and with power...healing all..." If healing was a significant part of Jesus' ministry, and He is living through us, then healing is also to be a significant part of *our* ministry. This is not complicated. It's easy to see that the gifts are still needed—and will continue to be needed—to carry out the ministry of Jesus Christ until He returns. We are ONE with Jesus and if He is Who we follow, then let's *follow*.

John 14:12

Most assuredly, I say to you, he who believes in Me*, the works that I do he will do also*; and greater works than these he will do, because I go to My Father.

Funny thing is, every time this verse is quoted, somebody wants to go off on a tangent and debate the meaning of "greater works." That's a fun guessing game; but it serves no useful purpose at this point in the Church's development. For now, let's focus on the first phase of the progression: "the works that I do." Let's not worry about the greater works—we'll cross that bridge when we get to it. First, let's get to where we've all got the *same* works that Jesus did. What works did He do? He healed *every* sick person that came to Him. What types of illness? You name it! What hindered Him from healing anyone, anytime? Nothing! Let's shoot for that standard first, and then we'll talk about what "greater works" means. Sure, that was Jesus; but that is not an excuse for us, as we are united to Him. "What God has joined together, let not man separate" (Matthew 19:6, Ephesians 5:31-32)! Even so, for the sake of argument, let's not only look at how He did ministry Himself. How did He train and command His *disciples* to do ministry?

Matthew 10:1, 7-8, 24-25
And when He had called His twelve disciples to Him, He gave them *power over unclean spirits, to cast them out, and to heal all kinds of sickness and all kinds of disease*... And as you go, preach, saying, 'The kingdom of heaven is at hand.' *Heal the sick, cleanse the lepers, raise the dead, cast out demons. Freely you have received, freely give*... A disciple is not above his teacher, nor a servant above his master. *It is enough for a disciple that he be like his teacher, and a servant like his master.*

Later, He commanded His disciples to teach *us* everything He had taught them. That includes the above commands and instruction in evangelism and ministry!

Matthew 28:19-20a
Go therefore and *make disciples* of all the nations, baptizing them in the name of the Father and of the Son and of the Holy Spirit, [20] *teaching them to observe all things that I have commanded you...*

> We should do ministry exactly like our Teacher and Master did it and taught it.

There is no way around it: We should do ministry exactly like our Teacher and Master did it and taught it. Listen, He didn't come and build the Jerusalem Central Hospital, He did miracles and cast out devils. Yes, He studied and knew the Scriptures, but He also had a living, breathing relationship with the Father. He followed Daddy's heart by doing and saying what He saw Our Father doing and saying. He was moved with compassion and healed the sick. He gave words of knowledge and words of wisdom and prophesied. He worked miracles, healings, signs and wonders by the power of the Spirit of God. He passed this supernatural, charismatic ministry baton on to His disciples, intending for it to continue until His final coming. Some folks might have dropped the baton along the way; but we're called to pick it up and run with it once again.

Hebrews 13:8
Jesus Christ is the same yesterday, today, and forever.

340

Jesus hasn't changed a bit. Nor has He changed the way He does ministry. We are His Body, and as such, we should be living a seamless continuation of the very life of Jesus "in whom we live, and move, and have our being." Jesus' character, nature, and ministry haven't changed just because now He's living through us! We simply must expect that Jesus is still "moved with compassion," and that He (through US) heals the sick among us (Matthew 14:14). We must believe that God is still Jehovah Rapha—"The LORD Who Heals"(Exodus 15:26b). It is His Name, His character, His very nature— It's just Who He is.

Why the Church is Uncomfortable with Spiritual Gifts

With miracles so prevalent in the Bible—that all Christians claim to believe—why is it that certain segments of the Church are so reluctant to allow for them to continue into today? It all goes back to the historic misunderstanding of the purpose of a miracle. Aquinas, Calvin, and Warfield all fell for the same false premise: that the *sole (*or at least the *primary) purpose* of a miracle is to *authenticate* the truth of the message it accompanies. They believed that miracles only came in conjunction with new revelation from God.

In the cessationist view, *all* revelation from God was solidified, complete, and finished with the closing of the Canon of Scripture. If miracles only confirm new doctrine—and there *is* no new doctrine—then there can be no legitimate new miracles. So to a cessationist, to admit to new miracles of God, would mean the miracle worker also speaks with Scripture-level authority (even if their doctrine isn't 100% right!), and must be obeyed and followed. This type of twisted view of a miracle-authority connection resulted in the abused authority in the Middle Ages Church, and that's why we needed the Protestant Reformation in the first place!

It's no wonder that the Evangelical Church is uncomfortable with miracles! They've been down that road before! The organized Church of the time said, "We have miracles. This proves we are God's sanctioned authority, so you have to obey us." In response, some of the Reformers and their descendants have swung the pendulum to the other extreme. Because of this mistaken concept of miracle-as-evidence—cessationism says that any miracles that do occur today must necessarily be counterfeit. Therefore, they feel that Christians who *do* experience miracles are deceived (or deceivers) and dangerous! Meanwhile, the Scriptures give us precisely the opposite warning:

2 Timothy 3:1-9
[1] But know this, that in the last days perilous times will come: [2] For men will be... despisers of good... [5] *having a form of godliness but denying its power.* And from such people turn away! ...so do these also resist the truth...*their folly will be manifest to all.*"

This Scripture plainly tells us that we ought to be wary of Christians who are "godly" but shut down the power (most often "dunamis" = miracle-working power, specifically). [25] It tells us to turn away from them! Then he encourages us with the message that eventually, everyone will know that they are wrong. I believe that this time is upon us. As miracles are becoming a more and more common occurrence in the lives of everyday Believers, the empty fallacy of cessationist theology becomes more and more obvious.

Cessationists do have some good motivations, honestly. They don't want to believe wrong doctrine, even if those who teach it have good intentions. And they certainly don't want to be deceived or led astray by those with bad motives, just because they work miracles. Obviously, it is much easier to rest in a "closed Canon" of Scripture, chant "Sola Scriptura," and follow the words in the

> A list of rules and principles set in stone (or a Canon) seems so much less complicated than an actual relationship with a Living God.

342

Book. But in my opinion, this is reminiscent of the Old Testament Israelites, "Moses, God is scary. You go talk to God for us, then just tell us what He says and we'll do it" (Exodus 20:18-21). A list of rules and principles set in stone (or a Canon) seems so much less complicated than an actual relationship with a Living God.

While the Scriptures are indeed a "prophetic word confirmed" (2 Peter 1:19), and are an unshakeable foundation and guide for all Believers—There are other issues at hand here. No writer in the New Testament gives any indication that they will be the last to hear from God. Of course the Scriptures are the plumb line by which all future revelation is judged; but is God now silent? Is He no longer interested in relationship with His people? Are we in union with Christ, or aren't we? Are we His sheep who hear His voice, or aren't we? Are we supposed to be like our Master and minister supernaturally—as He modeled and instructed—or not? God gave us guidelines in the Bible that we can't violate; but what about specific revelation for our individual lives? What about healing for our bodies? What about signs to the unbeliever? What about supernaturally-empowered communication with the Lord in other tongues? What about miracles? Cessationism says you can't have any. What do you believe? Either way, God's will is *always* healing!

Notes:

CHAPTER 17

SMALL POTATOES

Grasping at Straws

What is it in man—that makes us want so badly to find a reason we can stay sick or injured, or broke, or sad and depressed? Sometimes it's more comforting to find something to justify staying the devil's captive—than it is to believe that God has set us free, and we've been duped and deceived. It hurts to find out we've been fooled. On top of that, sickness can seem an insurmountable obstacle, and it can often be relentless, daunting, tiring, and wear a person out—especially the chronic, long-term health struggles that can partially define one's existence after awhile. It's so much easier and more comforting to find a Scripture that makes us feel OK about it, even if we have to misinterpret it to do so.

Ultimately, our minds are just trying to solve a puzzle: Why does our visible reality not look like the invisible one God says is mine? I think that's what these last few objections are—last-ditch efforts of our rational, logical minds to make sense of mystery and contradiction—to find a reason our lives are OK as they are. I realize that it can be uncomfortable to admit that there could possibly be more available in God than what we've already experienced. Let's humble ourselves and recognize that there are unsearchable riches available in Christ, and there is *always* more we can experience in Him.

None of these last few objections could justify a whole chapter on their own; but they do come up in people's minds occasionally. Lest someone is still grasping at these straws by this point in the book, here we are: facing the small potatoes.

SMALL POTATO #1:
Doesn't God Make the Handicapped?

One of the favorite, random, taken-out-of-context verses of the Hyper-Sovereignty "God is in control" folks (who think God's will includes sickness), is Exodus 4:11.

Exodus 4:11
So the LORD said to him, "Who has made man's mouth? Or who makes the mute, the deaf, the seeing, or the blind? Have not I, the LORD?

"See," they'll say, "It says right there that God made them that way. That *must* mean it's His will, right?" Wrong! Note first, God did *not* say He creates the *disabilities*, He said He makes the *people*—read it again to be sure. It doesn't say that He intended for these people to be blind, deaf or mute. So how could God *make* the blind people (for instance); but not *want* them to be blind? How might we interpret this one verse in a way that is consistent with the whole of the Bible?

- **A Look at Creation**

When you see someone blind, or crippled, or with some horrible birth defect or childhood illness—Did God do that? Did He "make" them that way? Only in the sense that He "makes" *all* men. That is, He created Adam and Eve, and designed the natural process by which they would reproduce. He told people to "Be fruitful and multiply." We do this through having sex, and procreating. God is the original source of life, but we cooperate to propagate it. When people do their part (sex), God has designed that life should come out of the process.

God made the blind, deaf and mute, *and everyone else*—in the *general* sense. He created the first people; and He created the process that would ultimately result in every person on earth. When He was done, He said, "It is good"—He didn't say, "It's a mess!" The "good" that God made and the "natural" processes He ordained were corrupted through the curse that came when

346

Man sinned—just like the weather patterns and everything else. The "multiplying" process is fallen, and as such—inconsistent, unpredictable, and subject to flaw. But it is not His will for their body to be less than His perfect design. God's design = God's plan. God's Plan = God's desire. God's desire = God's will. God's will = a perfectly functioning body! God's will is always healing! Remember, we can look in *two* places to find what the plan and will of God is for us—how He wants us to experience life: the Garden and Heaven. If there are things here on Earth now that we don't see in those two places, they aren't God's plan or will.

By contrast, however, if you want to see how God designed and created certain *body parts* (the way He planned and intended them to be formed before the Fall), I commend you to Proverbs...

Proverbs 20:12
The *hearing ear*, and the *seeing eye*, the Lord has made them both.

God designed parts that work perfectly. Listen, God is not sitting around putting each and every individual human body together, and making slip-ups and imperfections in the process. How involved is God in the actual physical formation of each human being's body? That could be debated from Scripture either way—and yes, I know what Job and the Psalms say (Ps.139:13 and Job 10:11, etc); but let's not forget they are poetry either.

We can see a parallel picture in, say, a tree. Did God make the tree outside your front door? Yes, ultimately—*if* you go back to the trees He spoke into the Garden, and the system of seedtime and harvest (reproduction and increase) He set in place. But did He take His own two hands and fashion THAT individual tree you're looking at? I don't believe He did. You planted the seed, and your cooperation in God's ordained process accesses the life He provided when He spoke in the Garden, and the tree grew.

However, if you want to argue that God directly forms each individual human body—I have some questions. Does God *directly* "knit together" conjoined twins purposely to be that way? What about miscarriages? Is that God's equivalent of crumbling up a messed up sketch? Did He make a *mistake*? What about stillborn babies? Did He take the time to *physically* mold and form their little bodies from physical matter, then breathe life into them—only to take it away before they even have a chance to be born—crushing the hopes and dreams of the expectant parents? What would be the point of *this* fruitless exercise? And what kind of personality would a God like that have to possess? What about kids born with missing limbs, or organs outside their bodies? To lead it back to Exodus 4:11— What about the blind, deaf, or mute? All of these questions have the same "big" answer: Natural processes were corrupted through the curse that came from Adam's sin.

> Natural processes were corrupted through the curse that came from Adam's sin.

The main reason for someone to be born handicapped may be too large of a concept for us to wrap our heads around. Let's bring it down to one smaller potential problem to use as an example. There are things we don't know, scientifically speaking. For example, certain medications that used to be recommended to women were later discovered to cause specific birth defects. Then we stopped using those medications. Others have yet to be discovered. We are exposed to all kinds of crazy things in our environment that can cause illness and problems in the reproduction processes. Think about it: cell phones, microwaves, radiation, power lines, chemicals in our food and water, medicines, personal care products, etc. All of these things may, or may not, have influence in our bodies. So even if we do *everything* right to the best of our ability and knowledge, there could still be something purely physical that we came into contact with that causes these things. Let's not be ridiculous and blame God for things He had nothing to do with. And let's not blame ourselves either. Healing and health is still a promise of God that belongs to us and our kids.

348

- ## A Look at Jesus

On another note regarding the blind, deaf, and mute specifically... Let's look at the will of God concerning them, as it is most clearly displayed—in the life of Jesus Christ.

Luke 4:18-19
"...the Spirit of the Lord God is upon me, because He has anointed me...to proclaim...recovery of sight to the blind.."

Some might say, "That's talking about the *spiritually* blind." Well, spiritual blindness is certainly *included*, but let's keep watching Jesus for clarification:

Matthew 15:30-31
"great multitudes came to Him, having with them the lame, blind, mute, maimed, and many others... and He healed them."

Mark 7:37
And they were astonished beyond measure, saying, "He has done all things well. He makes both the deaf to hear and the mute to speak."

The Bible is not talking about "spiritually lame", "spiritually blind", "spiritually mute", or "spiritually maimed." Jesus healed all of these *physical* infirmities consistently. So, my point: Was Jesus fighting against the will of God, ultimately fighting against Himself (since He is also God)??? Does God have two wills—One for the people to be blind, deaf and mute...and one for them to be well? Does God have multiple personality disorder? No!

The whole life and ministry of Jesus directly contradicts a misunderstanding of Exodus 4:11. If God allows sickness, then Jesus would also have to allow it. Yet we see just the opposite fact in Jesus' life and ministry. Why would Jesus heal the blind, deaf, and mute, if God the Father wanted or even allowed them to be that way?!?!?! Was Jesus fighting against the Father? How could it be that Jesus was anointed to "open the eyes of the blind"—when, according to the misinterpretation of Ex.4:11, they were made blind by the very same One sent to give them sight?

349

That is ridiculous and inconsistent!

- **A Look at the Context!!!**

So we can see how the "big picture" of God's sovereignty, and Man's authority, Sin and the Fall, answers one little verse in Exodus 4. However, for a much simpler analysis, let's look at the actual context!! God was about to send Moses back into Egypt to deliver the Israelites. God had just said to Moses, "I want you to go talk to Pharaoh for Me." Moses responded, "...but I'm a terrible speaker." Then verse 11 is God's response. In light of the context, it becomes obvious that God is actually saying, "Look, I made you. I know you. I know what you're good at, and I know what you're not good at. Even if you were completely mute, I know what I'm doing—So if I command you to talk for Me—you can do it!"

SMALL POTATO #2:
Does God Make People Sick Just to Heal Them?

Since we just looked at a non-ultra-sovereignty understanding of how people can end up sick without God being involved in it, I thought it a great place to clarify some things from John 9. We touched on this text briefly in Chapter 11; but I think it's important to look at it a little more in-depth here...

John 9:1-4
[1] Now as Jesus passed by, He saw a man who was blind from birth. [2] And His disciples asked Him, saying, "Rabbi, who sinned, this man or his parents, that he was born blind?" [3] Jesus answered, "Neither this man nor his parents sinned, but that the works of God should be revealed in him. [4] I must work the works of Him who sent Me while it is day; the night is coming when no one can work.

Some people read this text, and take Jesus' response to mean that *God* set this man up with a lifetime of blindness, just so one day Jesus could come walking along, heal him, and get God a little more glory. First, how cruel and narcissistic do we have to believe God is to get that interpretation? Does God need glory from people so much that He'd be willing to give someone a lifetime of misery to get it? God makes a mess, only to clean it up, all to get a little credit from man? This is a petty, needy view of God. Remember the "Hero or Criminal" parable from Chapter 10!

Second, that interpretation of John 9:3 does one of two things:

1) It would pit God the Father's will (making the man blind) *against* God the Son's will (healing him), thereby dividing the Trinity. Not possible! Or...

2) It would say that God is *inconsistent*. One day He wants you well, another day He wants you sick. This is totally against the Biblical picture of God's nature and character. He is immutable (unchangeable). In Him is light, and there is no darkness at all. Only good and perfect gifts come from Him. Period. He is (always) Jehovah Rapha—The Lord Who Heals. He is not Jehovah Rapha some days, and Jehovah Sicko—The Lord Who Makes Sick on other days. Sickness is always described in Scripture as a curse. God does not take part in a curse one day, and a blessing the next. This would mean one day God is a sweet fountain, and the next day He's a bitter fountain—which is not possible or godly, according to James 3:10-12.

Since anyone with even the most rudimentary understanding of God and Scripture knows that *neither* of those options is possible, then people must be misunderstanding the intent of John 9:1-4. So let's explore it some, shall we?

The argument sounds simple enough: They'll say, "It says the man was born blind 'so that' the works of God can be revealed in Him. See, God made the man blind, 'so that (with the will and intent)' He could get glory out of his blindness." The only problem is, the text doesn't say that *God made* the man blind.

We covered causes of illness in Small Potato #1. If you need to, please review now. Beyond that, let's delve into the text...

Did you know what the (at least) *two equally valid ways* that the Greek "hina + subjunctive aorist tense" grammar construction that we find in verse 3 can be interpreted as? Maybe not, so let's explore that together, shall we? I'm not a Greek scholar either, so we'll keep it fairly simple.

1) John 9:3 Translated as a Causative Clause

Several translations interpret it as a *causative* clause. In that case, it is roughly translated, "he was born blind SO THAT the works of God might be revealed in Him." This creates a cause-effect understanding of the verse. CAUSE: The man was born blind. INTENDED EFFECT: 'So that' God's works could be revealed.

It's easy to understand and explain this rendering (even though I don't personally believe it to be the best translation). Again, we only need to recognize one simple fact: *This Scripture does not say anywhere that GOD caused the man to be born blind.* Case closed right there, really. Recognizing this simple fact gets us over the "ultra-sovereignty hump."

> This Scripture does not say anywhere that GOD caused the man to be born blind. Case closed.

Once we realize that the man could have been born blind by purely natural, fallen Creation causes—or by demonic causes—then there is no problem understanding the text from that perspective. Jesus would be saying essentially, "His or his parents' sin had nothing to do with this. Stuff happens. Creation is a mess and he was born blind. Maybe his mom got really sick while she was pregnant with him and his eyes got messed up. Maybe a spirit of affliction was assigned to attack him. It doesn't matter how he got this way. Any way you slice it, it's just an opportunity for us to reveal the works of God by healing him."

This understanding of the verse is reflected nicely in the CEV (Contemporary English Version):

John 9:1-3 (CEV)
As Jesus walked along, he saw a man who had been blind since birth. [2] Jesus' disciples asked, "Teacher, why was this man born blind? Was it because he or his parents sinned?" [3] "No, it wasn't!" Jesus answered. "But because of his blindness, you will see God work a miracle for him.

2) John 9:3 Translated as a Command Clause

The second—and *equally valid* way to translate the Greek "hina + subjunctive aorist tense" is this: It can be a *command clause*. This would render the translation of the verse, "Neither he nor his parents sinned. Reveal the works of God in him." or "Neither he nor his parents sinned. Let the works of God be revealed in him (more polite-sounding command form)..."

This understanding shows Jesus correcting the disciples' wrong focus on the cause of the situation, and redirecting them to *their* calling in the situation—*fixing it!* "The cause is not our concern—the answer is. Now reveal God's glory and goodness!" I personally feel that this is the most likely translation, as it seems the most consistent with the rest of Jesus' life and ministry, the character and nature of God, and because it doesn't pit God the Father against God the Son in the situation (a division of the Trinity). We see this understanding of the text, for example, in the Message Version:

> "The cause is not our concern—the answer is. We aren't judges, we're liberators. Now reveal God's glory and goodness!"

John 9:3-4 (MSG)
Jesus said, "You're asking the wrong question. You're looking for someone to blame. There is no such cause-effect here. Look instead for what God can do. We need to be energetically at work for the One who sent me here, working while the sun shines. When night falls, the workday is over. For as long as I am in the world, there is plenty of light. I am the world's Light."

That being the case with the grammar in John 9, *neither the causative clause, nor the command clause translations can be proven from the Greek grammar alone. It's a 50/50 proposition,* and translators render it according to their understanding of God and the Bible. If a translator (or the approving organization) thinks God causes everything—and that He'll selfishly make messes only to fix them later to get glory—they render it as causative. However, if they see that the causative translation—at least with the false underlying belief that *God created* the man blind on purpose—wouldn't fit anything else in the life, teaching, or example of Jesus...(as I do) then they render it otherwise.

Since nobody can make the case from the grammar alone, the *only* way you know which way to translate it is by *context*. If there is no obvious clue in the context (and in this case, there isn't), then you must go back to another very basic rule of Bible interpretation, which is: "Let the Bible interpret itself." If the whole counsel of the Word supports the interpretation, then great. If not, try the other one.

But, you might say, that is the Message Version, which is not technically a "translation," but more of a "paraphrase." I understand. I don't always agree with the Message, and I don't necessarily use it for *studying the text*; but I do like to read it here and there for a more casual reading. So for you hardcore word-for-word study folks—here's yet another one for you:

Keep the Words, Change the Punctuation:

Even if you want to leave the *words* the same as the causative translation, you must also recognize that there is *no punctuation in the Greek*. That being the case, it is—yet again—left up to the translators and their particular theological understanding.

I was thinking about this Scripture's *punctuation* one day and looked at it another way, and asked myself, "If the punctuation were changed, could it possibly change the meaning? What if we switched a comma and a period??!!" Then, lo and behold, I discovered it's already been rendered that way in another translation:

John 9:3-5 (Common Edition New Testament)
Jesus answered, "Neither this man sinned nor his parents sinned. But that the works of God might be revealed in him, we must work the works of him who sent me, while it is day. Night is coming, when no one can work. As long as I am in the world, I am the light of the world."

Look at the *punctuation*. It makes all the difference in the world in this case! "Neither this man sinned nor his parents sinned. (Period. Switch gears. Redirect the disciples' attention). But that the works of God might be revealed in him, (comma, which connects the works of God being revealed to the next clause instead) we must work the works of Him who sent me." CAUSE: We work God's works. EFFECT: God's works are revealed. Again, with that punctuation change, there is no cause-effect demonstrated between His blindness and God's glory. This rendering, in a way, actually *reconciles both* the command clause understanding and the causative clause understanding of the text—a balanced view!

Most importantly, please remember this: It ultimately doesn't matter if you render it as causative or command form. What matters is that *the text itself doesn't blame GOD for the man's blindness*.

> The only thing in this text that reveals God's works—or will—is the man's healing!

That false understanding is only inserted into the text when one comes to it with ultra-sovereignty lenses on. The only thing in this text that we see God *actively engaged in,* is *healing* him. The only demonstration we have of God's will in the situation is this: Jesus (God in the flesh) healed the man. *The only thing in this text that reveals God's works—or will—is the man's healing,* period!

355

Another very similar Scripture that people will quote in trying to say that God makes people sick only to get glory out of them (gag!) is from John 11:

John 11: 1-4
Now a certain *man* was sick, Lazarus of Bethany, the town of Mary and her sister Martha. [2] It was *that* Mary who anointed the Lord with fragrant oil and wiped His feet with her hair, whose brother Lazarus was sick. [3] Therefore the sisters sent to Him, saying, "Lord, behold, he whom You love is sick." [4] When Jesus heard *that,* He said, "This sickness is not unto death, but for the glory of God, that the Son of God may be glorified through it."

So the Hyper-Sovereignty fans will say, "See, it says here that 'this sickness is... for the glory of God.'" Well, no, that's not what it says. Jesus said, "This sickness is not *unto* death..." The word "unto" here means the "end result." Jesus is simply saying "The end result of this situation won't be death; but the glory of God." Check out these other versions, I think they bring some clarity:

John 11:4 (CEV)
When Jesus heard this, he said, "His sickness won't end in death. It will bring glory to God and his Son."

John 11:4 (MSG)
When Jesus got the message, he said, "This sickness is not fatal. It will become an occasion to show God's glory by glorifying God's Son."

Here is the bottom line message we should take away from these passages in John 9 and 11: Lots of bad situations come up in life. God didn't create them. His desire is deliverance, healing, and freedom. But you can't have a miracle unless you first have a mess. Do you have a mess on your hands? Give it to Jesus. He'll bring a miracle that displays God's glory and goodness to all those around you.

> You can't have a miracle unless you first have a mess!

SMALL POTATO #3:
If Healing is Always Ours, Will We Never Die?

• Sickness is Not Earth's Exit Door

First, whoever asks this is implying that sickness is the only way to leave earth. Listen, sickness is *not* our exit door from life in the physical body. There is no "expiration date" on all of God's clear promises to heal us. We don't have to die from sickness. If you look at how the saints died in the Scripture, typically they just "breathed their last" (See Genesis 25:8, 17; 35:28-29; 49:33).

In the New Testament it became more common to be martyred for our faith. But even while being stoned to death, Stephen simply asked Jesus to receive his spirit (Acts 7:59). Paul was convinced that he had the *choice* about when, where and how he would depart. (Philippians 1:21-26). He made the choice to go to Jerusalem, even though he would be martyred there (Acts 21:13). Jesus also said, "No one takes it from Me, but I lay it down of Myself. I have power to lay it down, and I have power to take it again..." (John 10:18). He simply "committed" His Spirit into God's hands (Luke 23:46), "breathed His last" (Mark 15:37-39), and "gave up His Spirit" (Matthew 27:50, John 19:30). Last breath here, first breath there—this is the Biblical way for a Believer's life to end.

• Planting a Seed for a Glorified Body

Next, the Bible clearly says that all men *will* die, in the sense that our spirit will depart our body; and our earthly, natural existence will be over. God has ordained that we are here for a limited period of time—from 70-120 years (Genesis 6:3, Psalm 90:10). The limitation placed on our lifespan is a simple expression of God's mercy on us! This world is a mess, and once we see how great it

> The limitation placed on our lifespan is a simple expression of God's mercy on us!

is on the other side, we'll understand that, and be glad to get a break. While there are some notable variations in how we can leave—Enoch, Moses, Elijah, and the Believers who are alive at the Return of the Lord, for instance—Aside from those, most every man will face a natural death.

Physical "death" is not losing something, or having something stripped away from us. For the Believer, to be absent from the body is to be present with the Lord (2 Corinthians 5:8). Additionally, death is simply planting a seed to get a harvest. Isn't that exactly what Jesus modeled for us?

John 12:23-24
[23] But Jesus answered them, saying, "The hour has come that the Son of Man should be glorified. [24] Most assuredly, I say to you, unless a grain of wheat falls into the ground and dies, it remains alone; but if it dies, it produces much grain.

He said, "Guys, I'm about to be glorified; but I have to plant this seed to get the harvest!" Jesus was talking about planting His own life as a seed, so that God would reap many more children as a result.

However, if we are redeemed from sickness (death in an immature form) as we've talked about in other chapters, aren't we also redeemed from its mature form—death itself? The Bible says that our "outward man is perishing" (2 Corinthians 4:16). It also calls our bodies "mortal," which means they will die. However, let's not forget that the Holy Spirit does indeed "quicken" our mortal bodies—strengthening us with supernatural, Divine life (Romans 8:11). We always have the promise of healing and vitality. Nevertheless, for most of us, there will come a time when we will have finished our course— when we are satisfied with long life (Psalm 91:16). Then we will want to leave this body to step into our eternal reward.

1 Corinthians 15:53
[53] For this corruptible must put on incorruption, and this mortal *must* put on immortality.

It is only at physical death that we can "put on immortality." In fact, we must plant the seed of our natural, physical body to get the mature, spiritual, "glorified" body we are promised. We must plant a seed to get the harvest. And a seed only reproduces after it's kind. Sow a body, reap a new body.

1 Corinthians 15:35-44
[35] But someone will say, "How are the dead raised up? And with what body do they come?" [36] Foolish one, what you sow is not made alive unless it dies. [37] And what you sow, you do not sow that body that shall be, but mere grain—perhaps wheat or some other grain... [42] So also is the resurrection of the dead. The body is sown in corruption, it is raised in incorruption. [43] It is sown in dishonor, it is raised in glory. It is sown in weakness, it is raised in power. [44] It is sown a natural body, it is raised a spiritual body. There is a natural body, and there is a spiritual body...

Wait until you've done what God called and created you for. Wait until you've finished your course. Leave a blessing on your loved ones, choose your time, and commit your spirit into the hands of God. Don't let devils and diseases decide when you will leave! Get healed, and *then* cross over—if for nothing else than just to stick it to the devil one last time on the way out! Don't be afraid to plant your seed when the time comes—after all, you want the harvest of a glorified body. At the same time, don't let the thief steal your seed—Plant it yourself when you're good and ready!

> Don't let the thief steal your seed—Plant it yourself when you're good and ready!

- **Firstfruits vs. Full Manifestation**

While the Law of Sin and Death (The Curse from the Fall) is still in effect and has its results on the earth, Believers have already been set free from this Law (Romans 8:2)! Jesus has already purchased our bodies (1 Corinthians 6:19-20); but He doesn't pick them up (redeem them) until His Return (Romans 8:23).

Romans 8:15, 23

¹⁵ For you did not receive the spirit of bondage again to fear, but *you received the Spirit of adoption* by whom we cry out, "Abba, Father." ²³ Not only that, but we also who have the *firstfruits* of the Spirit, even we ourselves groan within ourselves, eagerly *waiting for the adoption*, the redemption of our body.

Here it says that we are *waiting* for the redemption of our bodies. Right now we do face an environment where sickness can illegally affect us, in that we *can* get sick—but we are *promised* healing! This is what Paul calls the "firstfruits" of our physical redemption. Healing is just the firstfruits. Nonstop, unchallenged, divine health is the full manifestation. How much of that full manifestation can we experience here and now? "According to your faith be it unto you!" However, after the full redemption of our bodies—when Jesus returns and we are made incorruptible, it will not even be *possible* to get sick! That is the difference between firstfruits and full manifestation.

> Healing is just the firstfruits. Nonstop, unchallenged, divine health is the full manifestation.

We can see that this interpretation is correct, if we simply follow the parallel Paul is making in the context. He is drawing an analogy between healing/health and being adopted/receiving the spirit of adoption. It says in verse 15 that we "have received" the spirit of adoption *already*. And yet it says in verse 23 that we are *waiting* for the full manifestation of our adoption. I doubt that any Christian would say that we are *not* already adopted by God, and yet they *will* argue that we are not already redeemed from sickness in our physical bodies! This argument is inconsistent with the parallel Paul has made here.

The Bible says that Jesus will return when His enemies are made His footstool (Matthew 22:44). It also says that the last enemy to be beaten will be death (1 Corinthians 15:26). Will *we* be the ones that enforce Jesus' victory, making death itself bow down to become His footstool—thus ushering in the Return of the

Lord? I believe we will. In the meantime, let's not let the fact that we still have a promise for the future (a glorified body) hinder us from receiving the promise we have for today— Healing!

SMALL POTATO #4:
What About "Suffering for Jesus?"

Some people think that sickness and disease is the Christian's promised "suffering." Yes, even in the New Testament, it is made perfectly clear that we *will* have suffering. However, I have looked up *every* reference to "suffer" (and its derivatives), in the New Testament—about 30 verses with numerous instances in some of them—and guess what? If you examine the context of them, *not one* of them have anything to do with physical illness.

Notably, on at least one occasion, it *specifically differentiates* sickness from suffering:

James 5:13-15
[13] Is anyone among you *suffering*? Let him *pray*. Is anyone cheerful? Let him sing psalms. [14] Is anyone among you *sick*? Let him *call for the elders* of the church, and let them pray over him, anointing him with oil in the name of the Lord. [15] And the prayer of faith will save the sick, and the Lord will raise him up. And if he has committed sins, he will be forgiven.

It's obvious in this particular text that sickness and suffering are two different things; because the Apostle James prescribes two different responses. He says if we're "suffering," *we* should pray. But he says if we're "sick," then we should call the elders and have *them* pray over us and anoint us with oil. If "suffering" and being "sick" were the same thing, there would only be one response expected of us. And of course, let's not fail to notice the obvious in this text: The only mention of sickness is made in conjunction with *a promise of healing*!

In *every* place where Christian sufferings are clarified or listed, it becomes clear that a Believer's "suffering" is *not* sickness. I'll just give a couple of examples:

1 Peter 2:19-23

[19] For this *is* commendable, if because of conscience toward God one endures *grief, suffering wrongfully.* [20] For what credit is it if, when you are *beaten* for your faults, you take it patiently? But when you do good and *suffer,* if you take it patiently, this is commendable before God. [21] For to this you were called, because Christ also *suffered* for us, leaving us an example, that you should follow His steps: [22] " Who committed no sin, nor was deceit found in His mouth"; [23] who, when He was *reviled,* did not revile in return; when He *suffered,* He did not threaten, but committed Himself to Him who judges righteously;

1 Peter 3:13-17

[13] And who is he who will harm you if you become followers of what is good? [14] But even if you should *suffer for righteousness' sake,* you are blessed. "And do not be afraid of their *threats,* nor be troubled." [15] But sanctify the Lord God in your hearts, and always be ready to give a defense to everyone who asks you a reason for the hope that is in you, with meekness and fear; [16] having a good conscience, that when they *defame* you as evildoers, those who *revile* your good conduct in Christ may be ashamed. [17] For it is better, if it is the will of God, to *suffer for doing good* than for doing evil.

> When we examine the context of any reference to "suffering" for the Christian—it is *never* referring to sickness.

It becomes quite obvious when we examine the context of any reference to "suffering" for the Christian—it is *never* referring to sickness. These 30-plus Scriptures define our suffering specifically as meaning the following: being concerned for others, sleeplessness, "fastings," shipwrecks, perils on land and sea, perils in the country and in the city, danger from strangers and "fellow countrymen" and "false brethren," being reviled and reproached, being defamed and spoken evil of, suffering "for righteousness' sake" or for doing good (how could this apply to sickness exactly?), suffering the loss of one's goods, being rejected, being imprisoned, being hated, being beaten, mocked, persecuted, or even executed for Christ. [1]

In *all* of these Scriptures, the Bible *never once* adds "sickness" or "disease" to the list of our promised sufferings! We've got to stick with the Bible! We are *not* promised sickness; but we *are* promised persecution, and we are *also* promised healing!

SMALL POTATO #5:
Timothy's Tummy

Another random verse people bring up when it comes to healing is in Paul's first letter to Timothy:

1 Timothy 5:23
No longer drink only water, but use a little wine for your stomach's sake and your frequent infirmities.

"See," they say, "even Timothy was *frequently* sick!" The first things we must remember are some of our "pillars" or "larger truths." Even if it's true that Timothy was frequently sick— *nobody's* personal experience can ever replace the clearly expressed will of God for us, found in His Word. *Nobody's* personal experience takes precedence over the full, radical provision for healing that Jesus made available through His finished work! Timothy's experience does not trump the fact that we are one with Jesus and hidden with Christ in God, where sickness is nowhere to be found!

Beyond that, let's look at what Paul is actually telling Timothy, since most westerners just have no clue. When I travel to other, "developing" countries that don't have advanced water treatment systems in place, I more or less

> *Nobody's* personal experience takes precedence over the full, radical provision for healing that Jesus made available through His finished work!

avoid drinking the water. Why? Because it's full of disease! Water-borne disease is one of the top killers around the world! Depending on the country, I may even avoid fresh fruit and vegetables because of the water used to grow them. Not only do

I drink only bottled water while there, I only brush my teeth with it too. There's no reason to be presumptuous and test the Lord. Now—if there's no other options, I certainly don't hesitate at all to "eat what's set before me" (Luke 10:8), bless it, drink it, and trust God that if I "drink any deadly thing, it will not harm (me)" (Mark 16:18).

Water may commonly be filled with disease-causing agents; but wine (yes, fermented wine), on the other hand, kills most of these organisms! Paul was *not* recommending wine as a *medical response* or "cure" to Timothy's sickness (instead of the far superior Divine Healing)! Paul was simply recommending that Timothy drink "a little" wine as a common sense *preventive measure* to keep from getting sick from the water. It's better to avoid getting sick in the first place, than to get sick unnecessarily and need healing. It's like washing your hands to keep from spreading germs, brushing your teeth to avoid tooth decay, or wearing a jacket not to catch a cold. It doesn't mean you don't believe in healing, it means, "an ounce of prevention is worth a pound of cure." Yes, we can receive God's healing if we get sick; but that's not license to be foolish or irresponsible.

> It's better to avoid getting sick in the first place, than to get sick unnecessarily and need healing.

SMALL POTATO #6: Trophimus Sick in Miletus

The final random Scripture I can think of that some people will take a last, desperate grasp at to try to say that God's will is sometimes sickness (I think I just threw up a little), is found in Paul's second letter to Timothy:

2 Timothy 4:20
Erastus stayed in Corinth, but Trophimus I have left in Miletus sick.

• Mis-Application #1

Some people will read this verse and make the leap that "Because this verse says that Paul left Trophimus sick in Miletus, Trophimus must not have gotten healed." We see *zero* indication whatsoever in this Scripture that Trophimus wasn't healed after Paul left. In fact, it seems quite the contrary, as you'll discover here. Paul had a pretty consistent healing ministry, so based on his track record, my guess is that Trophimus probably got healed in a day or two.

Here I will posit a theory. I call it a theory because scholars differ significantly on the timeline of Paul's travels and letters. So it's quite possible that this verse from 2 Timothy doesn't line up with Acts the way it would have to for this theory to be correct. But the theory sure makes a lot of sense, and would be consistent with Scriptural doctrine and personal experience in healing, so I'll put it here for your consideration.

Paul only left Trophimus sick in Miletus because he was on a tight schedule! He was in a rush to get to Jerusalem for Pentecost. How do we know this? Let's look at Acts, where it describes Trophimus and Miletus (potentially the same occasion mentioned in 2 Timothy):

Acts 20:4, 15-16
⁴ And Sopater of Berea accompanied him to Asia—also... *Trophimus* of Asia...
¹⁵ ...The next *day* we came to *Miletus.* ¹⁶ For *Paul had decided to sail past Ephesus, so that he would not have to spend time in Asia; for he was hurrying to be at Jerusalem*, if possible, on the Day of Pentecost.

Folks, Paul was in a hurry! While he may have cared deeply for Trophimus, Paul decided that didn't have the time to wait around for him to recover (even if dramatically accelerated by the gifts of healings)—he needed to get to Jerusalem in time to celebrate Pentecost—the Jewish Feast of Weeks/Shavuot.

Undoubtedly, Paul prayed for Trophimus' healing before he left—Paul was a healing machine! But remember, there is a difference between the gifts of healings, and the working of miracles (1 Cor. 12:9-10)—one tends to be instant, while the other is often more gradual in manifestation. Even Jesus sometimes saw gradual healing, or healing after repeated ministry (Please see Chapter 11 on "Jesus—Our Standard" if you need to review these facts). Paul prayed for Trophimus, left for Jerusalem, and within a day or two Trophimus was up and at 'em again. How can I say that? Because I read the story in Acts! Sometime within Paul's first *two or three days* in Jerusalem, Trophimus had already caught up with him there!

Paul arrived in Jerusalem in Acts 21, verse 17. Verse 18 says "on the following day," Paul went to see James and the church leaders there in Jerusalem. They told him to go to the temple and take some guys with him to participate in some religious rites during the seven days of purification that culminate with the day of Pentecost. Verse 26 says that he did it and "the next day" (day 3 in Jerusalem) he went with some guys to be purified, then went to the temple to announce the arrival of the Day of Pentecost (so Paul made it in time for Pentecost after all). In the temple, a bunch of Jews got mad at Paul. Why?

Acts 21:26-29
[26] Then Paul took the men, and *the next day*, having been purified with them, entered the temple to announce the expiration of the days of purification, at which time an offering should be made for each one of them. [27] When the *seven days* were nearly over, some Jews from the province of Asia saw Paul at the temple. They stirred up the whole crowd and seized him, [28] shouting, "Fellow Israelites, help us! This is the man who teaches everyone everywhere against our people and our law and this place. And besides, he has brought Greeks into the temple and defiled this holy place." [29] (*They had previously seen Trophimus the Ephesian in the city with Paul* and assumed that Paul had brought him into the temple.)

Here we clearly see that the Jews were mad because some time in the couple of days Paul was in Jerusalem, they had seen him with Trophimus (a Gentile from Ephesus), and assumed that he had brought him into the temple—a big Jewish no-no! But there we have it—Within a mere 2-3 days of his arrival in Jerusalem, Paul had already been seen publicly with Trophimus in Jerusalem!

So here's the theory: True indeed—back in Miletus, Trophimus had gotten sick. Paul prayed for Trophimus; but didn't have time to wait for him to get back on his feet, because he had to get to Jerusalem, so he left. Then, within three days of Paul's arrival in Jerusalem (at the longest), Trophimus had already rejoined Paul there—*after* having traveled from Miletus! Paul left Trophimus sick in Miletus, yes; but Trophimus also got healed and kept on trucking. He made it to Jerusalem only a day or two behind Paul—just in time to party with him on Pentecost.

Scholars disagree on the dating of 2 Timothy, and how exactly it aligns with Acts. It's possible that 2 Timothy was written 7-10 years after the events in Acts 21. So the theory above may or may not line up historically. But even so, there is another theory as to why Paul left Trophimus there. It is generally believed that Paul was (post-Acts) re-arrested in Troas (near Miletus), and taken to Rome, where tradition holds that he was beheaded. One of the most common sailing routes would have stopped in Miletus on the way to Rome from Troas. Paul could well have seen Trophimus there, ministered to him, and the prisoner boat had to keep sailing before Paul got to see his healing come to fruition. It would be perfectly logical to expect that a ship carrying prisoners would be on a set schedule.

However, even if we completely ignore these two theories from the text of Acts, and from post-Acts history—If we just read the verse in 2 Timothy, there is still *no reason* to make an anti-healing doctrine out of it. *That* would be mis-application #2...

• Mis-Application #2

Still others will read this one verse and say, "If Paul couldn't get Trophimus healed, then we shouldn't expect to see everyone healed either." Wrong! First, as we've already seen—Trophimus *was* probably healed! But just to play devil's advocate and teach a lesson—Even if Trophimus had never gotten healed, we *still* cannot say, "Let's take this one experience and create a doctrine out of it."

Paul was not teaching doctrine, he was simply telling a story about what happened in this case. We can't turn this experience into doctrine. We must always interpret if an experience recorded in the Bible is *descriptive* or *prescriptive*. In other words, is the Lord just describing what happened, or is He prescribing doctrine to set expectation for our own experience? Not everything is prescriptive. We can look at the rest of the same chapter (2 Timothy 4) and determine that. There we see that Demas forsook Paul (v.10). We also see that Alexander the coppersmith did Paul harm (v.14-15). Is God telling us to forsake people and do them harm? Of course not; but there they are—recorded as historical events in the Word of God— Descriptive vs. Prescriptive.

> Is the Lord just describing what happened, or is He prescribing doctrine to set expectation for our own experience?

Paul simply said that he left Trophimus sick in Miletus. He didn't say that it was God's will for Trophimus to get sick or stay sick. Paul didn't say that Trophimus must have sinned. He didn't say that Trophimus was reaping what he had sown. He didn't say, "Pray for the sick, and whatever happens, happens; because God is pretty unpredictable." No! Anywhere in the New Testament where we are being *taught* about healing and God's will, it is crystal clear that God's will is always healing. It's clear that Believers lay hands on the sick, and they recover. It is clear that our healing was paid for by the stripes of Jesus. It is clear that Jesus is our standard of expectation; because we are one with Him—and *everyone* He ministered to *always* got healed.

In the case of Trophimus being sick in Miletus, when looked at in the light of the full counsel of Scripture, it is clearly only *descriptive*. All of this is completely discounting the fact that Trophimus was most likely healed anyway, as we discussed.

Folks, I can't tell you how many times I've prayed for someone and didn't get to see the results *right away*. Then in a matter of moments, hours, or sometimes even a day or two—the healing completely manifested. But I had already "set sail!" Like Paul, I had "left them sick" at Walmart, in "Miletus", or wherever I ministered to them; but they *were* actually healed! Sometimes they contact me and tell me about it. Sometimes they don't, then I'll run into them a couple of years later and they'll say, "Oh, remember that time you prayed for healing of my chronic *(fill in the blank)*? Well the next day the pain left and it's never returned since." Thanks for telling me, so we could give God praise, buddy!

> Let's not build doctrinal castles on sand. God's will is always healing!!

These seven words about Paul leaving Trophimus sick in Miletus are not worthy of the weight they are sometimes given. He may have been healed in a day or two. He may not have. Either way, let's not build doctrinal castles on sand. God's will is *always* healing!!

369

Notes:

Final Thoughts

I'd like to say thank you to every person who took the time to read this book. It's long and has a ton of information in it. Much of it could be new to some people, and challenging to long-standing traditions and beliefs. Some might have agreed with me through the whole book, while others might still be upset with me at this point. They must not have done the chapter review questions! Hahaha! Relax, I'm kidding.

But seriously, I hope that we all walk away from this book with a few truths that have been established in our spiritual foundations, so that when life brings sickness or trouble to us—or those we minister to—we will always remember:

- Not everything that happens is God's will.
- We have the authority and responsibility to change the things that aren't.
- God wants things on earth to look like they do in Heaven.

Sometimes we fail; but we won't make up false theology to justify it; because we know:

- God is good, and the devil is bad.
- Sickness is a fruit of sin coming into the world, and is a work of the devil.
- Jesus was manifested to destroy the works of the devil, and so are we.

If we are ministering healing and people bring up various Scriptures to hinder healing, we'll know:

- Paul's "thorn" was persecution, not sickness.
- Job was in the Old Testament (we're not!), and he opened a door through fear.

- I'm not one with Job, I'm one with Jesus and His life and ministry is my standard of expectation.
- God is a loving Father, and He doesn't use sickness to teach us or make us more like Jesus.
- The Holy Spirit is our Teacher, and He uses His Word to teach us from the inside.
- The gifts of the Spirit have been in the Church for all Its history, and will continue until Jesus' final return.

When we find random Scriptures that make us go "Huh?" We will remember:

- Jesus is the perfect picture of the Father.
- Bible interpretation that creates a picture of God that doesn't look like Jesus' life and ministry is a wrong interpretation.
- Sometimes it was gradual, sometimes it took more than one prayer, sometimes it was instant; but Jesus healed everyone that ever came to Him. Without exception.
- Nothing could ever stop Him from healing them—not devils, not sin, not unbelief. Nothing. Ever.

When someone says to us, "Yeah, but that was Jesus!" We'll know that:

- As He is, so are we in the world.
- It's no longer us living, but Christ living through us.
- What God has joined together, let no man separate.
- The same works that He did, we'll do, and greater...

So we will never, ever settle for less than what Jesus experienced. We won't make excuses. We also won't get into condemnation. We will pick ourselves up, keep believing, and continue renewing our minds and being transformed until we re-present Jesus in every way. We will continue trusting and increasing in our experience of God's will here on earth. We will grow in revelation, and rise to the fullness of the stature of Christ.

When sickness presents itself—We won't have any question about if there's some mysterious "higher purpose" behind it. We won't wonder what we're supposed to "learn" from it. We won't die before we've run our race and fulfilled our destiny. Our healed bodies and blessed lives will give accurate witness to the goodness of God. When ministering to others, we will not accept sickness, disease or pain. We will not allow it. We will hate it and we will confidently and violently deal with it—all by trusting God's Word and resting in His superior reality.

We won't wonder about God's will, or God's timing. We'll know that every sickness and disease must bow to the Name above all names. We'll know that Jesus' stripes were more than enough. We'll know that He really did receive all authority, and that He really is the King seated on the throne! We'll know that we are anointed with the Holy Ghost and with power and are here to destroy the works of the devil! Sickness and every other enemy of Jesus *will* be made His footstool. The kingdoms of this world *will* become the kingdoms of our God and of His Christ, and He *will* reign forever!

Ultimately, I just wanted to encourage all of us, and stir our faith. Maybe we find ourselves sick, diseased, and in pain. Or, maybe we want to more accurately re-present Jesus by ministering Salvation and healing to others and setting the captives free—It's His will for every person, after all. Either way, let's keep our eyes on Jesus and what He's done. Let's allow those invisible truths to become our visible experience. Let's keep trusting His Word, and let's never settle for less than God's will. We are *one* with Jesus—the risen and exalted Lord of all. As He is, so are we in the world. Nothing can stop us! God's Will is Always Healing!!!

> Never, ever, settle for less than God's will. His will is *always* healing!

Prayer for Healing

God, I thank You for all you've done for us in Jesus Christ. Jesus, I thank You for coming and not only washing away our sins forever, but for providing physical healing in our great Salvation. Holy Spirit, I thank You for revealing to us the truth that God's will is *always* healing, and that it's already accomplished for us. Thank You that your power manifests the will of God in our lives as we trust Your Word above all else.

Devil, you are defeated and you know it. As a redeemed child of God— a higher authority than you—I order every demonic spirit of infirmity to leave this body in the authority of Jesus' Name! Go NOW! Leave this person and never return. Every work of the enemy must bow to the supremacy of Jesus and His Kingdom right now!

I curse every sickness and disease in the Name of Jesus! I command every sickness, virus, pain, disease-causing bacteria, and ungodly condition to die, disappear and leave this person's body. I command every malfunctioning part to be healed and restored to the perfection that God designed. Let missing parts be recreated in Jesus' Name. I command it to be on earth—in our bodies—just as it is in Heaven. There is no disease allowed in Heaven, so we don't allow it here anymore, in Jesus' Name.

Lord, we thank You that these bodies are Your temple. Lord, you completely fill your temple and drive out all sickness, pain, and work of the enemy. Your indwelling Spirit brings divine life into every cell, tissue and system. We thank you for making not only our spirits, but also our physical bodies, one with Christ Himself. As those united with the living, exalted King of Kings, we receive our inheritance as children of God! We trust that we are to enjoy the very life of Christ, seated at Your right hand! It's no longer us living, but Christ living in us. Thank You that Your power is at work in us—and our visible experience will align with the invisible Truth. We receive all You have accomplished and provided for us in Jesus' Mighty Name. Amen!

Endnotes/References

Introduction

1. Bosworth, F.F. (1973). *Christ the Healer.* Grand Rapids, MI. Fleming H. Regell.

Chapter 1

1. Power of attorney. (n.d.). *Collins English Dictionary – Complete & Unabridged 10th Edition.* Retrieved December 14, 2011, from Dictionary.com website: http://dictionary.reference.com/browse/power of attorney

Chapter 2

1. Hayford, J. (2002). *Prayer is Invading the Impossible.* Alachua, FL. Bridge Logos Foundation.
2. Yeomans, L. (2003). *His Healing Power: Four Classic Books on Healing, Complete in One Volume.* Tulsa, OK. Harrison House, Inc.

Chapter 3

1. Sovereign. (n.d.). *Dictionary.com Unabridged.* Retrieved December 14, 2011, from Dictionary.com website: http://dictionary.reference.com/browse/sovereign

Chapter 4

1. Torrey, R. (2003). *Difficulties in the Bible.* New Kensington, PA, Whitaker House.

Chapter 7

1. Blue Letter Bible. "Dictionary and Word Search for *sōzō (Strong's 4982)*". Blue Letter Bible. 1996-2011. 14 Dec 2011. http://www.blueletterbible.org/lang/lexicon/lexicon.cfm?Strongs=4982
2. Strong, J. (1990). The New Strong's Exhaustive Concordance of the Bible. Nashville, TN. Thomas Nelson, Inc. Publishers.
3. Atonement. (n.d.). *Dictionary.com Unabridged.* Retrieved December 14, 2011, from Dictionary.com website: http://dictionary.reference.com/browse/atonement
4. Blue Letter Bible. "Dictionary and Word Search for *choliy (Strong's 2483)*". Blue Letter Bible. 1996-2011. 15 Dec 2011. http://www.blueletterbible.org/lang/lexicon/lexicon.cfm?Strongs=H2483&t=NKJV
5. Blue Letter Bible. "Dictionary and Word Search for *mak'ob (Strong's 4341)*". Blue Letter Bible. 1996-2011. 15 Dec 2011. http://www.blueletterbible.org/lang/lexicon/lexicon.cfm?Strongs=H4341&t=NKJV
6. Scripture quotations marked HCSB are taken from the Holman Christian Standard Bible®, Copyright © 1999, 2000, 2002, 2003, 2009 by Holman Bible Publishers. Used by permission. Holman Christian Standard Bible®, Holman CSB®, and HCSB® are federally registered trademarks of Holman Bible Publishers.
7. Blue Letter Bible. "Dictionary and Word Search for *astheneia (Strong's 769)*". Blue Letter Bible. 1996-2011. 15 Dec 2011. http://www.blueletterbible.org/lang/lexicon/lexicon.cfm?Strongs=G769&t=NKJV
8. Blue Letter Bible. "Dictionary and Word Search for *nosos (Strong's 3554)*". Blue Letter Bible. 1996-2011. 15 Dec 2011. http://www.blueletterbible.org/lang/lexicon/lexicon.cfm?Strongs=G3554&t=NKJV
9. Blue Letter Bible. "Dictionary and Word Search for *nasa' (Strong's 5375)*". Blue Letter Bible. 1996-2011. 14 Dec 2011. http://www.blueletterbible.org/lang/lexicon/lexicon.cfm?Strongs=H5375&t=NKJV

10. Blue Letter Bible. "Dictionary and Word Search for *cabal (Strong's 5445)*". Blue Letter Bible. 1996-2011. 14 Dec 2011.
http://www.blueletterbible.org/lang/lexicon/lexicon.cfm?Strongs=H5445&t=NKJV
11. Blue Letter Bible. "Dictionary and Word Search for *plēroō (Strong's 4137)*". Blue Letter Bible. 1996-2011. 14 Dec 2011.
http://www.blueletterbible.org/lang/lexicon/lexicon.cfm?Strongs=G4137&t=NKJV

Chapter 8

1. Gordon, A.J. (1964). *In Christ or the Believer's Union with His Lord*. Grand Rapids, MI. Baker Book House

Chapter 9

1. Fried, R.N., & Schlamme, T. (1993). *So I Married an Axe Murderer*. USA: TriStar Pictures.

Chapter 10

1. Excerpts from: Good. (n.d.). *Dictionary.com Unabridged*. Retrieved December 14, 2011, from Dictionary.com website: http://dictionary.reference.com/browse/good
2. Wisenberg, S. & Clinton, W. (1998). *Videotaped Testimony of William Jefferson Clinton President of the United States Before the Grand Jury Empaneled for Independent Counsel Kenneth Starr*. Retrieved from the Jurist Legal News & Research website:
http://jurist.law.pitt.edu/transcr.htm
3. Finerman, W., & Zemeckis, R. (1994). *Forrest Gump*. USA: Paramount Pictures.
4. Torrey, R. (2003). *Difficulties in the Bible*. New Kensington, PA, Whitaker House.

Chapter 11

1. Bill Johnson – Bringing Heaven to Earth (Part 1/2). Retrieved from
http://www.youtube.com/watch?v=v0rsX3x98XE
2. Scripture taken from *The Message*. Copyright © 1993, 1994, 1995, 1996, 2000, 2001, 2002. Used by permission of NavPress Publishing Group.
3. Vine, W. E. "Apo and Ek", *Vine's Expository Dictionary of New Testament Words*. Blue Letter Bible. 1940. 24 June, 1996 15 Dec 2011.
http://www.blueletterbible.org/Search/Dictionary/viewTopic.cfm?type=GetTopic&Topic=Apo+and +Ek&DictList=9#Vine's

Chapter 13

1. Blue Letter Bible. "Dictionary and Word Search for *astheneia (Strong's 769)*". Blue Letter Bible. 1996-2011. 15 Dec 2011.
http://www.blueletterbible.org/lang/lexicon/lexicon.cfm?Strongs=G769&t=KJV
2. Luther, Martin. (1983). *Volume VII The Sermons of Martin Luther*. Grand Rapids, MI. Baker Book House. Accessed online at http://www.orlutheran.com/html/mlse2c11.html
3. Chrysostom, J. *Homily 26 on 2 Corinthians*. Translated by Talbot W. Chambers. From Nicene and Post-Nicene Fathers, First Series, Vol. 12. Edited by Philip Schaff. (Buffalo, NY: Christian Literature Publishing Co., 1889.) Revised and edited for New Advent by Kevin Knight.
http://www.newadvent.org/fathers/220226.htm.
4. Chrysostom, J. *Homily 9 on 2 Corinthians*. Translated by Talbot W. Chambers. From Nicene and Post-Nicene Fathers, First Series, Vol. 12. Edited by Philip Schaff. (Buffalo, NY: Christian Literature Publishing Co., 1889.) Revised and edited for New Advent by Kevin Knight.
http://www.newadvent.org/fathers/220209.htm.
5. Chrysostom, J. Homily 14 on Romans. Translated by J. Walker, J. Sheppard and H. Browne, and revised by George B. Stevens. From Nicene and Post-Nicene Fathers, First Series, Vol. 11.

Edited by Philip Schaff. (Buffalo, NY: Christian Literature Publishing Co., 1889.) Revised and edited for New Advent by Kevin Knight. http://www.newadvent.org/fathers/210214.htm

6. Chrysostom, J. *Letter to Olympias I*. Translated by W.R.W. Stephens. From Nicene and Post-Nicene Fathers, First Series, Vol. 9. Edited by Philip Schaff. (Buffalo, NY: Christian Literature Publishing Co., 1889.) Revised and edited for New Advent by Kevin Knight. http://www.newadvent.org/fathers/1916.htm

7. Unknown. Catholic Apologetics Information website. Accessed at http://www.catholicapologetics.info/scripture/newtestament/2ndcor1213.htm

8. Blue Letter Bible. "Dictionary and Word Search for *aggelos (Strong's 32)*". Blue Letter Bible. 1996-2011. 15 Dec 2011. http://www.blueletterbible.org/lang/lexicon/lexicon.cfm?Strongs=G32&t=KJV

9. Blue Letter Bible. "Dictionary and Word Search for *kolaphizō (Strong's 2852)*". Blue Letter Bible. 1996-2011. 15 Dec 2011. http://www.blueletterbible.org/lang/lexicon/lexicon.cfm?Strongs=G2852&t=KJV

10. Contumely. (n.d.). *Dictionary.com Unabridged*. Retrieved December 15, 2011, from Dictionary.com website: http://dictionary.reference.com/browse/contumely

11. Blue Letter Bible. "Dictionary and Word Search for *pēlikos (Strong's 4080)*". Blue Letter Bible. 1996-2011. 28 Dec 2011. http://www.blueletterbible.org/lang/lexicon/lexicon.cfm?Strongs=G4080&t=NKJV

12. Blue Letter Bible. "Dictionary and Word Search for *gramma (Strong's 1121)*". Blue Letter Bible. 1996-2011. 28 Dec 2011. http://www.blueletterbible.org/lang/lexicon/lexicon.cfm?Strongs=G1121&t=NKJV

Chapter 15

1. Blue Letter Bible. "Dictionary and Word Search for *paideia (Strong's 3809)*". Blue Letter Bible. 1996-2011. 15 Dec 2011. http://www.blueletterbible.org/lang/lexicon/lexicon.cfm?Strongs=G3809&t=NKJV

Chapter 16

1. Justin Martyr. *Dialogue with Trypho the Jew*. Origen. *Against Celsus*. Cited by Ruthven, J. in *On the Cessation of the Charismata: A Protestant Polemic on Post-Biblical Miracles*. Sheffield, UK. Sheffield University Academic Press.

2. Aquinas, T. *Summa Theologiae* and *Commentary on John*. Cited by Ruthven, J. (2008). *On the Cessation of the Charismata: A Protestant Polemic on Post-Biblical Miracles*. Sheffield, UK. Sheffield University Academic Press.

3. Calvin, J. *Institutes of the Christian Religion,* Prefatory Address, 3 (16). Cited by Ruthven, J. (2008). *On the Cessation of the Charismata: A Protestant Polemic on Post-Biblical Miracles*. Sheffield, UK. Sheffield University Academic Press.

4. Calvin, J. *Institutes of the Christian Religion,* vol.1, p.26. Cited by Warfield, B.B. (1918). *Counterfeit Miracles*. Accessed online at: http://www.christianbeliefs.org/books/cm/cm-contents.html

5. Calvin, J. *Institutes of the Christian Religion,* IV, 3, 4. Cited by Ruthven, J. (2008). *On the Cessation of the Charismata: A Protestant Polemic on Post-Biblical Miracles*. Sheffield, UK. Sheffield University Academic Press.

6. Warfield, B.B. (1918). *Counterfeit Miracles*. Accessed online at: http://www.christianbeliefs.org/books/cm/cm-contents.html

7. Warfield, B.B. (1918). *Counterfeit Miracles*. Accessed online at: http://www.christianbeliefs.org/books/cm/cm-contents.html

8. Epiphanius, *Against Panarion* 48. V. 4 (PG 41:855). Cited by Ruthven, J. (2008). *On the Cessation of the Charismata: A Protestant Polemic on Post-Biblical Miracles*. Sheffield, UK. Sheffield University Academic Press.

9. Eusebius, *Church History*, V,17,4 (*PNF*, 2nd ser., 1:234). Cited by Ruthven, J. (2008). *On the Cessation of the Charismata: A Protestant Polemic on Post-Biblical Miracles*. Sheffield, UK. Sheffield University Academic Press.

10. Ruthven, J. (2008). *On the Cessation of the Charismata: A Protestant Polemic on Post-Biblical Miracles*. Sheffield, UK. Sheffield University Academic Press.

11. Calvin, J. (1536). *Commentary on 1 Corinthians*. Accessed online at: http://www.ccel.org/ccel/calvin/calcom39.xx.iii.html

12. Calvin, J. (1536). *Commentary on 1 Corinthians*. Accessed online at: http://www.ccel.org/ccel/calvin/calcom39.xx.iii.html

13. Middleton, C. (1755). *Miscellaneous Works*. Cited by Warfield, B.B. (1918). *Counterfeit Miracles*. Accessed online at: http://www.christianbeliefs.org/books/cm/cm-contents.html

14. Warfield, B.B. (1918). *Counterfeit Miracles*. Accessed online at: http://www.christianbeliefs.org/books/cm/cm-contents.html

15. Warfield, B.B. (1918). *Counterfeit Miracles*. Accessed online at: http://www.christianbeliefs.org/books/cm/cm-contents.html

16. Warfield, B.B. (1918). *Counterfeit Miracles*. (Summarizing a thought from Conyers Middleton's works, *Remarks on Two Pamphlets...* and *A Free Inquiry...*) Accessed online at: http://www.christianbeliefs.org/books/cm/cm-contents.html

17. Warfield, B.B. (1918). *Counterfeit Miracles*. Accessed online at: http://www.christianbeliefs.org/books/cm/cm-contents.html

18. Warfield, B.B. (1918). *Counterfeit Miracles*. Accessed online at: http://www.christianbeliefs.org/books/cm/cm-contents.html

19. Warfield, B.B. (1918). *Counterfeit Miracles*. Accessed online at: http://www.christianbeliefs.org/books/cm/cm-contents.html

20. Calvin, J. *Institutes of the Christian Religion,* Prefatory Address, 3 (16). Cited by Ruthven, J. (2008). *On the Cessation of the Charismata: A Protestant Polemic on Post-Biblical Miracles.* Sheffield, UK. Sheffield University Academic Press.

21. Augustine. City of God. Cited by Warfield, B.B. (1918). *Counterfeit Miracles*. Accessed online at: http://www.christianbeliefs.org/books/cm/cm-contents.html

22. Ruthven, J. (2008). *On the Cessation of the Charismata: A Protestant Polemic on Post-Biblical Miracles*. Sheffield, UK. Sheffield University Academic Press.

23. Ruthven, J. (2008). *On the Cessation of the Charismata: A Protestant Polemic on Post-Biblical Miracles*. Sheffield, UK. Sheffield University Academic Press.

24. Ruthven, J. (2008). *On the Cessation of the Charismata: A Protestant Polemic on Post-Biblical Miracles*. Sheffield, UK. Sheffield University Academic Press.

25. Blue Letter Bible. "Dictionary and Word Search for *dynamis (Strong's 1411)*". Blue Letter Bible. 1996-2011. 22 Dec 2011. http:// www.blueletterbible.org/lang/lexicon/lexicon.cfm?Strongs=G1411&t=NKJV

Chapter 17

1. 2 Corinthians 11:22-29; Galatians 5:11, 6:12; Philippians 1:27-30; Philippians 3:7-11; 1 Thessalonians 2:2, 14, 3:4; 1 Timothy 4:10, 2 Timothy 1:8, 2:9, 3:12; Hebrews 2:9, 10:32-33; 1 Peter 4:12-16, 19; Revelation 2:10

378

STUDY GUIDE

Chapter 1

1. According to Genesis 1:26-28, and Psalm 8:4-6, what does Man have authority over? _____

   _____
   _____

2. Who owns the earth, according to Psalm 24:1? _____
   But according to Psalm 115:16, who has He given it to? _____

   _____

3. When Man sinned, he lost his authority. Please review 1 John 5:19, 2 Corinthians 4:3-4, Luke 4:5-7, John 12:31, John 14:30, and John 16:8-11. Who do these verses say gained that authority from Adam?

   _____

4. According to John 10:1-10 and Hebrews 2:14-18, why did Jesus have to come to Earth as a Man? _____

   _____
   _____

5. After reading Colossians 2:13-15, how would you describe the outcome of the "battle" between Jesus and Satan? _____

   _____
   _____

6. According to Revelation 1:18 and Matthew 28:18-20, Jesus got the "keys" and "all authority in heaven and earth" back. How much authority does that leave in the devil's hands? _____
   How should that impact *your* life? _____

   _____
   _____

7. Even before the Cross, Jesus operated in raw authority over nature, over sickness, and over devils. He also successfully commissioned at least 82 other people to do the same (See Matthew 10:1, Luke 9:1, Luke 10:19 and Matthew 16:19). How do you explain this? _____

   _____
   _____
   _____

8. Review Matthew 10:1, Luke 9:1, and Luke 10:19. What did Jesus give His disciples authority and power over? _____

    _____

    _____

9. Define "power of attorney." _____

    _____

10. Explain how Luke 19:12-13 gives a picture of this delegated authority. _____

    _____

    _____

    _____

11. Where do we see this same concept in Matthew 28? _____
    Who was Jesus talking to in this situation? _____
    Does this commission apply to us today then? Why or why not (Hint: the answer is in the same text)? _____

    _____

    _____

12. How can Jesus give us free reign to "Do business till I come?" Why does He trust us with this kind of authority? _____

    _____

    _____

Chapter 2

1. According to Ephesians 1:20-23 and 2:4-6, where are Believers currently sitting? _____
    What does that mean to you? _____

    _____

    _____

    _____

1. If we are the Body of Christ, then according to the above Scriptures, what is under our feet? _____
    According to Hebrews 2:8, what is *not* under our feet? _____

2. Even though we don't always see ourselves successfully operating in that level of authority (with our natural eyes and experiences), what should we do (according to Hebrews 2:8-10) to be reassured of what belongs to us? _____

What impact should *that* have on our expectations? _____
_____
_____

3. According to Hebrews 12:10-13 (See also Psalm 110:1; Acts 2:34-35;
    Hebrews 1:13; 1 Corinthians 15:25), how long will Jesus be sitting
    there waiting before He ultimately takes back full control of the
    Earth? _____
    Who do you think God will use to accomplish this? _____
    _____

4. If Believers are the Heirs of the Earth, left to "run the Family
    business", what does God Himself still control? _____
    _____
    _____

5. Read the parable of the talents in Matthew 25:14-30. What parallels
    do you see between this parable and the Kingdom? _____
    _____
    _____
    _____
    _____
    _____

6. How can you avoid the mistakes of the "unfaithful" or "lazy" servant?
    _____
    _____
    _____

7. Name two Scriptures that show that sometimes evil people get their
    way, against the will of God. _____
    Name two Scriptures that show that sometimes God's good will
    breaks in and overrides the plans that men make. _____
    _____

8. How do you explain that sometimes God can intervene and ruin evil
    plans, and other times the evil happens, even though it's against
    God's will? _____
    _____
    _____
    _____
    _____
    _____

9. After re-reading James 4:2-3 and 6, why do we not "have" some things that God has desired and promised to give us? _____

_____

_____

10. Review the CEV translation of Matthew 18:18. What things does God allow? _____
So who is it that determines on earth what is allowed—sickness, for instance? _____
How will you respond to this realization? _____

_____

_____

_____

11. What/Who does Ephesians 4:14-16 say that we are supposed to grow up into? _____ What would that look like in your own life?

_____

_____

_____

_____

_____

_____

_____

Chapter 3

1. What is the dictionary definition of "sovereign?" _____

_____

_____
Do you see anything about "controlling every detail?" _____

_____

2. If we say that God is in control of everything, and that He willed, decreed, or ordained for some evil thing to happen, do you think that would make God responsible (guilty) for that event? _____
Why or why not? _____

_____

_____

_____

3. After reading 1 Corinthians 2:9-12, why can we not claim that God works in mysterious ways? _____

_____

_____

Review John 15:15. If Christianity is a "relationship" like we claim, then what impact should relationship with God have on knowing His ways? _____

_____
_____

4. What is one thing that God has reserved to be under His sole authority? _____

_____

5. Do you think it would be just for God to tell us to "choose," if we had no free will, and He had really already decided for us? _____
Why or why not? _____

_____
_____

Would it make sense for there to be reward or punishment if people were not free to make—and responsible for their own decisions? ____
Why or why not? _____

_____
_____

6. In Luke 11:2, Jesus teaches us to pray that God's will would be on earth just as it is in Heaven. Do you think that implies that God's will is not already being done on Earth? _____
Why or why not? _____

_____
_____

7. What are some of the things that are currently being done on Earth, that are not allowed in Heaven? _____

_____
_____

Are these things, then, the will of God? _____
How are we to respond? _____

_____
_____

8. How do Matthew 16:19 and 18:18 confirm this understanding of the Lord's prayer? _____

_____
_____
_____
_____

9. What do 1 Timothy 2:3-4 and 2 Peter 3:9 clearly state that God's will is concerning salvation? _____

_____

Is there any qualifying statement about who God wants saved? _____

_____
_____

10. Explain why God must make *all* people, knowing in advance that *some* won't choose Him. _____

_____
_____
_____
_____
_____

11. Without freedom, there is no real loving relationship. Do you agree or disagree? _____
Explain. _____

_____
_____
_____
_____
_____

12. _____ is *not* God's will; but the _____ to sin *is*.

Chapter 4

1. Name at least two Scriptures where we see the devil/demons directly causing sickness. _____

2. According to James 4:7, what two things do we need to do to get the devil to flee? _____

3. According to John 10:10, what does the thief come to do? _____

_____

If the Master of the house approved or authorized this thief's activities, could we still call the thief a "thief"? _____
How should this impact our understanding of God's Sovereignty?

_____
_____
_____

4. Cite two Biblical examples of Creation being corrected, cursed, altered, or put in line by Jesus. _____

_____

_____

5. Explain how this clearly demonstrates that Nature is sometimes operating out-of-line with God's will. _____

_____

_____

6. Name at least two Scriptures where Jesus says that Believers can take authority over Nature and it will obey. _____

_____

How does this knowledge apply to Healing? _____

_____

_____

7. According to Romans 8:18-22, who or what is Creation waiting for, to help put it back in line with the way It was designed to function? ___

_____

What does that mean? _____

_____

8. What does Luke 13:1-5 tell you about both free will, and about "accidents?" _____

_____

_____

_____

9. Re-read Romans 9:14-24. Does it *seem* (on the surface) to say that God hardened Pharaoh's heart just to ultimately destroy him? _____
Please review Exodus, chapters 4-14 in detail. After reviewing the whole story in detail, which came first, God hardening Pharaoh's heart, or Pharaoh making a choice? _____

_____

10. To confirm this understanding, re-read Romans 1:21-28. Which comes first—God hardening someone's heart, or that person making their own choice? _____

_____

Why does God do this? _____

_____

_____

_____

11. In the story of the Prodigal Son, did the Father allow the younger son to make his own decisions—even though they were wrong? _____ Why did He do that? _____

_____

Does this make the Father responsible for the son's decisions? _____ Why or why not? _____

_____

_____

12. Name two Scriptures where Mankind limited God. _____ What were the two things the people in those Scriptures did that limited what God could do? _____

_____

Chapter 5

1. State the Law of Identification in one sentence: _____

_____

2. In Psalm 16, Psalm 88, and Acts 2, where does it say that Jesus' soul went? _____

3. According to Hebrews 4:15, did Jesus ever sin? _____ But according to 2 Corinthians 5:21, what *did* happen? _____

_____

4. In Romans 6:26, it says that, "the wages of sin is _____." In Colossians 1:18 and Revelation 1:5, Jesus is called the "Firstborn from the _____." Name at least 2 reasons why these cannot mean just "physically" dead: _____

_____

_____

5. What is the primary difference between Jesus' experience of spiritual death and separation from God, and the experience of anyone else?

_____

_____

6. According to Galatians 2:20, we have been _____ with Christ.

7. Read Colossians 2:11-15, Ephesians 2:5-6, and Colossians 3:1. These Scriptures say we have been _____ up together with Christ, made _____ together with Him, and have been made to _____ together with Him in _____ places—at the _____ _____ of God. Is there sickness allowed there? _____

8. If we have "put off the old man" and have "put on the new man" (Ephesians 4:21-24)... Then according to Romans 13:14 and Colossians 3:27, Who *is* that new man? _____ Describe that new man: _____

   _____
   _____
   _____
   _____

9. If we live, move, and have our being in Christ (Acts 17:28), then how does Galatians 2:20 in the Distilled Bible describe our "second existence"? _____ How does *your* translation describe it? _____

   _____
   _____

10. According to Romans 6:16,19 and 8:12-14, what do you see as one key in walking in the new man? _____

    _____
    _____

11. Describe the Great Exchange / The Ol' Switcheroo: _____

    _____
    _____
    _____

12. According to 1 Peter 2:24, what are we healed by? _____ What does that mean to you here and now? _____

    _____
    _____

Chapter 6

1. Look again at the section, "The Power of Past Tense." What is the power of recognizing past tense verbs in these Scriptures? _____

   _____
   _____

2. According to 1 Peter 2:24, what healed you? _____
   When? _____
   So when will God heal you? _____
   _____

3. According to Colossians 1:13, do you still need to be delivered from
   any powers of darkness? _____
   According to Romans 8:29-30, when will Believers be justified and
   glorified? _____

4. According to Ephesians 1:3, what spiritual blessings are you lacking?
   _____
   According to Colossians 2:8-10, if you're in Christ, what do you still
   need before you are complete? _____

5. According to Hebrews 4:10, what is God currently working on for us?
   _____
   _____
   What does God still need to do for anybody and everybody to be
   saved, healed, delivered, or blessed? _____
   _____

6. Is God deciding on a person-by-person basis whether or not He will
   save or heal or bless? _____
   Explain. _____
   _____
   _____
   _____

7. Does this increase or decrease your faith to minister to the sick?
   _____
   Why? _____
   _____
   _____

8. Reproduce the flowchart that describes the process of Christian
   "growth": _____
   _____
   _____

9. In light of 2 Peter 1:3, what is a key to receiving what Jesus has
   given? _____
   What is the only way the Bible tells us to have our lives transformed
   (See Romans 12:1-2)? _____

10. How can we see/learn more about the "unseen" things described in 2 Corinthians 4:18, Hebrews 11:1, and Colossians 3:1-2? _____

_____

_____

11. Describe what most New Testament Prayer should look like. _____

_____

In 2 Corinthians 1:18, what does it tell us is Jesus' response to our requests for God's promises to come to pass in our lives? _____

_____

12. If God didn't even spare His Own Son from us (Romans 8:32), do you think God is holding back some lesser blessing from you now? _____

Explain. _____

_____

_____

_____

Chapter 7

1. What is the Greek word for "saved," and what is included in the very definition of the word? _____ = "_____

_____"

How many New Testament instances of this word deal directly with physical healing? _____

2. Read Psalm 103. How many of God's benefits can you find listed? ___

Is physical healing included? _____

Since healing of our diseases was clearly a benefit under the Old Covenant, do you feel it also applies under the New Covenant? _____

Why or why not? _____

_____

_____

3. What are the best English translations of the words found in Isaiah 53:4, "choliy" and "mak'ob"? _____ and

_____. Name three Bible translations that

translate it this way. _____

What is the situation Matthew is applying Isaiah's prophecy to? ____

_____

_____

4. Does Matthew's application of Isaiah's prophecy confirm that Isaiah was referring specifically to physical sickness and disease? _____

389

Why or why not? _____

_____

_____

_____

5. Since these verbs describing Jesus' atoning work in verse 4 deal with physical sickness, and in verses 11-12 they deal with sin, what is the truth we learn from understanding that the same verbs apply to both sin and sickness? _____

   How does *this* answer the question, "If Jesus paid for my sickness, why am I still sick?" _____

   _____

   _____

   _____

   _____

   _____

6. Based on the relationship between Isaiah 53:4, Matthew 8:17 and 1 Peter 2:24, how can we know that when Peter says, "By His stripes you were healed" refers to physical healing? _____

   _____

   _____

   _____

   _____

7. What is one important Strong's Concordance definition of the Greek word for "fulfilled" that we find in Matthew 8:17? _____

   Does this word always mean "once and no more?" _____
   Give at least 2 other New Testament references where this same Greek word is used to describe a prophecy that will have multiple future fulfillments. _____

   _____

   _____

   _____

8. Name two references which either imply or state directly that the Israelites were healed when they were delivered from Egypt. _____

   Can you think of any other possible reason why God would suddenly identify Himself as "the God Who Heals You?" _____

   _____

   _____

9. In Communion, there are two elements we partake of. What are they? _____
    What element pays for our sins? _____

    If Communion was solely a celebration of our sins being forgiven and washed away, what is the purpose of the second element? _____
    _____
    _____
    _____

10. In Paul's 1 Corinthians 11 expounding of the Communion feast, what reason does he give for many being sick and dying prematurely? ____
    _____
    Paul defined partaking "in an unworthy manner" as "not discerning the Lord's Body." What do you think that means, *in context*? _____
    _____
    _____
    _____

11. We know from John 3:14 that the bronze serpent in Numbers 21:8-9 is a picture/type/shadow of Jesus on the cross. How is this truth an important confirmation that healing is in the atonement? _____
    _____
    _____
    _____

12. Explain the lessons learned from the Check Engine light in regards to symptoms vs. problems. _____
    _____
    How does *this* answer the question, "If Jesus paid for my sickness, why am I still sick?" _____
    _____
    _____
    _____
    _____
    _____

Chapter 8

1. In two words, what is the "signature of the Gospel"? "____ _____"

2. Naturally speaking, who had Paul been persecuting? _____
    _____

Who did *Jesus* say Paul was persecuting? _____

How do we account for this? _____

_____

_____

3. In 2 Corinthians 6:14-15, Christians are identified with what four things? _____

_____

4. According to Matthew 5:14, who is the light of the world? _____

_____

5. Does 1 John 4:17 say we are like Jesus *was*? _____

What *does* it say, and what is the importance of the distinction? _____

_____

_____

_____

6. 1 Corinthians 6:15-17 tells us that our _____ are members of Christ, and we are one _____ with Him.

1 Corinthians 2:16 tells us we have the _____ of Christ.

7. Review 2 Corinthians 4:16. Does it seem that physical death is nearly unavoidable? _____

Review 1 Corinthians 15:42-44, 53-54. What does it mean when our physical body is referred to as "corruptible?" _____

Review Romans 8:23. How do you think the concept of "firstfruits" applies to our physical bodies as Believers? _____

_____

_____

_____

8. However... In light of redemption, our bodies being "members of Christ," and the truth in Romans 8:11—How much benefit do you think could possibly be available for our physical bodies? _____

_____

_____

_____

If this is a benefit God has made available, do we receive it automatically? _____

How do we receive it then? _____

9. Philippians 2:5-8 commands us to think like Jesus in a couple of ways. Describe them. _____

_____

_____

_____

_____

_____

10. 2 Peter 1:4 says that through His _____, we are _____ of His Divine _____.

11. According to Colossians 1:27, what is the great "mystery" that is Christianity? "_____ in _____, the hope of _____."

12. Explain how the revelation of Union with Christ trumps any argument against Divine Healing. _____

_____

_____

_____

_____

_____

_____

_____

_____

Chapter 9

1. As we see in John 5:17-18, when someone calls God their Father, they are making themselves (in some sense) _____ with God.

2. According to Philippians 2:5-6, we are to think just like Jesus did in this matter: "In Christ, It's not a crime to be _____ with God."

3. In Romans 8:16-17, it says that if we are sons of God, then we are "_____ _____ with Christ."

4. In 1 Corinthians 3:21-23, we see that our inheritance as sons of God includes "_____ things." Is there any blessing you feel is not included in there? _____

_____

5. According to Ephesians 5:28-33, marriage is a picture of the "great mystery"—our relationship with _____. It says that in this relationship, the "two shall become _____ _____."

6. In Matthew 19:4-6, Jesus commands that "what God has _____ _____, let no man _____." What does that command mean to you, as it concerns your union with Him? _____
_____
_____
_____
_____
_____

7. In 1 Corinthians 6:17-19, it says that our _____ are members of Christ. Moreover, it says that whoever is joined to the Lord is "_____ _____ with Him."

8. As we see in Ephesians 1:20-23, "all things" are under Jesus' feet. If we are His Body, then where does that put "all things" in relationship to *us,* considering that we are the "_____ of Him who fills all in all?" _____
_____
_____

9. What does that mean to you personally? _____
_____
_____
_____
How should it affect your life? _____
_____
_____
_____
_____

10. According to Ephesians 4:14-15, we should "no longer be _____," but rather we should "_____ _____ in all things into Him who is the Head." What does this mean to you personally? _____
_____
_____
_____
_____

11. How does the truth of our union with Christ affect the issue of healing? _____

_____

_____

_____

_____

12. Any other idea that seems to contradict the fact that "God's will is always healing," must bow to the reality of our union with Christ. What does this mean to you? _____

_____

_____

_____

_____

_____

_____

Chapter 10

1. According to James 1:17, what kind of gifts does God give? _____ and _____. Does this verse allow for those gifts to come from any other source? _____
Does it allow for any *other* type of gifts to come from God? _____
In your opinion, does sickness, disease or pain meet the requirements to be considered as a good gift? _____

2. 1 John 1:5 says that God is _____, and in Him there is no _____ at all. How does this help us understand the nature of God's character, especially as it relates to healing?

_____

_____

_____

3. Under what circumstances do "all things work together for good" (Romans 8:26-28)? _____

_____

4. According to James 1:13, is God responsible for tempting anyone to sin? _____ So how does James 1:13 eliminate the possibility of "Hyper-Sovereignty", or God using the devil to do His will? _____

_____

_____

_____

5. Refer to the brief parable in this chapter. If someone creates a horrible situation, only to solve it so they can look good, are they a Hero or a Criminal? _____
   How does this relate to the subject of this chapter? _____
   _____
   _____

6. Read Matthew 12:33. If the devil produces good fruit (God's will), then would that make him a good tree, or a bad tree? _____
   Can that be correct? _____
   If the devil is a bad tree, then all of his fruit is _____.
   If God is a good tree, then all of His fruit is _____.

7. What is "The Kid-Check Theology Test"? _____
   _____
   _____
   Find a child 12 or under. Ask them, "Is sickness, disease and pain 'good' or 'bad'?" What did they say? _____
   Taking their answer, and the good fruit/bad fruit standard into account, where does sickness come from? _____

8. What Scripture is called "The Dividing Line of the Bible"? _____
   How can understanding the simple truth of this verse affect your everyday life? _____
   _____
   _____
   _____

9. According to Acts 10:38, everyone that Jesus healed was oppressed by whom? _____ According to 1 John 3:8, whose works was Jesus sent to destroy? _____
   Do you think that Jesus was destroying a work of Satan when He healed the sick? _____ Why or why not? _____
   _____
   _____

10. Review Matthew 12:22-32. Jesus basically says that when we say God's works are done by the devil, we are guilty of _____.
    Do you think the same thing would apply if someone says that the devil's works are being done by God? _____ Why or why not?
    _____
    _____
    _____

11. Name two negative results of allowing room in our thought life for an inconsistent, unreliable God. _____

_____

_____

_____

12. In what two places (environments) have we seen the will of God clearly displayed? _____
According to Matthew 6:10, what is supposed to be our decree as ambassadors of Christ? _____

_____

Do you believe it's really God's will that Earth reflect Heaven? _____
So what is God's will relating to healing here on earth? _____

_____

_____

Chapter 11

1. After reading 1 John 3:8b, Acts 10:38, and Luke 4:17-21, what are NINE descriptions of Jesus' Mission (and ours)? _____

_____

_____

_____

_____

_____

2. How does John 14:12 describe our mission? _____

_____

_____

3. Where in Scripture do we see the clearest, most accurate picture of God? _____
What should we do when we see one picture of God in Jesus, and a seemingly different one from somewhere else—even in Scripture?

_____

_____

_____

4. When our level of experience doesn't match up to that of Jesus, should we make up a reason why it doesn't? _____
What should we do instead? _____

_____

_____

5. Explain how Mark 9:14-27 eliminates the "We prayed and nothing happened" objection to healing. _____

_____

_____

_____

"Our own failure to get the _____ _____ is not a reflection of the _____ of _____."

6. Cite a Scripture passage that demonstrates that even unbelief won't stop the healing power of Jesus. _____
What kind of mighty works did Nazareth's unbelief stop? _____

_____

_____

7. If a person is afflicted by a demon, can a Believer cast out the demon even if the person wants to keep it? _____
Why or why not? _____
Would you recommend doing this? _____
Why or why not? Or, under what circumstances? _____

_____

_____

_____

8. Did sin in someone's life ever stop Jesus from healing them? _____
Should it stop us? _____ Why or why not?

_____

_____

9. Taking the situation in context, what is the meaning of Jesus' statement in John 9:3? Paraphrased: "We're not the _____, we're the _____."
Was God glorified in the man's sickness, or in the man's healing?

_____

10. Cite references that demonstrate three different ways Jesus saw healing manifest. Instant: _____
Gradual: _____ Repeated Prayer: _____
Why is it important to understand the truths contained in these passages? _____

_____

_____

_____

_____

11. Cite at least four references that show Jesus healing either: A) every sickness and disease, or B) every person that needed healing. _____

_____

Why is it important to understand that Jesus healed everyone that came to Him? _____

_____

_____

12. Since we are one with Christ, how does looking at the results of Jesus' healing ministry
affect what we should expect when ministering to the sick?

_____

_____

_____

_____

_____

_____

_____

Chapter 12

1. Whose performance determined one's relationship with God—and the covenant benefits enjoyed—in the Old Testament? _____
   What about in the New Testament? _____

2. Re-read Deuteronomy 28:1-2, and 15. How did people in the Old Covenant receive the blessings God has to offer? _____

   _____

   What happened if the people didn't obey and keep all the rules perfectly? _____
   Read the rest of Deuteronomy 28. Were sicknesses included in the list of curses for disobeying? _____

3. If sin is planted as a seed, it will produce a fruit called _____.
   Sickness and disease are simply immature forms of _____.
   Sickness will grow up to be _____ if left unchecked.

4. In light of James 2:10, and Romans 7, describe how the Law, although glorious, could be considered a curse. _____

   _____

   According to Galatians 3:13-14, what effect did Jesus have on this situation? _____

   _____

5. Does Romans 7 describe what it's like to be a Believer in Christ, living in the age of Grace? _____
Why or why not? (You may want to read Romans, chapters 6-8 for help.) _____
_____
_____
_____

6. Review the lengthy list of Old Testament Scriptures in which we see God "sending" sickness on people. Consider sowing and reaping, and sin and death, law and judgment. How do these concepts help you understand the Scriptures on that list? _____
_____
_____
_____
_____
_____

7. Explain why the results the people in those Scriptures received are not the results we are to experience in the New Covenant. What has changed? _____
_____
_____
_____

8. Review Romans 11:6. What is the New Covenant "If...Then" Agreement? _____
_____
_____
_____

9. Consider Romans 8:3-4. Why is it impossible for us as Believers to break the New Covenant, and thus, be punished for it? _____
_____
_____
_____

10. Revisit Romans 8:2, 10:4, and 5:20b-21. If one were to sin, "Rather than reaping the deserved harvest of _____,
_____ and death, they get more _____ than ever!!!" Do you believe this? _____ Why or why not?
_____
_____
_____

11. Explain the concept of being "perfect and being perfected," as seen in 2 Cor.5:17, Heb.10:14, Col.2:10, Phil.3:12, 2 Cor.13:4 and James 1:4

_____
_____
_____
_____

12. Give at least three Scriptures that confirm that neither God, nor Jesus, is pouring out judgment on individuals, groups, or nations—or counting our sins against us—in this age of Grace. _____

If these Scriptures are true, would it make any sense whatsoever for us to believe that God is "sending" or even "allowing" sickness, disease, pain, or disaster of any kind on people as a judgment for their sin? _____ Why or why not? _____

_____
_____
_____

Chapter 13

1. The Greek word "astheneia" can mean either "sickness" or "weakness." Which meaning does it have in *most* of its occurrences in the New Testament? _____
   Where do the chapters/verses, capitalization, and punctuation in our Bibles come from? _____
   Why might a translator select the word "infirmity" instead of the more accurate/precise "weakness" in this text? _____

   _____
   _____

2. Where is the first place we look for answers concerning the correct interpretation of a particular word, phrase, or verse? _____
   How does Paul define his "weakness" in 2 Corinthians 11:23-28 & 12:10? _____

   _____
   _____
   _____

3. In Bible Interpretation, what is the Law of First Mention? _____

   _____
   _____
   _____

4. Remember that _____ was Paul's mother tongue. Who/what were the "thorns" in Israel's side/eyes, from the Hebrew texts of Numbers 33:55, Judges 2:3 and Joshua 23:13? _____
    _____
    What English figure of speech roughly equates to the Hebrew figure of speech, "thorn in the flesh?" _____

5. Chrysostom, Theophylact, Theodoret, Ecumenius, Ambrose, Erasmus, and Martin Luther all agree that the thorn in the flesh was _____.
    Even John Calvin agreed that the thorn in the flesh was *not*
    _____.

6. In 2 Corinthians 12:7, the "thorn" is called a "messenger of _____."
    What Greek word is translated as "messenger," and how is it normally translated? "_____" = "_____"
    So, most likely, what was this messenger? _____
    What were the results of this messenger's work? _____
    _____
    _____

7. According to Matthew 5:11, Luke 21:12, and John 15:20, what are Christians promised to have? _____
    That being the case, what 2 things might "My grace is sufficient for you" mean? _____
    _____
    _____
    _____

8. How does this explain God's answer to Paul's prayer in verses 8-9?
    _____
    _____
    _____
    _____
    _____

9. Read Acts 8:1-4. What happened every time Believers were persecuted and fled to other places? _____
    Did the devil like this result? _____
    Could the removal of persecution result in people being "exalted above measure"? _____
    Describe the historical results of the removal of persecution from the Church. _____
    _____
    _____

10. Paul also says that the thorn was "for _____'s sake." Does it make any sense for *sickness* to be for Christ's sake, especially considering that He paid a very specific price to deliver us from it? __ On the other hand, would it make sense for *persecution* to be for Christ's sake? _____
_____

11. What does the word "buffet" ("kolaphizo") mean, every time it occurs in the New Testament? _____
What happens every time the power of Christ rests on someone who is "sick" in the NT? _____
Does it make any sense whatsoever in the context of Galatians 6:11 for Paul to comment on the size of his printing? _____
However, is it perfectly logical for him to refer to the length of his epistle? _____ Why or why not?
_____
_____
_____

12. What was the "physical infirmity" Paul had when he *first* preached in Lystra, Galatia? _____
In 2 Corinthians 11:30 and 12:5, would it make any sense to "boast in (his) infirmities," if it was a "sickness?" _____
What was Paul actually boasting in, and why? _____
_____
_____
_____
_____
_____

Chapter 14

1. In Job 1:1-6, what is unusual about the way we are introduced to Job? _____
_____
_____
_____

2. "Behold" just means "_____." With this understanding, does God's observation in Job 1:12 and 2:6 mean that He was giving Satan permission to afflict Job? _____
_____
_____

3. According to Job 1:10, God placed a _____ of _____ around Job's life, and all that he had. According to Job 1:12 and 2:7, who actually brought the calamities to Job's life? _____

4. Even while Job was totally susceptible to Satan's attacks, God in His goodness somehow managed to _____ the devil's destruction.

5. When the Bible records Job saying, "the Lord has taken away"—Does that mean his statement is the truth? _____ Why or why not? _____
_____
_____
_____

6. In Job 42:3, what does *Job* say about his own words? _____
_____
_____
In Job 38:2-3, what does *God* say about Job's words? _____
_____

7. _____ brings the will of the devil onto the scene, just like _____ brings God's will onto the scene.

8. In Job 3:25, what does Job admit had come upon him? _____
_____
_____

9. If that is the case, then what might have brought down God's hedge of protection? _____
_____

10. Should we blame Job for his own situation then? _____ Why or why not? _____
_____
_____
_____
_____

11. Even if Job did have a covenant with God (which we don't know)— Whose is better—his or ours? _____ That being the case, are we in the same situation as Job when it comes to our relationship with God, or when it comes to healing? ___ Is Job our template or standard? _____ If not, who is? _____

12. "When taken as a whole, the Bible _____ itself."
What are some of the larger truths that we see in the Bible (and this book) which prevent us from using the story of Job to think God would ever will or allow sickness to come upon someone today?

_____
_____
_____
_____

Chapter 15

1. Reread Hebrews 12:5-11. Who does the passage tell us gets to be chastened by the Father? _____
If sickness were chastening, then would unbelievers get sick? _____
Why or why not? _____

_____
_____

2. This passage also says that the chastening of the Lord is for our profit. How do these verses describe that profit? _____

_____
If sickness is the chastening of the Lord, shouldn't we see this profit in the lives of everyone that gets sick and diseased? ____ Do we? ____
Why or why not? _____

_____

3. List seven synonyms for "chastening," as seen in the Strong's Concordance definition of the Greek word, "paideia." _____

_____
_____

4. According to John 14:26 and 16:13, who is our Teacher? _____

_____
According to Romans 8:16, how does He communicate with us in the New Testament—internally or externally? _____ Is that consistent with the belief that God uses sickness to teach us? _____
Why or why not? _____

_____
_____
_____

5. According to Hebrews 10:14, 12:2a, and 13:20-21, Who is responsible for maturing and perfecting Believers and our faith? _____

_____

Name at least four Scriptures that say the Word of God is what He uses to clean up, instruct, correct, mature, or develop us: _____

_____

_____

6. Other than speaking His Word directly to our hearts, or through reading the Bible, according to Ephesians 4:11-15, what is another method God uses to get His Word to us and grow us up into Christ?

_____

_____

_____

7. According to Romans 2:4, what leads people to change their ways of thinking and acting (repentance)? _____

_____

What is the only thing necessary for the lost to be saved, and for Christians to grow up? _____

_____

_____

8. Consider Romans 8:28, and describe the difference between a set-up (a "push") and a teachable moment (a "fall"). _____

_____

_____

_____

Why is understanding this important in the context of healing? _____

_____

_____

_____

_____

9. Review John 10:10, Matthew 12:22-32, and compare those truths to the idea that God sends sickness to perfect us. Why must this idea be wrong? _____

_____

_____

_____

_____

_____

10. According to Mark 4:14-19, why do trials, tribulations, persecution and cares (worries) come to us? _____

_____

_____

How does this fact jibe with James 1:2-5? _____
_____
_____
_____
_____

11. Considering Hebrews 6:11-12 and James 1:22, describe the interaction of God's Word, faith, patience, works, and fulfilled promises. _____
_____
_____
_____

12. Review the section, "Some Challenges." Come up with at least two more logical ramifications of the idea that God sends sickness and disease to benefit His children (which therefore prove the idea false)?
_____
_____
_____
_____
_____
_____
_____
_____
_____

Chapter 16

1. According to Aquinas and Calvin, what are two notable exceptions to cessationism? _____
_____
_____
_____
_____

2. Explain how the historical setting contributed to Calvin's cessationist stand. _____
_____
_____
_____
_____
_____

3. What does 1 Corinthians 13:8-12 (in context) actually prove? _____

_____
_____
_____
_____

4. What is the "transmuting" theory of the charismata? Name two Scriptures that contradict this idea. _____

_____
_____
_____
_____

5. Name at least 6 Biblical examples that show that miracles do not necessarily attest to someone being in a mature relationship with Jesus, and/or having correct doctrine. _____

_____
_____
_____
_____

6. How does Galatians 3:5 explain how people who have imperfect doctrine and/or character can still do legitimate miracles of God.

_____
_____
_____
_____
_____

7. Name at least 10 Biblical purposes for the charismata, which have nothing at all to do with confirming doctrine or accrediting a messenger. _____

_____
_____
_____
_____
_____
_____
_____
_____

8. If the Biblical purposes of the charismata you just listed determine how long we will have the charismata, when will they "cease?" _____

_____
_____

9. What was Jesus' response to those who asked for a sign to accredit Him as God's messenger (See Matt.16:1,4)? _____

_____

_____

_____

_____

10. Name 4 Biblical commands that blatantly contradict cessationism. ___

_____

_____

_____

_____

11. If Jesus is our example for life and ministry, how did He do (and teach His disciples to do) ministry, according to Acts 10:38, John 14:12, and Matthew 10:1, 7-8, 24-25)? _____

_____

_____

_____

_____

_____

_____

12. What warning does 2 Timothy give us regarding those that have "a form of godliness," but deny its ("dunamis" miracle-working) power?

_____

_____

Chapter 17

1. Do you think God personally fashions each handicapped, stillborn, or diseased child's physical body? _____
What does it really mean that God "made" a particular person? _____

_____

_____

2. What is the ultimate cause of *every* physical imperfection, disease, and malfunction? _____
According to Proverbs 20:12, what kind of eyes and ears did the Lord design? _____

3. How do Luke 4:18-19, Matthew 15:30-31, and Mark 7:37 describe Jesus' response to the blind, deaf, and mute? _____

_____

How does this present a problem for the idea that God willed and made them to be that way? _____

_____
_____
_____
_____

4. Considering the full context, what is God actually saying to Moses in Exodus 4:11? _____

_____
_____
_____

5. Can you find anything in the Bible that suggests that sickness is supposed to be our exit door from earth? _____

_____

According to 1 Corinthians 15, what is the seedtime and harvest process in regards to us getting our glorified bodies? _____

_____
_____

6. Understanding the adoption analogy in Romans 8:15 & 23 ("received" and yet we are still "waiting" for adoption), describe the difference between "firstfruits" and full manifestation—in regards to healing and health. Firstfruits = _____ Full Manifestation = _____

_____

7. How can we determine from James 5:13-15 that "sickness" and "suffering" aren't the same thing? _____

_____
_____

8. Read 1 Peter 2:19-23 and 3:13-17. How does Peter describe the "suffering" that we are so often promised? _____

_____
_____
_____

9. Read 1 Timothy 5:23. Is this Paul giving Timothy advice of how to "cure" his infirmities, or how to "prevent" them in the first place? ___

_____

How do you know, and why is this important? _____

_____
_____
_____

410

10. Is 2 Timothy 4:20 descriptive or prescriptive? _____
    How do you know? _____
    _____
    _____
    _____

11. Why did Paul leave Miletus so quickly, based on the story as it is
    recorded in Acts 20:4, 15-16? _____
    _____
    _____
    _____

    What is some Biblical evidence that suggests Trophimus may have
    been healed? _____
    _____
    _____
    _____
    _____
    _____

12. Don't build doctrinal castles on _____.
    God's will is _____ healing!!!

APPENDIX A:
Scriptures Referenced

Bible Reference	Chapter
Genesis	
1:26	14
1:26-28	1
1:31	4
2:17	5
2:23	8
2:21-25	9
3:17	4
3:22-24	1
6:3	17
6:5-6	2
8:22	12
11:1-8	2
18:15	14
20:2	14
25:8, 17	17
35:28-29	17
49:33	17
50:20	2
Exodus	
4:11	17
7-12	12
14-15	7
15:26b	3, 14, 16
19:5	12
20:18-21	16
32:9-14	2
32:35	12
Leviticus	
14	7
17:11	7, 12
Numbers	
8:19	7
11:33	12
12:1-16	12
14:37	12
16:41-50	12
16:47-48	7
21:8-9	7
23:19	3, 6
25:6-13	7
33:55	13
Deuteronomy	
19:21	12
28:1-2, 15	12
28:21-22, 59-61	12

Bible Reference	Chapter
29:22	12
30:19	3
Joshua	
23:13	13
24:15	3
Judges	
2:3	13
1 Samuel	
5-6	12
12:15	12
2 Samuel	
12:14-19	12
16:12	12
24:10-25	12
2 Kings	
15:5	12
1 Chronicles	
21:1-30	12
2 Chronicles	
13:20	12
21:14-15	12
26:16-23	12
Job	
1:1-22	14
2:1-7	14
2:10	14
3:25	14
10:11	17
35:13-16	14
38:1-2	14
42:3	14
42:10	14
42:11	14
42:12-17	14
Psalms	
8:4-6	1
24:1	1
34:8	10
34:10	15
68:19	Intro, 7
78:41-42	4

Bible Reference	Chapter		Bible Reference	Chapter
Psalms (Cont.)			**Daniel**	
84:11	15		4:35	2
88:6-17	5			
89:34	3		**Hosea**	
90:10	17		2:16	9
91:16	17		3:5b	10
103:1-5	Intro, 7		4:6	Intro
103:2-3	16			
105:23-38	7		**Joel**	
110:1	2		2	7
115:3	2			
115:16	1		**Zephaniah**	
119:89	3		3:17	3
126:1-3	10			
139:13	17		**Zechariah**	
			2:8	3
Proverbs			14:12	12
1:32-33	15			
13:1	15		**Malachi**	
16:9	2		2:17	10
19:21	2			
20:12	17		**Matthew**	
			1:23	4
Ecclesiastes			3:16-17	9
7:14	2		4:23-24	16
			4:24	11
Isaiah			5:11-12	13
5:20	10		5:14	8
7:14	4		5:18	12
14:16-17	6		6:10	2, 5, 16
32:7-8	2		7:11	2
38:1-5	2		7:18	10
40:8	3		7:21-23	16
42:1-4	7		8:2-3	3
45:7	2		8:13	11
46:10	6, 12		8:16-17	7
53:4-5	7		9:5	7
53:5	14		9:32-34	10
53:11-12	7		9:35	11, 16
54:5	9		9:36	16
60:1-4	10		10:1	1, 16
62:5b	9		10:7-8	16
			10:8	11
Jeremiah			10:24-25	16
19:10	12		11:12	6
			12:17-21	7
			12:22-32	10, 15
			12:33	10
			12:35	2
Ezekiel			13:17	8
18:4, 20a	5		14:14	16
18:20	12		14:15-21	16
			14:33	16
			15:6-9	Intro

413

Bible Reference	Chapter	Bible Reference	Chapter
Matt (Cont.)		16:20	16
15:28	11		
15:30-31	17	**Luke**	
15:50	16	4	11
16:1, 4	16	4:5-7	1
16:19	1, 3	4:17-21	7, 11
17:14-21	10	4:18	16
17:20	11	4:18-19	17
18:2-3	10	4:40	11
18:18	2, 3	5:26	16
19:2	16	7:11-17	16
19:4-6	9	7:28	16
19:6	16	7:34	14
19:14	10	7:49	7
20:34	11, 16	8:22-25	4
21:14	17	8:36-37	16
21:18-22	4	9:1	1
22:44	17	9:11	11, 16
23:37	2	9:23	5
25:14-30	2	9:35	9
26:28	7	10:8	17
26:53	13	10:8-9	16
26:67-68	13	10:19	1, 11
27:46	5	10:21	10
27:50	17	11:2	3, 6, 10
28:18-20	1	11:14	10
28:19-20	16	11:15	14
		11:17	4
Mark		11:24-26	11
1:41	16	11:35	10
3:20-27	16	12:32	6
3:22	14	13:1-5	4
4:11	8	13:10-16	4
4:14-19	15	13:10-17	10
4:41	16	13:13	11
5:1-20	10	15:11-31	6
5:19	16	17:6	4
5:33	16	17:11-18	11
6:1-6	11	19:12-13	1
6:5	4	19:37	16
7:35	11	20:21	3
7:37	17	21:12-13	13
8:22-26	10	22:19-20	7
9:14-27	11	23:34	7, 13
9:17-18, 25-27	4	23:46	17
9:38-40	16		
11:26	12	**John**	
13:32	3	2:3-11	16
14:65	13	2:11a	16
15:37-39	17	2:23	16
16:15-20	16	3:2	16
16:17a	11	3:3, 6, 8	5
16:17-18	16	3:14	7
16:18	17	3:16	3, 7

414

Bible Reference	Chapter	Bible Reference	Chapter
John (Cont.)		2:22-32	5
4:19	3	2:23	10
5:1-15	11	2:34-35	2
5:9	11	2:38-29	16
5:14	11	2:43	16
5:17-18	9	3:1-10	11
5:19	11	3:10	16
5:19-20	4	4:16	16
5:19-37	9	4:27-28	10
5:22	12	5	14
5:39-40	11	5:12-16	16
6:2	16	7:28	8
8:11	7	7:59	17
John 8:11, 15	12	7:59-60	13
8:32	Intro	8:1-4	13
8:44	10	8:6-7	16
8:48	14	9:34	16
9:1-5	11, 17	10:38	10, 11, 16
9:5	8	11:1-18	16
10:1-10	1	12:1-19	13
10:10	4, 10, 15	13:30-34	5
10:18	13, 17	14:3	16
10:25, 37-38	16	15:8, 19-20	13
10:30	4, 11	15:12	16
10:30-39	9	16:16-31	13
10:41	16	17:28	5, 8
11:1-4	16, 17	19:11-17	16
11:22, 42	8	20:4, 15-16	17
11:40-44	16	20:23	13
12:23-24	17	21:10-11	13
12:31	1	21:13	17
12:47	12	21:12-14	13
12:48	12	21:26-29	17
14:6, 17	10	22:4-8	8
14:7-9	11	28:3-6	13
14:7-24	9		
14:9	4	**Romans**	
14:12	11, 16	1:21-28	4
14:26	15	1:27	12
14:30	1	2:4	10, 15
15:3	15	3:4	15
15:11-32	4	4:3	5
15:15	3	4:17b	12
15:20	13	5:17	2
16:8-11	1	5:20	11, 16
16:13	15	5:20b-21	12
17:20-23	8	6	5
17:22	9	6:1-4	12
19:28-30	12	6:16, 19	5
19:30	6, 17	6:23	5, 7, 12
		7:4-6	12
Acts		7:6	12
2	7	7:7-13	12
2:22	16	7:15, 19, 22-25	12

415

Bible Reference	Chapter	Bible Reference	Chapter
Romans (Cont.)		12:7	16
8:1	12	12:9	6
8:2	5, 12, 17	12:9-10	17
8:3-4	5, 12	12:12	9
8:11	5, 8, 17	13:8-12	16
8:12-14	5	14:1	16
8:13	5	14:3-5	16
8:15, 23	17	14:4	16
8:16	15	14:5	16
8:16-17	2, 9	14:14-15	16
8:17	6	14:15-17	16
8:18-22	4	14:16-17	16
8:23	8, 17	14:22	16
8:26-27	16	14:24-25	16
8:26-28	10	14:31	16
8:28	2, 15	14:39	16
8:29	5	15:23-28	2
8:29-30	6, 9	15:26	17
8:30	8	15:35-44	17
8:32	6	15:35-58	8
8:37	3	15:53	17
10:4	12		
10:17	6	**2 Corinthians**	
11:6	12	1:12-14	13
11:25	7	1:19-20	6
12:1-2	6, 8	3:6	6
12:2	10, 15	3:7-11	12
12:3b	4	4:3-4	1
12:5	9	4:7	8
13:14	5	4:16	8, 17
15:18-20	16	4:18	6, 9
19:4-24	4	5:8	17
		5:17	8, 12
1 Corinthians		5:18-19	6
1:17	16	5:18-20	12
1:25	16	5:20	2
1:25-29	8	5:21	5, 8
1:30	8	6:2	6
2:4-5	16	6:14-15	8
2:9-12	3	10:5	Intro
2:16	6, 8, 15	11:16-33	13
3:1-3	16	11:23-28	13
3:1-7	13	11:30	13
3:18-21	16	12:1-6, 11-15	13
3:21-22	9	12:2	3
4:11	13	12:5b	13
5:1	16	12:7-10	13
6:15-17	8, 9	12:10	13
6:17	5, 6, 8	12:11-12	16
6:19	5, 15	13:9	12
6:19-20	17		
6:20	8	**Galatians**	
11:23-26	7	2:6	3, 5
11:27-30	7	2:11-21	16

416

417

Bible Reference	Chapter	Bible Reference	Chapter
Hebrews (Cont.)		**2 Peter**	
11:35	13	1:1-4	8
12:2a	15	1:2-4	6
12:5-11	15	1:3-4	6
13:8	11, 16	1:4	5, 8, 15
13:20-21	15	1:5-8	6
		1:19	16
James		1:23	5
1:2-5	15	3:9	3
1:4	12		
1:13	10	**1 John**	
1:15b	12	1:5	10
1:16-17	10	1:7	10
1:17	Int, 2, 10, 14	3:1	5
2:1, 8-9	3	3:2	16
2:10	12	3:8	10, 11, 16
2:19	6	4:17	8, 11
2:22	15	4:18	3
2:23	7	5:1, 4	5
3:10-12	17	5:4-5	3
4:2-3, 6	2	5:14	6
4:7	4, 10	5:14-15	Intro, 8
4:10	13	5:19	1
4:17	14		
5:13-15	17	**3 John**	
5:14-15	15	1:2	3, 15
5:16b	2		
		Jude	
1 Peter		1:20	16
1:12	6		
2:19-23	17	**Revelation**	
2:20	13	1:5	5
2:24	5, 7, 13, 14	1:18	1, 2
2:24-25	6	2:7, 11, 17, 26	3
3:13-17	17	3:5, 12, 21	3
4:11	16	13:8	9, 10
5:6	13	13:14-15	13
5:8	4	21:6	3
		21:9	9

APPENDIX B:
Where to Find Answers to Specific Objections

Objection to Healing	Chapter(s)
Doesn't God control everything that happens on earth?	1-4
Is everything that happens God's will?	1-4, 10-11
Doesn't God *allow* the devil to run around hurting people?	1-4, 10-11
If "God's Will is Always Healing," then why am I sick?	1-4
If God's will was for me to be healed, then I'd be healed.	1-4
If God didn't want me sick, then I wouldn't be sick.	1-4
We prayed for (whoever) to be healed and they weren't.	1-4..
If God is good and loving, why is the world such a mess?	1-4
God *allows* sickness, so it must be part of His will.	1-4, 10-11, 14
It's *God's* responsibility to heal the sick, not mine.	1-4, 11
Healing is totally up to *God*, not me.	1-4, 11
"God is in control."	1-4, 10-11
How can you just *demand* healing? What about God's will?	1-4
If sickness isn't God's doing, then how did I get sick?	1-4, 10
I must have "done something" to *deserve* this sickness.	1-5
My sin *earned* me this disease. I'm reaping what I sowed.	1-5, 12
God *created* sickness, so it must be part of His plan.	1-4, 10-11
I opened a door for the devil, so he has a *right* to make me sick.	5
Sickness is only natural, and only *God* can control nature.	4, 11
Sickness and pain is just an unavoidable part of life on Earth.	5-12
My physical body is *not* affected by my salvation.	5-9
What about God's *timing*?	3, 5-7, 11
Maybe today's not my day.	3, 5-7, 11
I believe God *will* heal me, I just don't know *when*.	3, 5-7, 11
God will heal me when I get to Heaven.	3, 5-7, 11, 17
God chooses *when* someone will get their healing.	3, 5-7, 11
God picks and chooses *whom* He heals.	3, 5-7, 11
Healing is not promised like Salvation is.	5-7
Jesus did not specifically provide for my physical healing.	5-7
God *will* always save; but He *won't* always heal.	5-7
If Jesus paid for my healing, then why am I still sick?	1-7
Sure, Jesus had authority over sickness; but that was *Jesus!*	8-9, 11
Yes, Jesus isn't sick; but He's in Heaven, and we're on earth.	8-9, 11
Everybody has to be sick sometimes—we're only human.	8-9, 11, 17
Jesus was our example; but we can't *really* expect to be like Him.	8-9, 11
Sometimes God wants to heal, and sometimes He doesn't.	5-7, 11
We prayed and they weren't healed, so it must not be God's will.	1-11
Unbelief stops God's healing power.	11
Jesus always healed instantaneously.	11
Sometimes sin or demons can stop healing.	11
What about (some certain OT Scripture)???	12
Can't sickness be God's judgment on sin?	11, 12, 17
Didn't God make (whoever) sick in the Bible?	12

Objection to Healing	Chapter(s)
What about Paul's "thorn in the flesh?"	13
Doesn't God use sickness to keep someone humble?	13, 15
What About Job?	14
Doesn't God use sickness to teach and mature us?	15
Doesn't God use sickness and pain to chasten or discipline us?	15
Doesn't God use sickness to draw people closer to Him?	15
Isn't sickness part of the "trials and tribulations" we're promised?	15
Didn't the gifts of the Spirit stop a long time ago?	16
God doesn't do miracles anymore.	16
The early Church only had miracles to prove the gospel.	16
God did miracles to establish the Church. Now we don't need them.	16
We don't need miracles today—We have medical science.	16
I've seen messed up people do miracles, so it can't really be God.	16
God can't use me in healing until I get my act together and mature.	16
The so-called miracles today are just "lying signs and wonders."	16
If God makes people handicapped, He must want them that way.	17
God makes people sick, so He can heal them and get glory.	2-3, 10, 14-15, 17
If "God's Will is Always Healing," are you saying we'll never die?	17
Sickness is sometimes God's way of "calling us home."	17
Sickness can be part of our "suffering for Jesus."	17
What about Timothy's stomach problems?	17
Didn't Paul leave Trophimus sick in Miletus?	17

APPENDIX C:
"Astheneia" — Its New Testament Usage
(referenced in Chapters 7 and 13)

The word "astheneia" appears 24 times in Scripture.

14 times—weakness

9 times—sickness

1 time—debatable; but "weakness" more likely

Matthew 8:17	sickness	that it might be fulfilled which was spoken by Isaiah the prophet, saying: " He Himself took our *infirmities* And bore our sicknesses."
Luke 5:15	sickness	However, the report went around concerning Him all the more; and great multitudes came together to hear, and to be healed by Him of their *infirmities.*
Luke 8:2	sickness	and certain women who had been healed of evil spirits and *infirmities*—Mary called Magdalene, out of whom had come seven demons,
Luke 13:11	sickness	And behold, there was a woman who had a spirit of *infirmity* eighteen years, and was bent over and could in no way raise herself up.
Luke 13:12	sickness	But when Jesus saw her, He called her to Him and said to her, "Woman, you are loosed from your *infirmity.*"
John 5:5	sickness	Now a certain man was there who had an *infirmity* thirty-eight years.
John 11:4	sickness	When Jesus heard that, He said, "This *sickness* is not unto death, but for the glory of God, that the Son of God may be glorified through it."
Acts 28:9	sickness	So when this was done, the rest of those on the island who had *diseases* also came and were healed.
1 Timothy 5:23	sickness	No longer drink only water, but use a little wine for your stomach's sake and your frequent *infirmities.*
Romans 6:19	weakness	I speak in human terms because of the *weakness* of your flesh. For just as you presented your members as slaves of uncleanness, and of lawlessness leading to more lawlessness, so now present your members as slaves of righteousness for holiness.
Romans 8:26	weakness	Likewise the Spirit also helps in our *weaknesses.* For we do not know what we should pray for as we ought, but the Spirit Himself makes intercession for us with groanings which cannot be uttered.
1 Corinthians 2:3	weakness	I was with you in *weakness,* in fear, and in much trembling.
1 Corinthians 15:43	weakness	It is sown in dishonor, it is raised in glory. It is sown in *weakness,* it is raised in power.
2 Corinthians 11:30	weakness	If I must boast, I will boast in the things which concern my *infirmity.*
2 Corinthians 12:5	weakness	Of such a one I will boast; yet of myself I will not boast, except in my *infirmities.*
2 Corinthians 12:9a	weakness	And He said to me, "My grace is sufficient for you, for My strength is made perfect in *weakness.*" ...

2 Corinthians 12:9b	weakness	... Therefore most gladly I will rather boast in my *infirmities*, that the power of Christ may rest upon me.
2 Corinthians 12:10	weakness	Therefore I take pleasure in *infirmities*, in reproaches, in needs, in persecutions, in distresses, for Christ's sake. For when I am weak, then I am strong.
2 Corinthians 13:4	weakness	For though He was crucified in *weakness*, yet He lives by the power of God. For we also are weak in Him, but we shall live with Him by the power of God toward you.
Galatians 4:13	debatable; but physical "weakness" makes more sense considering Paul had been stoned probably to death there in Lystra, Galatia "at the first"	You know that because of physical *infirmity* I preached the gospel to you at the first.

About the Author

Joshua Greeson is a graduate of Bethel School of Supernatural Ministry, and holds a Bachelor's Degree in Organizational Leadership from Simpson University. He is married and has three wonderful kids. A former Missions Director, he has been privileged to travel to many cities and nations bringing the Kingdom of God, seeing many salvations, healings and miracles. His mission is to reveal the love and power of God, and train others to do the same. Originally from San Diego, he currently resides in Redding, California.

Connect with us via the book's Facebook page at:
www.facebook.com/GodsWillisAlwaysHealing

Comments, questions, testimonies or ministry requests?
Please email us at GodsWillisAlwaysHealing@gmail.com

Made in the USA
Middletown, DE
25 May 2020